Variation in Datives

OXFORD STUDIES IN COMPARATIVE SYNTAX II
Richard Kayne, General Editor

The Higher Functional Field: Evidence from North Italian Dialects
Cecilia Poletto

The Syntax of Verb-Initial Languages
Edited by Andrew Carnie and Eithne Guilfoyle

Parameters and Universals
Richard Kayne

Portuguese Syntax: New Comparative Studies
Edited by João Costa

XP-Adjunction in Universal Grammar: Scrambling and Binding in Hindi-Urdu
Ayesha Kidwai

Infinitive Constructions: A Syntactic Analysis of Romance Languages
Guido Mensching

Subject Inversion in Romance and the Theory of Universal Grammar
Edited by Aafke Hulk and Jean-Yves Pollock

Subjects, Expletives, and the EPP
Edited by Peter Svenonius

A Unified Theory of Verbal and Nominal Projections
Yoshiki Ogawa

Functional Structures in DP and IP: The Cartography of Syntactic Structures, Volume 1
Edited by Guglielmo Cinque

Syntactic Heads and Word Formation
Marit Julien

The Syntax of Italian Dialects
Christina Tortora

The Morphosyntax of Complement-Head Sequences: Clause Structure and Word Order Patterns in Kwa
Enoch Oladé Aboh

The Structure of CP and IP: The Cartography of Syntactic Structures, Volume 2
Edited by Luigi Rizzi

The Syntax of Anaphora
Ken Safir

Principles and Parameters in a VSO Language: A Case Study in Welsh
Ian G. Roberts

Structures and Beyond: The Cartography of Syntactic Structures, Volume 3
Edited by Adriana Belletti

Movement and Silence
Richard S. Kayne

Restructuring and Functional Heads: The Cartography of Syntactic Structures, Volume 4
Guglielmo Cinque

Scrambling, Remnant Movement and Restructuring in West Germanic
Roland Hinterhölzl

The Syntax of Ellipsis: Evidence from Dutch Dialects
Jeroen van Craenenbroeck

Mapping the Left Periphery: The Cartography of Syntactic Structures, Volume 5
Edited by Paola Benincà and Nicola Munaro

Mapping Spatial PPs: The Cartography of Syntactic Structures, Volume 6
Edited by Guglielmo Cinque and Luigi Rizzi

The Grammar of Q: Q-Particles, Wh-Movement, and Pied-Piping
Seth Cable

Comparisons and Contrasts
Richard S. Kayne

Discourse-Related Features and Functional Projections
Silvio Cruschina

Functional Heads: The Cartography of Syntactic Structures, Volume 7
Edited by Laura Brugé, Anna Cardinaletti, Giuliana Giusti, Nicola Munaro, Cecilia Poletto

Adverbial Clauses, Main Clause Phenomena and Composition of the Left Periphery: The Cartography of Syntactic Structures, Volume 8
Liliane Haegeman

Variation in Datives
Edited by Beatriz Fernández and Ricardo Etxepare

VARIATION IN DATIVES

A Microcomparative Perspective

Edited by Beatriz Fernández

and

Ricardo Etxepare

OXFORD
UNIVERSITY PRESS

OXFORD
UNIVERSITY PRESS

Oxford University Press, Inc., publishes works that further
Oxford University's objective of excellence
in research, scholarship, and education.

Oxford   New York
Auckland   Cape Town   Dar es Salaam   Hong Kong   Karachi
Kuala Lumpur   Madrid   Melbourne   Mexico City   Nairobi
New Delhi   Shanghai   Taipei   Toronto

With offices in
Argentina   Austria   Brazil   Chile   Czech Republic   France Greece
Guatemala   Hungary   Italy   Japan   Poland   Portugal   Singapore
South Korea   Switzerland   Thailand   Turkey   Ukraine   Vietnam

Oxford is a registered trademark of Oxford University Press in the UK and certain other
countries.

Published in the United States of America by
Oxford University Press
198 Madison Avenue, New York, NY 10016

© Oxford University Press 2013

Library of Congress Cataloging-in-Publication Data

Variation in datives : a micro-comparative perspective / edited by Beatriz Fernández and
Ricardo Etxepare.
      p. cm. — (Oxford studies in comparative syntax)
Includes bibliographical references and index.
ISBN 978–0–19–993738–7 (pbk. : alk. paper) — ISBN 978–0–19–993736–3 (alk. paper)
1. Grammar, Comparative and general—Syntax.   2. Grammar, Comparative and general—Case. 3.
Grammar, Comparative and general—Agreement.   I. Fernández, Beatriz.   II. Etxepare, Ricardo.
P201.V34 2013
415—dc23   2012011725

ISBN 978–0–19–993736–3
ISBN 978–0–19–993738–7

9 8 7 6 5 4 3 2 1
Printed in the United States of America
on acid-free paper

CONTENTS

Introduction   *vii*
Beatriz Fernández and Ricardo Etxepare

1. Evaluative Reflexions: Evaluative Dative Reflexive in
   Southeast Serbo-Croatian   *1*
   Boban Arsenijević (Universitat Pompeu Fabra)
2. Core and Noncore Datives in French   *22*
   *Nora Boneh and Léa Nash (The Hebrew Univ. of
   Jerusalem/Univ. of Paris VIII)*
3. Datives and Adpositions in Northeastern Basque   *50*
   Ricardo Etxepare and Bernard Oyhar Çabal (IKER)
4. Case in Disguise   *96*
   Hlíf Árnadóttir and Einar Freyr Sigurðsson (Univ. of Iceland)
5. Dative versus Accusative and the Nature of Inherent Case   *144*
   Jóhannes Gísli Jónsson (Univ. of Iceland)
6. Ideal Speakers and Other Speakers: The Case of
   Dative and Some Other Cases   *161*
   Höskuldur Thráinsson (Univ. of Iceland)
7. Feminine Bleeds Dative: The Syntax of a Syncretism Pattern   *189*
   Thomas Leu (Yale University)
8. Syntactic Microvariation: Dative Constructions in Greek   *212*
   Dimitris Michelioudakis and Ioanna Sitaridou (Univ. of Cambridge)
9. Dative Displacement in Basque   *256*
   Milan Rezac and Beatriz Fernández (Univ. of Paris VIII/UPV/EHU)
10. Accusative Datives in Spanish   *283*
    Juan Romero (Univ. of Cáceres)

Index   *301*

INTRODUCTION

This volume attempts to examine some of the issues related to the syntactic status of dative-marked DPs in the light of microsyntactic variation. Some of the central issues involved in characterizing dative-marked DPs in a larger grammatical context, such as the complementarity of dative case markers and adpositions, their relation to the lexical meaning of the verb, the animacy or definiteness restrictions that emerge in dative case marking, the range of functions available to dative-marked DPs and the way they are represented in the functional structure of the clause, their indexation in the finite verb, or the case alternations that arise between datives and other cases (accusative or nominative as well as so-called oblique cases), are addressed in this volume, in most cases from an angle that crucially involves syntactic comparison at a microvariation scale. The combination of a narrowly defined grammatical topic giving rise to some of the central interrogations in grammatical theory and a microcomparative approach addressing theoretically significant syntactic variation among closely related linguistic varieties characterizes this volume of the series.

1. MICROPARAMETERS IN THE CONTEXT OF PARAMETRIC VARIATION

The last twenty years in the area of generative grammar have seen a growing concern with progressively more inclusive comparative studies, on the one hand, and with an increasing focus on language internal variation, on the other. Both approaches directly stem from the principles and parameters model of the early 1980s and the notion of parameter that ensued: in this approach, Universal Grammar is an invariant system of abstract principles that constitute the species-specific language endowment and that permit a limited degree of variation in the form of parameters, unspecified options associated to a restricted set of grammatical loci, to be set by properties of the linguistic input. Early work in this model resulted in the formulation of large-scale parameters, the so-called *macroparameters* (Baker 2008) or *meta-parameters* (Pica 2001), such as the null subject parameter (Chomsky 1981,

Rizzi 1982)[1] or the polysynthesis parameter (Baker 1996), which involved a large number of languages and sweeping generalizations.

These long-range parameters are at the center of controversy nowadays. Newmeyer's (2004, 2005) recent work may be seen as a paradigmatic criticism of the notion of parameter embedded in the traditional Principles and Parameters (P&P) model.[2] Criticisms of this sort are usually based on the alleged failure of the parameter model to issue empirically correct typological generalizations. Other criticisms of the notion of parameter come from a different perspective: rather than focusing on the model's limited practical success, they note the problematic status of the concept in a minimalist framework, where the computational principles at work are subject to radical modularity, making it very difficult to integrate parameters into principles (Boeckx 2009, 2011). From this perspective, it is not easy to see how basic computational operations like *merge* or *copy* (previously implied in "movement"), for instance, could accommodate parametric variation of the sort that was apparent in, say, *subjacency* (but see Gallego 2010). One alternative approach that may be logically entertained is that parameters, rather than being overtly specified in the fabric of UG as binary options, follow from the underspecification of UG (see Boeckx 2009, Roberts and Roussou 2003). Under this view, the reason languages differ in the way they set the relative order of head and complement, for instance, follows not from the head-parameter, specified in UG as a binary choice in the directionality of recursion, but from the fact that merger, which produces hierarchical relations, does not specify order. Order is enforced by the externalization systems (PF), which must map hierarchical relations in time. Any of the possible options (head-complement or complement-head) optimally meet the interface requirements imposed by PF and therefore both become possible and are (roughly) evenly distributed.[3] Finally, some of the criticisms of the notion of parameter as understood in the original P&P model emerge from the area of language acquisition and language change. Recently, work by Yang (2002, 2010), who takes up and elaborates ideas first proposed by Kroch in the context of syntactic change, suggests that the learner is best modeled as having multiple grammars (associated to different weights) that compete among themselves to closely match the incoming input. It is the binary nature of the parameters, and the idea that the learner moves from one UG-defined grammar to another, that is replaced by a more flexible selectional model. This view of variation puts forward the idea that speakers

---

1 Although Baker (2008: 351–352) characterized it as a *medioparameter*.

2 See Roberts and Holmberg (2005) for a reply and Roberts and Holmberg (2010) for a (favourable) general discussion of the Principles and Parameters model.

3 We are simplifying deliberately. Issues related to nonharmonic orders become highly relevant.

may retain different parametric options as they develop their mature grammatical system. Höskuldur Thráinsson (this volume) provides evidence for this model on the basis of an ongoing change in Icelandic, so-called Dative Sickness. According to the corpus data he examines, the syntactic change in question (the spreading of the dative case in several verbal contexts) must be modeled in terms of an increasing factor of grammatical variability among the younger speakers, who accept (and use to different degrees) the two or more options involved in the change, as opposed to the older speakers. Intraspeaker variation of a microsyntactic type therefore becomes a revealing source of data and ideas for discussing the status of parameters.

The limited success of long-range parametric formulations has caused many linguists to turn their attention to more limited areas of variation, most notably to language internal variation.[4] This is where *microparameters* arise. As Kayne (2005: 8) graphically puts it, "The special status of micro-comparative syntax resides in the fact that it is the closest we can come, at the present time, to a controlled experiment in comparative syntax." Extending this image, Kayne (2000: 5) claims that

> comparative work on the syntax of a large number of closely related varieties/
> languages can be thought of as a new research tool, one that is capable of
> providing results of an unusually fine-grained and particularly solid character.
> If it were possible to experiment in languages, a syntactician would construct
> an experiment of the following type: take a language, alter a single one of its
> observable syntactic properties, and examine the result to see what, if any, other
> property has changed as a consequence. If some other property has changed,
> conclude that it and the property that was altered are linked to one another by
> some abstract parameter.

This approach to the study of syntactic variation is embedded in a particular notion of what parameters are. This notion can be defined in terms of what Baker (2008: 353–355) calls the Borer/Chomsky conjecture:

(1) The Borer/Chomsky conjecture
All parameters of variation are attributable to differences in the features of particular items (e.g. the functional heads) in the lexicon

(1) finds a stronger formulation in the idea that "every functional element made available by UG is associated with some syntactic parameter" (Kayne 2005: 11).

---

4 We take the opposition between I- and E-languages to apply not only to "languages" but also to "varieties," and only I-languages/varieties are amenable to scientific study. In other words, we find no reason not to identify "language" and "variety."

As Baker points out, this particular conception of parameter was first addressed by Borer (1984) and then adopted by Chomsky (1995) in the minimalist program and is tightly related to Kayne's (and others') microcomparative approach. If functional elements are responsible for cross-linguistic variation, then this variation resides in the component of grammar we learn from input data, that is, the lexicon. This way, acquiring the lexicon and idiosyncratic properties of functional elements means acquiring syntactic variation (Borer 1984: 29).

This view stands in contrast to the notion of macroparameters, as proposed by Baker (among others), which continue the original conception of parameter of the 1980s. The macroparametric view can be formulated as follows (Baker 2008: 354):

(2) There are some parameters within the statements of the general principles that shape natural language syntax.

(2) corresponds to the idea that something like being a polysynthetic language, for example, "seems to be more pervasive than can be attributed to any particular item" (Baker 1996). It is an open question whether parameters of the polysynthetic sort exist. An alternative view of such parameters is that they can be cashed out in terms of an aggregate of microparameters. As noted by Kayne (2005: 7), one of the key properties of polysynthetic languages—the obligatory appearance of a pronominal agreement element in addition to the (nonincorporated) lexical argument—is also found within languages like Italian. For example, the Italian clitic left-dislocation construction (Cinque 1990) requires the presence of a pronominal clitic in addition to the dislocated direct object argument. Although this property may ultimately be unconnected to the polysynthesis parameter, it could alternatively be the case that "the systematic obligatoriness of pronominal agreement morphemes in Mohawk is just an extreme example of what is found to a lesser extent in (some) Romance."

2. IDENTITY CRITERIA FOR PARAMETERS

The previous discussion on the status of parameters raises the issue of how we can distinguish bona fide parameters in the context of language variation, assuming that at least part of that variation will result from historical accident. Smith and Law (2009) propose a set of "identity criteria" for parameters that we may use as a useful heuristic to determine the existence of parameters at the microvariation scale. For Smith and Law, parameters present some characterizing properties amid more ordinary variation. Parameters must cover variation that is systematic, deterministic (in the sense that the input available to the child must be rich enough and explicit enough to guarantee that the parameter can be set), discrete (usually binary), and exclusive, such that the parametric variation gives rise to mutually exclusive options. Under an appropriate formulation, mutual exclusivity entails that the parametric options exhaust the hypothesis space in an interdependent way. That is, parameters are hierarchically nested (see Baker 2001).

As an example of how microparametric syntax uncovers significant aspects of syntactic variation in the sense suggested by Smith and Law (2009), consider the kind of systematic variation noted by Holmberg & Platzack between *Insular Scandinavian* languages (Icelandic, partly Faroese and Old Scandinavian) and *Mainland Scandinavian* ones (Danish, Norwegian, and Swedish).[5] As Holmberg & Platzack (2005: 420–421) point out, "In many respects these languages are no more different than dialects of a single language may be." All Scandinavian languages present a high degree of grammatical similarity (Holmberg & Platzack 2005: 421–424). However, some syntactic differences between Insular Scandinavian and Mainland Scandinavian are attested, as far as the left periphery (Rizzi 1997) is concerned (see section 3.4, 432–438). Apart from the intrinsic interest of the description of these syntactic differences attested in the languages under discussion, one of the most appealing aspects of Holmberg & Platzack's work lies in the simplicity and elegance of the theoretical explanation that underlies that variation. Assuming that in the left periphery, there is a Force Phrase, as in Rizzi 1997, and a Finite Phrase (FinP) that hosts an EPP feature (i.e., it must have a specifier), Holmberg & Platzack (2005: 433) propose that "the syntactic differences are the results of a single inflectional difference between these languages: the finite verb in Icelandic, but not in Mainland Scandinavian, is inflected for person." Holmberg & Platzack assume that "the person inflection hosts an uninterpretable finiteness feature uFin. For Mainland Scandinavian, which does not have person inflection, the feature uFin is contained in the nominative DP." Furthermore, as Scandinavian languages are verb-second languages, Fin° must be filled. A number of grammatical differences follow automatically from this parametric difference. Thus, Mainland Scandinavian must have a visible subject in all finite clauses, expletive or not, whereas Icelandic must have a visible element in front of the finite verb, but not necessarily a subject:

(1) a. Det   regnade igår   (Swedish)
    b. Það   rigndi   í gær   (Icelandic)
       it rained yesterday

(2) a. Igår   regnade *(det) (Swedish)
    b. Í gær rigndi   (*Það)   (Icelandic)
       yesterday rained it

5 Roberts and Holmberg (2005) use the same illustrative case.

Then, Insular Scandinavian, but not Mainland Scandinavian has stylistic front-ing. Here are the examples (from Icelandic) given in Holmberg & Platzack (2005: 436) from Jónsson (1991) and Holmberg (2000):

(1) a. Þetta er tilboð sem ekki er hœgt að hafna
       This is offer that not is possible to reject

    b. Þeir sem pessa erfiðu ákvörðun verða að taka
       those that this difficult decision have to take

Third, oblique subjects are available in Insular Scandinavian but not Mainland Scandinavian (from Icelandic):

(3) Hadfði mér Því leiðst Haraldur
    had me. DAT thus bored Harold. NOM

Finally, embedded subject questions compete with the complementizer in Insular Scandinavian, but not in Mainland Scandinavian:

(3) a. Hon frågade   vad *(som) låg   i byrån (Swedish)
    b. Hún spurði   hvað (*sem) lægi í skúffunni (Icelandic)
       she asked   what that was-lying in chest-the

A difference in the location of a noninterpretable feature (whether in Fin or in the nominative DP) gives rise to a set of clustering properties distinguish-ing two groups of dialects. The grammatical options addressed by the param-eter count as systematic, discrete, mutually exclusive, and deterministic.

Variation of that general form is to be found in several proposals along the volume. Most of the contributions in this volume are cast within an approach to parametric variation that is highly sympathetic to (1).

3. WHY DATIVES?

The volume focuses on the syntactic variation that arises in connection with dative-marked DPs. We define dative DPs as those DPs that typically occur as recipients of a caused motion event or a caused possession event (see Rappaport and Levin 2008, among many others) and that are identified by grammati-cal means that set them apart from the rest of the nominal arguments of a predicate. Those grammatical means may involve case-endings, dedicated mor-phology in the finite verb or auxiliary, or a special syntactic position vis-à-vis other DPs in the sentence (as can be deduced from binding and scope con-figurations or phrasal ordering). In addition, those means typically go beyond recipients of motion or change of possession events to characterize other DPs whose semantic contribution does not seem to be entailed by the lexical root or the basic thematic layer of the verb. This is one of the distinctive properties of dative-marked DPs, and one that sets apart dative-marked DPs from other case-marked DPs. Dative-marked DPs may occur as benefactives, as experiencers, as external possessors, as ethical datives, or as addressee-oriented markers, and their relation to selected datives is a source of permanent interrogation. The presence of nonselected datives has led to the hypothesis that datives in general are introduced in the clausal structure by indirect means, as arguments of an independent functional head, which could be inserted in different syntactic positions. The contribution of a dative-marked DP would therefore follow from the syntactic phrase to which this independent functional head merges. This intuition underlies much of the research on "high" and "low" datives (Pylkkänen 2008, Cuervo 2003, Anagnostopoulou 2003), which extends some of the findings on applicative constructions to languages that have no applicative morphology. Our volume contains two chapters that make specific contributions in this regard. Going beyond the usual discussion on the syntactic merger position of nonargumental datives, Nora Boneh and Léa Nash uncover several unnoticed asymmetries between core and noncore datives in French: the former must bind a variable inside the verbal phrase. By focusing on the relation between the high dative and its scope (the verbal domain), they are able to account for the range of DP-types that may occur inside the VP in combination with a nonselected dative and provide a convincing account of the uncovered restrictions. In his contribution, Boban Arsenijevic focuses on a relatively uncommon type of nonselected dative: the so-called evaluative dative, which he takes to be related to a head expressing evaluative mood. This particular type of dative can be shown to be licensed by the subject of the clause, therefore illustrating one of the cases of subject-involvement that make nonselected dative arguments so puzzling.

The ability of dative-marked DPs to occupy more than one structural position in such a prominent way raises a question as to the status of the dative marker, analyzed in many languages as a bona fide case-ending on the same level as, say, nominative/absolutive or ergative/accusative case-endings. The particular status of dative markers is apparent, however, in terminology (*oblique case*) that assimilates dative endings to other declensional types. There is an ongoing debate as to whether dative markers should be assimilated to adpositions. According to several authors (e.g., Asbury 2008), dative case markers are actually adpositions. In Caha's nanosyntactic approach (2009), prepositions and case-endings are distinguished as a result of NP movement. If the NP moves beyond a labeled feature, this feature will show up as a case-ending on the NP; if the movement does not reach the labeled feature, this feature will be realized as a preposition. Thus nothing substantial hinges on the adposition/case-ending distinction. That datives must be kept separate from nominative and accusative case (assumed to illustrate "abstract case") is shown by Tom Leu's chapter in the volume. In his analysis of the nominal inflection of Standard German and Swiss German, dative aligns with genitive case, not with nominative and accusative in several syncretism phenomena, and also aligns with the genitive in the position it occupies in the structure of the DP, different from nominative and accusative. Swiss German therefore becomes a source of evidence that dative case marking must be treated separately from undisputable instances of abstract case. On the other hand, many languages make clear distinctions between dative-marked endings and other declension classes, such as primary adpositions and other, more complex adpositional phrases. In Basque, for instance, dative-marked DPs typically agree in person and number with the inflected verb, just as absolutive and ergative-marked DPs do. Furthermore, dative-marked DPs share their agreement exponence with the ergative, an abstract case (see Rezac et al. for discussion). Dative DPs also enter into binding as legitimate antecedents, and they differ from primary adpositions in that they follow the determiner, unlike primary adpositions, which attach to the stem. Still, microvariation studies such as the one contributed by Ricardo Etxepare and Bernard Oyharçabal (this volume) present dialects that possess spatial datives along with the more general dative DPs. Those datives do not agree with the verb and occupy a position lower than agreeing ones. This type of dative, identical to ordinary dative DPs as to the form of the case-ending, exists along with the agreeing datives in those dialects, and thus offers an excellent window for discovering the minimal grammatical components that may determine the ultimate position of a dative-marked DP in the line that goes from case-marked DP to adpositional phrase.

The syntactic position of dative-marked DPs in case assignment configurations also sets dative DPs apart from other case-marked DPs. Dative DPs enter into dative alternations of different sorts. A common one presents an alternation between a case-marked high recipient that precedes the object, and a low prepositional recipient that follows the object (Greek, Anagnastopoulou 2003). Others express the prominent status of the dative-marked DP by clitic doubling (Spanish, Demonte 1995), or agreement (Etxepare 2011, in the context of northeastern dialects of Basque). English, on the other hand, presents no particular exponence for its first DP in the double object construction, but its prominent status can be tracked down by a number of syntactic asymmetries that distinguish the two objects. Microvariation studies can shed interesting light on several of the issues related to double object or alternating constructions. Dimitris Michelioudakis and Ioanna Sitaridou (this volume) compare the substitutes of the Ancient Greek dative in four different varieties of Greek and are able to establish some revealing correlations between their different syntactic properties. Thus, they show that those varieties where the dative DP exerts an intervention effect are also varieties that present a strong version of the PCC. Those are also the varieties that possess a dative alternation between a case-marked DP and a prepositional one. They propose a typology based on minimal distinctions in the specification of inherent case that elegantly accounts for the relevant differences. Juan Romero (this volume) presents a fresh look at an apparently low-level morphological variation in the gender specification of the dative clitic in some of the Iberian Spanish dialects: unlike in most of the Iberian Spanish dialects, northwestern ones seem to make a gender distinction (masculine/feminine) in the dative clitic paradigm. Interestingly, this feminine clitic, representing the indirect object, is possible only in those contexts where accusative is assigned. Romero convincingly argues that this restriction is related to the one we see in the double object construction in English, which has the indirect object receiving accusative case from the verb. A related asymmetry, but in a very different morphological setting, concerns so-called dative displacement in Basque, whereby a dative-marked argument ends up controlling the agreement slot in the inflected verb that corresponds to the absolutive. This phenomenon, like the Spanish feminine dative clitics, or the dative alternations examined by Michelioudakis and Sitaridou, is prompted by the presence of animacy or person features in the dative-marked DP. Unlike in the dative alternation constructions, however, the predicate does not have to be ditransitive. Dative displacement in those cases is highly reminiscent of Differential Object Marking phenomena. Milan Rezac and Beatriz Fernández (this volume) closely examine four Basque varieties that present dative displacement, and they use microsyntactic comparison to sketch a preliminary map of the grammatical variables that enter into the determination of the actual forms.

Differential Object Marking is typically associated to features that are not directly selected by the lexical predicate. Other cases of dative marking, however, seem to be related to the event structure associated to the lexical verb. Case alternations involving dative therefore become a good testing ground for the relation between event structure and case marking (see Svenonius 2002). Jóhannes Gísli Jónsson (this volume) and Hlíf Árnadóttir and Einar Freyr Sigurðsson (this volume) examine the distribution of dative and accusative cases in the context of different predicate classes in several varieties of Icelandic. This comparative work results in reconsideration of the status of inherent case.

4. CONTRIBUTIONS TO THE VOLUME

Most of the contributions in the volume are set in a microparametric perspective and examine two or more closely related dialectal variants. As such, the volume is able to provide very specific clues as to the exact factors that enter into the limited variation allowed in each case. In many cases, these chapters also include a reflection about the form of the parameters involved in variation as well as about the nature of parametric variation in general. We briefly summarize each of the chapters separately, stating their main contributions to the issues discussed in the book.

Boban Arsenijevic's article, "Evaluative Reflexions: Evaluative Dative Reflexive in Southeast Serbo-Croatian," focuses on a type of nonselected clitic dative form in southeastern dialects of Serbo-Croatian that the author calls "evaluative dative reflexive." The crucial component of this dative clitic is that it relates to the evaluative mood. The presence of the evaluative dative reflexive clitic contributes the meaning that the subject of the clause is a subject of evaluation of the underlying eventuality. The author argues that the relative position the evaluative dative reflexive occupies in the clause is highly reminiscent of evaluative mood as characterized by Cinque (1999). This evaluative reflexive is bound by the subject of the clause, which raises to a topic position. The author compares the Serbo-Croatian data with similar datives in English, Syrian Arabic, and Palestinian Arabic.

Nora Boneh and Léa Nash's article, "Core and Noncore Datives in French," analyzes nonselected or noncore datives, with particular focus on French. Against the widely held idea that noncore datives are selected by special applicative heads, they claim that those datives are merged as subjects of a stative predicate, itself part of a complex event with a resultant subevent or a locational endpoint. The extra noncore dative argument is licensed by a procedure of lambda abstraction over a variable provided by material in the lower subevent. Boneh and Nash uncover an interesting set of restrictions on the kind of DP or modifier that stays under the scope of the VP in the presence of noncore datives: the material inside the VP must be able to be bound by the null operator that triggers lambda abstraction. It thus follows that objects such as nonpossessive DPs, proper nouns, or modifiers not containing a pronominal element block the possibility of a noncore dative in French. Their analysis, inspired partly by Roberge and Troberg (2009), requires the noncore dative to bind a variable in the scope of the stative predicate.

Ricardo Etxepare and Bernard Oyharçabal's chapter, "Datives and Adpositions in Northeastern Basque," concentrates on two related differences that distinguish central and western Basque, on the one hand, and northeastern Basque, on the other. In the latter, the domain of dative case marking seems wider: it extends to DPs expressing purely spatial roles, such as goals of motion, and also to aspectual arguments such as complements of atelic aspectual verbs. In those contexts, the dative does not agree in person and number with the finite verb, an option that is otherwise not allowed for datives in Basque. This raises the question of the status of dative marking in those dialects. They argue that the spatial dative cases in northeastern Basque are not different from what we see in canonical dative DPs: they are case suffixes attached to nominal phrases and expressing purely syntactic relations. The only difference is that the kind of functional support necessary to license case in verbal predicates can also be found internal to adpositional phrases, within certain conditions. Concretely, they capitalize on recent work by Koopman (2000), Tortora (2009), and Den Dikken (2010) and argue that the spatial dative cases of northeastern Basque are licensed in an aspectual projection internal to a phrase headed by a directional adposition. The argument includes a detailed discussion of some of the aspects involved in the syntax of postpositional phrases in Basque.

Case in Disguise: The authors of this chapter, Hlíf Árnadóttir and Einar Freyr Sigurðsson, argue, following Legate (2008), that case assignment obeys potentially two conditions: a derivational one, whereby case relations are established in the syntax (abstract case), and an interface one (postsyntactic morphological case), which concerns its morphological realization. The latter is realized according to global morphological conditions that take into account the full set of morphologically realized cases in the sentence. Under this double determination of overt case, abstract case and morphological case may not be directly related. From this indirect relation arises the notion of "case in disguise," which may obscure the underlying case relations established in the syntactic component. The authors account for an ongoing change in the case pattern of DAT-NOM predicates into a DAT-ACC case pattern, where the dative case serves to "disguise" abstract nominative case.

Jóhannes Gísli Jónsson, in "Dative v. Accusative and the Nature of Nonstructural Case," examines the alternation between dative and accusative case in different predicate types in Icelandic and claims that case marking in Icelandic argues in favor of a case-marking typology that goes against the idea that inherent case cannot be assigned to themes (Woolford 2006). A subset of motion predicates in Icelandic (so-called predicates of translational motion) is shown to select only dative objects. While the semantic interpretation of those objects is entirely predictable, they are assigned inherent dative case. The chapter includes a discussion of dative/accusative alternations in the complements of Icelandic verbs.

Höskuldur Thráinsson's chapter, "Ideal Speakers and Other Speakers: The Case of Dative and Some Other Cases," is concerned with inter- and intraspeaker variation in the domain of subject and object case marking in Icelandic and Faroese. Based on the large-scale syntactic variation surveys IceDiasyn and FarDiaSyn, Thráinsson is able to point out some of the fine points of variation regarding the selection of case-endings in a population of speakers spanning from fifteen-year-olds to people between the ages of sixty and seventy. He observes that interspeaker variation in the time arrow, which brings about the spread of so-called Dative Sickness (the substitution of accusative case by dative in a particular class of so-called impersonal verbs), is accompanied by increasing intraspeaker variation. Thus, younger speakers tend overwhelmingly to accept both accusative and dative case-marking in the subject position of the relevant verbs, whereas older speakers tend to only accept accusative marking. Thráinsson examines this pattern of increasing intraspeaker variation in the light of recent proposals regarding the way parameters are set. For Thráinsson, the increasing intraspeaker variation observed in younger generations is hard to accommodate in a model of parameter setting that regards learners as settling relatively early in a grammar that is consistent and uniform in all respects. The data seem to point toward a model of parameter setting, advocated by Kroch (1989) and more recently (Yang 2000, 2004, 2010), that proceeds in a probabilistic fashion (within a limited hypothesis space) and may involve a degree of indeterminacy in the grammatical knowledge that is acquired, in the sense that the latter may involve more than one grammatical option, or differently put, more than one grammar.

Tom Leu's chapter, "Feminine Bleeds Dative: The Syntax of a Syncretism Pattern," focuses on the morphological paradigm of case- and agreement-marking in German (singular) DPs. He argues that the patterns of syncretism that arise from the combination of case and gender feature exponence are better analyzed by postulating different syntactic positions for dative and genitive case-markers (gathered under the category oblique), on the one hand, and nominative-accusative ones, on the other; the latter are merged lower in the DP structure and are part of what is called adjectival agreement. Part of the evidence presented capitalizes on dialectal variation internal to German, with particular attention to Swiss German. One important conclusion of the analysis is that the correct analysis of adjectival agreement must be stated in the grammar independently of the distribution of dative/genitive morphology.

Dimitris Michelioudakis and Ioanna Sitaridou's chapter, "Syntactic Microvariation: Dative Constructions in Greek," is a careful comparison of the status of the IO (the descent of the classical Greek dative) in several closely related varieties and subvarieties of Greek (particularly Pontic Greek). Michelioudakis and Sitaridou manage to scrutinize some of the most prominent theoretical issues regarding the relation between case-marked and PP IOs on the basis of minimally contrasting varieties and reach conclusions that, in the light of comparison, have general import. Their work thus constitutes a good example of a microvariation study. Michelioudakis and Sitaridou examine some of the basic aspects of cross-dialectal variation in Greek, such as the availability of dative alternations, the relative syntactic position of objects and indirect objects, the existence of minimality effects in Agree/Move operations in the context of dative constructions, and the presence of PCC effects of varying strength. The correlations they find between those different aspects of variation suggest that the differences must be related to the nature of the case feature associated with the dative argument: the authors distinguish between bona fide inherent cases, and inherent cases that seem to participate in Agree/Move relations. They also defend the idea that applicative morphemes do not select or introduce datives but, rather, attract DPs with an active case originating in a thematic position related to the verbal root.

Milan Rezac and Beatriz Fernández's chapter, "Dative Displacement in Basque," discusses differences across Basque dialects in the accessibility of datives to absolutive-type agreement. In most varieties, including Standard Basque, datives control a dedicated series of dative suffixes. In some varieties, however, their agreement "displaces" to take over morphology otherwise reserved for the absolutive, a phenomenon known as *dative displacement*. Rezac and Fernández examine in detail four dative displacement dialects in Basque with the aim of distinguishing the syntactic and the morphological factors that may enter in the determination of the forms showing displacement. Although they show that in many cases the arising forms could be accounted for by invoking either syntactic or purely morphological operations, some conditioning factors are irreducibly syntactic. This corresponds to those cases where dative displacement is limited to particular subclasses of datives (goals of motion, or indirect objects of causativized verbs) whose marking is indistinguishable from that of other datives in the morphology.

Juan Romero's chapter, "Accusative Datives in Spanish," explores the phenomenon of "laísmo" (the use of feminine dative clitics) in a subset of peninsular Spanish dialects. He shows that the traditional analysis of this phenomenon, traditionally interpreted as a low-level morphological variation, is related in a nontrivial way to other syntactic dimensions of ditransitive constructions, such as the animate/inanimate status of the dative, the case-assigning properties of the predicate, and the argumental nature of the dative, all of them unexpected if only a gender distinction is at stake. Romero provides a convincing analysis of laista dialects that builds on some well-established properties of double object constructions: the idea that the object and the indirect object are part of a small clause, that the head of the small clause incorporates onto the verb, and that the higher verb only has a case to assign. In this context, standard dialects of Spanish incorporate the head of the indirect object to the verb in the form of the clitic *le*. On the basis of the ambiguous status of *le* as both a dative and an accusative clitic in standard Spanish, laísta dialects have reanalyzed certain instances of dative case/agreement involving feminine gender as cases of incorporation. In this sense, laista dialects are a subset of leista ones, and the relation between the different varieties can be described in terms of a "nested" microparametric option.

ACKNOWLEDGMENTS

This work has been partially supported by the following grants: Basque Government HM-2009-1-25, IT4-14-10 and GIC07/144-IT-210-07; Ministerio de Ciencia e Innovación FFI2008-00240/FILO and FFI2011-26906; Agence Nationale de la Recherche ANR-07-CORP-033.

REFERENCES

Anagnostopoulou, Elena. 2003. *The syntax of ditransitives*. Berlin: Mouton de Gruyter.

Asbury, Anna. 2008. "The morphosyntax of case and adpositions." PhD diss., Utrecht University.

Baker, Mark. 1996. *The polysynthesis parameter*. New York: Oxford University Press.

Baker, Mark. 2001. *The atoms of language*. New York: Basic Books.

Baker, Mark. 2008. "The macroparameter in a microparametric world." In Theresa Biberauer (ed.), *The limits of syntactic variation*, 351–374. Amsterdam: John Benjamins.

Boeckx, Cedric. 2009. *Bare syntax*. Oxford: Oxford University Press

Boeckx, Cedric. 2011. "Approaching parameters from below." In Cedric Boeckx and Anna M. di Sciullo (eds.), *The biolinguistic enterprise: New perspectives on the evolution and nature of the human language faculty*, 205–221. Oxford: Oxford University Press.

Borer, Hagit. 1984. *Parametric syntax: Case studies in Semitic and Romance languages*. Dordrecht: Foris.

Caha, Pavel. 2009. "The nanosyntax of case." PhD diss., Tromso.

Chomsky, Noam. 1981. *Lectures on government and binding*. Dordrecht: Foris.

Chomsky, Noam. 1995. *The minimalist program*. Cambridge, MA: MIT Press.

Cinque, Guglielmo. 1990. *Types of A-dependencies*. Cambridge, MA: MIT Press.

Cinque, Guglielmo. 1999. *Adverbs and functional heads*. Oxford: Oxford University Press.

Cuervo, Maria Cristina. 2003. *Datives at large*. Cambridge, MA: MIT Press.

Demonte, Violeta. 1995. "Dative alternation in Spanish." *Probus* 7: 5–30.

Den Dikken, Marcel. 2010. "On the functional structure of locative and directional PPs." In Cuglielmo Cinque and Luigi Rizzi (eds.), *Mapping spatial PPs: The cartography of syntactic structures*, vol. 6, 74–126. Oxford Studies in Comparative Syntax. New York: Oxford University Press.

Etxepare, Ricardo. 2011. "Contact and change in a restrictive theory of parameters." To appear in C. Picallo (ed.), *Parameters and linguistic variation*. New York: Oxford University Press.

Gallego, Angel. 2010. *Phase theory*. Amsterdam: John Benjamins.

Holmberg, Anders. 2000. "Scandinavian stylistic fronting: How any category can become an expletive." *Linguistic Inquiry* 31: 445–484.

Holmberg, Anders. 2010. "Parameters in minimalist theory: The case of Scandinavian." *Theoretical Linguistics* 36(1): 1–48.

Holmberg, Anders, and Christer Platzack. 2005. "The Scandinavian languages." In Guglielmo Cinque and Richard S. Kayne (eds.), *The Oxford handbook of comparative syntax*, 420–458. New York: Oxford University Press.

Jónsson, Johánnes Gisli. 1991. "Stylistic fronting in Icelandic." *Working Papers in Scandinavian Syntax* (Lund University) 48: 1–43.

Kayne, Richard S. 1996. "Microparametric syntax: Some introductory remarks." In J. Black and V. Montapanyane (eds.), *Microparametric syntax and dialect variation*, ix–xvii. Amsterdam: John Benjamins. Reprinted in Kayne 2000: 3–9.

Kayne, Richard S. 2000. *Parameters and universals*. New York: Oxford University Press.

Kayne, Richard S. 2005. "Some notes on comparative syntax, with special reference to English and French." In Guglielmo Cinque and Richard S. Kayne (eds.), *The Oxford handbook of comparative syntax*, 3–69. New York: Oxford University Press.

Koopman, Hilda. 2000. "Prepositions, postpositions, circumpositions and particles." In Hilda Koopman (ed.), *The syntax of specifiers and heads*, 204–260. London: Routledge.

Kroch, Anthony. 1989. "Reflexes of grammar in patterns of language change." *Language Variation and Change* 1: 199–244.

Legate, Julie Anne. 2008. "Morphological and abstract case." *Linguistic Inquiry*. 39 (1): 55–101.

Newmeyer, Frederick J. 2004. "Against a parameter-setting approach to language variation." In Pierre Pica, Johan Rooryck, and Jeroen van Craenenbroek (eds.), *Language Variation Yearbook*, 4: 181–234. Amsterdam: John Benjamins.

Newmeyer, Frederick J. 2005. *Possible and probable languages. A generative perspective on Linguistic Typology*. New York: Oxford University Press.

Newmeyer, Frederick J. 2006. "A rejoinder to 'On the role of parameters in Universal Grammar: A reply to Newmeyer' by Ian Roberts and Anders Holmberg." Available online: http://ling.auf.net/lingBuzz/000248.

Ormazabal, Javier, and Juan Romero. 2007. "The object agreement constraint." *NLLT* 25 (2): 315–347.

Pica, Pierre. 2001. "Introduction." *Linguistic Variation Yearbook* 1: v–xii.

Pylkkänen, Lyna. 2008. *Introducing arguments*. Cambridge, MA: MIT Press.

Rappaport, Hovav M., and Beth Levin. 2008. "The English dative alternation: The case for verb sensitivity." *Journal of Linguistics* 44: 129–167.

Rezac, Milan, Pablo Albizu, and Ricardo Etxepare. 2011. "Abstract ergative case." Ms. CNRS–University of the Basque Country.

Rizzi, Luigi. 1997. "The fine structure of the Left Periphery." In Liliane Haegeman (ed.), *Elements of grammar: Handbook in generative syntax*, 281–337. Dordrecht: Kluwer.

Rizzi, Luigi. 1982. *Issues in Italian syntax*. Dordrecht: Foris.

Roberge, Yves, and Michelle Troberg. 2009. "The high applicative syntax of the dativus commondi/incommodi in Romance." *Probus* 21: 249–289.

Roberts, Ian, and Anders Holmberg. 2005. "On the role of parameters in Universal Grammar: A reply to Newmeyer." In Hans Broekhuis, Norbert Corver, Riny Huybregts, Ursula Kleinhenz, and Jan Koster (eds.), *Organizing grammar: Linguistic studies in honor of Henk van Riemsdijk*, 538–553. Berlin: Mouton de Gruyter.

Roberts, Ian, and Anders Holmberg. 2010. "Introduction: Parameters in minimalist theory." In Theresa Biberauer, Anders Holmberg, Ian Roberts, and Michelle Sheehan (eds.), *Parametric variation: Null subjects in minimalist theory*, 1–57. New York: Cambridge University Press.

Roberts, Ian, and Anna Roussou. 2003. *Syntactic change: A minimalist approach to grammaticalisation*. Cambridge: Cambridge University Press.

Smith, Neil, and Ann Law. 2009. "On parametric (and non-parametric) variation." *Biolinguistics* 3 (4): 332–343.

Svenonius, Peter. 2002. "Icelandic case and the structure of events." *Journal of Comparative Germanic Linguistics* 5: 197–225.

Tortora, C. 2009. "Aspect inside PLACE PPs." In Anna Asbury, Jakub Dotlacil, Berit Gehrke, and Rick Nouwen (eds.), *Syntax and semantics of Spatial P*, 273–301. Amsterdam: John Benjamins.

Woolford, Ellen. 2006. "Lexical case, inherent Case, and argument structure." *Linguistic Inquiry* 37 (1): 111–130.

Yang, Charles. 2000. "Internal and external forces in language change." *Language Variation and Change* 12 (3): 231–250.

Yang, Charles. 2002. "Knowledge and learning in natural language." Oxford: Oxford University Press.

Yang, Charles. 2004. "Universal grammar, statistics or both?" *Trends in Cognitive Sciences* 8 (10): 451–456.

Yang, Charles. 2010. "Three factors in language variation." *Lingua* 120: 1160–1177.

Variation in Datives

CHAPTER 1

Evaluative Reflexions: Evaluative Đative Reflexive in Southeast Serbo-Croatian

BOBAN ARSENIJEVIĆ

1. INTRODUCTION

The aim of this article is to present the relevant data and propose an analysis for the expression that I refer to as the Evaluative Dative Reflexive (EDR), as it is used in the southeastern dialects of Serbo-Croatian (SESC). This expression belongs to the class of nonselected datives and is characterized by the semantic effects of a positive evaluation of the underlying eventuality, a low value on a certain scale (small quantity of the eventuality, its low informational relevance, etc.), and some additional restrictions introduced in section 3. I argue for an analysis at the syntax-semantics interface, in which the crucial component of this dative is that it relates to the evaluative mood, specifying that the subject of the clause is also the subject of evaluation. I show how this analysis, which focuses on specifying the evaluative aspect of the semantic contribution of EDR, derives other semantic effects as well as the syntactic properties of the expression.

The article is organized as follows. In section 2, I present the class of nonselected datives—dative constituents which are not specified as typical participants in the kind of eventualities denoted by the verb. Section 3 introduces data from SESC about a special type of nonselected datives—the Evaluative Dative Reflexive. Section 4 presents an analysis that I propose for this expression, and section 5 shows how the analysis copes with the properties presented in section 3. Section 6 concludes.

2. NONSELECTED DATIVES

Dative case, both cross-linguistically and in Serbo-Croatian (S-C), a dialect of which is in the center of interest of this article, shows a tendency to appear on both selected and nonselected constituents. It is selected when the meaning of the verb (the type of eventualities it denotes) somehow introduces the presence of a participant that it expresses, and it is nonselected when no such relation with the verb can be observed. A typical use of the former type is to mark the recipient (1a) or the direction of some movement (1b), while a typical use of the latter is to mark the benefactive/malfactive meaning (1c, d).

(1) a. Jovan   daje   knjigu   *Mariji.*   S-C
     J.Nom   gives   book.Acc   M.Dat
     "Jovan gives/is giving a/the book to Marija."

   b. Jovan   ide   *lekaru.*
     J.Nom   goes   doctor.Dat
     "Jovan is going to (see) the doctor."

   c. Jovan   je   otvorio   vrata   *Mariji.*
     J.Nom   Aux   opened   door.Acc   M.Dat
     "Jovan opened the door for Marija."

   d. Jovan   je   *Mariji*   postavio   zamku.
     J.Nom   Aux   M.Dat   set   trap.Acc
     "J set a trap for Marija."

Other nonselected datives include the possessive dative (2a), the ethical dative (2b), the dative of interest (2c), and others (Horn 2008, Al Zahre & Boneh 2010).

(2) a. Marija   *mu*   je   videla   sestru.   S-C
     M.Nom   he.DatCl   Aux   seen   sister.Acc
     "Marija saw his sister."

   b. Kako   si   *mi?*
     how   Aux.2Sg   me.Dat
     lit. "How are you to/for me?"

   c. Ja   *ti*   onda   krenem   na   put.
     I   you.DatCl   then   start_going   on   trip.Acc
     "And then I took a trip [information in which you are interested]."

These traditional classes of nonselected datives are closely related to each other and are often hard to differentiate. This is already obvious in (2b and c), where the ethical dative could be seen as a pragmatically colored version of the benefactive (the speaker presents the well-being of the hearer as something that she is concerned about, hence benefactive/malfactive, i.e., the speaker takes the information he is conveying to directly bear on the hearer, again as a kind of benefactive/malfactive role in this respect). Moreover, most examples of benefactive and malfactive datives involve the meaning of possession and vice versa, as illustrated in (3).

(3) a. Jovan   je   *Mariji*   slomio   olovku.
        J.Nom   Aux   M.Dat   broken   pen.Acc
        "Jovan broke Marija's pen [at her damage]."

    b. Marija   je   *Jovanu*   namestila   zglob.
        M.Nom   Aux   J.Dat   set   joint.Acc
        "Marija relocated Jovan's joint [for his benefit]."

Yet another type of nonselected datives is the Evaluative Dative Reflexive (EDR), as I call it in this article, also known as the Coreferential Dative (CD; Berman 1982, Al Zahre & Boneh 2010), Reflexive Dative (Borer 2005), Personal Dative (Horn 2008), and so on. (For arguments that EDR belongs to nonselected datives, see especially Horn 2008.) I decide to introduce a new term for the same element to an already long list, because I think that none of the existing terms points to an exclusive property of the phenomenon observed and hence is a potential source of confusion. It is indeed coreferential and reflexive, but indirect objects and benefactives can also be coreferential (with another nominal expression in the clause, or even just the subject) and reflexive; it involves a "personal attitude," but this is not so straightforwardly read of the term Personal Dative and so on. As will be argued in this article, its evaluative contribution is its core characteristic, and along with its reflexivity, this characteristic distinguishes it from all other datives.

While rare or totally absent in the standard S-C, EDR is highly frequent in some of its dialects, especially in the southeastern dialects of S-C (SESC). (From here on, unless otherwise specified, all examples are from this group of dialects, which behave uniformly in respect of the construction under discussion; most of the examples are from the dialect of the city of Niš, with around four hundred thousand inhabitants, which represents nearly half of the speakers of SESC.)

(4) a. Jovan   *si*   sedi   i   gleda   *si*   film.
        J.Nom Refl.Dat sits   and   watches   Refl.Dat movie.Acc
        "Jovan's sitting and watching a movie [+EDR *effects]*."[1]

1 To specify the additional meaning contributed by the EDR, which is not contained in the English translation, I add "[+EDR effects]" to each translation rather than trying to paraphrase the effects.

b. Dao   sam   *si*   još   jedan   ispit.
given   Aux.1Sg   Refl.Dat   more   one   exam
"I took one more exam *[+EDR effects]*."

It is in most relevant respects similar to the EDR in most other languages in which this phenomenon exists, as it is described in, among others, Horn (2008), for English, and Al Zahre & Boneh (2010) for Syrian Arabic and Modern Hebrew. Throughout the article, I consider EDR in different languages essentially the same phenomenon, but with certain variations. In some cases, the differences may well be a matter of (im)precise observations or descriptions, the risk of which is great due to the sociolinguistic and pragmatic aspects playing a significant role in the use and interpretation of these expressions. Compared to the situation in other languages, SESC shows a greater variety of verbs (or verb classes) that appear in the EDR construction. This pattern of variation is not exceptional: it resembles the patterns in other domains, such as that of the classes of verbs used as inaccusatives, as presented in Sorace (2000).

While it is closely related to some of them, none of the traditional classes of nonselected datives may fully accommodate EDR, as it both escapes certain properties of each of them and has properties of its own that are not typical for any of these classes. The following section lists its typical properties, some of which are already described in the literature, and some of which are either observed for the first time, or characteristic only of the EDR as it is used in SESC.

3. PROPERTIES OF EDR

As Horn (2008) describes it, EDR does not bear on the truth conditions of the sentence it appears in. The sentence is fully grammatical and semantically sound without the EDR. Yet, with the reflexive, its meaning is somewhat different. The difference—that is, the contribution of the reflexive—can be informally described through a number of components. Horn (2008: 172) provides the following:

(5) a. They always co-occur with a quantified (patient/theme) direct object.

     b. They cannot be separated from the verb that precedes and case-marks them.

     c. They are most frequent/natural with monosyllabic "down-home"-type verbs (e.g., *buy, get, build, shoot, get, catch, write, hire, cook*).

d. They lack any external (PP) pronominal counterpart.

e. They can occur in positions where a true indirect object is ruled out and can co-occur with (rather than substituting for) overt dative/indirect object.

f. They are weak pronouns (Cardinaletti & Starke 1996, 1999; Bresnan 2001) and cannot be stressed or conjoined.

g. They have no full NP counterpart.

h. There's no consistent thematic role for these elements.

i. Most speakers have no absolute restriction against third-person pronominals, but some exhibit a residual person-based asymmetry: first > second > third

j. They are nonarguments coreferring with the subject.

k. They do not combine well with negated verbs.

In what follows, I describe a number of properties of EDRs in SESC. Some of the properties given here (e.g., (5b, d, f, g, i, j)) are trivial or nonapplicable in SESC because it uses a reflexive, not a pronoun. Moreover, as will be shown, EDRs in SESC do not share all the properties of their English counterpart described by Horn—for instance, they can occur with any verb (against (5a, c, k)). The list in (6) summarizes the properties of EDR in SESC presented in this section (as specified in the following discussion, most of them have been observed for other languages where EDR is in use, by other authors).

(6) a. They are always realized by a reflexive.

b. The subject they are bound by has to involve some kind of intentionality.

c. The eventuality in the respective clause is positively evaluated by the subject.

d. They do not combine well with focal elements with an evaluative interpretation.

e. Information conveyed by the respective sentence is implied to be of low relevance.

f. The subject binding the EDR must be topical.

g. The subject binding the EDR must be referential.

f. They resist distribution over plural subjects.

I first describe the semantic and pragmatic ones, and then those that are (also) related to the syntax of this expression.

Unlike its English counterparts described by Horn, but on a par with its counterparts in most other languages that display this phenomenon, EDR in SESC is always realized as a reflexive: that is, it is always anaphoric and bound by the clausal subject. Again on a par with its counterparts in other languages (Borer & Grodzinsky 1986), EDR in SESC cannot be stressed. And since pronominal elements that cannot take stress in SESC are realized as clitics, EDR in SESC is always a clitic. In other words, there is only one lexical item that realizes EDR in SESC: the dative form of the reflexive clitic, *si*.

Al Zahre & Boneh (2010: 9) observe that EDR comes with an interpretation "involving some intentionality attributed to the referent of the subject DP." Even when the subject is the undergoer or some other participant, its involvement still assumes some kind of intentionality, some awareness of the underlying eventuality.[2]

(7) a. Pera   si   zna   odgovor.
     P   Refl.Dat   knows   answer
     "Pera is having the answer ready *[+EDR effects]*."
     not the more literal: "Pera knows the answer *[+EDR effects]*."

     b. Grana   (#si)   plovi   rekom.
     branch   Refl.Dat   sail   river.Inst
     "The branch is floating down the river *[+EDR effects]*."
     [This sentence improves if the branch is personified.]

Horn (2008: 181) talks about the following interpretive effect of the use of EDRs: "The speaker assumes that the action expressed has or would have a positive effect on the subject, typically satisfying the subject's perceived intention or goals." I argue that this is actually an evaluative effect: the subject POSITIVELY EVALUATES the eventuality, or more precisely the meaning of the entire PolP (the eventuality located with respect to the reference time

---

2 Borer & Grodzinsky (1986) argue that EDRs may only be used with a verb that has an external argument, and Al Zahre & Boneh (2010) show that this is actually not correct. It may be that Borer and Grodzinsky were misled exactly by the component of control described here, which is similar to the control typical of certain external arguments but is at the epistemic level rather than the level of event-participants. To illustrate the difference, let me note that, as Al Zahre and Boneh show, in Modern Hebrew, even stative and nonverbal predicates, including the individual-level ones, can be used with an EDR, as long as the subject holds some rather vague intentional control over them (though it is clearly not a controller in the sense of agency). The same holds in SESC.

and assigned a polarity). Information with a negative bias is pragmatically degraded, often infelicitous with the EDR.[3]

(8) a. Upao   sam   (*#si*)   u   rupu.
      fallen   Aux.1Sg Refl.Dat in   hole
      "I fell into a hole."

    b. Pera   (#si)   slomio   nogu.
      P.Nom   Refl.Dat broken   leg
      "Pera had his leg broken."

Both these examples are fine in contexts in which their subjects consider it good for themselves to fall into a hole and broke a leg, respectively. Nevertheless, I provide arguments that this is rather a tendency, with a significant number of exceptions. Not all negatively biased examples sound so bad with an EDR (see section 5 for examples and a discussion).

To further illustrate the evaluative effect, observe the examples in (9). When the sentences are pronounced with a strong stress on *mnogo* "much," they get an interpretation of a strong subjective evaluation that the newspaper is judged as highly interesting. Intensifiers of this type do not combine with EDRs, because the EDR requires an evaluative interpretation but the evaluative interpretation is already reserved for the focal intensifier.[4]

(9) a. Čitam   (#si)   MNOGO interesantne novine!
      read   Refl.Dat much   interesting   newspaper
      "I'm reading SUCH an interesting newspaper."

    b. Pera   (#si)   video   MNOGO dobar   sat!
      P   Refl.Dat saw   much   good   watch
      "Pera saw SUCH a good watch."
      [The sentence improves with a possessive/benefactive reading of the reflexive.]

There is one more interpretive effect of EDR that involves attitude and is common for its use in all languages in which it is found. The speaker uttering the sentence containing the EDR considers the information conveyed by it to bear LITTLE RELEVANCE for the collocutors. In SESC, sentences

---

3 As pointed out by an anonymous reviewer, the evaluational restriction is another property that can be observed on other types of expressions as well. For instance, epithets tend to carry a negative evaluation, even though positively evaluated uses are not fully excluded. The source of the restriction is probably pragmatic in both cases, even though it is linked to different syntactic and semantic phenomena.

4 More precisely, the problem is that the EDR takes one subject of evaluation (the clausal subject) and the evaluative focal element another one (the speaker), which yields a conflict. See sections 4 and 5 for an explanation.

containing EDR have a kind of marginal, parenthetical intonation. They cannot be exclamative, and cannot involve a strong focal stress on the clausal polarity or one of the arguments.

(10) a. Dobio   sam   *si*   sat.   /no strong focal stress/
        gotten   Aux1Sg   Refl.Dat   watch
        "I got a watch [+EDR *effects*]."

   b. #DOBIO   SAM   SI   SAT! /strong focal stress on the sentence/
        gotten   Aux1Sg   Refl.Dat   watch

   c. #Dobio   sam   *si*   SAT. /contrastive focal stress/
        gotten   Aux1Sg   Refl.Dat   watch

In other words, a sentence involving EDR cannot be felicitously used in a context where it brings in the information that the hearer is wondering about. Its content is always somehow digressive—beside the main line of exchange of information. Although the speaker assumes that the information is not relevant to the hearer, the hearer may well show interest in the information conveyed, and this is exactly what usually happens, and what probably is one prominent purpose of EDR—to smuggle into the discourse information that might be pragmatically (socially) inadequate, by attributing it a lower degree of relevance (usually simply because the speaker may be judged egocentric for introducing such information without a ground in the current set of topical issues).

Al Zahre and Boneh (2010) report that in Syrian Arabic, EDRs can only be used if the eventuality involved is modified to have a SMALL QUANTITY (by adverbs and quantifiers such as *šway* "little," *kam* "several," or numerals marking a relatively small quantity). In other languages that display instances of EDR there is a similar tendency, though not necessarily with an overt marking. This is probably just a consequence of the marginal informational relevance of the contents of sentences involving EDRs. Observe the example in (11), where it is obvious that the quantification introduces only pragmatic information, without real quantity entailments.

(11) a. Šta   si   radeo   juče?
        what   Aux2Sg   done   yesterday
        "What did you do yesterday?"

   b. *Malo*   sam   si   jeo   palačinke.
        little   Aux1Sg   Refl.Dat   eaten   pancakes
        "I ate pancakes [+EDR *effects*]."

   c. Kolko   si   pojeo?
        how_much   Aux2Sg   eaten_up
        "How much/many did you have?"

d. Uuu,   *mnogo,*   *najmanje*   20.
      many,   fewest   20
  "Huh, a lot, at least 20."

Finally, as an illustration of the pragmatic nature of this type of quantification, observe a typical exchange in the beginning of a colloquial conversation in SESC in (12).

(12) a. Šta   se   radi?
    what   Refl.Acc   does
    "What's up?" / "What's going on?" / "What are you doing?"

  b. Evo   malo.
    Prtl.Deic[5]   little
    lit. "Here, a little." [semantically empty, pragmatic content only]

The response does not say what the person is doing; it only says that it is a little of whatever it is. There seems to be a pragmatic convention, the mechanisms of which should be looked for in sociolinguistics, that whatever one is saying about oneself, it is by default of little relevance in the ongoing discourse, and one of the ways to express this is by a low degree quantification.

This property interacts with the level of aspect. In SESC (and generally in S-C), only sentences involving imperfective verb forms can include an explicit quantification with an adverb such as *malo* "little." With perfective verbs, this yields unacceptability.

(13) a. Malo   sam   gledao   TV.
    little   Aux1Sg   watched   TV
    "I watched TV for a little while."

  b. */#   Malo   sam   pročitao   novine.
      little   Aux1Sg   read_out   newspaper
   ~"I read the newspaper for a little while."

However, when the sentence involves an EDR (or even when it does not, but the respective reading of *malo* "little" is suggested by the context or by the intonation), THE USE OF *MALO* "LITTLE" no longer depends on the aspectual properties of the verb. In such cases, *malo* "little" clearly specifies the degree of relevance of the information conveyed.

---

5 *Evo* is a deictic particle, similar in meaning to the Italian *ecco*. It refers to something that the speaker is showing or presenting, and it can be used ostensively, but also in a more abstract way, to refer to some discourse-prominent object, event, temporal interval, or spatial location.

(14) a. Malo   sam   si   gledao   TV.
little   Aux1Sg   Refl.Dat   watched   TV
"I watched TV a little [+EDR effects]."

b. Malo   sam   si   pročitao   novine.
little   Aux1Sg   Refl.Dat   read_out   newspaper
"I read the newspaper a little [+EDR effects]."

These facts can be interpreted in two ways. One conclusion would be that EDR has nothing to do with aspect, as the quantification that is related to its meaning is at the level of informational relevance rather than at the level of aspect. The other would be that the use of EDR shifts the aspectual status of the verb to imperfective, thus making it compatible with the adverbs of the type of *malo* "little." Again, only a precise description of the aspectual restrictions imposed by EDRs could provide an answer to this question, and as I propose an analysis that is orthogonal to the issues of aspect (although certain interactions are obvious), I do not devote a more elaborate discussion to this problem.

Sentences involving an EDR come with restrictions on their information structure. The SUBJECT MUST BE TOPICAL. This is already illustrated in (10), where the subject is a first-person *pro* that must be topical. Topic on other constituents yields unacceptability, as illustrated in (15) and (16).[6]

(15) a. Znaš   onaj   *sat*$_i$ što   smo   videli?
know.2Sg   that   watch   Comp   Aux1Pl   seen
"You know that watch that we saw?"

b. Znam.   *Pera*   (#si)   *ga*$_i$ kupio![7]
know.1Sg   Pera   Refl.Dat   it.AccCl   bought
"I know. Pera bought it!"

(16) a. *On* si   pije   kafu. /(contrastive) topic on the subject/
he   Refl.Dat   drinks   coffee
"He is drinking coffee [+EDR effects]."

b. *pro* Pije   si   kafu. /topic on the subject, which is dropped/
pro drinks Refl.Dat coffee.
"He is drinking coffee [+EDR effects]."

---

6 The type of topic in all these cases is the aboutness topic, which preferably coincides with the familiarity topic, in terms of Reinhart (1981). For more information on the structural "side effects" of topical constituents in S-C, see Arsenijević (2009).

7 In this article, I assume the EDR use for each dative reflexive used in the examples. Sometimes another interpretation is available and yields different acceptability judgments (e.g., in this case, the example improves with a recipient interpretation of the dative reflexive clitic), but these other readings are ignored.

c. *Kafu* (#si)   pije   (on).   /topical object/
   coffee Refl.Dat   drinks he
   "Coffee, he drinks."

Al Zahre & Boneh (2010: 17) find this requirement for a topical subject so striking that they "speculate that the CD [their term for EDR] is actually related to a topic in an A<prime>-position, itself associated with a thematic-argument."

As Al Zahre & Boneh (2010) observe, the SUBJECT of a clause involving an EDR must BE REFERENTIAL—that is, it cannot be arbitrary or generic. This is confirmed in SESC, as shown in literal translations of their Syrian Arabic and Modern Hebrew examples. The sentence in (17), on the intended interpretation with an arbitrary subject, cannot combine with an EDR. The EDR is fine if *pro* is interpreted as referential.

(17) pro$_{ARB}$ popravili (#si)   klimu.
                    fixed   Refl.Dat   aircondition
      "They fixed the aircondition." [on an arbitrary agent reading]

EDRs seem to RESIST DISTRIBUTION OVER SUBJECTS and probably even DISTRIBUTION IN GENERAL. They involve an effect of singularity: whatever interpretation is derived for the eventuality and its participants, the EDR subjects it to one evaluation. More precisely, they never combine with distributed or iterative referential eventualities. The example in (18a) can be interpreted in only one way: that the speaker answered correctly each time and the speech therefore displays the positive evaluation, lower informational relevance, and other EDR effects. The other reading—in which for every relevant event in which the speaker gives the correct answer, the speech displays the positive evaluation, lower informational relevance, and other EDR effects—is not available. The example in (18b) is similar: only the collective interpretation is available for the conjoined constituents (as a group, they are solving crosswords). The distributive interpretation, where each is solving crosswords, and each of these facts is evaluated as positive and marginally relevant—is out. In section 4, I speculate that this is a consequence of the tight relation between the evaluative effects and the discourse update.

(18) a. Ja   sam   si   svaki   put   tačno odgovorio.
        I   Aux1Sg   Refl.Dat each   time   correct answered
        "[EDR effects](I answered correctly each time)."
        *"Each time, [EDR effects](I answered correctly)."

     b. Pera i   Mika   si   rešavaju ukrštene reči.
        P   and M   Refl.Dat solve   crossed   words
        "[EDR effects](Pera and Mika are solving crosswords)."
        *"[EDR effects](Pera is solving crosswords) and [EDR effects]
        (Mika is solving crosswords)."

While other authors do not make similar observations on the use of EDR in other languages, there are some observations that I consider related to this one. In particular, Borer & Grodzinsky (1986) note that EDRs (Reflexive Datives in their terminology) cannot be coordinated, Al Zahre & Boneh show that they cannot be associated with a group of coordinated verbs, and Borer (2005) argues that they only occur with atelic interpretations (but see Al Zahre & Boneh, who show that telicity does not play a role in the use of EDRs in Modern Hebrew). While the ban on coordination of EDRs cannot be tested in SESC, where EDR is a clitic and clitics generally do not coordinate, its ban in languages in which otherwise it would be expected, as well as the ban on coordination of eventualities, needs an explanation. As for the aspectual facts, the empirical situation is still quite unclear (see Al Zahre & Boneh), but it would not be surprising to find that they also derive from the singularity restriction on the evaluation time.

Horn observes that in English, EDRs do not go well with NEGATION. Although certain examples are attested, they are all licensed by what Horn refers to as a syntagmatic priming (the expression involving an EDR is literally repeated in the negated sentence, from a sentence from the preceding discourse). Horn's evidence is based on the quantitative data about antonym verbs as well as examples involving explicit negation, rather than on the unacceptability of negated examples, and I refer the reader to Horn's article for the precise data.

In SESC, EDRs are not (so) sensitive to negation, as long as it does not affect the positive evaluation of the sentential content by the subject. Examples of the type in (19) are well formed, although some speakers find some of them slightly degraded.

(19) a. Ja   si   danas   ne   odo   na   poso.
        I   Refl.Dat today   not   went   on   work
        "I didn't go to work today [+EDR effects]."

     b. Pera si   ni   ogrebotinu   ne   dobi.
        P   refl.Dat n_even   scratch   not   got
        "Pera wasn't even scratched [+EDR effects]."

4. THE ANALYSIS

Previous accounts of the EDR were mostly based on the data from Modern Hebrew (Berman 1982, Borer & Grodzinsky 1986), with the exception of Al Zahre & Boneh (2010), who compare the Modern Hebrew data with those from Syrian Arabic, and Horn (2008), who uses the data from English. These analyses form two groups: the first tries to explain the effects of EDR in terms of conventional implicature (Horn, and to some extent Al Zahre & Boneh); and the second links the EDR to the aspectual and argument structure (all other accounts). An exception is the work of Al Zahre and Boneh, the aim of which is not to offer an analysis but to systematize the data, adding important new observations and generalizations, and correcting some old ones that turned out to be wrong. They show that at least the accounts focusing on the aspectual and argument structure are based on incomplete data and actually fail to explain the facts. Finally, the analysis in this article is similar in spirit to the analysis of Boneh and Nash (2010), who target French and who also argue that the dative element brings in a sense of affectedness, and that its attachment site is crucial for its interpretation. From the information available about their analysis, the main differences are that they assume the subject in EDR constructions to be the agent, which is not necessarily the case in SESC, and their analysis generates EDRs no higher than TP, while in the present analysis it goes to MoodP, or even ForceP; as will be presented soon, the present analysis also goes into more detail about the mechanics deriving the effects observed. For reasons of space, I do not discuss the earlier accounts in more detail; instead I refer the reader to Al Zahre & Boneh (2010), who provide a detailed discussion.

In deriving the analysis of EDR in SESC, and probably also more universally, I depart from the analysis proposed in Boneh and Nash (2010). Boneh and Nash argue convincingly that EDR (CDC in their terminology) is generated somewhere at the level of TP, that is, higher than vP and lower than CP. In this section, I first offer some additional arguments for the same claim and then propose a more precise location for EDRs: the projection of the evaluative mood (Cinque 1999's Mood$_{evaluative}$P). In section 5 I show how the particular syntactic and semantic properties of EDR presented in sections 3 and 4 follow from generating EDR in this position.

As shown in section 3, EDR has several pragmatic effects, including the marking of a low informational relevance. This effect is often employed to serve certain social relations between the speaker and the hearer, such as the introduction of oneself as a topic. In this way, EDR is similar to the interested speaker dative (which is often grouped together with the ethical dative), expressed in S-C by a first-person dative clitic, and to the interested hearer dative (IHD), expressed by a second-person dative clitic. IHD thus refers to the hearer, indicating that the information conveyed, or the process of conveying it, is of a high relevance for the hearer, or even takes place for her benefit. The entire narration that includes (20) is somehow dedicated to the hearer.

(20) Pera *ti*   onda dohvati jabuku i   baci   je kroz   prozor.
     P you.DatCl then catches apple and throws it through window
     "[FYI] Pera then catches the apple and throws it through the window."

In SESC, in addition to the hearer-oriented relevance, it also marks a special social relation between the speaker and the hearer—they are in a close, almost intimate relation (a typical gesture that comes with the IHD is putting an arm on the hearer's arm or shoulder). Note, in illustration, that IHD cannot take the form of a polite second person.

(21) #Pera   *Vam*   dohvati   jabuku
     P   you_polite.Dat.Cl   catches   apple
     i   baci   je   kroz   prozor.
     and   throws   it   through   window
     "[FYI] Pera catches the apple and throws it through the window."

Next to the relevance and socially related effects, EDR and IHD are also similar in being restricted to the expression by only one lexical item. EDR is always lexically realized as a dative reflexive, and IHD as a dative-second person clitic. Strong pronouns, lexical nominals, or any other items are excluded.

Assuming that IHD is expressing a set of features in the projection responsible for the performative force of the clause (ForceP), marking thus that the force of the clause goes in the hearer's direction, we may speculate that EDR expresses a similar type of features, but specifying the direction of the clausal subject.

This parallel explains (a) the restriction to clitics: clitics are light elements without lexical content, realizing bundles of functional features, and that is why they have the capacity to realize not only arguments, but also contents of higher functional heads, such as Force; and (b) the restriction on EDRs to use in clauses where the subject is topical: only a topical subject may bind a reflexive generated in a position as high as ForceP. In semantic terms, while IHD marks that the force of the clause is directed toward the hearer, and hence of a special relevance for her, the orientation toward the subject, especially when the subject is in first person, marks that the information is relevant to the speaker, hence at least by implicature not particularly relevant to the hearer.

There are, however, also certain facts indicating that these two elements are neither syntactically nor semantically identical. First, IHDs and EDRs may occur in the same sentence.

(22) Mika   *ti*   *si*   ustane   i   ode.
     M   you.DatCl   Refl.Dat   gets_up   and   leaves
     "[FYI] Mika gets up and leaves [+EDR effect]."

If they were generated in the same position, and contributing semantics of the same type, they should never co-occur in a sentence unless they were coordinated.

Second, while EDR frequently appears in embedded clauses, IHD never embeds.

(23) Mika kaže da   (*ti)   (si)   on lepo ustane i   ode.
     M says comp you.DatCl Refl.Dat he nice gets_up and leaves
     "Mika says that [*FYI] he simply gets up and leaves [+EDR effect]."

Since embedded clauses lack a fully specified force, this minimal pair suggests that IHD is indeed force-related, but that EDR sits not in ForceP but in some lower functional projection, as indicated by example (23), and also by example (24), which shows that the IHD cannot surface after the EDR.

(24) Mika (ti)   si   (*ti)   ustane i   ode.
     M   you.DatCl Refl.Dat you.DatCl gets_up and leaves
     "[FYI] Mika gets up and leaves [+EDR effect]."

The lower bound can be determined by another type of nonselected dative— the benefactive. Let us assume with Pylkkänen (2002) that benefactives are generated somewhere at the level of vP, and observe (25).

(25) Ček da   si   mu   otvorim   vrata.
     wait Comp Refl.Dat he.DatCl   open   door
     "Wait till I open the door for him [+EDR effect]."

Finally, one sentence can have all three types of datives above, but only in the strict order IHD<EDR<Benefactive.

(26) Ja ti   si   mu   otvorim   vrata...
     I   you.Dat.Cl Refl.Dat he.DatCl   open   door
     "[FYI] I open the door for him [+EDR effect]."

This tells us that indeed, as argued by Boneh and Nash (2010), EDR is base generated somewhere between CP (or, more precisely, ForceP) and vP—that is, within the IP layer (which I assume, with Rizzi 1997, Cinque 1999, and a lot of subsequent work, to be constituted by the specification of the components such as polarity, mood, tense, and outer aspect, i.e., different types of MoodP, PolP, TP, AspP, and perhaps other related projections).

The asymmetries are not really unexpected, considering that the description of EDR involved specifying a number of different properties, some of which have nothing to do with force, while IHD seems to be restricted to the force-related effects. Moreover, the possibility of combining IHD and EDR in the same sentence, without a conflict, indicates that the relevance-related effect of one of them at the very least has to be cancelable; otherwise in some cases the same sentence would be specified for contributing information that is at the same time relevant and irrelevant for the hearer.

I propose, based on the semantics of EDRs, that, in a finer analysis of the IP layer, the right projection to generate them is $\text{Mood}^0_{\text{evaluative}}$ (which specifies the evaluative aspect of the mood; see Cinque 1999, and especially Liu 2007 for an implementation). The dative reflexive in this head introduces a variable that is bound by a c-commanding nominative subject and specifies the subject of evaluation (i.e., the one who evaluates the semantic contents of the structure in the complement). The direct interpretive effect is that the predicate of the eventuality is evaluated by the clausal subject. Other evaluators determined overtly or in the discourse are allowed, as long as the subject is also involved, and as long as the evaluation by the subject is exempted from any more general evaluation. We arrive at the analysis in (27a), illustrated by an example in (27b).

(27) a. $[\text{Subj}_i \; [_{\text{ForceP}} \; [\text{IHD}] \quad \dots \quad [_{\text{MoodPeval}} \; [\text{EDR}]_i \; [_{vP}$
$[v] \quad [_{\text{ApplP}} \quad [\text{Benefactive}]]]]]$

b. Ja   ti   si   mu   otvorim   vrata…
   I   you.Dat.Cl   Refl.Dat   he.DatCl   open   door
   "[FYI] I open the door for him [+EDR effect]."
   $[_{\text{TopicP}} \; Ja \; [_{\text{ForceP}} \; [ti] \dots [_{\text{MoodP}} \; [si] \; [_{\text{PolP}} \dots [_{vP} \; Ja \; [v] \; [_{\text{ApplP}} \; [mu] \; [otvorim$
   $vrata]]]]]]]$

This, I argue, is the semantic entailment of the EDR: The eventuality is evaluated, and it is evaluated by the clausal subject. Other semantic and pragmatic effects, in particular: that this evaluation is positive, the lower degree of relevance of the information, the small quantity of the eventuality, the intentionality of the subject, and the ban on distributive interpretations all derive from this core property.

5. EXPLAINING (AND REEXAMINING) THE PROPERTIES OF EDR

The positive interpretation of the eventuality is only an implicature from specifying that the subject is also a subject of evaluation, and of giving the subject's evaluation a special status in this way. In over 70 percent of nearly 300 examples excerpted using Google, the subject is also the agent, and the controller of the evaluated eventuality. It is natural that if the evaluator holds control over the evaluated eventuality, she evaluates the eventuality as positive for herself (else she would have stopped it, or controlledly pushed it in another direction). Sentences with EDRs involving other types of subjects inherit this generalized positive evaluation interpretation from those which make a majority (note that the asymmetry in frequency is so strong that Borer & Grodzinsky 1986 had made a generalization that only eventualities with an external argument license the use of EDR; Al Zahre & Boneh 2010 showed that this generalization was wrong). In any case, the positive evaluation of the eventuality is not an absolute condition for the use of EDRs, as shown in the examples in (28), where those in (28b–f) are found via Google, and (28a) is from a live conversation.

(28) a. Pao   sam   si   ispit,   sa'ću vi'm šta ću radim.
       fallen   Aux1Sg   Refl.Dat   exam   now I'll see what to do
       "I failed the exam, now I'll see what to do [+EDR *effects*]."

   b. Nego, nema   veze,   teb   si   ide   to   na savest...
      but   n_have connection you.Dat Refl.Dat goes that on conscience
      "But, never mind, it goes to your conscience [+EDR *effects*]..."

   c. Kome   se   ne   svidja   nek   si   ide!!
      who.Dat   Refl.Acc   not   like   let   Refl.Dat   go.3Sg
      "Those who don't like it may leave [+EDR *effects*]."

   d. Iz   ovaj li   moj   dom   da   si   idem?
      from   this Q_Part mine   home   Comp   Refl.Dat go.1Sg
      "Is it this home of mine that I have to leave? [+EDR *effects*]"

   e. ipak   džabe   Raka uči,   on si   ide   kući...
      nevertheless in_vain   R   learns he Refl.Dat   goes   home
      "Nevertheless, Raka's learning is in vain, he's going home [+EDR *effects*]..."

   f. Nek   si   ide   život...
      let   Refl.Dat   goes   life
      lit. "Let go the life [+EDR *effects*]..."
      "Let my life be sacrificed (for a contextually given reward) [+EDR *effects*]."
      (used when a great sacrifice has to be made for a rather hedonist reason)

In fact, almost one-third of the examples excerpted from the Internet can be judged more or less negative for the subject. In all these cases, however, there is a sense of the negative facts being (a) evaluated and (b) "none of the business of anyone else than the subject." This is actually a rather general effect that comes with EDRs and that is also observed (though not as a general one, but as one of the pragmatic options) by Al Zahre & Boneh (2010: 25) as an "isolation effect." This effect naturally follows from the present analysis, more precisely from the specification of the subject as a (singled-out, hence isolated) subject of evaluation.

I argue that exactly this effect of isolation of the clausal subject as a subject of evaluation is what triggers the effect of a lower informational relevance of the sentence containing an EDR. As the subject is taken aside, as an evaluator, from the other relevant subjects of evaluation (most importantly the interlocutors as the default evaluators), the information conveyed receives a special status in the discourse. It carries an evaluation that is not (necessarily) shared by the speaker and/or the hearer, and therefore less directly updates the discourse (i.e., updates it not with an evaluation of the facts, but with information about the subject's evaluation of the facts). Moreover, the MoodP$_{evaluative}$ projection is closely related to the projection introducing evidentiality specification, MoodP$_{evidential}$ (see Liu 2007 for empirical evidence). Unless the evidential status of the sentence is explicitly specified, this brings about an effect of indicating that the subject is the source of information.

In itself, this gives a weak lower relevance effect, which can be made stronger when the pragmatic conditions are fulfilled, that is, when the speaker intends to make a stronger effect of this kind. One way to overtly mark this status is through adverbs and quantifiers that introduce the values from the lower sections of a scale. This is illustrated in (29), where the sentence with the adverbial *malo* "little" sounds more natural than the one without it, although both are fully acceptable.

(29) a. Malo   sam   si   jeo   palačinke.
      little   Aux1Sg   Refl.Dat   eaten   pancakes
      "I ate pancakes a little [+EDR *effects*]."

    b. Jeo   sam   si   palačinke.
      eaten   Aux1Sg   Refl.Dat   pancakes
      "I ate pancakes [+EDR *effects*]."

The sentence in (29a) is more appropriate when it is a digression or introduces a new topic into the discourse (which gives it a stronger low relevance effect). The one in (29b) is more natural as an answer to the question "What were you doing (at the relevant time)?"—that is, in a context in which it has some informational relevance (answers a question), which it degrades by its own implicature of low relevance. In languages like Syrian Arabic, where EDR necessarily requires the presence of an adverb or quantifier of this kind (Al Zahre & Boneh 2010), EDR has probably become part of a construction specialized to express meanings with a strong low relevance effect.

The component of intentionality of the subject that binds the EDR (Al Zahre & Boneh 2010: 9) directly follows from the specification of the subject as an (isolated) evaluator: trivially, intentionality is a necessary property of any possible subject of evaluation—it is a prerequisite of evaluation. The very fact that the subject binds a variable that represents the evaluator forces an interpretation that attributes intentionality to the subject, even when the actual referent normally does not display intentionality, as illustrated by the example in (7b), repeated here as (30).

(30) Grana   (#si)   plovi   rekom.
     branch   Refl.Dat sail   river.Inst
     "The branch is floating down the river (#[+EDR effects])."
     [This sentence improves if the branch is personified.]

EDR effects do not distribute over subjects or times, as already discussed in section 3 in relation to examples in (18), repeated here as (31). Several other restrictions, such as the ban on coordination both of EDRs and of the respective eventualities (Borer and Grodzinsky 1986), as well as the referentiality restrictions described in Al Zahre & Boneh (2010), subsume under this one. I speculate that the discourse status of evaluative attitudes is responsible for these effects. More precisely, (the discourse-representation of) the set of beliefs of the subject has to be updated by the evaluation introduced by EDR, and this effect cannot distribute (similar to the fact that force does not distribute).

(31) a. Ja   sam   si   svaki   put   tačno   odgovorio.
        I   Aux1Sg   Refl.Dat each   time   correct   answered
        "I answered correctly each time [+EDR effects]."

     b. Pera i   Mika   si   rešavaju ukrštene reči.
        P   and   M   Refl.Dat solve   crossed   words
        "Pera and Mika are solving crosswords [+EDR effects]."[8]

This is also part of the explanation of a final property of EDRs discussed in this section, namely that the subject that binds the EDR has to be topical. The direct discourse update of clauses involving an EDR (e.g., in the sense of file-card semantics of Heim 1982) are in the domain of the beliefs of the subject. If any other event participant were topical, that should also be the referent directly targeted by the discourse update, and the semantic contribution of EDR could not be realized.

   The restriction of EDRs' realization by a reflexive is not an effect; rather, it is a core property of EDRs. Hence, rather than explaining why it holds, one could speculate on the ways in which it led to the independent establishing of this element in mutually unrelated languages. The reasons are more pragmatic than grammatical. As Horn (2008) indicates, there was probably

---

8 Note, in further support of the weak low informational relevance effects, that this sentence cannot combine with adverbs such as *malo* "little," and only in a very remote sense displays the low relevance effect.

a fortunate match between a niche in the set of frequent pragmatic patterns and the entailments of the particular syntactic structure with a referent with the evaluative capacity being both the evaluator and the controller of an event. This guaranteed a high frequency of the configuration, leading to its establishment as a construction, with the set of restrictions less directly related to its entailment varying across languages.

There is also a syntactic condition that is fulfilled by the topical interpretation of the subject. In order to bind the dative reflexive, the subject needs to be higher than $MoodP_{evaluative}$. Assuming that the subject normally moves only as high as TP, which is lower than $MoodP_{evaluative}$ (Cinque 1999), the subject must move higher up to get into a c-command relation with the EDR. This is achieved by its movement to TopicP.

6. CONCLUSION

In this article, I presented the data about the Evaluative Dative Reflexive as it is used in southeastern Serbo-Croatian. It shares most of its properties with its counterparts from Modern Hebrew, Syrian Arabic, French, or dialects of English, but also differs from them in some interesting ways. I proposed an analysis according to which the semantic contribution of EDR is in specifying that the subject of the clause is a subject of evaluation of the underlying eventuality. Syntactically, it is generated in $MoodP_{evaluative}$, where it realizes its semantic contribution and is bound by the subject, which moves up to TopicP. I showed how this analysis accounts for other presented properties of the EDR: the positive nature of the evaluation, the intentionality and the topical and collective interpretation of the subject, the low relevance of the information conveyed, and the reflexive nature of the EDR. The analysis should also apply to EDRs in other languages—possibly with small modifications in the domains of variation (e.g., the obligatory use of a small-quantity adverb in Palestinian Arabic, as in Al Zahre & Boneh 2010), hopefully motivated by the different setting of syntactic parameters in these languages.

ACKNOWLEDGMENTS

I am indebted to the editors of this volume, and the organizers of the workshop at which it was initiated for providing a great venue for the research on the aspects of variation in the use of datives, and to two anonymous reviewers for comments that have helped me to improve the article considerably. Funding from the following grants is gratefully acknowledged: "The origins of truth" (NWO 360-20-150) and "Natural language ontology and the semantic representation of abstract objects" (MICINN, FFI2010-15006, and JCI-2008-2699).

REFERENCES

Al-Zahre, Nisrine, and Nora Boneh. 2010. "Coreferential dative constructions in Syrian Arabic and Modern Hebrew." *Brill's Annual of Afroasiatic Languages and Linguistics* 2, 248–282.

Arsenijević, Boban. 2009. "{Relative {conditional {correlative clauses}}}." In Aniko Liptak (ed.), *Correlatives crosslinguistically*, 131–156. Amsterdam: John Benjamins.

Berman, Ruth. 1982. "Dative marking of the affectee role: Data from Modern Hebrew." *Hebrew Annual Review* 6: 35–59.

Boneh, Nora, and Lea Nash. 2010. "Getting high." Paper presented at the *Colloquium on Generative Grammar*, Barcelona, March 18–20, 2010.

Borer, Hagit. 2005. *Structuring sense.* Oxford: Oxford University Press.

Borer, Hagit, and Yosef Grodzinsky. 1986. "Syntactic cliticization and lexical cliticization: The case of Hebrew dative clitics." In Hagit Borer (ed.), *Syntax and semantics 19*, 175–215. New York: Academic Press.

Bresnan, Joan. 2001. "The emergence of the unmarked pronoun." In Geraldine Legendre, Jane Grimshaw, and Sten Vikner (eds.), *Optimality-theoretic syntax*, 113–142. Cambridge, MA: MIT Press.

Cardinaletti, Anna, and Michal Starke. 1996. "Deficient pronouns: A view from Germanic. A study in the unified description of Germanic and Romance." In Hoskuldur Thräinsson, Samuel Epstein, and Steve Peter (eds.), *Studies in Comparative Syntax II*, 21–65. Dordrecht: Kluwer.

Cardinaletti, Anna, and Michal Starke. 1999. "The typology of structural deficiency: A case study of the three classes of pronouns." In Henk van Riemsdijk (ed.), *Clitics in the languages of Europe*, 145–233. Berlin: Mouton de Gruyter.

Cinque, Guglielmo. 1999. *Adverbs and functional heads.* Oxford: Oxford University Press.

Heim, Irene. 1982. "The semantics of definite and indefinite noun phrases." PhD diss., University of Massachusetts, Amherst.

Horn, Laurence R. 2008. "'I love me some him': The landscape of nonargument datives." In Olivier Bonami and Patricia Cabredo-Hofherr (eds.), *Empirical issues in syntax and semantics 7*, 169–192. Available at www.cssp.cnrs.fr/eiss7/index_en.html.

Liu, Chen-Sheng Luther. 2007. "The V-qilai evaluative construction in Chinese." *UST Working Papers in Linguistics* 3: 43–62.

Pylkkänen, Liina. 2002. "Introducing arguments." PhD diss., Massachusetts Institute of Technology, Cambridge, MA.

Reinhart, Tanya. 1981. "Pragmatics and linguistics: An analysis of sentence topics." *Philosophica* 27: 53–94.

Rizzi, Luigi. 1997. "The fine structure of the Left Periphery." In Lilliane Haegeman (ed.), *Elements of grammar*, 281–337. Dordrecht, The Netherlands: Kluwer.

Sorace, Antonella. 2000. "Gradients in auxiliary selection with intransitive verbs." *Language* 76 (4): 859–890.

CHAPTER 2
Core and Noncore Datives in French

NORA BONEH & LÉA NASH

1. INTRODUCTION

1.1 Distinguishing Properties

Like many other languages, French expresses the goal argument of ditransitive verbs (1) and the optional dative, which is not thematically selected by the verb (2) in the same fashion, by means of a dative clitic. In what follows we refer to optional datives as noncore datives, and to those attached to canonical ditransitive verbs as core datives.

(1) a. Le syndic   leur   a envoyé des lettres recommendées.
       The property manager 3P.DAT sent   letters registered
       "The property manager sent them registered letters."

   b. Marie   lui   a donné   un baiser.
      Marie   3S.DAT   gave   a kiss
      "Marie gave her/him a kiss."

   c. Il   lui   a dit   la vérité.
      He   3S.DAT   told   the truth.
      "He told her/him the truth."

   d. Le directrice   lui   a attribué   une tache difficile.
      The headmistress 3S.DAT   allocated   a task difficult
      "The headmistress gave her/him a difficult task."

(2) a. Le plombier   leur   a vidé   un chauffe-eau.
       The plumber   3P.DAT   emptied   a water-heater
       "The plumber emptied a water-heater for them."

b. La teinturier   lui   a massacré   une chemise.
   The dry-cleaner 3S.DAT   destroyed   a shirt
   "The dry-cleaner ruined her/his shirt (on her/him)."

c. Hélène   lui   a peint   son portail.
   Hélène   3S.DAT   painted   his gate
   "Hélène painted the gate for her/him."

d. Marie   lui   a vomi   sur ses coussins.
   Marie   3S.DAT   vomited   on his cushions
   "Marie vomited on her/his cushions."

e. Elle   lui   a tiré   dans le ventre.
   She   3S.DAT   shot   in the belly
   "She shot her/him in the belly."

The constructions in (1) and (2) are also alike in that the datives co-occur in both sentences with direct objects. It has been long noted that noncore datives cannot appear when the verb is a bare intransitive, lacking VP additional material (see Leclère 1976, Morin 1981, Herslund 1988, Rooryck 1988, Authier & Reed 1992, Lamiroy & Delbecque 1998, Roberge & Troberg 2007, Jouitteau & Rezac 2007):

(3) a. Marie   lui   a bu   *(trois pastis).
        Marie   3S.DAT   drank   (three pastis)
        "Marie drank three glasses of pastis (on her/him)."

     b. Hélène   lui   a chanté   *(sous ses fenêtres).
        Hélène   3S.DAT   sang   (beneath his windows)
        "Hélène sang beneath her/his window (on her/him)."

     c. Marie   lui   a mangé   *(avec les doigts)/(*rapidement).
        Marie   3S.DAT   ate   (with the fingers)/(quickly)
        "Marie ate with her fingers (on her/him, aggravating her/him)."

     d. *Jean   lui   a chanté   tout l'après-midi.
        Jean   3S.DAT   sang   all afternoon long

     e. *Jean lui   a chanté parce qu'il ne pouvait pas s'en empêcher.
        Jean 3S.DAT sang   because he couldn't refrain from it

     f. *Jean   lui   a bu   pour choquer ses invités.
        Jean   3S.DAT   drank   to shock the guests

The examples, adapted from Authier & Reed (1992), show that VP material has to be of a specific categorial and semantic type. Alongside DP arguments (3a), location and manner PPs are allowed (3b–c), but manner adverbial phrases (3c), temporal adjuncts (3d), causation adjuncts (3e), or purpose clauses (3f) are not suitable VP material. Note that in the absence of a dative clitic, bare intransitives are fully acceptable.

(4) a. Marie a bu (rapidement).
   "Marie drank quickly."

   b. Hélène a chanté.
   "Hélène sang."

Beyond the superficial similarities in the form of the dative clitic and the obligatoriness of a certain type of VP material, core and noncore datives differ in several respects. The most proclaimed feature setting them apart is the ability to appear as full *à*-DPs (Leclère 1976, Rouveret & Vergnaud 1980, Barnes 1985, Rooryck 1988, Herschensohn 1992, Authier & Reed 1992, Roberge & Troberg 2009 a.o.). Whereas there are no restrictions on the availability of full *à*-DPs for core datives, noncore datives are most natural as clitics; full *à*-DPs are awkward or plainly ungrammatical.[1]

(5) a. Le syndic a envoyé des lettres recommendées *aux co-propriétaires*.
   "The property manager sent registered letters to the apartment-owners."

   b. Marie a donné un baiser *à Jean*.
   "Marie gave a kiss to Jean."

   c. Il a dit la vérité *à Jean*.
   "He told the truth to Jean."

(6) a. *Le plombier a vidé un chauffe-eau *aux co-propriétaires*.
   The plumber emptied a water-heater to the apartment-owners

   b. *La teinturier a massacré une chemise *à Marie*.
   The dry-cleaner ruined a shirt to Marie

   c. *Ton fils a encore décapité trois poupées Barbie *à ses petites camarades*.
   Your son has again decapitated three Barbie dolls to/on his little friends

   d. *Marie a embrassé le front *à Jean*.
   Marie kissed the forehead to Jean

   e. *Elle a tiré dans le ventre *à Jean*.
   She shot in the belly to Jean

---

1 Like the other authors, we distinguish between clause-level *à*-DPs and adnominal ones. The latter is qualified as substandard French, e.g., *la pipe à papa* "Dad's pipe."

Second, core datives can appear in nominalizations (7a), but noncore datives cannot (7b–c):

(7) a. l'envoi   des lettres   *aux co-propriétaires*
        the sending the letters   to the apartment-owners
        "the sending of the letters to the apartment-owners"

      b. *la vidange   d'un chauffe-eau   *aux co-propriétaires*
          the emptying   of a water-heater   to the apartment-owners

      c. *le repassage   des chemises   *à nos fidèles clients*
          the ironing   of shirts   to our devoted customers

Third, noncore datives seem to differ from core datives in that they imply a notion of affectedness: the extra noncore participant is taken to be affected by the underlying event. In the examples above, this is reflected in the English translation by the expression "on her/him."[2]

1.2 Previous Analyses

Previous analyses tried to account for licensing conditions of noncore datives in the absence of semantic selection, or theta-role assignment. Positing an applicative analysis whereby an applicative head selects and licenses the noncore dative has gained popularity since the publication of Pylkkänen's work (2002/2008). She establishes two kinds of applicatives: low applicatives, relating two individuals and high applicatives relating an individual to an event. It has been shown on several grounds that assuming low applicatives fails to account for phenomena attesting that the introduced argument is in fact higher in the structural hierarchy (Nash 2006, Georgala et al. 2008), or does not take

---

2 Core and noncore datives also seem to differ as to whether or not they allow passivization of the internal argument (Rooryck 1988, ex. 9). Core datives, in (i), can co-occur with theme subjects in passives, but noncore datives, in (ii), cannot. However, speakers do not seem to be unanimous about these facts (Authier & Reed 1992).

(i)   a. Un livre   lui   a été donné.
          A book   3S.DAT   was given
          "A book was given to her/him."

      b. Cet emploi   lui   a été attribué.
          This job   3S.DAT   was allocated
          "This job was allocated to her/him."

(ii) a. *Un gâteau   leur   a été cuit.
          A cake   3P.DAT   was cooked

      b. *Ce pull   lui   a été déchiré   (par le gosse).
          This sweater 3S.DAT   was torn   (by the kid)

into consideration interpretative issues (Larson 2010). The option of introducing noncore datives via a low applicative projection has been dismissed for French by Boneh & Nash (2010). A high applicative analysis for French seems more plausible and has been proposed by Roberge & Troberg (2009), Boneh & Nash (2010), and Bosse & Bruening (2010).[3] However, positing a high applicative head is problematic for French, since according to Pylkkänen's predictions, high applicatives are indiscriminate as to the type of VPs they select, and they impose no transitivity requirements. As shown in (3), this state of affairs does not hold in French, where the the noncore dative can only attach to a *nonbare* VP with the direct object or a specific PP complement.

The question, then, is how to reconcile, within an applicative analysis or otherwise, the mixture of "high" and "low" properties of noncore datives: on the one hand, they are attached to an event; on the other it is felt that the individual denoted by the noncore dative is somehow linked to an element in the VP, by a somewhat vague notion of possession.

A raising analysis for noncore datives, suggested in the writings of Kayne (1993, 2004, 2010) for possessors and datives in general, captures this duality. However, it seems to be most suitable for accounting to a specific set of data involving possession relying on the part-whole relation. Empirically it is difficult to find evidence for the syntactic reality of the low position (cf. Landau 1999). A proposal within the applicative framework that implements the spirit of Kayne's possessor-raising analysis has been advanced by Georgala et al. (2008), whereby the dative argument is introduced low but needs to rise to the Spec of ApplP projection in order to get licensed. Apart from theory-internal issues that this type of analysis may raise (i.e., what it means to posit an applicative head that introduces *no* argument), it seems to be inapplicable to French, since it does not clearly discriminate between core and noncore datives.

Roberge & Troberg (2009), from a comparative perspective placing French noncore datives in opposition to other Romance languages, also opt for a high applicative analysis but build into it the relation between the noncore dative and VP material without resorting to raising. According to them, the applicative head, merged above *v*P, is instantiated by the clitic; a prepositional full *à*-DP cannot appear in the specifier position, since it is only reserved for DPs, thus an expletive operator is merged in this position. The operator binds material in its scope, therefore the VP has to contain referential material. This is how Roberge & Troberg (2009) account for the mixture of high and low properties characterizing French noncore datives.

3 An applicative analysis has been also proposed for a variety of other languages. For instance: Cuervo (2003, 2010) for Spanish; Georgala (2010) and McIntyre (2007) for German; Georgala et al. (2008) for Mandarin; Grashchenkov & Markman (2008) for Russian; Folli & Harley (2006) for Italian.

Crucial to them, for assuming an expletive null operator, is the fact that the noncore dative is manifest only as a clitic.

In what follows, we adopt the spirit of Roberge & Troberg's analysis by maintaining the operator-variable relation related to the presence of a noncore dative. However, we will claim that it is established via a procedure of λ-abstraction, not involving a dedicated head, selecting and licensing the noncore dative. We reject several details in their analysis by unveiling new data. Importantly, we show in the next section (1.3) that noncore datives are not attested only as clitics but can also be found as full à-DPs. Second, we show in section 2.3 that there is no conclusive evidence in support of the prepositional status of à-DP constituents; hence, nothing should prevent them from being merged in a specifier position, the element à being a case marker. Finally, in section 2.2 we bring new evidence for the operator-variable relation and thus confirm a nonraising analysis.

1.3 New Data

To the best of our knowledge, previous literature does not fully recognize that the ban on the availability of noncore full à-DP is far from being absolute and is actually quite limited. It has been already noted by Kayne (1975) for datives of inalienable possession that while à-DP is not attested in a declarative, the interrogative is fully acceptable:

(8) a. Marie   lui   a embrassé   le front.
       Marie   3s.DAT   kissed   the forehead
       "Marie kissed him on the forehead."

     b. *Marie   a embrassé   le front   à Jean
        Marie   kissed   the forehead   to Jean

     c. A qui   elle   a embrassé   le front?
        To whom   she   kissed   the forehead
        "Whose forehead did she kiss?"

Additionally, Rooryck (1988) provides an example, while discussing other issues, where a noncore à-DP is possible (9b), when not in rightmost position:

(9) a. *Les gosses ont dessiné des ânes sur tous les murs à Marie.
       The kids   drew   donkies on all the wall   to Marie

     b. (?)Les gosses ont déssiné à Marie des ânes sur tous les murs.
        The kids   drew   to Marie donkies on all the walls
        "The kids drew donkies on all the walls to Marie."

These pieces of data are confirmed by our informants:

(10) a. Le plombier a enfin vidé aux co-propriétaires leur chauffe-eau.
"The plumber finally emptied to(for) the apartment-owners their water-heater."

b. La nouvelle stagiaire a massacré à Monsieur le Député un imper tout neuf.
"The new trainee ruined (to) the honorable Member of Parliament his brand-new raincoat."

c. Ton fils a encore décapité à ses petites camarades trois poupées Barbie.
"Your son has again decapitated to his little friends three Barbie dolls."

A more general inquiry revealed that what is actually banned is the occurrence of a full *à*-DP in the position in which one expects to find a goal/recipient argument of a canonical ditransitive verb (11). In every other position, and especially in A-bar positions, *à*-DPs are fully attested, as exemplified in (12).

(11) *Le teinturier a massacré une chemise à Marie.
The dry-cleaner ruined a shirt to Marie

(12) a. A qui le teinturier a massacré une chemise?
To whom the dry-cleaner ruined a shirt.

b. C'est à Marie que le teinturier a massacré une chemise.
It is to Marie that the dry-cleaner ruined a shirt.

c. ?A Marie, le teinturier a massacré une chemise.
To Marie, the dry-cleaner ruined a shirt.

d. Le teinturier a massacré une chemise, à Marie.
The dry-cleaner ruined a shirt, to Marie.

e. Le teinturier a massacré une chemise à ma nouvelle voisine de palier.
The dry-cleaner ruined a shirt to my new floor neighbor.

As in (8c) above from Kayne, a full *à*-DP can appear as *wh*-extracted also in cases not involving a body-part and a part-whole relation (12a). A full *à*-DP can be the focal element in cleft sentences (12b); it can be dislocated to the left or to the right (12c–d). Finally, a noncore *à*-DP can appear at the rightmost position in the clause, similarly to a goal/recipient dative argument, *only* if the noncore dative is phonologically heavy (12e). Here is an additional set of examples:

(13)   *Le plombier a vidé un chauffe-eau aux co-propriétaires.
       The plumber emptied a water-heater to the apartment-owners.

(14) a. A qui le plombier a vidé un chauffe-eau?
        To whom did the plumber empty a water-heater?

     b. C'est aux co-propriétaires que le plombier a vidé un chauffe-eau.
        It is to the apartment-owners that the plumber emptied a
        water-heater.

     c. Aux co-propriétaires, le plombier a vidé un chauffe-eau.
        To the apartment-owners, the plumber emptied a water-heater.

     d. Le plombier a vidé un chauffe-eau, aux co-propriétaires.
        The plumber emptied a water-heater, to the apartment-owners.

     e. Le plombier a vidé un chauffe-eau aux co-propriétaires du
        bâtiment A.
        The plumber emptied a water-heater to the apartment-owners
        of building A.

In all these examples a full *à*-DP can appear in positions that imply movement or external merge to a hierarchically high position. Under the assumption that clitics in French, including the dative clitic (e.g., *lui, leur* in the
examples above), *also* move from their base position, theta-position, to
attach to an inflecting element, the puzzle is this: what base position does a
noncore dative rise from, if it is not a theta-bearing DP? And if there is a
position that is like the one reserved for recipient/goal in the VP, why can't
a noncore dative *à*-DP freely appear in that position? The examples in (10)
will be taken to be indicative of the base position for this type of noncore
datives. In the next section we turn to spelling out our analysis.

2. THE ANALYSIS

In this section we present our analysis of core and noncore datives in
French. We start in 2.1 with the structure adopted for core datives, which
coincides with the standard treatment of prepositional *to*-goals in English.
In section 2.2 we put forward our analysis of noncore datives and show
how they differ structurally from core datives. In the subsections of 2.2 we
discuss particular cases of noncore datives. We claim that the dative is the
same element but that it attaches to slightly different chunks of structure.
Section 2.3 presents some thoughts on the indeterminate status of the element *à*.

2.1 Core Datives

We suggest the following underlying structure for core datives, representing the structure of a bieventive extended VP with different types of little vPs.[4]

(15)   Marie a envoyé la lettre à Céline.
       "Marie sent the letter to Céline."

(16)

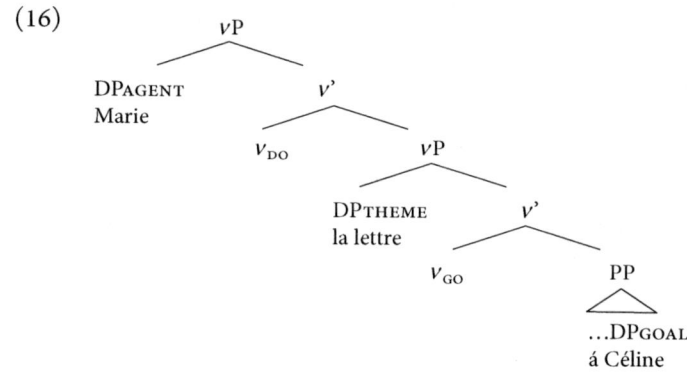

This analysis is not different from the one suggested for English ditransitive verbs with prepositional *to* (e.g., Larson 1988, 1990, Pesetsky 1995, Harley 2002). We assume that French ditransitives are essentially CAUSED-MOTION constructions and that this applies across the board, and also to verbs such as *give*. The CAUSED subevent is structurally represented by v_{DO}, and the lower MOTION subevent, temporally concomitant with the upper subevent, is represented in syntax by v_{GO}. Although Rappaport-Hovav & Levin (2008) convincingly show that *give* in English should be analyzed only as a CAUSED-POSSESSION type predicate, while *send* is compatible with both CAUSED-MOTION and CAUSED-POSSESSION frames, we will not adopt the same logic for the French *donner* "give." A notorious difference between French and English concerns the absence of double object constructions in the former. We attribute this gap to the unavailability in French of the light abstract predicate v_{HAVE} heading a lower POSSESSION subevent in English double object constructions. Because a MOTION subevent licenses spatial goals, some of which are recipients (i.e., animate spatial goals), CAUSED-POSSESSION can in principle be expressed in the subset of CAUSED-MOTION structures, as in (16). Therefore, we take *envoyer* "send" and *donner* "give" to share

---

4 Marantz (2005) convincingly argues for a slightly different configuration, disposing of light verb heads such as v_{DO}, v_{GO}. For ease of exposition we do not implement his view here.

not only the same upper v_{DO} head but also the underlying v_{GO} MOTION *sub*structure in French.

2.2 Noncore Datives

We suggest that noncore datives are attached as a secondary subject to a stative predication, embedded in a bieventive construction via a procedure of λ-abstraction over a variable provided by material in the lower subevent (cf. Cuervo 2003, 2010, where the Spanish high applicative is placed in this intermediate position).

(17) a. Le teinturier lui a massacré sa chemise.
   "The dry-cleaner ruined her/his shirt on her/him."
   b. Marie lui a vomi sur ses coussins.
   "Marie vomited on her/his cushions on her/him."

(18) a.

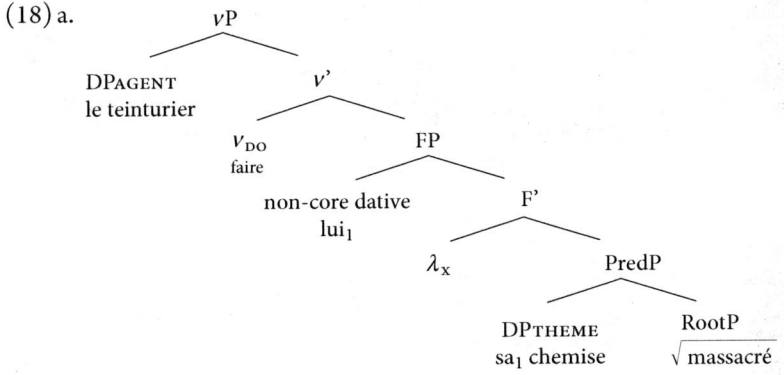

b.

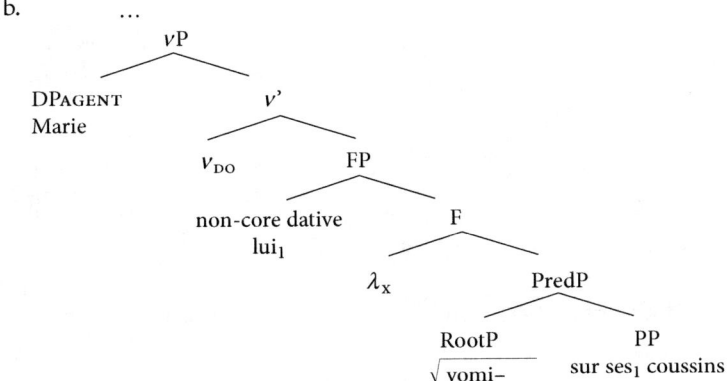

Some precisions on the lexical meaning and the corresponding structure of verbs that allow noncore datives are in order. Transitive verbs that express a change of state have a common CAUSE-RESULT frame with v_{DO}, which heads an upper causative subevent and selects for a stative temporally nonconcomitant subevent PredP. In (18a) PredP indicates a result state lexicalized by the verb root, where the theme DP, understood to have undergone a change of state, functions as its subject; alternatively, PredP can be locative (18b), appearing with unergative verbs and thus creating bieventivity (cf. Hoekstra & Mulder 1990). The locational PP expresses the endpoint of a path, which is another type of result phrase (cf. Levin & Rappaport-Hovav 2006). Here the cognate object (Root) of the unergative verb functions as the subject of the resulting state (18b).

Before elaborating on the procedure of λ-abstraction, we first present evidence for the relative hierarchy of the participants, agent > noncore datives > theme > core dative, starting first with the relative order of the noncore dative and the theme. For reasons of clarity, our arguments relate to the change-of-state construction in (17a)/(18a).

Variable binding facts show that the noncore dative is hierarchically higher than the theme, contrary to the state of affairs with core datives in (16). French instantiates a clear structural difference between core goal datives and noncore benefactive datives in terms of the c-command relations holding between theme and dative argument.

(19) a. La maîtresse a rendu   son cartable   à chaque élève.
        The teacher   gave-back   his schoolbag   to every pupil.

    b. La maîtresse a rendu   chaque cartable   à son propriétaire.
        The teacher   gave-back   every schoolbag   to its owner.

(20) a. Marie   a peint   à chaque locataire   sa maison.
        Mary   painted   to every tenant   his house.

    b. *Marie   a peint   à son locataire   chaque maison.
        Mary   painted   to its tenant   every house

(21) a. Marie a peint sa maison à chaque nouveau habitant du village.
        Mary painted his house   to every new inhabitant of the village.

    b. *Marie a peint chaque maison à son anxieux locataire de longue date.
        Mary painted every house   to its worried tenant of long duration

The contrast in (19–21) shows that core dative and the theme are not hierarchically ordered (19) and that the noncore argument asymmetrically c-commands the theme irrespective of word-order, that is, both in environments when it *precedes* the theme (20), which we claim to be its basic position, and in environments where it follows the theme due to its phonological heaviness (21). Here are additional examples.

(22) a. Il faudra que Marie présente son patient à chaque interne.
It is necessary that Marie present her patient to each intern.

b. Il faudra que Marie présente chaque patient à son médecin traitant.
It is necessary that Marie present each patient to his general practitioner.

(23) a. Il faudra que Jean nettoie à chaque chauffeur son camion.
It is necessary that Jean clean to each driver his truck.

b. *Il faudra que Jean nettoie à son chauffeur chaque camion.
It is necessary that Jean clean to his driver each truck

(24) a. Il faudra que Jean gare sa voiture à chaque assistante parlementaire.
It is necessary that Jean park her car to each parliament assistant

b. *Il faudra que Jean gare chaque voiture à son propriétaire exaspéré.
It is necessary that Jean park each car to its exasperated owner

Next, we provide support for attaching the noncore dative lower than an agent DP. This goes against the analysis proposed by Roberge & Troberg (2009), who suggest that the ApplP containing the noncore dative is attached above vP introducing the agent. Two arguments, adapted from Bosse & Bruening (2010), support this assumption. The first one concerns variable binding facts, this time between the agent and the noncore dative.

(25) a. Chaque propriétaire a peint un portail à son locataire préféré.
"Each landlord painted a gate for his tenant."

b. *Son propriétaire a peint un portail à chaque nouveau locataire.
His landlord painted a gate for each new tenant

The quantifier in the agent DP can bind into the noncore dative (25a), but the opposite is not true (25b). There is asymmetric c-command between the agent DP and the noncore datives.

The second argument indicating that the noncore dative is merged below the agent DP concerns available readings related to the scope of the adverb *de nouveau* "again":

(26)   Marie a peint un portail à tous les voisins   de nouveau.
       "Marie painted a gate   for all the neighbors again."

This multiply ambiguous sentence gives rise to the following readings: (i) *again* has scope over the lower subevent: the gate is painted again; (ii) *again* has scope over the entire extended *v*P: someone painted the gate for all the neighbors and now Marie did it for them again; or, similarly, (iii) Marie has painted the gate for them and now she does it again. One reading, however, is *not* available, where *again* has the agent in its scope to the exclusion of the noncore dative: (iv) #Marie has painted the gate before, and she does it again but for the first time for the neighbors. Importantly, this particular reading is not available even if the place *de nouveau* before the dative argument. This leads us to the conclusion that the agent DP is *always* hierarchically higher than the noncore dative DP.

2.2.1 Motivation for λ-Abstraction

Generally, there are two procedures in grammar for adding arguments: by a theta-marking head or by predication derived by λ-abstraction (cf. Landau 2009 on λ-abstracting over CPs and references therein). Under this procedure, a null operator is merged to an untensed propositional-like element, which is the complement of a selected head. Our PredP in (18) answers these criteria: it is untensed and selected by a higher *v*. Similarly to Roberge & Troberg (2009), we assume that a noncore dative implies the merger of a null operator. According to these authors, the presence of a null operator is justified because it causes crossover effects: the theme cannot be *wh*-extracted in questions containing a noncore dative (27b).

(27) a. Paul   lui   a bu   la meilleure bouteille.
      Paul   3S.DAT   drank   the best bottle.
      "Paul drank the best bottle on him."

    b. *Qu'est-ce que   Paul   lui   a bu?
       What   Paul   3S.DAT   drank
       Intended: "What did Paul drink on him?"

    c. Qu'est-ce que   Paul   a bu?
       What   Paul   drank?
       "What did Paul drink?" (Roberge & Troberg 2009, ex. 51)

The same holds for our λ-abstraction operation: if the theme is part of a phrase that has undergone abstraction and is bound into, we do not expect it to be able to rise outside of that constituent.

Roberge & Troberg (2009) link the presence of their null expletive operator to the fact that noncore datives in French are part of structures involving obligatorily VP material. They take the operator to bind into the VP, given the ban on vacuous quantification. However, they do not actually show *which material* in the VP gets bound by the operator. We try to address this issue below and present constraints on the type of VP material allowed when a noncore dative is present. To our knowledge these constraints have not been explicitly noted before. We show that noncore datives are licit when VP material succeeds to provide a variable for binding.

Consider first the following pair.

(28) a. Marie   lui   a peint   *son* portail   en orange.
      Marie   3S.DAT   painted   his gate   orange

    b. #Marie   lui   a peint   *le* portail   en orange.
      Marie   3S.DAT   painted   the gate   orange

A possessive pronoun is fine as the determiner of the theme DP, while a definite article is not.[5] The possessive pronoun clearly provides a variable to be bound by the operator, a definite article does not. Note further that this distinction is not relevant for core datives:

(29) a. Marie   lui   a envoyé   *ses* affaires.
      Marie   3S.DAT   sent   his stuff
      "Marie sent him his stuff."

    b. Marie   lui   a envoyé   *les* affaires.
      Marie   3S.DAT   sent   the stuff
      "Marie sent him the stuff."

A pronoun (e.g., *le*) or a proper name in theme position do not provide a variable to be bound, and a noncore dative cannot be available:

(30) a. *Le plombier   l'a enfin   vidé   aux co-propriétaires.
      The plumber   it finally   emptied   to the apartment-owners
      Intended: "The plumber finally emptied it for them."

    b. *Luc les   a decapitées à Pauline Escure (*les* = *les poupées* "the dolls")
      Luc them decapitated to Pauline Escure.
      Intended: "Luc decapitated them on Pauline Escure."

(31) a. *Marie   lui   a peint   Paul.
      Marie   3S.DAT   painted   Paul
      Intended: "Marie painted Paul on him."

---

5 Example (28b) with the definite article is fine only under a list reading.

b. *Marie   lui   a brûlé   Paris.
   Marie   3s.DAT   burnt   Paris
   Intended: "Marie burnt down Paris on him."

The following example is an attested one—a proper name is possible in theme position, when a noncore dative is present in the structure, only if it is preceded by a possessive pronoun (32a), presumably providing a variable to be bound; otherwise the sentence is ungrammatical (32b):

(32) a. Ce prof   m'   a détruit   ma Paulinette
        This teacher 1s.DAT   destroyed   my Paulinette (on me).
        "This teacher destroyed my Paulinette on me."

     b. *Ce prof   m'   a détruit   Paulinette.
        This teacher 1s.DAT   destroyed   Paulinette

Other types of theme DPs that seem to provide a variable are indefinites and quantified expressions:

(33) a. Le plombier   leur   a vidé   un/*le chauffe-eau.
        The plumber   3p.DAT   emptied   a/the water-heater
        "The plumber emptied a water-heater for them."

     b. Le plombier   leur   a vidé   tous les chauffe-eaux.
        The plumber   3p.DAT   emptied   all the water-heaters
        "The plumber emptied all the water-heater for them."

Curiously, demonstratives are suitable in constructions containing noncore datives, contrary to (referring) definite articles.[6]

(34) a. Le teinturier   lui   a massacré   cette chemise.
        The dry-cleaner 3s.DAT   ruined   this shirt
        "The dry-cleaner ruined this shirt on her/him."

     b. Marie   lui   a peint   ce portailen orange.
        Marie   3s.DAT   painted   this gate orange
        "Marie painted this gate orange for her/him."

Lepore & Ludwig (2000) suggest that complex demonstratives are like quantified NPs. Whether this is the right explanation for the observed pattern will have to await future work. Restricting ourselves, at this stage, to the interplay between the possessive pronoun and the definite article, it can also

---

6 Lucien Kupferman (p.c.) notes that this is possible only when the demonstrative has a deictic reading and not an anaphoric one.

be shown that a verb that is not a classical ditransitive like *écrire* "write" is interpreted as one when the theme is introduced by a definite article:

(35) Marie   lui   a écrit   la lettre.
      Marie   3S.DAT   wrote   the letter
      "Marie addressed the letter to him."
      Not: #Marie wrote the letter for him.

It is as if the choice of determiner facilitates a lexical drift in the meaning of the verb. Finally, in the case of examples like (17b)/(18b), with unergative verbs containing a locational PP, the same constraint seems to be at play:

(36) Marie   lui   a vomi   sur ses coussins/??les coussins.
      Marie   3S.DAT   vomited   on his cushions/the cushions
      "Marie vomited on his cushions."

Here too, it appears, VP material must provide a variable that can be abstracted over.

To sum up, the type of determiner allowed with core and noncore datives is an additional feature setting them apart. It lends support to our analysis in terms of λ-abstraction over a variable. To the best of our knowledge this empirical fact has not been previously acknowledged.

2.2.2 Body-Parts as Predicates

In the previous section we have shown how lexical semantic properties of the predicate condition the availability of noncore datives in French: noncore datives are attached when the extended *v*P contains a stative subevent. This implies that extended *v*Ps lacking such a subevent would be excluded from appearing with noncore datives:

(37) a. *Marie   lui   a embrassé   son voisin.
        Marie   3S.DAT   kissed   his neighbor

    b. *Marie   lui   a touché   un livre.
        Marie   3S.DAT   touched   a book

    c. *Marie   lui   a rencontré un passant.
        Marie   3S.DAT   met   a passerby

    d. *Marie   lui   a attendu   le plombier qui ne venait pas.
        Marie   3S.DAT   waited   the plumber that didn't show up

However, for a subset of the sentences in (37), having a relational "part" as the head of the object (theme) licenses a noncore dative as the "whole" argument.

(38) a. Marie   lui   a embrassé   la main.
    Marie   3S.DAT   kissed   the hand
    "Marie kissed her/his hand/kissed her/him on the hand."

     b. Marie   lui   a touché   le visage.
    Marie   3S.DAT   touched   the face
    "Marie touched her/his face on her/him."

We contend that noncore datives added to a structure with an inalienable theme are derived via a specialized configuration, namely possessor raising. The dative DP is the argument of a nominal predicate, and it rises from within the DP containing it to the clause level for case reasons (Kayne 1993, Szabolcsi 1983, 1994, Landau 1999).

Interpretatively speaking, this is the only case involving noncore datives where a possession relation between the theme and the dative DP is entailed and not implied:

(39) a. Jeanne   lui   a peint   *les sourcils*   en orange.
    Jeanne   3S.DAT   painted   the eyebrows   orange
    "Jeanne painted her/his eyebrows orange (on/for her/him)."

     b. Jeanne   lui   a peint   *son portail*   en orange.
    Jeanne   3S.DAT   painted   his gate   orange
    "Jeanne painted her/his gate orange (on/for her/him)."

When the theme may be understood in a part-whole relation with the applied argument, a possessive reading seems the most salient reading (39a). However, when no part-whole relation exists between the dative and the accusative arguments, any reading—possessive, benefactive, malefactive—is available depending on the context, (39b). In other words, possessor raising constructions differ from noncore datives discussed above in that the dative element is indeed understood as composing with the theme. In (38a) the dative DP denotes an individual that received a kiss on *his/her* body-part (= hand). In (39a) the dative DP denotes an individual who has orange paint *on him* (whose part is orange). This is not the case in examples such as (39b), where the dative DP does not itself undergo the change of state in question.

There are several pieces of evidence that the head nominal constituting the theme argument of the verb acts as a predicate at the DP level (Kayne 1975, Vergnaud & Zubizarreta 1992). First, the theme noun cannot be freely pluralized: compare (40a), where the body-part is interpreted distributively, to (40b), which has a plural theme that prevents inalienable reading:

(40) a. Le médecin leur   a radiographié l'estomac, (aux gosses).
         The doctor   3P.DAT X-rayed   the stomach, (to.the kids)

     b. #Le médecin leur   a radiographié les estomacs, (aux gosses).
         The doctor   3P.DAT X-rayed   the stomachs, (to.the kids)

Second, the definite article in this case is an expletive form: it is attached to a type denoting expression, yielding a nondenoting DP (Vergnaud & Zubizarreta 1992). A possessive pronoun is not available in these constructions, further suggesting that the head-noun, the "part," is predicatively related to the noncore dative, its "whole" argument; a possessive pronoun would saturate the predicate's empty slot and render a fully referential DP.

(41) *Le médecin lui   a radiographié   son estomac.
        The doctor   3S.DAT   X-rayed   his stomach

We suggest the following analysis for noncore datives related to a part predicate. The noncore dative originates inside the DP containing the part predicate and rises to an intermediate position for case reasons.

(42)   Marie lui embrasse la main.
       "Marie is kissing her/him on the hand."

(43)

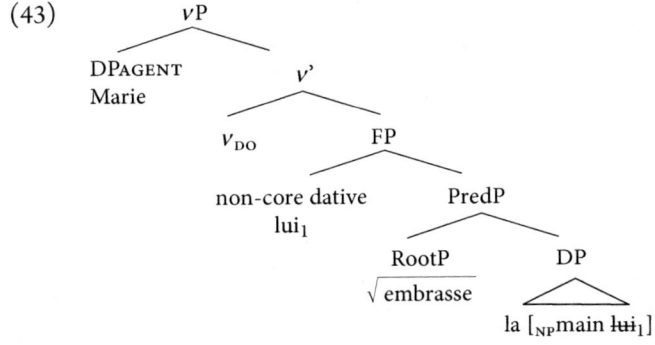

Crucially, a "whole" argument can rise only from a lower subevent. This means that a noncore dative cannot be added if the part predicate is the head of the agent argument. The prediction is confirmed by sound emission verbs:

(44)   *L'oreille   lui   siffle.
        the ear   3S.DAT   whistles
        Intended: "Her/his ear whistles."

With unaccusative verbs, just as with transitive change-of-state verbs, body-part themes are perfect:

(45) a. La tête   lui   tourne.
      the head   3s.DAT   spins
      "Her/his head spins."

   b. Les yeux   lui   brûlent.
      the eyes   3s.DAT   burn
      "Her/his eyes are burning her/him."

Here, the noncore dative rises from within the theme DP to the intermediate FP position, to be case licensed. The theme residue can subsequently become a derived subject. Interestingly, noncore datives are not allowed with unaccusative verbs in the absence of a relational noun in the theme position, (46).[7]

(46) a. *Le/*son ballon   lui   tourne.
      the ball   3s.DAT   spins
      Intended: "His ball spins."
   b. *Les/*ses cahiers   lui   brûlent.
      the notebooks   3s.DAT   burn
      "His notebooks are burning."

Finally, it should be noted that plain mono-eventive stative *v*Ps are not a proper environment for adding a noncore dative, even with a body-part predicate.

(47) a. *Elle   lui   hait   le nez.
      She   3s.DAT   hates   the nose
      Intended: "She hates his nose."
   b. *Elle   lui   a oublié   le visage.
      She   3s.DAT   forgot   the face
      Intended: "She forgot his face."

This is due presumably to the unavailability of an FP as a case-licensing position in such configurations (see Landau 1999).

To sum up, noncore datives related to theme DPs denoting body-parts have a wider distribution. They are naturally found with transitive verbs

---

7 This suggests that a noncore dative cannot be added via λ-abstraction in unaccusative structures, maybe because their change-of-state component fails to be stativized as in transitive structures.

expressing a change of state and with unergative VPs with a locational PP (48), since they can provide a classical argument to abstract over.

(48) a. Marie   lui   a coupé   les cheveux.
        Marie   3S.DAT   cut   the hairs
        "Marie cut his hair."

    b. Elle   lui   a tiré   dans le ventre.
          She   3S.DAT   shot   in the belly
          "She shot him in the belly."

Last, noncore datives related to a body-part, and to a somewhat lesser degree other noncore datives, involve affectedness, unlike core datives. This stems directly from the way noncore datives become part of the syntactic structure, whether by λ-abstraction or possessor raising. As a result of λ-abstraction, noncore datives come to be the subjects of the result-state predicates containing an argument that has undergone change of state. λ-abstraction requires that this affected argument be coindexed with the c-commanding noncore dative. Consequently, the two become referentially dependent and also share the property of being affected by the change of state. The tighter the semantic link between the two is, in terms of (in)alienability or part-whole relations, the stronger the affectedness of the non-core is implied (cf. Labelle 2002).

2.3 The Indeterminate Status of à-DPs

This analysis implies that à in à-DPs spells out two distinct linguistic objects. In core dative constructions à functions as a preposition that selects its DP complement, whereas in noncore datives it is a morphological marker (case) of the additional argument. This duality characterizes the treatment à-DPs received in the literature, where it is debated whether à-DPs should be best analyzed as PPs or as DPs. Most authors seem to agree that à-DPs are actually DPs (Authier & Reed 1992, Anagnostopoulou 2003). Here we review the evidence that has been provided to make such a claim. We show that this evidence is not conclusive, which enables us to tolerate the indeterminate status of à-DPs reflected in our analysis.

It should first be noted that, semantically, à is locative, not specified for direction or path:

(49) a. Jean   rentre   à la maison   PATH
        Jean   returns   a the home
        "Jean goes home."

b. Marie   vit   à Amsterdam   LOCATION
   Marie   lives   *a* Amsterdam
   "Marie lives in Amsterdam."

Additionally, when *à*-DP is merged as the complement of v_{GO}, where it is prepositionlike, it can be substituted, in certain environments by a true PP:

(50) a. J'ai lancé le ballon à Marie.
     "I threw the ball to Marie."

   b. J'ai lancé le ballon sur mon adversaire.
      "I threw the ball on/at my opponent."

It is true that the substitutability manifest in (50) is not available or restricted for different types of verbs (e.g., *give*, *send*; but cf. *J'ai envoyé les enfants chez mes amis* "I sent the children to my friends"). Therefore, we are not taking a clear stand on whether core *à*-DPs are always available as the complement PPs of a DIRECTED-MOTION predicate, or whether they are unselected PPs. This state of affairs is also due to the lack of conclusiveness of tests that have been previously proposed in the literature to determine whether or not *à*-DPs are prepositionlike.

First, it has been claimed that *à* differs from other prepositions in a specific binding environment (Authier & Reed 1992). However, according to our informants, *à*, whether pronominalizable as *lui* or *y*, behaves like other prepositions.

(51) a. Jean$_1$ ne parle que [de lui$_1$].
        Jean   ne talks only of him(self).

   b. Jean$_1$ ne compte   que   [sur lui$_1$].
      Jean ne counts   only   on him(self).

   c. Jean$_1$ ne pense qu'[à lui$_1$]. compare: Jean y/*lui pense
      Jean   ne thinks only of him(self).

   d. Jean$_1$ n'écrit   qu'[à lui$_1$]. compare: Jean lui/*y écrit
      Jean   ne writes   only to him(self).

Second, Anagnostopoulou (2003) uses a coordination test to show that distributionally *à* is not like other prepositions. Whereas true prepositions do not require the preposition to be repeated under coordination, *à* does. This leads Anagnostopoulou to suggest that *à* is not prepositional. However, careful examination of the data reveals that some prepositions must be repeated in the second conjunct, just like *à*, while others may do so.

(52) Nous avons présenté notre demande **au** ministre et *****(à)** la vieille milliardaire.
We presented our demand to.the minster and (to.the) old billionaire.

(53) Nous avons parlé **du** ministre et *****(de)** la vieille milliardaire.
We talked of the minister and (of) the old billionaire.

(54) J'ai déjà acheté des chocolats **chez** Hermé et *****(chez)** Ladurée.
I already bought chocolates at Hermé and (at) Ladurée.

(55) Nous avons discuté **avec** le ministre et **(avec)** la vieille milliardaire.
We talked with the minister and (with) the old billionaire.

(56) J'ai déjà acheté un cadeau **pour** Eric et **(pour)** ma milliardaire préférée.
I already bought a gift for Eric and (for) my favorite billionaire.

Thus *à* patterns exactly like *de* "of/from" or *chez* "at," while *avec* "with" and *pour* "for" are truly prepositional according to this test. This state of affairs leads us to conclude that this test too is not viable.

In the absence of conclusive evidence for determining whether or not *à* is prepositional, we contend that this duality is related to the syntactic configuration in which it is found. As for noncore datives, once an argument is added via λ-abstraction, the extended *v*P becomes "ditransitive," in the sense that it has two internal DPs. General case-dependency mechanism ensures that the dative case be assigned to the second argument (cf. Marantz 1991, Baker & Vinokurova 2010).

3. IMPLICATIONS

3.1 Co-occurrence with Core Datives

Core and noncore datives are licensed by different subevent types, according to our analysis. The question arises as to why they should not co-occur—why the sentence in (57), describing a situation whereby Pierre distributes candy to children and does this for the sake of a third party, *lui*, is ungrammatical:

(57) *Pierre lui   a distribué   des bonbons   aux enfants
     Pierre 3s.DAT distributed   candy   to.the children

In order to generate (57), the lower subevent must be λ-abstracted (to license *lui*) over a dynamic MOTION subevent that ensures a reading whereby candy "goes" to the children. As this yields an unacceptable outcome, the question is why vP_{GO}, expressing MOTION, cannot be λ-abstracted over.

The generalization seems to be that λ-abstraction operates on *stative* elements. We have shown that RESULT predicates that express a change of state head stative subevents. So do small clauses that contain locations expressing the place of result. Compare (57) with (58a–b). A SC in (58a), containing a cognate object (root), "vomit," and a PP, *sur ses coussins* "on her/his cushions," expressing the result, can be compared to a more transparent (58b).

(58) a. Paul   lui   a vomi   [$_{SC}$ vomi sur ses coussins].
       Paul   3S.DAT   vomited   [vomit on her/his cushions]

    b. Paul   lui   a remis   [$_{SC}$ un livre sur son étagère].
       Paul   3S.DAT   returned   [a book on hre/his shelf]

Importantly, (58), unlike (57), does *not* contain a vP_{GO} subevent, which implies a dynamic subevent concomitant with the causing event (Svenonius 2002). Dynamic subevents express (the beginning of) movement of the theme along the path but not the endpoint place it reaches, which is a state caused by movement. This is best exemplified by the contrast in (59), where (59a) contains a SC involving movement, and (59b) contains a stative SC.

(59) a. *L'électriciens   leur   a installé   [$_{SC}$ un radiateur à la jeune fille au pair].
       The electrician   3P.DAT installed   [a radiator to the au pair]

    b. Paul   leur   a installé   [$_{SC}$ un radiateur sous la fenêtre].
       Paul   3P.DAT installed   [a water-heater under the window]

So the ingredients necessary for noncore datives to appear are bieventive vPs, whose lower part is a λ-abstracted stative predicate, syntactically expressed as a change-of-state verb or a result-location PP.

3.2 Differences between French and English

Now that we have defined noncore datives in French as "second" subjects of the lower RESULT-STATE subevent, we turn to the issue of cross-linguistic variation concerning the linguistic expression of these optional arguments. It has been often observed that the range of possible noncore datives is much larger in Romance languages than in English; for example, French equivalents of (60) are all well formed. Why this should be the case, however, is rarely discussed in the literature.

(60) a. *I'll fix you the radiator.

b. *John opened Mary the door.

c. *Mother crumbled the baby his cookie.

d. *Mary (accidentally) burned John the steak.

Pesetsky (1995: 153) observes that double object constructions are found only with non-change-of-state predicates. Indeed, the same verb may appear in a double object construction if the entire event is conceived as "creation" or "coming into possession," and may be unacceptable in the same configuration if the entire event is conceived as a change of state, as shown by the contrast between (60a) and (61a), or between (60b) and (61b).

(61) a. I'll fix you a sandwich (= I'll make you a sandwich)

b. John opened Mary a beer (= John handed Mary a beer, created Mary a drink)

Not only does English disallow double objects with change-of-state verbs but it also disallows them with most Latinate verbs, and the latter fact received more attention. We would like to tie these two gaps in English double object constructions and claim that they are interrelated (cf. Nash 2006, Marantz 2005).

First, we adopt a quite common conception of English double object constructions (cf. Pesetsky 1995, Harley 2002, Rappaport-Hovav & Levin 2008) according to which these configurations involve CAUSE-TO-POSSESS event structure, where the lower POSSESS subevent is headed by an empty (abstract) HAVE (G_{have}) predicate that relates the dative possessor subject and the theme possessee complement. Such a structure can be considered to license a noncore argument if the verb's semantics does not necessarily imply the existence of a recipient (e.g., creation verbs like *bake, make, write, draw*). Structurally, this can be translated as follows: while a lower subevent headed by HAVE is obligatory with ditransitive verbs, it can be optionally added with creation verbs.

(62) a. John wrote Mary a poem => John DO$_{write}$ [Mary HAVE a poem]

b. John wrote a poem => John DO$_{write}$ a poem

We saw above that change-of-state verbs must contain a lower RESULT subevent where the theme that undergoes a change of state serves as a subject to the stative predicate that expresses a result. Clearly, two stative subevents, the HAVE subevent and the RESULT subevent, "compete" for the same position with respect to the upper causative subevent, and this accounts for their mutual incompatibility. As Latinate verbs have a resultative subcomponent in them, visible through polymorphemic verb stems, their incompatibility with abstract HAVE subevent follows (cf. Marantz 2005 and Giannikadou & Merchant 1999, who attribute the lack of resultative clauses in Greek to the same factor). In other words, the presence of robust verb derivation affixes in Latinate stems imposes the lexicalization of the lower subevent, notwithstanding whether the verb is interpreted as a change-of-state verb or a creation verb semantically compatible with MOTION subevent (cf. Levin & Rappaport-Hovav 2006).[8]

Our analysis leads us to the conclusion that languages similar to English, namely those that allow double accusative case-array and lack visible applicative affixes, should disallow noncore datives with verbs that unambiguously express change of state. We think that this constraint owes its *raison d'être* to case-assigning mechanisms. Marking two arguments with identical morphological means, as is the case in English, should be possible only under very strict locality conditions that confine the two DPs to the same minimal domain—this condition is satisfied in the small clause headed by the abstract HAVE. On the other hand, languages, like French, that have a morphological means to differentiate a noncore argument from the theme by case markers (or by extra morphology on the verb) have more freedom to merge a noncore argument in a different domain in the extended *v*P. One of its manifestations is λ-abstraction on stative result predicates heading the lower subevent of transitive verbs that express change of state. This operation makes it possible for noncore datives to be merged as second subjects that bind into the predicate.

4. CONCLUSION

This article investigated the syntactic and semantic properties of core and noncore datives in French. While most of the cross-linguistic work done on datives focuses either on core or on noncore datives, the present analysis sought to contrast the two to improve our understanding of the ingredients involved in their derivation. We showed that despite their superficial similarity, core and noncore datives present several distinctive properties, some of which were not previously noted for French. We proposed that core and noncore datives have their origin in different underlying structures:

8 Krifka (1999) proposes a constraint according to which verbs that impose the lexicalization of the lower subevent by the manner component are banned in double object constructions. The verbs *whisper* and *shout* differ from *tell* in that the latter expresses the manner-of-message communication, i.e., MOTION. So an environment where the lower subevent must be lexicalized is incompatible with empty light HAVE stative subevent. This explanation brings Latinate verbs and manner-of-motion verbs under the common denominator.

the former originate as the complement of a MOTION subevent of transitive verbs, whereas the latter are "second" subjects of a stative predicate, either base-generated in this position, or rised out of a theme that contains a part-noun. The analysis reaches generalizations concerning the lexico-semantic decomposition of verbal predicates appearing with core and noncore datives. It departs from the received applicative typology of functional heads introducing dative arguments.

ACKNOWLEDGMENTS

We are grateful to Richard S. Kayne, Ivy Sichel and Anne Zribi-Hertz for discussing various parts of this paper with us. We thank also the organizers and audience of the 4th European Dialect Syntax Meeting held in 2010 in Donostia/San Sebastian, the audiences of the linguistics colloquium at the Hebrew University of Jerusalem, and at Tel-Aviv University, and the audience at the Séminaire Architecture Grammaticale at Université Paris 8. Special thanks to Marie-Laurence Knittel, Laurent Roussarie, Isabelle Roy, Florence Villoing, for their help with the French data. All errors are our own. The paper was supported by ISF grant 1157/10 to Nora Boneh.

REFERENCES

Anagnostopoulou, Elena. 2003. "Cross-linguistics and cross-categorial variation of datives." In Melita Stavrou and Arhonto Terzi (eds.), *Recent advances in Greek Generative Grammar: Festshrift for Dimitra Theophanopoulou-Kontou*, 46–118, Amsterdam: John Benjamins.

Authier, Marc J., and Lisa Reed. 1992. "Case theory, theta theory, and the distribution of French affected clitics." In Bates Dawn (ed.), *Proceedings of the West Coast Conference on Fromal Linguistics* 10: 27–39. Somerville, MA: Cascadilla Press.

Baker, Marc C., and Nadya Vinokurova. 2010. "Two modalities of case assignment: Case in Sakha." *Natural Language and Linguistic Theory* 28: 593–642.

Barnes, Betsy. 1985. "A functional explanation of French nonlexical datives." *Studies in Language* 9: 159–195.

Boneh, Nora, and Léa Nash. 2010. "A higher applicative: Evidence from French." In *Proceedings of Israel Association for Theoretical Linguistics* 25, available at http://linguistics.huji.ac.il/IATL/25/Boneh_Nash.pdf.

Bosse, Solveig, and Benjamin Bruening. 2011. "Benefactive versus experiencer datives." In Mary Byram Washburn et al. (eds.), *Proceedings of the 28th West Coast Conference on Formal Linguistcs*, 69–77. Somerville, MA: Cascadilla Proceedings Project.

Cuervo, María Cristina. 2003. "Datives at large." PhD diss., MIT.

Cuervo, María Cristina. 2010. "Against ditransitivity." *Probus* 22: 151–180.

Folli, Raffaella, and Heidi Harley. 2006. "Benefactives aren't goals in Italian." In Jenny Doetjes and Paz Gonzalez (eds.), *Romance languages and linguistic theory 2004*, 121–142. Amsterdam: John Benjamins.

Georgala, Effi. 2010. "Why German is not an exception to the universal base order of double object constructions." Handout for *28th West Coast Conference on Formal Linguistics*.

Georgala, Effi, Waltraud Paul, and John Whitman. 2008. "Expletive and thematic applicatives." In Charles B. Chang and Hannah J. Haynie (eds.), *Proceedings of the 26th West Coast Conference on Formal Linguistics*, 181–189. Somerville, MA: Cascadilla Proceedings Project.

Giannakidou, Anastasia, and Jason Merchant. 1999. "Why Giannis can't scrub his plate clean: On the absence of resultative secondary predication in Greek". In Amalia Mozer (ed.), *Greek Linguistics '97: Proceedings of the 3rd International Conference on Greek Linguistics. Ellinika Grammata*, 122–134, Athens.

Grashchenkov, Pavel, and Vita G. Markman. 2008. "Noncore arguments in verbal and nominal predication: High and low applicatives and possessor raising." In Natasha Abner and Jason Bishop (eds.), *Proceedings of the 27th West Coast Conference on Formal Linguistics*, 185–193. Somerville, MA: Cascadilla Proceedings Project.

Harley, Heidi. 2002. "Possession and the double object construction." *Yearbook of Linguistic Variation* 2: 29–68.

Herschensohn, Julia. 1992. "On the economy of Romance non-lexical datives." In Paul Hirschbühler and Konrad Koerner (eds.), *Romance languages and modern linguistic theory*, 123–134. Amsterdam: John Benjamins.

Herslund, Michael. 1988. *Le datif en français*. Paris: Louvain.

Hoekstra, Teun, and René Mulder. 1990. "Unergatives as copular verbs: Locational and existential predication." *Linguistic Review* 7: 1–79.

Jouitteau, Mélanie, and Milan Rezac. 2007. "The French ethical dative: 13 syntactic tests." *Bucharest Working Papers in Linguistics* 9(1): 97–108.

Kayne, Richard S. 1975. *French syntax: The transformational cycle*. Cambridge, MA: MIT Press.

Kayne, Richard S. 1993/2000. "Towards a modular theory of auxiliary selection." In *Parameters and Universals*, 107–130. Oxford: Oxford University Press.

Kayne, Richard S. 2004. "Prepositions as probes." In Adriana Belletti (ed.), *Structures and beyond: The cartography of syntactic structures*, vol. 3, 192–212. Oxford: Oxford University Press.

Kayne, Richard S. 2010. "The DP-internal origin of datives." Talk presented at the *4th European Dialect Syntax Meeting* June 21–23 2010 in Donostia/San-Sebastian, Spain.

Krifka, Manfred. 1999. "Manner in Dative Alternation". In Sonya Bird, Andrew Carnie, Jason D. Haugen, and Peter Norquest (eds.), *18th Proceedings of the West Coast Conference on Formal Linguistics* 1–14. Somerville, MA.: Cascadilla Prceedings Project.

Labelle, Marie. 2002. "The French noncanonical passive in *se faire*." In Shosuke Haraguchi, Bohumil Palek, and Osamu Fujimura (eds.), *Proceedings of Linguistics and Phonetics 2002*. Tokyo: Charles University Press and Meikai University.

Lamiroy, Béatrice, and Nicole Delbecque. 1998. "The possessive dative in Romance and Germanic." In W. Van Langendonck and W. Van Belle (eds.), *The Dative*, vol. 2: *Theoretical and Contrastive Studies*, 29–74. Amsterdam: John Benjamins.

Landau, Idan. 1999. "Possessor raising and the structure of VP." *Lingua* 107: 1–37.

Landau, Idan. 2009. "Predication vs. aboutness in copy raising." Unpublished ms.

Larson, Richard K. 1988. "On the double object constructions." *Linguistic Inquiry* 19: 335–391.

Larson, Richard K. 1990. "Double objects revisited: Reply to Jackendoff." *Linguistic Inquiry* 21(4): 589–632.

Larson, Richard, K. 2010. "On Pylkkänen's Semantics for Low Applicatives". *Linguistic Inquiry* 41(4):701–704.

Leclère, Christian. 1976. "Datifs syntaxiques et datifs éthiques." In J.-C. Chevalier and M. Gross (eds.), *Méthodes en grammaire française*, 73–96. Paris: Klincksieck.

Lerpore, Ernest, and Kirk Ludwig. 2000. "The Semantics and Pragmatics of Complex Demonstratives". *Mind* 109: 199–240.

Levin, Beth, and Malka Rappaport-Hovav. 2006. "Constraints on the complexity of verb meaning and VP structure." In H.-M. Gaertner, R. Eckardt, R. Musan, and B. Stiebels (eds.), *Between 40 and 60 puzzles for Krifka*. Available at www.zas.gwz-berlin.de/file-admin/material/40–60-puzzles-for-krifka/pdf/levin_and_rappaport.pdf.

Marantz, Alec. 1991. "Case and licensing." In *Proceedings of ESCOL*, 234–253. Ithaca, NY: Cornell Linguistics Club. Republished in Eric Reuland (ed.), *Arguments and case: Explaining Burzio's generalization*, 11–30. Amsterdam: John Benjamins, 2000.

Marantz, Alec. 2005. "Objects out of the lexicon: Objects as events." Unpublished ms.

McIntyre, Andrew. 2007. "High and low datives in German." Unbublished Ms.

Morin, Y.-C. 1981. "Some myths about pronominal clitics in French." *Linguistic Analysis* 8: 95–109.

Nash, Léa. 2006. "Structuring VP: Goals." EALING lectures, September 2006, Ecole Normale Supérieure, Paris.

Pesetsky, David. 1995. *Zero syntax*. Cambridge, MA: MIT Press.

Pylkkänen, Liina. 2008. *Introducing arguments*. Cambridge, MA: MIT Press.

Rappaport-Hovav, Malka, and Beth Levin. 2008. "The English dative alternation: The case of verb sensitivity." *Journal of Linguistics* 44: 129–167.

Roberge, Yves, and Michelle Troberg. 2007. "Les objets indirects non thématiques en français." *Actes du congrès annuel de l'Association canadienne de linguistique 2007. Proceedings of the 2007 annual conference of the Canadian Linguistic Association.* Available at http://homes.chass.utoronto.ca/~cla-acl/actes2007/actes2007.html.

Roberge, Yves, and Michelle Troberg. 2009. "The high applicative syntax of the dativus commondi/incommodi in Romance." *Probus* 21: 249–289.

Rooryck, Johan. 1988. "Formal aspects of French nonlexical datives." *Folia Linguistica* 22: 373–386.

Rouveret, Alain, and Jean-Roger Vergnaud. 1980. "Specifying reference to the subject: French causatives and conditions on representations." *Linguistic Inquiry* 11: 97–202.

Svenonious, Peter. 2002. "Icelandic case and the structure of events." *Journal of Comparative Germanic Linguistics* 5: 197–225.

Szabolcsi, Anna. 1983. "The possessor that ran away from home." *Linguistic Review* 3: 89–102.

Szabolcsi, Anna. 1994. "The noun phrase." In Ferenc Kiefer and Katalin É. Kiss (eds.), *Syntax and Semantics 27: The Syntactic Structure of Hungarian*, 179–274. San Diego, CA: Academic Press.

Vergnaud, Jean-Roger, and Maria Luisa Zubizarreta. 1992. "The definite determiner in French and in English." *Linguistic Inquiry* 23: 595–652.

CHAPTER 3

Datives and Adpositions in Northeastern Basque

RICARDO ETXEPARE AND BERNARD OYHAR ÇABAL

INTRODUCTION

Many languages show a degree of overlapping between the distinct categories of adpositions and cases.[1] Case markers typically used to express

1 In Basque, case suffixes and primary adpositions differ in several important regards.
Descriptively, whereas case suffixes are both morphologically and semantically phrasal,
in the sense that they relate an entire syntactic phrase to a verbal predicate, adpositions
are semantically phrasal, but seem to behave morphologically as affixes. That is, their
morphological scope is word bound. Consider in this regard the following contrast
between a (nonagreeing) dative case suffix and the ablative adposition, that illustrates a
general contrast between so-called "declension" suffixes and case suffixes:

(i)   a. [[Arte-a-ri]   eta   [zientzi-a-ri]]   interesatzen da
         art-D-dat   and   science-D-dat   interest-hab is
         "She/he is interested in art and in science."
      b. [[Artea]   eta   [zientzia]-ri]   interesatzen da
         art-D   and   science-D-dat   interest-hab is
         "She/he is interested in art and science."
(ii) a. *[[Etxe]   eta [herri]]-tik   urrundu da
          house   and village-abl   go-away is
          "She/he went away from (the) house and (the) village"
      b. [[Etxe-tik]   eta   [herri-tik]]   urrundu da
         house-abl   and   village-abl   go-away is
         "She/he went away from (the) house and (the) village."

Whereas coordination can target a phrasal constituent internal to the case projection,
as in (32b), the declension suffix cannot be merged to a coordinate phrase, as shown
in (33b). The ablative suffix must be repeated in each of the conjuncts. The ablative,
on the other hand, takes semantic scope over phrasal objects, as shown by the fact
that it can mark the source of complex relations, as possessive ones:

(iii)   Xabier   [bere etxe]-tik   urrundu da
         Xabier-abs   his house-abl   go-away is
         "Xabier went away from his house."

Note also that the dative case suffix is merged to a DP, whereas the postpositions
seem to merge directly to the stem.

grammatical relations may also extend to cover semantic roles that are typically expressed by adpositions. Spatial roles, such as locations, goals of motion, or sources, are a case in point. A common approach to this general phenomenon assimilates dative case-suffixes to adpositions, and specifies in the lexicon the relation between particular spatial roles and the two types of entities. In northeastern varieties of Basque, datives can express spatial roles, such as targets of motion or locations. Basque is a particularly intriguing case of overlap, in that its dative case-suffix behaves as a bona fide case marker outside the spatial cases, on the same level as absolutive and ergative cases, triggering agreement with the auxiliary and showing behavior typical of DPs. We will argue that the spatial dative cases in northeastern Basque are not different from what we see in canonical dative DPs: they are case suffixes, attached to nominal phrases, and expressing purely syntactic relations. The only difference is that the kind of functional support necessary to license case in verbal predicates can also be found internal to adpositional phrases, within certain conditions. Concretely, we will capitalize on recent work by Koopman (2000), Tortora (2009), and Den Dikken (2010) and argue that the spatial dative cases of northeastern Basque are licensed in an aspectual projection internal to a phrase headed by a Path adposition. The argument will require a detailed discussion of some of the aspects involved in the syntax of postpositional phrases in Basque.

Crucial for the analysis of spatial datives here is the idea that lexically realized postpositions encode complex spatial properties and that their semantic richness is a function of phrasal Spell Out, in the sense of Starke (2005, 2010): overtly realized adpositions in Basque lexicalize complex arrays of spatial features under conditions of adjacency. In the spirit of Koopman (2000) and much subsequent work, we take Place and Path adpositions to be able to project their own functional structure, in a way parallel to other lexical categories such as nouns or verbs. The lexical description for the insertion rule of overt adpositions, however, may prevent intermediate functional heads to project. Non–overtly realized adpositions, on the other hand, only spell out a feature and are therefore insensitive to adjacency conditions. Functional projections in the complement domain of a silent adposition can project and attract embedded DPs to their Spec. The presence of spatial datives is related to the presence of an intermediate aspectual head in between the Path and the Place spatial features, occupied by the dative-marked phrase. From this point of view, the distribution of the spatial dative case in northeastern dialects arises as the combined outcome of two interacting factors: the presence of a null Path adposition, available in northeastern dialects, and lexicalization patterns common to all Basque varieties.

The discussion is based on data drawn from two different sources: a corpus of Navarro-labourdin writings of the second half of the twentieth century,[2] and the answers of informants gathered in the developing database Basyque, which aims at building a syntactic database of the different dialectal varieties spread across the Basque domain. The Navarro-Labourdin variety is the largest subvariety of northeastern Basque (the set of Basque varieties spoken in the French side of the Basque Country and bordering areas along the Pyrenees), and the one that has been best represented in written form since the nineteenth century.[3]

1. SOME GENERAL PROPERTIES OF DATIVE CASE IN BASQUE

Dative is one of the so-called grammatical cases in Basque.[4] It shares this property with ergative and absolutive cases. Dative DPs agree with the auxiliary in number and person. The dative usually marks the recipient or beneficiary of the action:

(1) a. Jonek   Mikeli   eskutitz   bat   bidali dio
       Jon-erg Mikel-dat letter   one-abs   sent aux[ditransitive]
       "Jon sent a letter to Mary."

    b. Jonek   Mikeli   autoa   konpondu dio
       Jon-erg Mikel-dat car-the-abs   fixed aux[ditransitive]
       "Jon fixed the car for Mikel."

Basque also employs dative marking for some nonparticipant roles in ditransitive constructions, such as ethical datives, datives of interest (2b), and possessor-raising constructions (2a). Dative case also marks subjects of psychological predicates of the *piacere* class (2c) (Belletti and Rizzi 1988):

(2) a. Jonek   Mikeli   besoa   hautsi dio
       Jon-erg Mikel-dat arm-D-abs   broken aux[3sA-3sD-3sE]
       "Jon broke Mikel's arm."

    b. Esneak   Mireni   gaindi egin   dio/*du
       milk   Miren-dat over   done   aux[1sE-3sD-3sA]/[1sE-3sA]
       "The milk boiled over on Miren."

    c. Joni   liburuak   gustatzen   zaizkio
       Jon-dat   books-abs   like-hab   aux[3plA-3sD]
       "Jon likes books."

2 The written output of the authors examined expands from the early 1950s to the late 1980s. The authors referenced in the corpus started to write before the advent of the normative pressure related to the expansion of standard Basque in the 1970s, and showed little concern to accommodate to the standard norm.

3 See Lafitte (1944) and Arotçarena (1951) for two descriptive grammars.

4 "Grammatical case" is a descriptive notion employed in the Basque grammatical tradition to refer to suffixes that are associated to grammatical functions, can be merged to a DP, and allow the DP they merge with to agree with the inflected auxiliary.

Dative case and agreement are not the only means by which Basque marks the presence of a dative argument. Finite sentences containing a dative argument require a particular affix (-i-/-ki- see Trask 1995) in the inflected auxiliary. This affix has been variously called *dative-flag* (Rezac 2006) or *pre-dative affix* (Hualde 2003). The dative-flag precedes the agreement affix cross-referencing the dative argument. Take an unaccusative verb like *nator* "I come":

(3) N-ator
    1sA-root
    "I come."

The form in (3) can be extended to include reference to a dative argument, the endpoint or beneficiary of the coming event. In that case, the agreement affix corresponding to the dative argument is preceded by the pre-dative affix (Hualde 2003: 207):

(4) N-ator-**ki**-zu
    1sA-root-predat-2sD
    "I come to you."

In other words, the presence of a dative argument in a Basque finite sentence requires three things: (i) a dative case suffix; (ii) agreement in person and number; and (iii) an independent inflectional head which signals that the sentence has a dative.

It is generally admitted that dative arguments in Basque are case-marked DPs. Only DPs trigger agreement on the verb, and datives, as we saw, do. Only DPs enter into binding relations as antecedents, and this is the case with dative DPs too. Compare in this regard (5a), with a dative argument, and (5b), with a postpositional phrase:

(5) a. Jonek   Mireni$_i$ bere$_i$ buruaz   hitzegin dio
       Jon-erg   Miren-dat   poss head   talked aux[3sA-3sD-3sE]
       "Jon talked to Miren about herself."

    b. *Jonek   Mirenekin$_i$ bere$_i$ buruaz   hitzegin zuen
       Jon-erg   Miren-with poss head-instr   talked aux[3sA-3sE]
       "Jon talked with Miren about herself."

As indirectly shown by the examples in (1–2), the dative argument typically precedes (and c-commands) the theme in Basque (see Fernandez 1997 and Elordieta 2001 for a thorough discussion).

2. NORTHEASTERN VARIETIES

The northeastern varieties of Basque spoken in France present a series of contrasting properties in both the distribution of the case marker and its agreement properties. First, the semantic scope of the dative case suffix expands to include the marking of spatial functions of different sorts (sections 2.1 and 2.2), as well as the aspectual status of the event as unbounded (section 2.3).[5]

2.1 Spatial Datives

In northeastern varieties, the dative marks the spatial goal of the event or situation:

(6) a. Erretora badoa elizako atearen gakoari (Lz.I, 235)
    Priest-D goes church-gen door-gen lock-dat
    "The priest goes to the door-lock of the church."

   b. Balkoin bat, bideari emaiten duena (Etc. OM, 130)
    balcony one, road-dat give-hab aux[tr]-rel-D
    "A balcony that looks onto the road."

   c. Alemanen tankak oldartzen zirela Maginot harresiari
    (Lz, VII, 53)
    German-gen tanks charge-ger aux-Comp Maginot fence-dat
    "As the German tanks charged against the Maginot line"

   d. Hurbiltzen da poliki-poliki bonetari (LZ, I, 113)
    approach-ger is slowly beret-dat
    "She/he slowly approaches the beret."

Central and western varieties only admit spatial postpositions or complex postpositional phrases (see next subsection) in that case:

(7) a. Erretora badoa elizako ate gakora
    Priest-D goes church-gen door lock-all
    "The priest goes to the door-lock."

   b. Balkoin bat, bidera ematen duena
    balcony one, road-all give-hab aux[tr]-rel-D
    "A balcony that looks over the road."

5 Those contrasting properties arise together in the nineteenth century in the Navarro-Labourdin variety examined here. For the diachronic development of this phenomenon with particular reference to the Navarro-Labourdin subvariety, see Etxepare (2011).

d. Alemanen   tankeak oldartzen zirela   Maginot harresia **ren kontra**
German-gen tanks charge   aux-Comp Maginot fence-gen   against
"As the German tanks charged against the Maginot line."

e. Hurbiltzen da   poliki-poliki   txapela**ren**   **ingurura**
draw-near aux   slowly   beret-gen   vicinity-all
"She/he slowly approaches the beret."

Spatial datives do not agree with the auxiliary. (8) is an illustration:

(8) *Balkoin bat   bideari   ematen   diona
balcony one,   road-dat   give-hab   aux[3erg-3dat-3abs]-rel-D

2.2 Datives in Complex Postpositions

There is a set of postpositions in Basque that encode directional paths. Some of those postpositions select DP Grounds that are marked with a dative case suffix in the Navarro-Labourdin variety:

(9) a. Mendia-**ri** gora
Mountain-dat up
"Up the mountain"

b. Mendia-**ri** behera
mountain-dat down
"Down the mountain"

d. Pareta-**ri** kontra
wall-dat against
"Against the wall"

e. Jujea-**ri** bisean-bis
judge-dat vis-à-vis
"Vis-à-vis the judge"

f. Etxea-**ri** parrez-par
House-dat face-to-face
"Facing the house"

g. Har-**i** buruz
That-dat toward
"Toward him/her"

In those same contexts, the Ground is marked by inessive postpositions or genitive cases in the rest of the Basque varieties:

(10) a. Mendia-**n** gora
Mountain-in up
"Up the mountain"

b. Mendia-**n** behera
mountain-in down
"Down the mountain"

c. Pareta-**ren** kontra
wall-gen against
"Against the wall"

d. Jujea-**ren** aurrez-aurre
judge-gen vis-à-vis
"In front of the judge"

e. Etxea-**ren** parrez-par
house-gen face-instr-face
"In front of the house"

f. Har-**en-gana**
She-gen-ine-all
"Toward her/him"

2.3 Datives in Complements of Aspectual Verbs

Aspectual verbs of the atelic sort select for dative nominalized clauses in Navarro-Labourdin (see section 3.1), as the progressive and inchoative aspectual verbs in (10):[6]

> (11) a. Eta   horren   ahultzeari   *ari* zirezte
>   and   that-gen   weaken-Nom-D-dat   prog are
>   "And you are weakening that."

>   b. Josteari   *lotu*   da
>   sew-nom-dat   tied   is
>   "He/she started sewing."

Dative aspectual complements do not agree either with the auxiliary, as shown in the examples.

2.4 Summary

Nonagreeing datives arise in the complement position of aspectual verbs, as the complement of some postpositions expressing a directional notion, and in DPs that express the target of a motion or path. Datives in the complement of an aspectual verb and dative complements of directional postpositions will be discussed in section 4 (particularly in sections 4.3 and 4.4.). The next section examines in detail the distribution of nonagreeing datives in their spatial roles as they combine with lexical verbs.

3. SPATIAL DATIVES AND PREDICATE CLASSES

The northeastern spatial dative occurs across a variety of predicate types: motion verbs (3.1), stative verbs (3.2), oriented change-of-state verbs (3.3), verbs of comparison (3.4), and verbs of contact (3.5).

3.1 Motion Verbs and Unbounded Paths

As a starting point in the examination of the conditions that allow the presence of a spatial dative in motion predicates, let us consider the verb *itzuli*.

---

6 The dative also shows up in the object of a handful of unergative and semelfactive predicates (see Etxepare 2011 for an aspect-oriented analysis of the presence of the dative in those cases):

> (i) a. Horr-**i** pentsatu   b. Atea-**ri** jo
>   That-dat think   door-dat knock
>   "To think about that"   "Knock on the door"

This verb has two related meanings in Basque: it means either "return, come back," or "turn toward something." In its first reading, it takes an allative DP as the target of motion (12a). In its second meaning, it takes a dative DP as the target of an oriented path (12b):

(12) a. Maiterenganat   itzuli   zen
      Maite-gen-ine-all   turned   was
      "He/she returned to (where) Maite (was)."

     b. Itzuli   zen   Maiteri   (Etchepare 1958: 94)
       Turned was   Maite-dat
       "He/she turned toward Maite."

Jackendoff (1990) provides the following conceptual schema for the "turn toward" meaning:

(13)   *Itzuli*   "Turn toward"
      $[_{\text{EVENT}}$ INCH $([_{\text{STATE}}$ ORIENT $([_{\text{Thing}}$ Subject], $[_{\text{Path}}$ Object])])]

Compared to the basic conceptual function GO underlying the "return" reading of the verb, the conceptual representation of "turn toward" contains the basic conceptual function ORIENT, which does not imply motion into a goal. ORIENT has two arguments, one being the Figure of the relation, and the other one being a directional or unbounded Path, which in turn selects a spatial Ground. The above contrast suggests the following hypothesis: spatial datives occur with those predicates that do not represent a transfer of the Figure into the Goal. The turning motion leaves the Theme in a certain position vis-à-vis the spatial goal (*Maite*, in 12b), but does not take it into the spatial Goal. The latter spatial relation requires an overt adposition (12a).

Bihurtu in (14) is another verb that obeys a similar pattern. *Bihurtu* also has two different meanings: it means either "return" or "to turn against." The first meaning requires an allative goal and entails that the theme has moved to a physical or abstract place. The second one does not give rise to such an entailment; it only means that the subject stands in a resisting or rebelling attitude vis-à-vis a certain goal:

(14) a. Gaizkira   bihurtu   da
      Evil-all   turned-back   is
      "She/he returned to evil(-doing)."

     b. Gaizkiari   bihurtzen   delarik
       evil-dat   turn-against-ger is-Comp-part
       "As she/he turns against evil"

Abiatu "depart, to set in motion to a goal" can take an allative or a dative goal. The two cases do not have an identical meaning:

(15) a. Bidera   abiatu   da
       road-all   moved   is
       "She/he moved to the road."

    b. Bideari   abiatu da
       road-dat   moved is
       "She/he set out on his/her way."

With the allative postposition, the predicate expresses a motion taking the theme to a physical space, the road. With the dative, it means that the subject has set out on her or his way, with no further implication that a goal has been attained.

The verb *erori* provides a further example of the alternation between the dative and the allative. With an allative postposition *erori* means "fall," and the Ground marks the physical space where the falling ends (16a). Our corpus also shows the variant in (16b), with a dative Ground, where *erori* means "fall under" or "be inclined to/toward." In the latter case, no motion is entailed, and the Ground is marked dative:

(16) a. Lurrera   erori da
       Floor-all   fallen is
       "She/he fell on the floor."

    b. Jainkoaren nahi sainduari erortzen diren   arima jenerosak
       God-gen   will holy-dat   fall-hab aux-comp   spirit generous-D-pl
       "Those generous spirits who are inclined toward God's holy will"

Verbs like *jarraiki/segitu* "follow" or *hurbildu* "approach," which lexically entail that the theme has not reached the goal but are nevertheless goal-oriented, require dative:

(17) a. Etsenplu oneri...   jarraiki da bere...urhatsetan
       Example good-dat   follow in his steps-loc
       "She/he follows the good examples in all his steps."

    b. Hurbiltzen   da   polliki   bonetari
       approach-ger   is   slowly   beret-dat
       "She/he slowly approaches the beret."

If this is what underlies the use of dative Ground DPs, we can make sense of the fact that verbs like *arrive* or *come*, which denote an attained spatial goal, are incompatible with the dative:

(18) a. *Etxeari   liburua   heldu da
      House-dat   book-D   arrived is
      "The book arrived to the house."

    b. *Etxeari   eskale   bat etorri da
      house-dat   beggar   one come is
      "A beggar came home."

The data suggest the following partition in the set of Path exponents in Basque:

(19) a. Allative -> Bounded Path (Spatial Goal, TO)
    b. Dative -> Unbounded Path (Oriented Path, TOWARD)

3.2 Stative Verbs

The directional element associated to the dative suffix is particularly prominent when the predicate itself is such that it cannot contribute one. Stative verbs like (20a,b) are a case in point.

(20) a. Balkoin bat...   bideari   emaiten duena   (Etc. OM, 130)
      Balcony one   road-dat   give-hab aux   (tr)-rel-D
      "A balcony that looks onto the road."

    b. Lehena salbu, oro Kaliforniako   itsasoari dagoen lur zerrendan (G, 52)
      first   except all California-gen sea-dat is-rel   land stretch-loc
      "Except the first one, all of them in the stretch of land looking (lit. *which is*) onto California"

(20a) presents a complex predicate formed by the light verb *eman* "give" and a dative goal. The complex verb is a stative predicate that does not involve motion. The directional component is directly contributed by the dative Ground. An even clearer case is (20b), where the copula *egon* "to be" physically locates the subject *oro* "all," but contributes nothing that could be interpreted as an orientation function. Jackendoff (1983: 173) proposes the following conceptual structure for cases like "to look onto":

(21) $[_{\text{STATE}} \text{ ORIENT } ([_{\text{Thing}} x], [_{\text{Path}} y])]$

Since in (20a, b) the predicate does not contribute by itself the orientation function, it is the presence of the dative Ground that adds the directional component.

3.3 Directed Change of State

Consider the following cases:

(22) a. Heien egitateeri begiak hetsi ditut (LZ II, 74)
   Their deeds-dat eyes close aux(tr)
   "I closed the eyes to their deeds."

   b. Aphal dezagun burua jainkoaren nahi sainduari (Etc. FE, 179)
   lower aux(tr) head-D God's will holy-dat
   "Let us bow to God's holy will."

   c. Haien erranari behar dugu nahitaez plegatu
   their words-dat must aux(tr) obligatorily yield
   "We must submit to what they say."

In all cases, the absolutive argument (the Figure) undergoes a change of state, and this change leaves it in a particular orientation vis-à-vis the Reference Point (someone else's deeds, God's will, or someone else's words in (22a–c)). But there is no movement that will take the Figure into the Ground. I assume that a relevant part of the conceptual structure underlying those predicates involves the function ORIENT, as in the previous cases:

(23) $[_{\text{EVENT}}$ CAUSE $([_{\text{Thing}}...], [_{\text{STATE}}$ ORIENT $([_{\text{Thing}}...], [_{\text{Path}}...])])]$

3.4 Verbs of Comparison

Verbs of comparison are another class that show a dative suffix in the DP expressing the reference term of the comparison:

(24) a. Hiru medaileri, hamabi nausi dituk (LZ III, 79)
   three medals-dat twelve superior are
   "Three medals win over twelve."

   b. Hoik zure semeari preferatzen dituzu (LZ I, 45)
   those your son-dat prefer-ger aux
   "You prefer those to your son."

c. Lore hari zuen Lotik bere burua parekatzen   (LZ V, 135)
   flower that-dat Loti-erg   himself level-hab
   "Loti used to compare himself to that flower."

We follow Broadwell (1996) in the idea that all verbs of comparison possess an abstract Path in their conceptual structure that ends in the term of comparison (see also Pasicki 1988). In this case, however, the Path must be supplemented with reference to a set of vertical and horizontal axes that will determine whether the Figure is higher or lower than the reference term, or whether it is before or behind it. The latter cases can be assimilated to ordinary comparative relations. They also bear a dative reference term in northeastern varieties:

(25) Suprefetari   aintzinduz   (LZ I, 110)
     subprefect-dat   advancing
     "Anticipating to the subprefect."

We will take verbs of comparison to need three conceptual components: a Figure (that which is compared), a Ground or Reference Term (the term to which it is being compared), and a set of axes that will determine their relative positions in the comparison relation, roughly, whether the latter holds in a horizontal (before, after) or vertical scale (higher, lower). The Figure is marked absolute. The Ground is marked Dative.

(26) $[_{STATE}\ GO_{Comparison}\ ([_{Thing}...],\ [_{Path}\ TO\ [_{Place}\ AT_{axial\ relation}\ [_{Thing}...]]])]$

3.5 Verbs of Contact

Dative DPs also surface as the support term for verbs expressing attachment:

(27) a. Estekatzen   dute   kadiraren   bizkarrari   (LZ IV, 312)
        tie-ger   aux   armchair-gen back-dat
        "They tie him to the back of the armchair."

     d. Iragana josi nahi   zuen zetorrenari   (LZ VII, 128)
        past   sew   want   aux   come-Rel-D-dat
        "He wanted to sew the past to the things that were coming."

     c. ...Canal de Suez   bi itsaso   elgarri   juntatzen
        canal de Suez   two seas   each-other-dat   unit-ger
           ur-bidea   (Etc. O, 194)
        dituen aux-Relchannel
        "The Suez Canal, a channel that unites two seas."

According to Jackendoff (1990: 106–116), verbs of attachment contribute a predication about a state, which contains a locative function AT. This locative function is enriched with the diacritic [+contact], which specifies that the Figure and the reference term are in contact. For the inchoative case, Jackendoff proposes the following conceptual structure (1990: 109):

(28) $[_{\text{EVENT}}$ INCH $[_{\text{STATE}}$ $([_{\text{Thing}}\ldots], [_{\text{Place}}$ AT$_{\text{contact}}$ $[_{\text{Thing}}\ldots]])]]$

3.6 Summary

The set of conceptual representations that capture the distribution of spatial, nonagreeing datives can be summarized by means of the following table:

(29) a. $[_{\text{EVENT}}$ INCH $([\text{ORIENT}\ ([_{\text{Thing}}\ldots], [_{\text{Path}}\ldots])])]$
(oriented motion)

    b. $[_{\text{EVENT}}$ CAUSE $([_{\text{Thing}}\ldots], [_{\text{STATE}}$ ORIENT$])\ ([_{\text{Thing}}\ldots], [_{\text{Path}}\ldots])]$
(oriented change of state)

    c. $[_{\text{EVENT}}$ CAUSE $[_{\text{STATE}}$ GO $([_{\text{Thing}}\ldots], [_{\text{Path}}$ TO $[_{\text{Place}}$ AT$_{\text{axial relation}}$ $[_{\text{Thing}}\ldots]]])]]$
(comparison)

    d. $[_{\text{EVENT}}$ INCH $[_{\text{STATE}}$ AT$_{\text{contact}}$ $([_{\text{Thing}}\ldots], [_{\text{Place}}\ldots])]]$
(verbs of joining)

    e. $[_{\text{STATE}}$ ORIENT $([_{\text{Thing}}\ldots], [_{\text{Path}}\ldots])]$
(stative verbs of orientation)

If we concentrate on the portions of the conceptual structure that directly represent the goal, we can further simplify (29) into (30):

(30) a. $[_{\text{STATE}}$ ORIENT $([_{\text{Thing}}\ldots], [_{\text{Path}}\ldots])]$
    b. $[_{\text{STATE}}$ GO $[_{\text{PLACE}}$ AT$_{\text{axial relation}}$ $([_{\text{Thing}}\ldots], [_{\text{Place}}\ldots])]]$
    c. $[_{\text{STATE}}$ AT$_{\text{contact}}$ $([_{\text{Thing}}\ldots], [_{\text{Place}}\ldots])]$

The relation between the Figure and the Reference Term or Ground can be resumed in the following three cases: (i) the Figure is or becomes oriented to the dative Reference Term; (ii) the Figure is or ends up in a relative position vis-à-vis the Reference Term determined by a set of horizontal and vertical axes projected from the Reference Term; or (iii) the Figure is or ends up being in surface contact with the dative Reference Term. As shown by the stative function heading the locative relations, none of the conceptual structures entails actual motion.[7]

  7 For an explanation of the distribution of the dative, see section 7. We keep the discussion at a descriptive level here.

4. HOW DOES THE DATIVE ARISE?

One obvious question regarding spatial datives is exactly how they compare to adpositions, or, in other words, what regulates the alternative use of an adposition and a Case suffix in the expression of spatial relations. The conceptual analysis entertained in section 3 provides a potential answer: since the dative is associated to a well-defined set of spatial relations, the proper grammatical place to locate the alternation between adpositions and nonagreeing datives should be the lexicon. The idea can be spelled out as follows: if the spatial relation is one that denotes an orientation path toward a reference term, a contact situation between Figure and Ground, or a comparative relation, then the dative is the morphological exponent of the Ground term in those cases. Allatives in turn will lexicalize the Ground in other sorts of relations, and so will inessives. In this view, the Basque spatial lexicon would be arbitrarily divided between lexical exponents of category P and morphological cases, each of the categories encoding a subset of the (linguistically) available spatial relations. The dative suffix would be listed in the lexicon as encoding the following spatial semantic relations:

(31)   Dative Grounds = {Targets of unbounded directional paths, supporting entities in contact situations, reference terms in comparisons}

This assimilates the nonagreeing, spatial dative suffix to the set of postpositions. In fact, some authors (see Albizu 2001 for an elaboration of this idea) have directly identified the nonagreeing dative of eastern dialects to postpositional phrases. The fact that agreement is impossible with spatial dative goals would further add to the plausibility of this connection: postpositional phrases in Basque do not trigger agreement. The idea is in line with Asbury (2008), who takes oblique cases to lexicalize adpositional heads. Despite its initial plausibility (somehow weakened by the heterogeneous nature of the spatial notions involved) we will try to show that the hypothesis that dative suffixes are postpositional heads directly encoding a spatial role in the cases at hand is misleading.

As we will see, dative Grounds arise also in the domain of postpositional phrases, under the presence of overt postpositions that convey the kind of spatial notions covered by (30). The consequence of this observation is clear: if the spatial relations invoked in (30) are expressed by independent postpositions, then they cannot be directly encoded by the dative suffix. The argument requires a comparison of the three basic postpositional structures of Basque, which we develop in the following sections.

4.1 Locational Nouns and Spatial Suffixes

The domain of spatial relations in Basque is expressed by means of three sets of grammatical formatives: (i) suffixes; (ii) locational nouns (De Rijk 1990, Eguzkitza 1997, Aurnague 1996, 2001, Hualde 2002); and (iii) non-inflected postpositions derived from locational nouns or adpositional sources (Aurnague 2001, Hualde 2002). The set of suffixes in Basque contains three basic forms: the inessive (32a), the allative (32b), and the ablative (33c).[8]

(32) a. Etxea-**n**   b. Etxe-**ra**   c. Etxe-**tik**
     home-D-iness   home-all   home-abl
     "In/at the house"   "to the house"   "from the house"

In addition to this limited set of spatial suffixes, Basque also has a rich inventory of locational nouns that allow a more flexible localization of the Figure and combine with the previous suffixes (see Euskaltzaindia 1985, De Rijk 1990, Eguzkitza 1997, Hualde 2002). An example is provided below:

(33) a. Etxe-a-ren   **aurre**-a-n
     House-D-gen   front-D-loc
     "In front of the house"

    b. Zuhaitz-en   **arte**-tik
      trees-gen   among-from
      "From among the trees"

    c. Ohe-a-ren   **azpi**-ra
      bed-D-gen   under-all
      "(To) Under the bed"

    d. Erreka-a-ren   **ondo**-tik
      river-D-gen   next-through
      "Through the space next to the river"

    e. Errekaren   **inguru**-a-n
      river-gen   space-around-det-loc
      "Around the river"

According to De Rijk (1990), locational nouns behave as regular nouns: they require a complement with a genitive suffix, as binominal structures typically do, and bear suffixes that usually attach to nouns, such as the inessive postposition. This is illustrated in (34). Locational nouns participate in noun compounding (see De Rijk 1990 and below), and many

---

8 Plus other complex suffixes formed on the basis of the allative. See Hualde (2002).

of them have a referential use and can be followed by a determiner, as shown in (35):

(34) Etxearen   aurre-a-n
      House-gen   front-D-iness
      "In front of the house"

(35) a. Etxearen   **aurrea/aitzina**   konpondu beharra dago
        House-gen   front fix   need is
        "The front/façade of the house should be fixed."

   b. **Inguru**   hura   arras   hondatua   zen
      area   that   completely   ruined   was
      "That area was completely ruined."

   c. **Ondo** hetan   ibiltzen   ginen
      place that-in   walk-hab   aux[1plA]
      "We used to see that place quite often."

This referential use of locational nouns, however, gives rise to some subtle shifts in meaning. It is clear that *aurre/aitzin* "front" identifies very different spatial entities in (36a) and (36b):

(36) a. Etxearen   aurre-a
        House-gen   front-D
        "The façade/front side of the house"

   b. Etxearen   aurre-a-n
      house   front-D-loc
      "In front of the house"
      "On the façade/front side of the house"

Under the "referential" use in (36a), the only interpretation of the noun *aurre* is "façade"(that is, a part of the house). In (36b), its meaning is ambiguous between "space in front of the house" (thus, not a part of the house itself) and "façade of the house." The ambiguity disappears if we force a syntactic structure that goes beyond a bare noun. For instance, adjectival modification is only possible under the "referential." Interpretation:

(37) Etxearen   aurre   hondatuan
      house-gen   front   ruined-iness
      "In the ruined façade of the house"
      "*In the ruined front of the house"

Adding a plural also forces a referential reading:

(38) Etxearen   aurreetan
     house-gen   façade-pl-iness
     "In the façades of the house"

On the other hand, not all locational nouns admit a referential use. The nonreferential interpretation is the only possible one for some of those nouns. This is the case for *arte* "space in between," as shown in (39):[9]

(39) a. *Hango   arteak meharregi ematen   du
        that-gen space-in-between   narrow-too looks aux[3sE-3sA]
        "That space in between looks too narrow."

    b. Besoen   artean   gorde   du
       arms   between   kept   aux[3sE-3sA]
       "She kept it between her arms."

The only possible meaning for the noun *arte* is that of "space in between, projected from a Ground or reference object embracing that space." Let us call this type of interpretation a "projective interpretation." Locational nouns thus define spatial regions projected from their DP complement (Aurnague 1996). Projective interpretations are a characterizing feature of locational nouns when they are embedded in simple postpositional constructions. For Svenonius (2010), the syntactic differences between true nouns and locational nouns in their projective interpretation justifies defining the latter as a distinct functional item. Locational nouns with a projective meaning lexicalize a particular syntactic head, distinct from both the Ground (represented by the complement DP) and the Place (represented by an adpositional head), that he calls Axial Part. The semantic content of the category can be described according to the following definition of axial parts by Jackendoff (1996: 14): "The axial parts of an object—its *top, bottom, front, back, sides,* and *ends*—..., unlike standard parts such as *handle* or a *leg,*...have no distinctive shape. Rather, they are regions of the object (or its boundary) determined by their relation to the object's axes. The up-down axis determines top and bottom, the front/back axis determines front and back, and a complex set of criteria distinguishing horizontal axes determines sides and ends." Axial Parts constitute a semantically distinct spatial notion and a syntactically autonomous functional category. Axial Parts are selected by a Place

9 Under the spatial reading. *Arte* may also refer to a temporal interval, in which case it can be used as an independent noun, in eastern dialects:
(i) Arte hortan,   finituko   dugu
    interim that-in   finish-fut   aux[1plE-3sA]
    "In that interim, we'll finish it"

denoting adposition, and they in turn select a reference object or Ground (40). This structure is lexicalized in the same way in all Basque varieties.

(40) $[_{PlaceP}$ Place^0 $[_{AxialP}$ AxialP^0 $[_{DPground}$ D^0 NP]]]

In Basque the axial part is a bare noun, with no functional structure beyond its category feature itself. The nominal properties of the axial part head in this structure have a reflex in Case assignment. The axial noun receives case from the adposition. The Ground term either receives genitive case (41a) or forms a compound with the axial noun (41b):

(41) a. Etxearen   aurrean
    house-gen   front-Det-Loc
    "In front of the house"

   b. Etxe-   aurrean
    house   front-D-Loc
    "In front of the house"

The two options are syntactically represented as follows:[10]

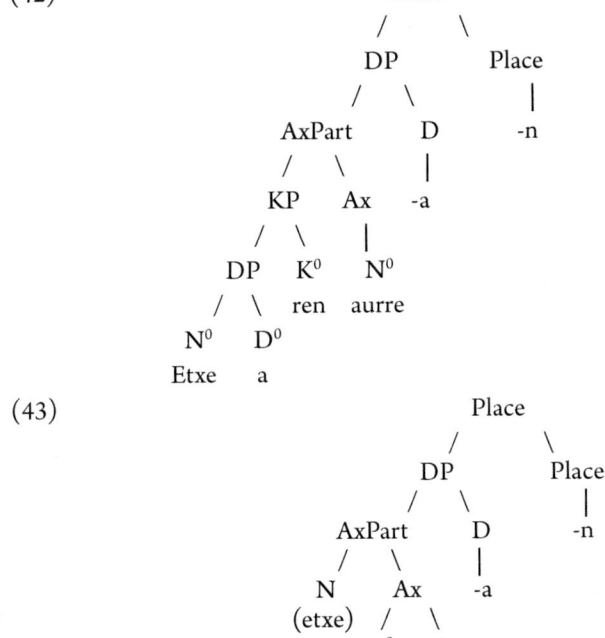

(42)

(43)

10 For the sake of exposition, I adopt a head-final representation for the adpositional phrases here. For the antisymmetry hypothesis as it applies to Basque, see Haddican (2001, 2004), and the papers in Arteatx et al. (2008).

4.2 Invariant Postpositions

Basque has another complex postpositional construction where the head of the construction is an invariant form expressing some abstract directional concept. The following is an example:[11]

(44) a. Etxearen **kontra**
    House-D-gen against
    "Against the house"

b. Aldapan **gora**
    Slope-D-in up
    "Up the slope"

c. Aldapan **behera**
    Slope-D-in down
    "Down the slope"

d. Basoan **barna**
    Wood-D-in into
    "Into the woods"

e. Basoan **zehar**
    wood-D-in across
    "Across the woods"

f. Basoaz **kanpo/landa**
    Wood-D-instr out
    "Out of the woods"

These invariant forms have different sources: some of them are borrowings from Romance prepositions (Spanish *contra* "against") or nouns (Spanish *campo*; Gascon *land/lande* "open space"); most are derived from native locational nouns that have lost their autonomy as nouns and mostly occur as a frozen part of the morphologically complex postposition. This is the case of *gora* "up," *behera* "down," *barna* "into," and *zehar* "across." In the sample[12]. *Gora* and *behera* also function independently as adverbs:[13]

(45) a. Gora joan da
    upperside-all gone is
    "He/she/it went up."

b. Behera joan da
    low-side-all gone is
    "He/she/it went up."

Morphologically, the adverbs *behera* and *gora* are composed by a locational noun, *behe* "low side" or *goi* "upper side," plus a simple spatial suffix, the allative *-ra* "to." The locational noun can be anaphorically referred to in the adverbial cases:[14]

(46)   Gora/behera joan da, baina (behealde/goikalde hura) ikaragarri bustia zegoen
        up/down   gone is but (low side/upperside that) terribly wet-D was
        "He/she went up/down, but that low area was terribly wet."

---

11 For the directional component embedded in *kontra* "against," see the discussion on French *contre* "against" in Vandeloise (1990).

12 *Gora, behera* and *barna*, are formed by the nouns *goi, behe* and *barren*, plus an allative suffix.

13 *Barna* "through" cannot be used as an adverb. It is a phonologically shortened form of *barren(er)a*, which means not "through" but "to the interior of something." In *barrena*, the locational noun *barren* "inside" is easily identifiable, unlike in the shortened form. *Barren(er)a* can function as an adverb. *Barna* cannot.

14 The parentheses are meant to indicate the possibility of *pro-drop*. Basque is a *pro-drop* language for the three arguments ergative, absolutive and dative.

In its adverbial function, the complex postpositional phrase can also be questioned:

(47) a. Nora   joan   da?
        Where   gone   is
        "Where is she/he gone?"

   b. Gora/behera
      Up/down

When the postposition is part of the complex directional postpositional phrase, on the other hand, anaphoric reference to it becomes impossible (48a), as well as questioning the invariant postposition (48b):

(48) a. Mendian behera joan   da,   #baina (behealde hura)   ikaragarri bustia   zegoen
        mountain-iness down gone is   but (low-side) that   terribly   wet   was
        "He/she went up/down the mountain, but that area was terribly wet."

   b. *Mendian   nora/nola   joan   da?
       Mountain-iness   where/how   gone   is
       "How/which direction in the mountain he/she went?"

The fact that anaphoric reference to the locational noun is impossible and that questioning it by a wh-phrase is not possible either, suggests that the invariant postposition, unlike the adverb, does not possess an independent nominal part, but that the whole complex item is a head expressing direction. This difference between adverbial and nonadverbial complex postpositions is confirmed by the following fact: adverbial postpositional phrases admit noun compounding; nonadverbial ones do not. Thus, one can compound the locational noun *behe* or *goi* with another locational noun in the adverbial cases:

(49) a. Behe-aldera   joan   gara
        low-side-all   gone   we-are
        "We went to the low side."

   b. Goi-aldean   hotz   zen
      up-side-iness   cold   was
      "It was cold on the high side."

But noun compounding is impossible in the nonadverbial cases:

(50) a. *Mendian   behe-aldera joan   gara
        mountain-iness   low-side-all gone we-are
        "We went down to a low place in the mountain."

b. *Mendian   goi-aldera   joan   gara
    mountain-iness   up-side-all   gone   we-are
    "We went up to a high place in the mountain."

From the point of view of selection, invariant directional postpositions select spatial Grounds that are themselves headed by a postposition, normally the inessive (44b, c, d, and e), and not genitive Grounds (with the noticeable exception of *kontra* "against," but see section 7.1), as we would expect if they included a locational noun.

4.3 Dialectal Variation

The ground terms of invariant directional postpositions are not uniformly realized in the Basque area: northeastern dialects show a dative suffix where the central and western dialects have inessives and genitive. Our corpus presents the following cases:[15]

(51) a. Paret**ari** kontra
     Wall-D-dat against
     "Against the wall"

b. Patarr**ari** behera
    slope-D-dat down
    "Down the slope"

c. Patarr**ari** gora
    slope-D-dat up
    "Up the slope"

d. Juje**ari** bisean-bis/parrez-par
    judge-dat face-to-face
    "Face-to-face with the judge"

e. Etxe**ari** buruz
    house-D-dat head-instr
    "Toward the house"

f. Etxe**ari** begira
    house-dat looking
    "Looking at the house"

Interestingly, not all bare postpositions take a dative Ground. Some of them, like *kanpo, at, zehar,* or *barna,* in our corpus, take postpositional Grounds, not dative ones:

(52) a. Etxeaz/tik kanpo
     house-instr/abl outside
     "Outside the house"

b. Mendietan zehar
    mountains across
    "Across the mountains"

c. Basoan barna
    wood-in through
    "Through the wood"

d. Etxetik at
    house-abl out
    "Out of the house"

---

15 (51f) is actually well attested in the central and western dialects too. The invariant postposition in this case is the stem-form of the verb *begiratu* "look at" that we translated as the gerundive "looking." The verb itself takes a dative object in both eastern and central dialects.

The bare postpositions that take dative Grounds are easily identifiable in semantic terms: they are conceptually akin to the spatial relations that license dative goals in the verbal domain. They encode orientation (53), location vis-à-vis a set of axial vectors (54), and location plus surface contact (55).

(53) a. Etxeari buruz/begira   a. $[_{\text{STATE}}\ \text{ORIENT}\ ([_{\text{Thing}}\ldots],\ [_{\text{Path}}\ldots])]$
      house   toward/looking
      "Toward the house"

(54) a. Jujeari bisean-bis   b. $[_{\text{STATE}}\ \text{AT}_{\text{axial relation}}\ ([_{\text{Thing}}\ldots],\ [_{\text{Place}}\ldots])]$
      judge-dat face-to-face
      "Face-to-face to the judge"

(55) a. Paretari kontra   c. $[_{\text{STATE}}\ \text{AT}_{\text{contact}}\ ([_{\text{Thing}}\ldots],\ [_{\text{Place}}\ldots]])]$
      wall-dat against
      "Against the wall"

To recapitulate: we have presented three different adpositional structures in Basque. One of them involves what we called primary adpositions (*inessive*, *allative*, and *ablative*), that is morphologically simple suffixes that express basic spatial notions such as location, path and source. The second one involves location nouns, which following Svenonius (2010) we take to head an independent functional projection Axial Part. The last type of postpositional phrase is headed by a set of invariant postpositions, which, unlike simple suffixes, can stand by themselves, and typically express some directional notion. Those independent postpositions also select for complements that seem to be headed by either a primary postposition or a genitive suffix. It is in this last complex type that dialectal variation arises: in northeastern varieties a subset of the invariant postpositions takes dative complements, instead of taking complements headed by the genitive or a primary adposition. The relevant subset can be defined along conceptual representations that are entirely parallel to those capturing the distribution of spatial datives in the context of main verbal predicates.

4.4 Aspectual Datives in the Postpositional System

To the set in (53)–(55) we must add the invariant postpositions *gora* "up" and *behera* "down." Those postpositions present the following intriguing properties: (i) they are only possible with motion predicates, as shown by the contrast in (56), and (ii) they are atelic, as shown by the fact that motion predicates supplemented with those invariant postpositions cannot be measured (57).

(56) a. *Etxea   mendiari   behera dago
       house-det mountain-dat down   is
       "The house is down the mountain."

   b. Mendiari   behera joan gara
      mountain-dat down   go   aux[1plA]
      "We went down the mountain."

(57)   *Mendiari   behera bortz minututan joan gara
        mountain-dat down   five minute-loc go   aux[1plA]
        "We went down the mountain in five minutes."

Gora and *behera* plus a dative Ground, unlike their adverbial counterparts, are also incompatible with predicates that lexically entail the end of a Path, such as *arribatu* "arrive":

(58) a. Mendira   arribatu gara
       mountain-all arrived we-are
       "We got to the mountain."

   b. *Mendiari   behera   arribatu gara
      mountain-dat down-all   arrived   we-are
      "We got down the mountain."

The aspectual restrictions related to *gora* and *behera* in their invariant postpositional form suggest that their meaning contribution occurs in a higher syntactic layer, one that is able to condition the aspectual interpretation of the higher predicate. We will elaborate on this idea in section 7.2.

4.5 On the Contribution of the Dative

Let us now have a second look at the postpositional contructions showing a dative Ground, represented in (59):

(59) a. Etxeari buruz   b. $[_{STATE}$ ORIENT $([_{Thing}\ldots], [_{Path}\ldots])$
       house toward
       "Toward the house"

(59) constitutes a powerful argument against a lexical approach to spatial datives as sketched in the beginning of the section. In the contexts above, the directional spatial component is overtly lexicalized by the invariant postposition. To the extent this is true, the dative cannot directly encode the Path function involved in those cases. In other words, although the dative

is somehow associated to the Path conceptual function, it does not directly express it. In the context of verbal predicates, we will assume the underlying presence of a tacit Path head c-commanding the dative-marked Ground in some local domain (60b). This silent Path head is the tacit equivalent of the invariant postpositions lexicalizing the Path head in the adpositional domain (60a).

(60) a. $[_{PathP} [_{KP}$ etxea-ri$]$ buruz ~~etxeari~~

   b. $[_{vP}$ v $\ldots [_{PPath}$ P$^0 \ldots [_{Ground}$ DP$]]]$

The tacit Path adposition is manifest in those cases where the predicate does not contain a Path denoting component, as in the purely stative predicate *egon* "(locative) be":

(61) a. Itsasoari dago
      sea-dat it-is
      "It is facing the seaside."

   b. $\ldots$ BE $[\emptyset_{PATH}$ [the sea $_{DAT}] \ldots]$

5. TOPOLOGICAL CONDITIONS ON SPATIAL SUFFIXES

If (61) underlies what we called spatial datives, we must wonder about the following: assuming that P in a structure like (61) instantiates an orientation path, why is (62) impossible?

(62)   *Trena Parisi   doa
       Train   Paris-dat   goes
       "The train is going to/toward Paris."

There is in principle nothing wrong with (62): if the relevant adposition is one that expresses an orientation path, and orientation paths license the dative in postpositional phrases, then we would expect (62) to be possible. We think that (62) actually provides an important clue to the conditions under which the dative is licensed. The proper way to express (62) includes an allative:

(63)   Trena Pariserat (buruz)   doa
       Train Paris-all (toward) goes
       "The train is going to/toward Paris."

There is an important difference between lexical postpositions and the purported abstract, unrealized one. Aurnague (2001) notes that the allative imposes certain topological restrictions in the relations between the Ground and the Figure. He notes, for instance, that the Ground selected by an allative postposition must be such as to be able to include or to serve as a support for the Figure. A clause like (64) is odd because no such relation can be envisioned (Aurnague 2001: 197):

(64) ??Ganibetara joan da
      knife-all   gone is
      "He/she went to the knife."

We note here that the few cases where the eastern dative occurs in the place of the allative are cases where such a relation cannot be established. Compare in this regard (65a, b) and (66a, b):

(65) a. Erretora joan da atearen   gakoari
        priest   gone is door-gen   lock-dat
        "The priest went to the door-lock."

     b. ??Erretora joan da atearen   gakora
        priest   gone is door-gen lock-all
        "The priest went to the door-lock."

(66) a. Beharri guziak solas   berri bati   zoazin
        ear   all-D conversation new one-dat   went
        "All ears went to a new conversation."

     b. ??Beharri guziak solas   berri batera zoazin
        ear   all-D conversation new one-all went
        "All ears went to a new conversation."

In (65a), the reference object (the door-lock) cannot be interpreted as including or supporting the Figure (the priest). And in (66b), the ears do not end up in a new conversation but are somehow oriented to it. In this case, the Path component is realized not overtly, by the allative postposition, but by dative marking of the Ground DP. The contrasts in (65–66) suggest that the allative and the dative do not freely alternate: the contexts where the allative suffix is used are topologically richer than those where the dative case suffix is used. In an explicit syntactic representation of the underlying spatial relations, it means that they are featurally more complex. The rich spatial content of the simple suffixes probably also explains why they cannot be directly merged with animate DPs, which do not easily yield to a purely spatial conception (see Aristar 1996). Dative case-suffixes, on the other hand, can. We summarize the contexts of use for the allative and the nonagreeing dative in the following table:

(67)   Path$_{\text{inclusion}}$ Path

	Path$_{\text{inclusion}}$	Path
Animate	**-ri**	**-ri**
Inanimate	**-ra**	**-ri**

We will provide a syntactic analysis of (67) that associates dative and allative suffixes with different structural configurations. Capitalizing on the idea, elaborated in the nanosyntax program (Starke 2010), that lexical items can spell out nonterminals, we will argue that the allative suffix lexicalizes adpositional structures that contain both a Path and a Place feature, whereas the latter is lacking in those structural configurations lexicalized by the dative. As we will see in the next section, this will force us to revise some of the received views on the syntactic structure of Basque adpositional phrases.

6. LEXICALIZING THE ADPOSITIONAL FIELD

In the following, we construct an argument for the phrasal Spell Out of adpositional structures that is based on two well-known observations. One is the similar topological restrictions that delimit the range of objects the simple spatial suffixes (inessive, allative, and ablative) can combine with (section 6.1). The other one is the syntactic asymmetries that arise between the inessive and the other two spatial suffixes in their ability to combine with other functional heads (6.2), a classic problem in Basque adpositional syntax.

6.1 Topological Restrictions in Simple Postpositions

We start by noting that the topological restrictions that arise in the case of the allative are also shown by the inessive. Thus, the inessive suffix (68b), exactly as the allative one (68a), cannot be directly merged to an animate DP:

(68) a. *Zu-ra   b. *Zu-n
      you-all   you-iness
      "To you"   "In you"

Aurnague (2001: 103–112) shows that the inessive in Basque imposes relatively specific constraints in the relation between the Figure and the Ground. Roughly, the entity represented by a Ground with an inessive suffix is such that it must either include or support the Figure. Those conditions are the same that govern the presence of the allative. A simple way of making sense of the parallel restrictions shown by the allative and the inessive in contexts like (68a, b) is to say that the allative inherits the restrictions imposed by the inessive—in other words, that the allative lexicalizes both Path and Place features. As shown by an increasing amount of cartographic work, in complex directional postpositions the Path feature seems to select the Place feature (see Koopman 2000, Kracht 2002, Svenonius 2006, Pantcheva 2008, Caha 2009 a.o.), a fact that is expected on conceptual grounds (see Jackendoff 1990):

(69)   PathP
        /   \
     Path   PlaceP
        /   \
    Place   DP

Some dialectal variants of northeastern Basque, as the Souletin variety, overtly realize both the allative suffix and the inessive one, so that the two features Path and Place are independently lexicalized. In (70), the inessive is not overtly visible, due to the impossibility of /nl/ sequences in Basque, but is manifest in the presence of the determiner, which cannot otherwise precede the allative:[16]

(70)   Etxe-a(*n)-lat
        house-D-iness-all

The order of the affixes, with the inessive closer to the stem than the allative, supports the hierarchical structure in (69).

6.2 Asymmetries in the Complement of P

The syntactic structure of the adpositional domain, as schematized in (69), coupled with the idea that the allative lexicalizes both the Path and the Place features can help us understand a long-standing puzzle in the domain of adpositional syntax in Basque: the fact that whereas inessives seem to take DP complements (81a), the complements of allatives and ablatives must be bare (81b, c).

16 The suffix -lat in Souletin is actually the allomorph of the general eastern allative -ra(t), the lateral consonant being weakened to/r/between vowels. The presence of an underlying nasal consonant in (70) representing the inessive provides the right phonological context for the strong form of the starting consonant.

(71) a. Etxe-a-n   b. Etxe-(*a)-ra   c. Etxe-(*a)-tik
      house-D-iness   house-D-all   house-D-ablative

We saw that both the conceptual structure of Paths, as well as dialectal evidence internal to Basque, point to a syntactic structure in which Path denoting features (allatives and ablatives) dominate Place denoting ones. If this conclusion is correct, it is unclear why the addition of a Path feature on top of Place should cause the disappearance of the article. Whatever the relevant relation, it cannot be stated in terms of selection. The Souletin example in (70) suggests the following generalization:

(72)   If the Path and the Place features are independently lexicalized, the Ground can be a DP

We would like to connect this generalization with the idea that the article that one sees in the nominal complements of inessive postpositions is actually external to the Place postposition. First, note that the purported determiner, which in Basque is associated to familiarity and definiteness (see Etxeberria 2005), is compatible with an overt indefinite article in the context of Ground complements, and this with a clear indefinite interpretation:

(73)   Liburua   mahai   bat-e-a-n   dago
        book-the   table   one-D-iness   is
        "The book is on a/*the table."

Sequences of indefinite and definite determiners are possible in Basque, with the meaning of "one of the," and clear definite (and distributive) interpretation (74), none of which properties are manifest in the Ground case:

(74)   Bat-a-k   100 orrialde   zituen,   beste-a-k   150
        one-D-erg   100 page   had,   other-D-erg   150
        "One of the books had 100 pages, the other one 150."

We can add to this the nonreferential interpretation of the determiner when it occurs in between an overt nominal locative and the inessive (75a), which should be contrasted with the referential uses of -a when it heads a DP (75b):

(75) a. Etxearen   aurre-a-n
      house-gen   front-D-iness
      "In front of the house"

     b. Etxearen   aurre-a
      house-gen   façade-D
      "The façade of the house"

Besides the fact that the determiner preceding the inessive presents semantic properties unlike those in normal nominal contexts, it also shows syntactic restrictions that are unlike those found in canonical DPs. Etxeberria (2005) has shown that the determiner -a in Basque selects a number head, which is affixed into the determiner at PF, giving rise to the affix order D-Number. When the number is plural, the complex determiner head has the form -ak in (76):

(76) Liburu-a-k
      book-D-Number
      "Books/the books"

The ground complements of inessive suffixes, and of spatial suffixes in general, have the intriguing property of not accepting the plural determiner:

(77) *Liburu-a-k-e-n
      book-D-Num-inessive
      "In the books"

Number in the complement of spatial suffixes in Basque is carried by a special suffix that directly attaches to the nominal stem:

(78) Liburu-eta-n
      book-pl-iness
      "In the books"

In fact, plural Grounds do not admit determiners either: the distinction between definite and indefinite plurals is realized via allomorphy: the suffix -eta- encodes definiteness and plurality; the suffix -ta- encodes indefiniteness and plurality:

(79) a. Etxe-eta-n   b. (Hainbat) etxe-ta-n
        house-pl-iness   so-many house-pl-iness
        "In the houses"   "In so many houses"

The asymmetry between plural and singular determiners remains mysterious under the idea that the inessive postposition takes a complement headed by the determiner -a. But if -a is not the canonical determiner one finds in definite DPs in Basque, what is its status in the inessive cases? Since Koopman's seminal paper (2000) on the Dutch adpositional system, we know that the structure of simple PPs must be extended to provide room for various functional projections. The idea behind Koopman's analysis is that in the same way that nouns and verbs project functional structure, lexical adpositions can also be shown to do so. In Den Dikken's elaboration of this idea, both Place and Path adpositions project a functional structure akin to the one found in nominal and verbal phrases. Concretely, Den Dikken (2010: 100) proposes the following parallel functional skeleton for all lexical categories N, V, and P:

(80) a. $[_{CP}$ $C^{[FORCE]}$ $[_{DxP}$ $Dx^{[TENSE]}$ $[_{AspP}$ $Asp^{[EVENT]}$ $[_{VP}$ $V...]]]]$

   b. $[_{CP}$ $C^{[DEF]}$ $[_{DxP}$ $Dx^{[PERSON]}$ $[_{AspP}$ $Asp^{[NUMBER]}$ $[_{NP}$ $N...]]]]$

   c. $[_{CP}$ $C^{[SPACE]}$ $[_{DxP}$ $Dx^{[SPACE]}$ $[_{AspP}$ $Asp^{[SPACE]}$ $[_{PP}$ $P...]]]]$

In the adpositional field, the C-layer is involved in the extraction of adpositional heads out of the PP (Van Riemsdijk 1978), DxP is related to deixis, and the aspectual head to the bounded/unbounded status of the location or path. The deictic layer represents how the location or path is oriented vis-à-vis the speaker. Thus, locative adpositions distinguish whether the location is at the speaker's location (here) or away from it (there). In Path adpositions, the head expresses whether the path is oriented toward or away from the speaker. Basque has a deictic contrast in the context of plural determiners. Thus, only in the plural (81b), the determiner -a (unmarked for proximity) contrasts with the proximate determiner -o- (a marked form expressing proximity to the speaker):

(81) a. Etxe-a/-*o   b. Lagun-a-k/-o-k
     house-D/proximate   house-D-pl/proximate-pl
     "The house"   "The houses/the houses here"

In the context of adpositional phrases, the proximate suffix -o- is in complementary distribution with -e-, unmarked for proximity, that encodes plurality:

(82) a. Etxe-e-ta-n   b. Etxe-o-ta-n
     house-SC-suffix-iness   house-proximate-suffix-inessive
     "In the houses"   "In the houses here"

The absence of a proximate singular determiner alternating with -a suggests that the determiner and the proximate deictic affix do not occupy the same syntactic position. The proximate affix is involved in the deictic location of the noun it is associated to, and it syncretically expresses number in the inessive cases. The dependency of the proximate deictic determiner on number suggests it selects a number feature, as argued by Den Dikken:

(83) $...[_{DeicP}$ -o $[_{NumP}$ -k $[_{NP}$ N...]]]$

Both -e- and -o-, on the other hand, may trigger the definite interpretation of the Ground (this is the most natural interpretation in (82a, b)). We will conclude that the affixes in question can syncretically realize Definite D in the complement domain of the Place head. This, on the other hand, constitutes further evidence that the determiner -a in the inessive cases is an external functional projection, not related to definiteness.

The separation of the Determiner -a from the functional set associated to the Ground yields the following structure:[17]

(84) $[$-a...$[_{\text{PlaceP}}$ -n $[_{\text{DP}}$ D $[_{\text{DeicP}}$ -o $[_{\text{NumP}}$ -k $[_{\text{NP}}$ N...$]]]]]]$

The external status of the determiner -a in the inessive constructions is not surprising. The Basque determiner -a is known to operate at very different syntactic levels. As shown by Artiagoitia (1995), it can encode tense in clausal nominalizations (see also Etxepare 2006). Consider the following minimal pair:

(85) a. Patatak ja-te-n   joango   gara
        potatoes eat-Nom-iness   go   we-are
        "We will leave eating (the) potatoes."

     b. Patatak ja-te-a-n, joango   gara
        potatoes eat-Nom-Det-iness, go-fut   we-are
        "We will leave when we eat (the) potatoes."

(85a) presents a gerundive clause. It is composed at least by the VP *patatak jan* "eat potatoes," a nominalizing affix -te normally associated to clausal nominalizations, and the inessive suffix -n, which selects an interval within the time boundaries of the eating event (see Demirdache & Uribe-Etxebarria 2000, 2002, 2004, for an analysis of progressive forms in the context of a topological approach to tense and aspect relations). Minimally contrasting with (85a) is (85b), which involves the same nominalized base as (85a) but contains a determiner between the nominalizing suffix and the inessive. The determiner picks up a contextually salient temporal event, that specifies the interval denoted by the matrix future temporal morpheme. Interestingly, when the determiner picks up a temporal interval, plural marking is excluded. Consider the following minimal pair, adapted from Etxepare (2006):

(86)   Xabier etortzea   eta Miren joatea   nahi dut/*ditut
       Xabier come-nom-D   and Miren leave-nom-D   want aux(sing)/aux(pl)
       "I want Xabier to come and Mary to leave."

17 Note that there is no way to state the "external" position of the determiner in simple minded head-final representation, in which the inessive selects the article. See note 13 for references on the antisymmetry debate in Basque.

If the D layer had a singular number feature, we would expect conjunction of the nominalized clauses to trigger plural agreement in the auxiliary. Since this is not possible, it must be that D, and the nominalized clause it heads, do not possess number features. The determiner -a in clausal nominalizations is also involved in licensing overt subjects (possible in (85b), but not in (85a). San Martin (2001) and Etxepare (2006) take -a to lexicalize T/C.

The unlikely behavior of the determiner following the inessive in the light of DP structure in Basque, as well as the restriction on number that assimilates -a to the kind of left-peripheral article occurring in clausal nominalizations, suggests an analysis whereby -a does not belong in the complement of the Place adposition, but is generated outside it, in the extended projection of P. We will follow Koopman (2002) and Den Dikken (2006) in the idea that lexical adpositions project a number of functional projections, akin to other lexical categories such as nouns and verbs. Capitalizing on the well-established status of Basque -a as a multifunctional head expressing various notions related to temporal and individual deixis, we will locate -a in the extended functional domain of the Place adposition, as related to Den Dikken's C. If this is correct, the determiner would actually dominate the Place adposition. Let us represent this projection as follows:

(87) $[_{\text{CP/DeicticP}}$ -a $[_{\text{PlaceP}}$ -n [NP]]]

The NP raises to the external functional projection C/D, yielding (88):

(88) $[_{\text{CP/DeictiP}}$ etxe -a $[_{\text{PlaceP}}$ -n ~~etxe~~]]

6.3 Adding Path

Consider the idea that directional Paths select (88):

(89) $[_{\text{PathP}}$ Path^0 $[_{\text{CP}}$ -a $[_{\text{PlaceP}}$ Place^0 [NP]]]]

The result of moving the NP to the external D projection will be (90):

(90) $[_{\text{PathP}}$ Path^0 $[_{\text{CP}}$ NP-a $[_{\text{PlaceP}}$ Place^0 [~~NP~~]]]]

Now imagine that the insertion context of the allative suffix is the following:

(91)   all $\Longrightarrow$ PathP
                /   \
            Path   PlaceP
                    /
                Place

The configuration in (90) does not allow the insertion of the allative, since the DP intervenes. A possible way out would be pied-piping the whole DP projection to the Spec of the Path Phrase:

(92) $[_{\text{PathP}} \; [_{\text{CP}} \; \text{NP -a} \; [_{\text{PlaceP}} \; \text{Place}^0 \ldots] \; \text{Path}^{0 \ldots}]]$

But in this case the syntactic configuration does not license the insertion of the allative, either. The Place feature having been removed from the complement domain of the Path head, (92) does not represent (91). In other words, there is no way to comply with the insertion context of the allative if the DP raises to a functional projection intervening between the Path and the Place heads. The Place head will not have the same problem. Consider the relevant structure:

(93) $[_{\text{CP}} \; D^0 \; [_{\text{PP}} \; \text{Place}^0 \; [\text{NP}]]$

If the inessive only lexicalizes the Place feature, the DP cannot intervene in any relevant way.

The proximate and number features do not produce the kind of intervention effect we observed for the determiner -a:

(94) a. Etxe-o-ta-ra   b. Etxe-e-ta-ra
        house-proximate-suf-all   house-pl-suf-all
        "To the houses here"   "To the houses"

This is unsurprising if those features are lower than the inessive and raise together with the nominal Ground to the Spec of the allative:

(95) $[_{\text{PathP}} \; [_{\text{DP}} \; \text{Etxe-e/o-ta}] \; \text{-ra} \ldots]$

The lexicalization rule in (91) for the allative addresses an obvious question that arises once we accept that the adpositional domain is hierarchically structured in terms of features encoding different aspects of spatial configurations. If Path features are represented as selecting Place features, we must wonder why the Basque suffixes representing Place and Path are in complementary distribution, in all varieties except Souletin. The idea that in those varieties, the allative lexicalizes something more than Path provides a plausible answer. The ablatives representing sources in Basque show the same animacy restrictions as allatives and inessives, and they impose the same restrictions on the nominal complement as allatives do. If we follow Pantcheva (2008) in the idea that sources dominate Paths, it is reasonable to think that ablatives inherit their semantic restrictions in the same way as allatives do. We will take them to lexicalize the whole adpositional field:

(96) abl —> SourceP
```
              /        \
          PathP       Source
          /    \
       Path   PlaceP
                /
              Place
```

Again, an intervening functional projection hosting the Ground DP would destroy the syntactic configuration for lexical insertion.

In other words, only the lowest adpositional head will be able to license a higher functional projection, because only in those cases the adpositional form lexicalizes a single feature, and no intervention effect arises. (97) recapitulates in a schematic way the lexicalization patterns of simple spatial suffixes:

(97) Inessive —> {Place}
    Allative —> {Path, Place}
    Ablative —> {Source, Path, Place}

7. SILENT PATHS AND DATIVE CASE

Silent Path adpositions seem to select fully fledged nominal Grounds. Unlike with the allative suffix, the silent Path requires a DP Ground, which furthermore surfaces with dative case:

(98) a. Oro itsasoari   daude
     all   sea-D-dat   are-loc
     "All of them are looking at/facing the sea."

   b. ...BE $[\emptyset_{PATH}$ [the sea $_{DAT}]$...]

If the previous analysis that accounted for the obligatory bare status of NP Grounds with allatives and ablatives was on the right track, it must be that the silent Path does not lexicalize together the Path and the Place features. Since it doesn't, there is no reason why the nominal Ground of an adposition should be bare. The issues raised by the structure in (98) are of a different sort. First, there is the question of why the construction in (98) is bound to a limited set of spatial relations ranging from unbounded directional paths to configurations of surface contact between the Figure and the Ground. Then, if (98a) follows from the fact that the Path adposition is independently lexicalized, there is the question of why the Place feature is not overtly lexicalized by the inessive -*n*. As we will see, the two issues are related.

7.1 Spatial Datives

There is at least one respect in which dative marked Grounds differ from the Grounds in inessive phrases. The Ground in the dative cases is clearly a regular DP. There is, for instance, no available sequence of indefinite and definite determiners in the Ground of invariant postpositions, unlike in the case of inessives (99a). The indefinite determiner *bat* "one/a" is in complementary distribution with the article -*a*, expressing definiteness and familiarity in this case (99b, c):

(99) a. Etxe   bat-e-a-n   b. *Etxe bat-e-a-ri   c. Etxe bat-i
       house   one-D-iness   house one-D-dat   house one-dat
       "In a house"   "To a house"   "To a house"

Remember that (99a) was possible because the overt article -*a* is external to the Place adposition, exerting a function closer to that of a complementizer:

(100) $[_{CP}$ -a $[... [_{PlaceP}$ -n $[_{DP}$ etxe bat$]]$

By the same reasoning, the determiner in the dative case cannot be external in this sense. It must belong in the same extended domain that includes the number feature. We conclude that the internal structure of Path-related dative Grounds lacks the external C projection:

(101) * $[_{PathP}$ Ø $[_{CP}$ -a $[...$DP-dat$...]]]$

Note that the inessive did not allow the presence of -*a* in the DP Ground: a syncretic affix -*e*- or the proximate determiner -*o*- were taken to lexicalize D in those cases. The simplest way to address the lack of an overt inessive suffix and the presence of -*a* in the dative cases, is to say that the inessive is simply absent. This constitutes a problematic move under the premises that the inessive is a lexical adposition that contributes the basic locative function associated to the structure. But consider again the derivation in (88), repeated below:

(102) a. $[_{CP}$ -a $[_{PlaceP}$ -n [NP]$]]$ -> raising of NP to Spec of CP
      b. $[_{CP}$ etxe -a $[_{PlaceP}$ -n ~~etxe~~$]]$

The bare Ground selected by the Place adposition raises to the Spec of the external C head, apparently stranding the lexical preposition behind. Basque, however, does not have preposition stranding. The status of the inessive, we think, fits better in the overall picture if it, like the external determiner -*a*, is a functional head. We know independently that the inessive in Basque is used to encode aspect, with a meaning akin to its spatial meaning (see 85a). Let us therefore amend our structure in (100) into something like (103):

(103) $[_{\text{CP/DP}}$ -a $[_{\text{AspP}}$ -n [NP]]]

The absence of the inessive in the dative cases corresponds therefore to the absence of a (given) lexical instantiation of the aspectual head in the locative domain.[18]

The dative cases must nevertheless possess some locative content different from the Ground itself. Take, for instance, the orientation function of adverbs such as *bisean-bis* "face-to-face." The relevant spatial relation does not only specify a directional path from the Figure to the Ground, but also a particular way of locating the Figure with respect to the Ground: someone who is face-to-face to a reference term stands in relation to a certain projected space from that reference term. A projected space is defined on the basis of the inherent directed vertical and horizontal axes of the Ground (Jackendoff 1992: 111). This projected region is syntactically represented by means of a feature encoding projected space: the Axial Part head. We will therefore conclude that the relation between the Path head and the nominal Ground is mediated by a syntactic head encoding projected space. The Axial Part selects a nominal Ground that can project up to D:

(104) $[_{\text{PathP}}$ Ø...$[_{\text{AxP}}$ Ax $[_{\text{DP}}$...NP]]]

From the standpoint of (104), we may wonder what the effect of eliminating the inessive suffix would have in the overall meaning of the spatial structure. Aurnague (2001) provides a detailed examination of the different semantic values that the inessive adopts. They are basically two: inclusion and support. Let us consider the first notion. The addition of an inclusion relation in a Path structure should have as a result the bounded interpretation of the Path. The elimination of the inclusion relation linking the Path to the projected region from the Ground basically means that the Figure does not attain the spatial Goal. This captures immediately all those spatial relations that we described under the concept of oriented paths. Oriented

18 This entails that the lexicalization rule that targets the Path and the aspectual feature denoted by the inessive lexicalizes together lexical and functional material. For the factual availability of this option, see recently Dekanyi (2009) and her analysis of Hungarian postpositions.

paths, by definition, do not lead the Figure to the Ground. The following invariant postpositions can be seen to fall under the notion of oriented path:

(105) Etxeari   buruz/begira/bisean-bis
      house-D-dat toward/looking/face-to-face
      "Toward the house/looking at the house/facing the house"

In all those cases, the absence of the inessive allows the unbounded interpretation of the directional Path introduced by the invariant postpositions.

The aspectual contrast associated to the alternation between dative and inessive Grounds suggest they both represent different values of a same aspectual category. Whereas the inessive, via an inclusion spatial feature, would force the meaning that the Figure is included within the Ground, the dative would be associated to unbounded aspect. The latter conclusion is supported by the presence of the dative in complements of atelic aspectual verbs, as seen in section 2.3. We thus extend the structure in (104) to include an aspectual head that specifies the bounded or unbounded status of the Path:[19]

(106) $[_{PathP} \: \emptyset \: [_{AspP} \: \text{-n/-ri} \: [_{AxP} \: Ax^0 \: [_{DP} ... NP]]]]$

Let us consider now the second basic semantic value of the inessive suffix, the expression of support. As Aurnague notes (2001: 107, n. 6), not any support configuration is expressed by the inessive. For the inessive to be felicitously used, the Ground must be the only stabilizer of the Figure. Thus, we would use the inessive to describe a set of bookcases fixed to a wall, but not to describe one that is lying on the floor and against the wall. For the latter case, northeastern Basque employs *kontra* "against" plus a dative Ground. (107a, b) illustrate the difference:

(107) a. Ipini ezazu   apalategia   paretan
         put   imperative bookcase-D wall-D-on
         "Fix the bookcase to the wall."

      b. Ipini ezazu   apalategia   paretari kontra
         put   imperative bookcase-D wall-dat against
         "Put the bookcase against the wall."

---

19 For the sake of concreteness, I take the dative suffix to lexicalize the aspectual head. It could be that the dative is just the spell out of a morphological case directly merged to the DP. Nothing in this article hinges on that. In the nanosyntax approach, as developed by Caha (2009), cases are independent features heading their own projection, and stacked in a hierarchical order above a nominal phrase.

(107b) shows one of the dative taking invariant postpositions of Basque. Interestingly, *kontra* only occurs with a dative Ground when the overall meaning of the spatial relation clearly includes location. Purely directional cases are not enough. Consider in this regard the contrast arising in northeastern varieties between the following two cases:

(108) a. Berlingo   harresiaren kontra   mintzatu da
         Berlin-gen wall-gen   against talked   is
         "He/she talked against the Berlin Wall (she/he criticized it)."

      b. Berlingo   harresiari kontra   mintzatu da
         Berlin-gen wall-D-dat against   talked   is
         "She/he talked as she/he was resting against the Berlin Wall."

Support configurations are expressed by those verbs that represent contact, such as the verbs of attachment or union discussed in section 4.5. All those verbs take dative Grounds in northeastern varieties. In all those cases, the supporting entity (the Ground) is not the only stabilizing agent in the relation. Other elements, such as ties and ropes, play a crucial role as stabilizers. In those cases, the inessive is excluded.

The hypothetical aspectual basis of the alternation between the dative and the inessive is more difficult to discern in the case of supporting configurations. Although the notion of inclusion extends naturally to the domain of aspectual ontology, the notion of support does not. We think the complementary distribution of the dative and the inessive suffixes makes sense if the aspectual projection in the locative domain is sensitive to the notion of spatial overlap between the Figure and (a projected region from) the Ground. In the inclusion relation, the Figure is exhaustively included in the region projected from the Ground. In the support relation, the inessive surfaces only if the Figure is located in such a way that its contact area is fully within the space projected from the Ground. In this case, the inclusion relation is relativized to those areas that stand in a contact configuration. Jackendoff (1990) proposes that verbs of attachment must be represented in the lexicon as locative configurations specified by a diacritic expressing contact (see (28)). We claim that the relevant aspectual relations are computed relative to the spatial areas of the Figure that are specified as being in contact with the Ground.

7.2 Aspectual Datives

Our analysis of the alternation between the inessive and the dative suffixes extends in a straightforward fashion to the domain of aspectual datives.

Since the Dative suffix lexicalizes unbounded aspect, it is only natural to find it in the complement of atelic aspectual verbs like the progressive *ari*:

(109)   Eta horren   ahultzeari   *ari*   zirezte
         and that-gen weaken-Nom-D-dat prog are
         "And you are weakening that."

In Etxepare (forthcoming) I argue that the syntactic structure of aspectual complements includes a silent Path adposition that selects a nominalized clause. Under the analysis proposed here, the structure of the aspectual cases must be as in (110), with the nominalized clause in the Spec of the unbounded aspectual head:

(110) $\emptyset_{PATH}$ $[_{AspP}$ $[_{Nominalized\ Clause}\ ...V...]$ $Asp_{DAT...}]$

A different case is that of Basque directional postpositions *gora* "up" and *behera* "down," which have the property of enforcing the atelic reading of the predicates they merge with. In other words, unlike in English, they cannot be used to point to a location in the path:

(111) a. *Etxea   mendiari   behera dago
          house-det mountain-dat down   is
          "The house is down the mountain."

      b. Mendiari   behera joan gara
          mountain-dat down   go   aux[1plA]
          "We went down the mountain."

This property goes together with another one: unlike the spatial datives examined in the preceding section, the DP-Ground of directional postpositions can show up as (i) a bare noun (112a), (ii) an absolutive DP (112b), or (iii) a dative DP (112c). Compare in this regard (112a–c), illustrating the various structural options available to Grounds of directional postpositions, with the rigid (113), corresponding to the unbounded locative ones:

(112) a. Mendi behera   b. Mendi-a behera
         mountain-down   mountain-D down
         "Down the mountain"   "Down the mountain"

      c. Mendi-a-ri behera
         mountain-D-dat down
         "Down the mountain"

(113) Paret*(ari) kontra/buruz/bisean-bis
       wall D-dat against/toward/face-to-face
       "Against/toward/facing the wall"

The different structural options represented in (112) show that the inner aspectual projection associated to location is not necessary for the unbounded interpretation of the whole postpositional phrase. (112a, b) indicate that the aspectual head is lacking. (112a) presumably represents a case where a bare Ground incorporates into the Axial head, and (112b) a case where a fully fledged DP Ground raises to the specifier of the Axial Phrase:

(114) a. $[_{PathP}\ Ø\ [_{AxP}\ N + Ax...]]$

    b. $[_{PathP}\ Ø\ [_{AxP}\ DP\ Ax...]]$

(112c) represents the case where the DP raises to the specifier of the aspectual phrase:

(115) $[_{PathP}\ Ø\ [_{AspP}\ DP\text{-}ri...]]$

We will claim, therefore, that the aspectual contribution of *gora* and *behera* happens in a higher layer of structure, the one projected by the invariant Path postposition. The conclusion is reminiscent of Den Dikken's analysis of the accusative/dative alternation in the domain of spatial adpositions in Germanic. Under this analysis, the dative case is licensed in the extended functional domain of a Place adposition, whereas accusative case is licensed in the extended domain of a directional postposition (Den Dikken 2010: 114). In the spirit of Den Dikken's proposal, the absolutive nominal Grounds in (112a, b) are licensed in the domain of the invariant directional postposition:[20]

(116) $[_{AspP}\ DP\text{-absolutive Asp}\ [_{PathP}\ behera/gora\ [_{AxP}\ Ax...]]]$

We must wonder now why the aspectual reading that arises in the above cases is of the unbounded type. There is nothing per se in the projection of an aspectual head that forces an unbounded reading: witness the aspectual alternation between the inessive and the dative in the locative domain. We think a comparison of the above cases with the adverbial cases can shed some light in what is going on. Remember that the adverbial cases behave for all purposes as regular allative adpositional phrases with an underlying

---

20 For the dative DP cases, we will assume the whole aspectual phrase pied-pipes to the Spec of the Path aspectual Phrase.

Axial Part Noun. This axial noun can constitute an antecedent for anaphora and provide the basis for nominal compounding. In our terms, this means that the underlying structure of the adverbial cases is the following:

(117) $[_{PathP}$ Path $[_{PlaceP}$ Place $[_{AxP}$ locational noun$]]]$

Along the syntactic derivation, the nominal *behe* "downside" raises to a syntactic position that is beyond the Path head. The syntactic configuration is one that licenses the lexicalization of the Path and Place heads as the allative *-ra*:

(118)   [locational noun...$[_{PathP}$ Path $[_{PlaceP}$ Place ~~behe~~$]]]$

One question that immediately arises is how the axial noun gets its case. Since there is no intervening aspectual projection in the Place domain, there is no functional structure to license case there. The case of the axial part must therefore be licensed in the domain of the directional adposition. Let us say that the directional adposition, as in the *gora* and *behera* cases, projects an aspectual head that licenses the axial noun:

(119) $[_{AspP}$ locational noun Asp $[_{PathP}$ Path $[_{PlaceP}$ Place ~~locational noun~~$]]$

The adverbial structure in (119) is not that different from the one we proposed for the invariant postpositional phrases with absolutive Grounds, repeated below:

(120) $[_{AspP}$ DP Asp $[_{PathP}$ behera/gora $[_{AxP}$ Ax...$]]$

In one important regard, however, the two structures differ: (119), but not (120), possesses a Place feature, associated to the expression of bounded aspect. The simple allative, furthermore, is a bound form that occurs on the locational noun. Let us say that the simple allative adposition adjoins to the aspectual head and that aspect calculus takes place there. In that case we will have a feature complex composed by a directional feature and a bounded locative one, expressing an inclusion relation, in the aspectual head. The presence of the bounded Place feature triggers the bound interpretation of the adverbial cases.

(121) $[_{AspP}$ behe Asp + $ra_{\{Path, bounded\ Place\}...}]$

In the case of invariant postpositions, the underlying structure does not include a bounded aspect head (see (120)). In this case, adjunction of the

Path head to the aspect head does not yield the type of feature complex resulting from the adjunction of the allative Path head:

(122) $[_{AspP}$ DP Asp + behera/gora$_{Path}$ $[_{PathP}$ ~~behera/gora~~ $[_{AxP}$ Ax...$]]$

In the absence of the Place/aspect feature, the Path will interpreted as unbounded. The unbounded interpretation of the Path, on the other hand, forces the atelic interpretation of the predicate it combines with.

7.3 Animacy

As shown in table (65), simple suffixes such as the inessive and the allative cannot be directly combined with animate DPs. In our analysis, this means that animate Grounds in Basque do not constitute appropriate landmarks to sustain inclusion or support relations. Dative goals therefore project an aspectual phrase of the unbounded type in the locative domain:

(123) a. Jon-i   b. $[_{AspP}$ Jon-i Asp $[_{AxP}$ Ax...$]]$
      Jon-dat
      "to Jon"

7.4 A Note on Case, Aspect, and Number

Our examination of the Place adpositional domain in Basque yields the maximal structure in (124):

(124) $[_{C/T}$ -a $[_{AspP}$ -n/-ri $[_{AxP}$ Ax^0 $[_{DP}$ D^0 $[_{DeicticP}$ Deixis^0 $[_{NumP}$ Num^0 NP$]]$

However, not all conceivable structural instantiations of the syntactic elements in (124) are possible. One important restriction concerns the relation between the Place-external -article a and the category of the Ground. Bare nominal Grounds, as well as indefinite ones headed by bat "one," obligatorily raise to C/T:

(125) a. Etxe-a-n   b. Etxe bat-e-a-n
      house-D-iness   house one-D-iness
      "In the house/at home"   "In a house"

Raising to unbounded Asp is impossible for those elements:

(126) a. *Etxe-n   b. *Etxe bat-e- n   c. *[$_{AspP}$ NP–n/-ri...]
         house-iness   house one-iness

The crucial element in the availability of raising to unbounded aspect seems to be (overt) number. We note first that plural indefinite Grounds do raise to aspect:

(127) a. Hainbat etxetan   b. [$_{AspP}$ hainbat etxeta -n...]
         so-many houses
         "In so many houses"

Unlike the singular indefinite *bat* "one," the plural indefinite determiner *batzu* "some" forces raising to unbounded aspect:

(128) a. Etxe batzutan   b. [$_{AspP}$ etxe batzuta -n...]
         house some-iness
         "In some houses"

On the basis of this, we can state the restriction as follows:

(129)   If the complement of AxP includes Number, then the Ground raises to unbounded AspP.

The connection between aspect and number is well established in the domain of case and agreement (see Svenonius 2002 and Pesetsky & Torrego 2004, for two different views). For Basque, Etxepare (2006, 2009) shows, in the context of Long Distance Agreement in Basque, that that number features must occupy a position lower than person features. This position, he claims, is an aspectual head within the (small) VP.

The generalization in (129) must be supplemented with the following one:

(130) If the complement of AxP raises to AspP, T/C is not projected.

In other words, Place-external -a is projected only when the Ground is such that it cannot be licensed in AspP. Combining (128) and (129), we reach the following condition on the economy of representations (see Boskovic 1995):

(131) Project as much structure as you need for Case licensing.

ACKNOWLEDGMENTS

The authors acknowledge financial support from the following projects: Basque Government HM-2009-1-25 and IT4-14-10; Ministerio de Ciencia e Innovación FFI2008-00240/FILO and FFI2011-26906; Agence Nationale de la Recherche ANR-07-CORP-033, Grupos consolidados de investigación del sistema universitario vasco (GIC07/144-IT-210-07).

REFERENCES

1. Literary Corpus
Etcheberry, J. B. 1980. *Berriz ere beretarik.* Bayonne: Imprimerie Cordeliers.
Etcheberry, J. B. 1966. *Frantziako erregina.* Bayonne: Imprimerie Cordeliers.
Etcheberry, J. B. 1978. *Han-Hemenka.* Bayonne: Imprimerie Cordeliers.
Etcheberry, J. B. 1981. *Hazparneko misionestak.* Bayonne: Imprimerie Cordeliers.
Etcheberry, J. B. 1969. *Obrak mintzo.* Bayonne: Imprimerie Cordeliers.
Larzabal, Piarres. 1991–1998. *Lan guztiak* (Complete works). Edited by Piarres Xarriton. 8 vols. Donostia: Elkar.
Pochelu, Leon [Garralda ezizenez]. 2008 [1947–1951]. *Jakitatez jakitate.* Erroteta argitaletxea.
Sallaberry, Etienne. 1978. *Ene sinestea.* Itxaropena: Zarautz.

2. Database Basyque
http://ixa2.si.ehu.es/atlas2/index.php?lang=eu

3. Theoretical Bibliography
Albizu, Pablo. 2001. "Datibo sintagmen egitura sintaktikoaren inguruan:eztabaidarako oinarrizko zenbait datu." In Beatriz Fernandez and Pablo Albizu (eds.), *Kasu eta komunztaduraren gainean (On case and agreement)*, 49–70 Bilbao: University of the Basque Country.
Aristar, Anthony R. 1996. "The relationship between dative and locative: Kurylowicz's argument from a typological perspective." *Diachronica* XIII (2): 207–224.
Arotçarena, A. 1951. *Grammaire Basque. Dialectes Navarro-Labourdins.* Bayonne: Librairie Le Porche.
Arteatx, Iñigo, Xabier Artiagoitia, and Arantzazu Elordieta, eds. 2008. *Antisimetriaren hipotesia vs. Buru parametroa: Euskararen oinarrizko hitz hurrenkera ezbaian.* Bilbao: University of the Basque Country.
Artiagoitia, Xabier. 1995. Verbal projections in Basque and Minimal Structure. *Anuario del Seminario de Filologia Vasca "Julio de Urquijo"* 28(2): 341–504.
Asbury, Anna. 2008. "*The morphosyntax of case and adpositions.*" Utrecht: LOT dissertation series.
Aurnague, Michel. 1996. "Les noms de localisation interne: Tentative de caracterisation sémantique à partir des données du basque et du français." *Cahiers de lexicologie* 69: 159–192.
Aurnague, Michel. 2001. "Entités et relations dans les descriptions spatiales: L'espace et son expression en basque et en français." Mémoire d'habilitation, Université de Toulouse–Le Mirail.
Belletti, Adriana, and Luigi Rizzi. 1988. "Psych-verbs and θ-theory." *Natural Language and Linguistic Theory* 6: 291–352.
Boskovic, Zeljko. 1995. *The syntax of non-finite complementation.* Cambridge, MA: MIT Press.

Broadwell, George A. 1996. "Directionals as complex predicates in Choctaw." In M. Butt and T. Holloway (eds.), *Proceedings of the LFG98 Conference*. Stanford: CSLI Publications.

Caha, Pavel. 2009. "The nanosyntax of case." PhD diss., University of Tromso.

De Rijk, Rudolf. 1990. "Location nouns in standard basque." *ASJU* 24.1: 3–20.

Dékány, Éva. 2009. "The nanosyntax of Hungarian Postpositions." *Nordlyd 36.1*, special issue on Nanosyntax, In Peter Svenonius, Gillian Ramchand, Michal Starke, and Knut Taraldsen (eds.) *Nordlyd 36.1*, special issue on Nanosyntax, 41–76. Tromsoe: CASTL.

Demirdache, Hamida, and Myriam Uribe-Etxebarria. 2000. "The primitives in temporal relations." In R. Martin, D. Michaels, and J. Uriagereka (eds.), *Step by step: Essays on minimalist syntax in honor of Howard Lasnik*. Cambridge, MA: MIT Press.

Demirdache, Hamida, and Myriam Uribe-Etxebarria. 2002. "La grammaire des prédicats spatio-temporels: Temps, aspect et adverbes de temps." In Brenda Laca (ed.), *Temps et aspect. De la morphologie àl' interprétation*, 125–176. Paris: Presses Universitaires de Vincennes.

Demirdache, Hamida, and Uribe-Etxebarria, Myriam Uribe-Etxebarria 2004. "The syntax of time adverbs." In Jacqueline Guéron and Alexander Lecarme (eds.), *The Syntax of Time*, 143–180. Cambridge, MA: MIT Press.

Den Dikken, Marcel. 2006. *"Relators and linkers." The syntax of predication, predicate inversion, and copulas*. Linguistic Inquiry Monograph 47. Cambridge, Mass.: MIT Press.

Den Dikken, Marcel. 2010. "On the functional structure of locative and directional PPs." In Guglielmo Cinque and Luigi Rizzi (eds.), *Cartography of syntactic structures*, 74–126. New York: Oxford University Press.

Eguzkitza, Andolin. 1997. "Kasuak eta Postposizioak: deklinabidea eta postposiziobidea." *Hizpide* 40. 39–52.

Elordieta, Arantzazu. 2001. *Verb movement and constituent permutation in Basque*. Utrecht: LOT Dissertation series.

Etxeberria, Urtzi. 2005. "Quantification and domain restriction in Basque." PhD diss., Vitoria, Gasteiz, University of the Basque Country.

Etxepare, R. 2006. "Number long distance agreement in (sub-standard) Basque." *Anuario del Seminario de Filologia Vasca "Julio de Uriquijo"* 40(1–2): 303–350.

Etchepare, J. 1958. *Iturraldea*. Erroteta.

Etxepare, Ricardo. 2009. "Case and long distance agreement in Basque." Ms. IKER (UMR5478).

Etxepare, Ricardo. 2011. "Case and long distance agreement in Basque" Ms. IKER (UMR5478).

Etxepare, Ricardo. Forthcoming. "Contact and change in a restrictive theory of parameters." In Carme Picallo and Jose María Brucart (eds.), *Linguistic variation and minimalism*. Oxford: Oxford University Press.

Euskaltzaindia. 1985. *Euskal Gramatika Lehen Urratsak* I. Bilbo: Euskaltzaindia.

Fernandez, Beatriz. 1997. *Egiturazko kasuaren erkaketa euskaraz*. PhD diss., University of the Basque Country.

Fernandez, Beatriz, and Jon Ortiz de Urbina. 2008. *Datiboa hiztegian*. Bilbao: University of the Basque Country.

Haddican, William. 2001. "Basque functional heads." Linguistics in the Big Apple. City University of New York/New York University Working Papers in Linguistics.

Haddican, William. 2004. "Sentence polarity and word order in Basque." *Linguistic Review* 21(2): 81–124.

Hualde, Jose Ignacio. 2002. "Regarding Basque postpositions and related matters." In Xabier Artiagoitia, Patxi Goenaga, and Joseba A. Lakarra (eds.), *Erramu boneta: Festschrift for Rudolf P. G. De Rijk*, 325–340. ASJU Supplements 44. Bilbao: University of the Basque Country.

Hualde, Jose Ignacio. 2003. "Postpositions." In Jose Ignacio Hualde and Jon Ortiz de Urbina (eds). *A grammar of Basque*, 187–190. Berlin: Mouton.

Jackendoff, Ray. 1983. *Semantics and cognition*. Cambridge, MA: MIT Press.

Jackendoff, Ray. 1990. *Semantic structures*. Cambridge, MA: MIT Press.

Jackendoff, Ray. 1996. "The architecture of the Linguistic-Spatial Interface." In Paul Bloom, Mary Peterson, Lynn Nadell, and Merrill F. Garrett (eds.), *Language and space*, 1–30. Cambridge, MA: MIT Press.

Jackendoff, Ray, and Barbara Landau. 1992. "Spatial language and spatial cognition.""In Ray Jackendoff, *Languages of the mind. Essays on mental representation*, 99–124. Cambridge, MA: MIT Press.

Koopman, Hilda. 2000. "Prepositions, postpositions, circumpositions and particles." In Hilda Koopman (ed.), *The syntax of specifiers and heads*, 204–260. London: Routledge.

Koopman, Hilda. 2002. "The Dutch PP." In Guglielmo Cinque and Luigi Rizzi (eds.), *The cartography of PPs*. Oxford University Press.

Kracht, Marcus. 2002. "On the semantics of locatives." *Linguistics and Philosophy* 25: 157–232.

Lafitte, Pierre. 1979 [1944]. *Grammaire Basque*. Baiona: Elkar.

Pantcheva, Marina. 2008. "The place of PLACE in Persian." In A. Asbury, J. Dotlacil, B. Gehrke, and R. Nouwen (eds.), *Syntax and semantics of Spatial P*, 305–330. Amsterdam: John Benjamins.

Pasicki, Adam. 1996. "Meanings of the Dative Case in Old English." In Van Belle, W. and Van Langendonck, W. (eds.), *The Dative*, Vol. 2, 113–142. Amsterdam: John Benjamins Publishing Company.

Pesetsky, David, and Esther Torrego. 2004a. "Tense, case, and the nature of syntactic categories." In Jacqueline Guéron and Jacqueline Lecarme (eds.), *The syntax of time*, 495–537, Cambridge, Mass.: MIT Press.

Rezac, Milan 2006. *Basque morphosyntax*. Unpublished ms. University of Nantes/Centre National de la Recherche Scientifique.

San Martin, Itziar. 2004. On the interpretation and the distribution of PRO. PhD diss. University of Maryland.

Starke, Michal. 2005. "Nanosyntax." Seminar taught at CASTL, University of Tromsø.

Starke, Michal. 2010. "One more go at the trigger problem: Nanosyntax and post-syntactic filtering." Paper presented at the workshop *Linguistic Variation in the Minimalist Framework*, Barcelona, January 14–15.

Svenonius, Peter. 2002. "Icelandic case and the structure of events." *Journal of Comparative Germanic Linguistics* 5: 197–225.

Svenonius, P. 2006. "The emergence of axial parts." In *Tromsø Working Papers in Language and Linguistics (Nordlyd)* 33.1: 49–77.

Svenonius, Peter. 2010. "Spatial P in English." In Guglielmo Cinque and Luigi Rizzi (eds.), *Cartography of syntactic structures*, 127–160. New York: Oxford University Press.

Tortora, Christina. 2009. "Aspect inside PLACE PPs." In A. Asbury, J. Dotlacil, B. Gehrke, and R. Nouwen (eds.), *Syntax and semantics of Spatial P*. Amsterdam: John Benjamins.

Trask, Robert L. 1995. "On the history of the non-finite verb-forms in Basque." In Jose Ignacio Hualde, Joseba A. Lakarra, and Robert L. Trask (eds.), *Towards a History of the Basque Language*. John Benjamins.

van Riemsdijk, Henk. 1978. *A case study in syntactic markedness: The binding nature of prepositional phrases*. Dordrecht: Peter De Ridder.

Vandeloise, Claude. 1991. *Spatial prepositions. A case study from French*. Chicago: University of Chicago Press.

CHAPTER 4

Case in Disguise

HLÍF ÁRNADÓTTIR AND EINAR FREYR SIGURÐSSON

1. INTRODUCTION

As is well known, Icelandic has not only nominative case[1] subjects but also oblique subjects (see, e.g., Andrews 1976, Thráinsson 1979, and Zaenen, Maling, & Thráinsson 1985). In this article, we focus on the dative-nominative (DAT-NOM) construction, where the subject gets dative case and the object nominative case. In examples (1) and (2), the dative argument *mér* "me" is the subject and the nominative argument *bílarnir* "the cars" the object:[2]

(1) Mér   líka   bílarnir
    me.DAT   like.3PL   cars.the.PL.NOM
    "I like the cars."

In (1) the verb agrees in number (plural) with the nominative object. The verb agreement with the object in the example above is optional for many speakers, as shown by the nonagreement in (2), where the verb is in the default third-person singular (3SG):

(2) Mér   líkar   bílarnir
    me.DAT   likes.3SG   cars.the.PL.NOM
    "I like the cars."

---

1 As has become usual within generative linguistics, we use lowercase "case" when we talk about morphological case; when we use the capitalized form, "Case," we are referring to abstract Case.

2 We use the following abbreviations where we gloss linguistic examples: NOM = nominative, ACC = accusative, DAT = dative, GEN = genitive, 1 = first-person, 2 = second-person, 3 = third-person, SG = singular, PL = plural, DEF = default third-person singular neuter form on the passive participle, M = masculine, F = feminine, EXPL = expletive, INF = infinitive, PRO = unexpressed argument in a control infinitive.

H. Á. Sigurðsson and Holmberg (2008) discuss three varieties of Icelandic (A, B, and C) with respect to the DAT-NOM construction: Icelandic A speakers prefer agreement with nominative objects, while for Icelandic B speakers agreement is optional, but in the C variety only nonagreement is allowed (the finite verb then always turns up in the default 3SG).

However, as noted by Árnadóttir and E. F. Sigurðsson (2008), there are some indications of an interspeaker variation in the object case of DAT-NOM verbs—for some speakers the object is in the accusative case instead of the standard nominative case. We show examples of this in (3), taken from a blog and a newspaper, respectively:

(3) a.

En	hey,	hljómsveitin	er	samt	ekki	slæm
But	hey	band.the.F	is	still	not	bad
þó	mér	líkar	**hana**	ekki		
though	me.DAT	likes.3SG	her.ACC	not		

"But hey, the band isn't bad although I don't like it."
www.hugi.is/rokk/articles.php?page=view&contentId=4940211, posted May 28, 2007

b.

og	er	hún	fyrsta	hljómsveitin	sem
and	is	she	first	band.the	which
hlotnast	**þann**	**heiður**			
acquires.3SG	that.ACC	honor.ACC			

"It is the first band that acquires this honor."
Tíminn [newspaper], August 5, 1989, p. 4

For most speakers, this use of an accusative object with the DAT-NOM verbs *líka* "like" (*mér líkar hana* in (3a)) and *hlotnast* "acquire" (*hlotnast þann heiður* in (3b)) is ungrammatical.[3]

The DAT-NOM > DAT-ACC change has received little attention in the literature. Therefore we conducted a small study in 2009 to test whether there really is a variation in the object case of DAT-NOM verbs. The results show that there

---

3 It should be noted that instead of the nominative object of *líka* "like," a prepositional phrase, headed by *við* "to, with," is frequently used (see (i-a) below). Thus, one might draw the conclusion from an example such as *Mér líkar hana* "me.DAT like her.ACC" that this was some kind of an error in writing where the preposition is not written. That is ruled out, however, in (3a) above, where an accusative argument of *líka* precedes the negation (Object Shift). As shown in (i-b) below, a PP argument of *líka* cannot precede the negation.

(i) a.

Mér	líkar	ekki	við	hana
me.DAT	like.3SG	not	to	her

"I don't like her."

b.

*Mér	líkar	við	hana	ekki
me.DAT	like.3SG	to	her	not

definitely is a variation in this respect among young speakers, and another survey from 2010 also conducted among young speakers shows the same (see section 2). We believe that this is an ongoing change at an early stage.

Dative subjects appear in the passive voice of many verbs, both monotransitives (4) and ditransitives (5). DAT-NOM constructions are thus also used in the passive: see (5b), where the dative argument raises to the subject position (Spec,T).[4]

(4) a. Í gær   bjargaði hún   mér   *active of a*
       yesterday saved   she.NOM   me.DAT   *monotransitive*
       "Yesterday, she saved me."

   b. Í gær   var   mér   bjargað   *passive of a*
      yesterday was.3SG   me.DAT   saved.DEF   *monotransitive*
      "Yesterday, I was saved."

(5) a. Í gær   gaf   hún   mér   bílana   *active of a*
       yesterday gave   she.NOM me.DAT cars.the.PL.ACC   *ditransitive*
       "Yesterday, she gave me the cars."

   b. Í gær   voru   mér   gefnir   *passive of a*
      yesterday were.3PL   me.DAT   given.M.PL.NOM   *ditransitive*
      bílarnir
      cars.the.M.PL.NOM
      "Yesterday, I was given the cars."

Unlike the DAT-NOM construction in the active, agreement with a nominative object is obligatory with a passivized ditransitive. The passive participle agrees with the nominative object in number and gender, and the finite verb agrees with it in number. Therefore, in example (6) below, it is ungrammatical to use the finite verb in third-person singular and the passive participle in default third-person neuter (marked as DEF in glosses).

(6) *Í gær   var   mér   gefið   bílarnir
      yesterday was.3SG   me.DAT   given.DEF   cars.the.M.PL.NOM
      "Yesterday, I was given the cars."

However, DAT-ACC has recently been discovered in the ditransitive passive (Jónsson 2009a). It is ungrammatical to most speakers; those who do find it grammatical are mainly younger speakers.

---

4 Icelandic is a V2 language with T-to-C movement. If, for example, an adverbial phrase or a prepositional phrase, e.g., *í gær* "yesterday" is topicalized, as in (4)–(5), then the verb immediately precedes the subject, which is in Spec,T.

(7) Í   gær   var   mér   gefið   bílana
     yesterday   was.3SG   me.DAT   given.DEF   cars.the.M.PL.ACC
     "Yesterday, I was given the cars."

In all the DAT-NOM examples above involving a morphological change, the case of the object changes from nominative to accusative, while the dative case of the subject remains stable. However, there has been a lively discussion of morphological changes of oblique subjects in the active in Icelandic. It has mainly revolved around two phenomena: dative substitution (DS) and nominative substitution (NS) (see, e.g., Svavarsdóttir 1982, Eythórsson 2002, Jónsson 2003, Ingason 2010, and many others). In short, as Eythórsson (2002: 197) argues, "NS is motivated by syntax (structure) but DS is motivated by semantics (thematic roles)."[5] We will only discuss NS, since DS is beyond the scope of the article.

NS (mainly) affects oblique theme subjects (accusative and dative) of monadic verbs, rather than dyadic verbs.

(8) a. Bátana   rak   > Bátarnir   ráku
        boats.the.PL.ACC drifted.3SG   boats.the.PL.NOM drifted.3PL
        "The boats drifted."

     b. Bátunum   hvolfdi   > Bátarnir   hvolfdu
        boats.the.PL.DAT capsized.3SG   boats.the.PL.NOM capsized.3PL
        "The boats capsized."

The reason for NS not affecting subjects of DAT-NOM verbs seems to be that nominative is only assigned to one argument (e.g., Yip, Maling, & Jackendoff 1987), and in the case of DAT-NOM verbs, nominative has already been assigned to the object, therefore the oblique subject is not affected by NS. This is discussed further in section 4.

NS does not seem to affect oblique subjects of monotransitives in the passive voice.

(9) a. Í   gær   var   honum   hjálpað
        yesterday   was.3SG   him.DAT   helped.DEF
        "Yesterday, he was helped."

     b. *Í gær   var   hann   hjálpaður
        yesterday   was.3SG   he.M.SG.NOM   helped.M.SG.NOM

---

5 The term "DS" is used for a change in the case marking of experiencer subjects, mainly when an accusative subject is replaced by dative.

According to the examples sketched above, some speakers use nominative subjects with many monadic verbs in the active with which other speakers use an oblique subject: see (8). This is not the case with subjects of monotransitive verbs in the passive: see (9). In the active and passive DAT-NOM constructions, a change has been observed on the object but not the subject: see (3) and (7), respectively.

The goal of this article is twofold. First, we claim that there is an ongoing change of DAT-NOM verbs in Icelandic, not only in the passive, as has already been shown by Jónsson (2009a), but also in the active. We also claim that this change is expected, as can be seen when Icelandic is compared to other related languages. Second, we propose that this change must be explained in the syntax where Case is established, but then case is realized in a postsyntactic morphology (Legate 2008). Since we believe case realization derivationally follows Case establishment, covert NOM-ACC Case can be disguised as morphological DAT-NOM or DAT-ACC case.

The article is organized as follows: In section 2 we present the results of a written questionnaire we conducted, in which we focused on the DAT-NOM construction. Section 3 involves a comparison between Icelandic and some other Germanic languages. In section 4 we sketch an analysis of the change, and in section 5 we conclude the article.

To sum up we show in (10) and (11) the constructions discussed in this section (sometimes the examples are simplified).

(10) DAT-NOM and DAT-ACC constructions

Active			Passive			
a. DAT-agreement-NOM						
i. Mér	líka	bílarnir	ii. Mér	voru	gefnir	
me.DAT	like.3PL	cars.the.PL.NOM	me.DAT	were.3PL	given.M.PL.NOM	
"I like the cars."			bílarnir			
			cars.the.M.PL.NOM			
			"I was given the cars."			
b. DAT-nonagreement-NOM						
i. Mér	líkar	bílarnir	ii. *Mér	var	gefið	bílarnir
me.DAT	likes.3SG	cars.the.PL.NOM	me.DAT	was.3SG	given.DEF	cars.the.M.PL.NOM
c. DAT-ACC						
i. Mér	líkar	bílana	ii. Mér	var	gefið	bílana
me.DAT	likes.3SG	cars.the.PL.ACC	me.DAT	was.3SG	given.DEF	cars.the.M.PL.ACC

(11) Nominative substitution (NS)

Active			Passive		
a. DAT subject					
i. Bátunum	hvolfdi	ii.	Honum	var	hjálpað
boats.the.PL.DAT	capsized.3SG		him.DAT	was.3SG	helped.DEF
"The boats capsized."			"He was helped."		
b. NOM subject (NS)					
i. Bátarnir	hvolfdu	ii.	*Hann	var	hjálpaður
boats.the.PL.NOM	capsized.3PL		he.M.SG.NOM	was.3sg	helped.M.SG.NOM

Now we turn to the results of our questionnaire.

2. A DAT-NOM QUESTIONNAIRE

2.1 The Questionnaire

In March 2009 we conducted a written questionnaire where we tested whether the DAT-ACC case pattern (instead of regular DAT-NOM) is accepted at all in Icelandic. We made the survey with Google docs (https://docs.google.com) and sent an invitation via Facebook (http://facebook.com). This way we got thirty-six participants: twenty-five male speakers and eleven female speakers. The youngest participant was seventeen years old (b. 1992) and the oldest one thirty (b. 1979), but most of them were around the age of twenty-five.[6]

The majority of the questionnaire revolved around a judgment task where the participants were asked to judge sentences. Three choices were given: *yes* "I could say this,"? "I could hardly say this," and *no* "I could not say this." Part of the survey had two, three, or four similar sentences where the participants were asked to mark the ones they could use. A few sentences had gaps where the speakers were asked to fill in the correct word form.

The main purpose of the survey was to test our suspicion that a change is taking place in DAT-NOM verbs, since we had already found several

---

6 Since we believe that the change from DAT-NOM case to DAT-ACC is at an early stage, as it only recently was noticed, we mostly focused on getting younger partici-pants. Thus the group tested is homogenous with regard to the age of the speakers. For this reason we cannot say that the participants are representative of the Icelandic population. Neither can we state that they are representative of this particular age group. We do not think that this is a problem, since the main goal of the study was to test whether the DAT-ACC pattern is accepted in the active voice in Icelandic. A test group consisting of older speakers would, however, be ideal for comparison.

DAT-ACC examples in the active on the Internet. This had not been tested for Icelandic. The test sentences focused on DAT-NOM versus DAT-ACC pattern and agreement versus nonagreement, both in active and in passive of ditransitives. Interestingly, the speakers in the study accepted the DAT-ACC construction in the active a lot more than would be expected if the DAT-NOM pattern is as robust as has been described in the literature. However, some DAT-NOM verbs are much more accepted than others, as outlined below— some verbs, like *berast* "receive" and *leiðast* "be bored by," were rejected with an accusative object by almost everyone, whereas nearly half of the participants produced an accusative case object with the verb *nægja* "suffice." Although we believe that there is a change under way in case marking among DAT-NOM verbs, the results must be taken with care because only thirty-six speakers participated in the study.

We now present the results of our questionnaire.

2.2 DAT-ACC in the Active

In short, the results of the study indicate that there is an ongoing DAT-NOM > DAT-ACC change at an early stage in Icelandic.[7] Sentences with the DAT-ACC pattern were accepted by a considerable number of participants, and some speakers even produced an accusative object in a fill-in sentence with a dative subject (see (12) below). In that sentence, we tested the case of the object of the DAT-NOM verb *nægja* "suffice." The speakers were asked to write with letters the correct word form instead of the number 2. In general, the participants either wrote the nominative form of two, *tveir*, or the accusative form, *tvo*. Interestingly, a large number of the participants, sixteen speakers, produced accusative with *nægja*.[8]

(12) Results for the object case of *nægja* "suffice"			NOM	ACC	other
Bjarni: Þarf	landsliðið	ekki	þrjá	sigra?	
Bjarni: needs	national.team.the	not	three	wins	

---

7 When we talk about the change from DAT-NOM case pattern to DAT-ACC pattern, we talk about the DAT-NOM > DAT-ACC change. We also talk about the DAT > NOM case change when we discuss the change from dative subjects to nominative subjects in general (both for monadic and dyadic verbs in the active, and monotransitives and ditransitives in the passive).

8 In (12), Bjarni (a proper name of a man) asks Gunna (a proper name of a woman) whether it isn't right that the national team (in some sport, presumably) only needs three wins. Gunna answers with the DAT-NOM verb *nægja* "suffice" that the two wins will be enough (to qualify for the next round or to win a competition, presumably). Note that *nægi* in (12) is the present tense, subjunctive mood of the verb *nægja*. The morphology is the same for third-person singular and plural, which means that number agreement is not a factor.

"Does not the national team need three wins?"

Gunna:	Nei,	ég	held	að	liðinu	nægi	2	19	16	1
Gunna:	no	I	think	that	team.the.DAT	suffice.SG/PL	2			

"No, I think two [wins] will be enough for the team."

However, only one speaker accepted accusative object with *líka* "like" (*mér líkar* **hana**; answering options: *yes/?/no*):

<table>
<tr><td colspan="8">(13) Results for an accusative object with líka "like"</td><td>yes</td><td>?</td><td>no</td></tr>
<tr><td>Hljómsveitin</td><td>er</td><td>fín</td><td>en</td><td>mér</td><td>líkar</td><td>hana</td><td>samt</td><td>ekki</td><td>1</td><td>1</td><td>34</td></tr>
<tr><td>band.the.F</td><td>is</td><td>fine</td><td>but</td><td>me.DAT</td><td>likes.3SG</td><td>her.ACC</td><td>still</td><td>not</td><td></td><td></td><td></td></tr>
</table>

"The band is OK but I still don't like it."

The difference between the results for the accusative object for *nægja* (12) and *líka* (13) is very clear (not taking into account the different methods to test these sentences). These verbs differ in at least two ways that might in part explain this difference. First, *nægja* is an alternating verb (or symmetric, e.g., Wood 2011), meaning that not only the dative argument, but also the nominative argument, can move to the subject position, as seen in (14). *Líka*, however, is not an alternating verb (it is asymmetric, e.g., Wood 2011, or "pure" DAT-NOM verb), hence the nominative is always the object, as seen in (15).[9]

(14) a.
Liðinu	mun	ekki	nægja	þessi	sigur
team.the.DAT	will.3SG	not	suffice.INF	this.NOM	win.NOM

"This victory will not be enough for the team."

b.
Þessi	sigur	mun	ekki	nægja	liðinu
this.NOM	win.NOM	will.3SG	not	suffice.INF	team.the.DAT

(15) a.
Mér	hefur	aldrei	líkað	hljómsveitin
me.DAT	have.3SG	never	liked	band.the.NOM

"I have never liked the band."

b.
*Hljómsveitin	hefur	aldrei	líkað	mér
band.the.NOM	have.3SG	never	liked	me.DAT

This does not seem to explain why accusative case on objects is more acceptable with *nægja* than *líka*. In fact, some other alternating verbs, like *berast* "receive" and *henta* "suit," seem to be more resistant to this change than pure (nonalternating) DAT-NOM verbs, as seen by the fact that only two

9 The use of the auxiliaries *munu* "will" and *hafa* "have" in (14b) and (15b) excludes the possibility that the nominative argument is topicalized; it must be interpreted as the subject since the dative argument does not move out of the VP.

speakers accepted DAT-ACC in (16) with *berast* and three accepted DAT-ACC in (17c) with *henta*. In (17) and other similar examples, where the speakers could choose more than one sentence, the numbers at the end indicate how many marked that they could say that sentence.

(16) Results for an accusative object with *berast* "receive"

						yes	?	no
Lögreglunni	barst	eina	ábendingu	um	ferðir	2	1	33
police.the.DAT	received.3SG	one.ACC	tip.ACC	about	tours			
grunsamlegs	manns	við	skólalóðina					
suspicious	man	at	schoolyard.the					
"The police got one tip about a suspicious man at the schoolyard."								

(17) Results for *henta* "suit"

						accepted by
a.	Pétri	hentar	ekki	sjálfskiptir	bílar	15
	Peter.DAT	suits.3SG	not	automatic.PL.NOM	cars.PL.NOM	
	"Automatic cars do not suit Peter."					
b.	Pétri	henta	ekki	sjálfskiptir	bílar	15
	Peter.DAT	suit.3PL	not	automatic.PL.NOM	cars.PL.NOM	
c.	Pétri	hentar	ekki	sjálfskipta	bíla	3
	Peter.DAT	suits.3SG	not	automatic.PL.ACC	cars.PL.ACC	
d.	Pétri	henta	ekki	sjálfskipta	bíla	1
	Peter.DAT	suit.3PL	not	automatic.PL.ACC	cars.PL.ACC	
					answered by:	31

The second difference between the verbs *nægja* "suffice" and *líka* "like" is that the subject of *líka* is an experiencer, but the dative argument of *nægja* is a beneficiary.[10] Let us, then, take a look at another DAT-NOM verb that takes an experiencer subject, *leiðast* "be bored by."

(18) Results for an accusative object with *leiðast* "be bored by"

					yes	?	no
Páli	leiðist	handbolta	mjög	mikið	3	7	26
Paul.DAT	is.bored.by.3SG	handball.ACC	very	much			
"Paul does not like handball at all."							

10 Note that the theta role of the dative argument of alternating verbs like *nægja* "suffice" has been analyzed as an experiencer (Jónsson 1997–1998: 20, Thráinsson 2005: 333). We believe, however, that it more accurately bears the role of beneficiary, as can be seen from the fact that it may be replaced with a PP with the preposition *fyrir* "for," which also bears the role of beneficiary:

(i) Þetta   nægði   mér   / fyrir   mig
this.NOM   sufficed.3SG me.DAT   / for   me.ACC

If the dative argument of *nægja* is a beneficiary, we expect *nægja* to have more in common with other beneficiary verbs or recipient verbs (e.g., *áskotnast* "acquire") than experiencer verbs like *líka* "like."

As in the case of *líka*, very few accept accusative object with *leiðast*. If the thematic role of the subject matters, then accusative object could be more acceptable with a pure DAT-NOM verb that takes a recipient subject than with *líka* and *leiðast*, since recipients and beneficiaries are closely related roles (a beneficiary is often described as an intended recipient). Such a verb is *áskotnast* "acquire."

(19)	Results for an accusative object with *áskotnast* "acquire"						yes	?	no
	Maríu	áskotnaðist	glænýjan	bíl	á	dögunum	6	3	27
	Mary.DAT	acquired.3SG	brand.new.ACC	car.ACC	on	days.the			
	"María recently got a brand new car."								

When we compare (19) to the results in (13) and (18), we see that accusative case object with *áskotnast* is, in fact, more readily accepted than with *líka* and *leiðast*. However, we must be cautious in drawing conclusions.

We tested another DAT-ACC example of *áskotnast*. There the participants were given four similar sentences. They were asked to choose the ones they could say: that is, they could choose more than one (see (20)). In (20a) there is nonagreement with a nominative object; in (20b), the verb assigns accusative to the object; in (20c) there is agreement with a nominative object; and in (20d) there is agreement with an accusative object.

(20)		Results for *áskotnast* "acquire"					accepted by
	a.	Kristjáni	áskotnaðist	tveir	miðar	á	tónleika	6
		K.DAT	acquired.3SG	two.PL.NOM	tickets.PL.NOM	at	concert	
		í		Laugardalshöll				
		in		Laugardalshöll				
		"Kristján got two tickets to a concert in Laugardalshöll."						
	b.	Kristjáni	áskotnaðist	tvo	miða	á	tónleika	9
		K.DAT	acquired.3SG	two.PL.ACC	tickets.PL.ACC	at	concert	
		í		Laugardalshöll				
		in		Laugardalshöll				
	c.	Kristjáni	áskotnuðust	tveir	miðar	á	tónleika	24
		K.DAT	acquired.3PL	two.PL.NOM	tickets.PL.NOM	at	concert	
		í		Laugardalshöll				
		in		Laugardalshöll				
	d.	Kristjáni	áskotnuðust	tvo	miða	á	tónleika	0
		K.DAT	acquired.3PL	two.PL.ACC	tickets.PL.ACC	at	concert	
		í		Laugardalshöll				
		in		Laugardalshöll				
							answered by:	34

More speakers accepted the DAT-ACC sentence in (20b) than in (19). These results indicate that *áskotnast* "acquire," which takes a recipient subject, more readily takes an accusative object than *líka* "like" and *leiðast* "be bored by," which take an experiencer subject.[11]

Since rather few speakers filled out our questionnaire, we present, in (21)–(22) below, results from a survey conducted in 2010 in the project "Linguistic change in real time in Icelandic phonology and syntax" (REAL; Höskuldur Thráinsson, PI). One goal of the survey was to test speakers who participated in Maling and Sigurjónsdóttir's (2002) survey on the New Passive and compare the results in those two surveys. As of the writing of this article, forty-five speakers, all born in 1984, have filled out the REAL judgment task. Among the sentences that were tested (with the same response options as in our survey, i.e., *yes,?* and *no*) were two with DAT-NOM verbs showing the DAT-ACC case pattern, *hlotnast* "acquire," see (3b) above, and *líka* "like." Note that these two sentences were not among the sentences tested in Maling and Sigurjónsdóttir's study.

(21) Results for an accusative object with *hlotnast* "acquire" in REAL

								yes ?	*no*
Honum	hafði	ekki	hlotnast	þann	heiður	áður		18 10 16	
him.DAT	had.3SG	not	acquired	that.ACC	honor.ACC	before			

"He had not acquired that honor before."

(22) Results for an accusative object with *líka* "like" in REAL

						yes ?	*no*
Honum	líkar	nýju	tölvuna	ekki		9 3 33	
him.DAT	likes.3SG	new.ACC	computer.the.ACC	not			

"He doesn't like the new computer."

Just as in our study, the results from REAL indicate that there really is a change under way in the case marking of DAT-NOM verbs. If there were no signs of such a change, we would expect that almost all speakers would reject both the sentences. The majority did reject the sentence with *líka* in (22), similar to our survey (see (13)), although it was accepted a bit more in REAL than in our survey (nine speakers, or 20 percent, in REAL, but only one speaker accepted the sentence in our survey). Twice as many, eighteen speakers (41 percent), accepted an accusative object with *hlotnast* (see (21)). That is a much higher acceptance rate than would be expected if DAT-ACC in the active was ungrammatical to all, or almost all, speakers of Icelandic.

11 As pointed out to us by Jim Wood, there is another difference between *líka* and *nægja* in that the dative argument is optional for *nægja* (*Þetta nægir* "This is enough"), whereas it is obligatory for *líka*. This aspect could be addressed more properly with a bigger survey.

In (23) we show a compilation of the sentence types we tested (and also the two sentences that were tested in REAL) and discussed in this subsection. Note that we have simplified the sentences for sake of clarity, always using the dative *mér* "me" as the subject and either *hún/hana* "she.NOM/her.ACC" or *bílar/bíla* "cars.PL.NOM/ACC" as the nominative/accusative object (this should make comparison between different verbs easier for the reader).

(23)	Verb	Construction	Example		See full example
a.	*nægja*	DAT-NOM/ACC	Mér	nægir	hún/hana 12
	"suffice"		me.DAT	suffices.3SG	she.NOM/her.ACC
b.	*líka*	DAT-ACC	Mér	líkar	hana 13/22
	"like"		me.DAT	likes.3SG	her.ACC
c.	*berast*	DAT-ACC	Mér	barst	hana 16
	"receive"		me.DAT	recieved.3SG	her.ACC
d.	*henta*	DAT-NOM/ACC	Mér	henta/r	hún/hana 17
	"suit"	+/− agreement	me.DAT	suit.3PL/SG	she.NOM/her.ACC
e.	*leiðast*	DAT-ACC	Mér	leiðist	hana 18
	"be bored by"		me.DAT	is.bored.by.3SG	her.ACC
f.	*áskotnast*	DAT-NOM/ACC	Mér	áskotnaðist/áskotnuðust	bíla/r 19/20
	"acquire"	+/− agreement	me.DAT	acquired.3SG/PL	cars.PL.NOM/ACC
g.	*hlotnast*	DAT-ACC	Mér	hlotnaðist	hana 21
	"acquire"		me.DAT	acquired.3SG	her.ACC

We also showed an alternating verb (*nægja* "suffice") that can have either argument as the subject, versus a nonalternating verb (*líka* "like") that can only take a dative case subject (again, the examples are simplified, see full version in (14–15)):

(24)		Alternating				Nonalternating		
				DAT-NOM				
a.	i.	Mér	mun	nægja	hún	ii. Mér	mun	líka	hún
		me.DAT	will.3SG	suffice.INF	she.NOM	me.DAT	will.3SG	like.INF	she.NOM
				NOM-DAT				
b.	i.	Hún	mun	nægja	mér	ii. *Hún	mun	líka	mér
		she.NOM	will.3SG	suffice	me.DAT	she.NOM	will.3SG	like.INF	me.DAT

2.3 Nonagreement with Nominative Objects

Number agreement with a nominative object in the DAT-NOM construction is sometimes considered optional, and for many speakers it is. As mentioned in the introduction above (section 1), H. Á. Sigurðsson and Holmberg (2008) divide Icelandic into three varieties with respect to number agreement in the DAT-NOM construction. In Icelandic B number agreement with the nominative object is optional; it is preferred in Icelandic A but disallowed in Icelandic C.

There was an obvious preference for nonagreement with the verb *líka* "like" in our survey—(25a) shows nonagreement, which the majority accepted, and (25b) shows number agreement, which only three speakers accepted.

(25)	Results for agreement with *líka* "like"				*yes*	?	*no*
a.	Stefáni	líkar	ekki	súrsaðir	hrútspungar	20	8	7
	Stefán.DAT	likes.3SG	not	pickled.PL.NOM	sheep.testicles.PL.NOM			
	"Stefán does not like pickled sheep testicles."							
b.	Jóhönnu	líka	ekki	gosdrykkir		3	8	25
	Jóhanna.DAT	like.3PL	not	soft.drinks.PL.NOM				
	"Jóhanna does not like soft drinks."							

Fifteen of those who accepted the sentence in (25a) rejected (25b), three of them found (25b) questionable (they could hardly say it), but two speakers accepted them both. This clearly shows that number agreement with the nominative object is not optional for all speakers—at least not with the DAT-NOM verb *líka* "like" where the subject is an experiencer.

This suggests that most of the participants in our questionnaire were Icelandic C speakers. However, number agreement with some DAT-NOM verbs is more readily accepted if the dative subject is a recipient or a beneficiary. This applies to both the pure DAT-NOM verb *áskotnast* "acquire" (see results in (20c) above), and the alternating verb *henta* "suit" (see (17b)).[12] In addition to this, the vast majority accepted number agreement with the alternating verb *berast* "receive" (see (26b)), whereas a little less than half of the speakers accepted nonagreement (see (26a)). Note that the nominative forms in (26a) *tvö tilboð* "two offers" and (26b) *þrjár umsóknir* "three applications" are not morphologically distinct from the accusative form.

(26)	Results for *berast* "receive"						*yes*	?	*no*
a.	Önnu	barst	tvö	tilboð	í	húsið	15	4	17
	Anna.DAT	received.3SG	two.PL.NOM	offers.PL.NOM	in	house.the			
	"Anna received two offers for her house."								

12 It might seem strange that DAT-ACC is more readily accepted with a verb like *áskotnast* "acquire" than *líka* "like" at the same time as number agreement with a nominative object of *áskotnast* is also more accepted. However, we need to look at intraspeaker judgments: Nine speakers accepted DAT-ACC case pattern with *áskotnast* in (20) above. Eight of them did not accept number agreement with a nominative plural object.

b. Fyrirtækinu   bárust   þrjár   umsóknir   30   4   2

company.the.DAT   received.3PL   three.PL.NOM   applications.PL.NOM

um   starfið

on   job.the

"The company received three applications for the job."

Based on these results, where thirty accepted number agreement in (26b) with *berast*, the vast majority (83 percent) are either Icelandic A or Icelandic B speakers with respect to this particular verb. Given the results above, it is interesting to compare (26) to DAT-ACC with *berast* (16), which only two speakers accepted—that is no coincidence: if number agreeement is optional or preferred in a particular variety, then DAT-ACC is disallowed.

As is seen when (25) and (26) are compared, it certainly matters what verb, or what kind of a verb, we look at when we discuss the three varieties, Icelandic A, B, and C; if someone is an Icelandic C speaker with respect to a verb like *líka* "like" we cannot automatically draw the conclusion that she or he doesn't like number agreement with any kind of a DAT-NOM verb.[13]

Before we look at results for the DAT-ACC construction in the passive, we want to mention that it is important to investigate the intraspeaker variation with respect to Icelandic C and the DAT-ACC variety. Although we argue that there is a relationship between Icelandic C and the DAT-ACC variety (and not between Icelandic A/B and DAT-ACC) our data is not rich enough to draw

13 In one of the surveys conducted in the project "Variation in syntax" more than seven hundred speakers in four age groups were asked to give judgments (answering options *yes/?/no*) on sentences with number agreement (Thráinsson, Angantýsson, & E. F. Sigurðsson 2011). The speakers were divided into four age groups: 15, 20–25, 40–45, and 65–70. Let's take a look at the number agreement sentences in (i):

(i) Number agreement in "Variation in syntax" ($N = 702$)
   a. Honum   leiddust   tónleikarnir   mjög   mikið
      him.DAT   was.bored.by.3PL   concert.PL.NOM   very   much
      "He found the concert really boring."

   b. Henni   hafa   alltaf   leiðst   langar   bíómyndir
      her.DAT   have.3PL   always   been.bored.by   long.PL.NOM   movies.PL.NOM
      "She has always found long movies to be boring."

   c. Það   hafa   mörgum   blöskrað   þessi   ummæli
      EXPL   have.3PL   many.PL.DAT   been.shocked.by   these.PL.NOM   statements.PL.NOM
      "Many people are shocked at these statements."

Two of three sentences in (i) have the main verb *leiðast* "be bored by" and one *blöskra* "be shocked by." Both these verbs take experiencer subjects and are nonalternating (the subject is never the nominative argument).

Only 9 out of 702 speakers rejected all three sentences. That indicates that rather few are Icelandic C speakers. However, 227 speakers found all the sentences in (i) to be grammatical. According to H. Á. Sigurðsson and Holmberg (2008) sentences like (i-c) above with "dative intervention" are ungrammatical to other than Icelandic A speakers. Out of 712 speakers, 368 found (i-c) to be grammatical, but 187 rejected it. Based on this, most speakers are either Icelandic A or B speakers.

firm conclusions in these matters. To give an example of this, with *áskotnast* "acquire" in (20) we expected some speakers to accept both (20a) (nonagreement) and (20b) (DAT-ACC) but none of them did. However, four out of six speakers who accepted (20a) also accepted (20c) (number agreement). For those speakers number agreement with *áskotnast* is optional (Icelandic B).

2.4 DAT-ACC in the Passive

As has been pointed out recently by Jónsson (2009a), some speakers, mainly younger ones, use accusative objects instead of nominative in the passive of ditransitives (DAT-NOM > DAT-ACC passive). This change looks like the DAT-NOM > DAT-ACC change in the active. The DAT-ACC passive was, however, less accepted than some DAT-ACC active sentences in our survey.

(27) Results for accusative with *senda* "send"							yes	?	no
Mér	var	sent	þessa	mynd	í	tölvupósti	4	3	28
me.DAT	was.3SG	sent.DEF	this.ACC	photo.ACC	in	e-mail			
"This photo was sent to me by e-mail."									

Árnadóttir and E. F. Sigurðsson (2008) argue that an intermediate stage in this change is when the verb and the passive participle do not agree with the nominative object—just like nonagreement with the nominative object of DAT-NOM verbs in the active seems to be an intermediate stage in the development of DAT-NOM to DAT-ACC. However, most speakers in the survey did not like the nonagreement in the ditransitive passive either (the canonical passive would have a passive participle agreeing with the nominative object, i.e., *sendur grunsamlegur pakki* "sent.M.NOM suspicious.M.NOM package.M.NOM").

(28) Results for nonagreeement with nominative for senda "send"					yes	?	no
Forsetanum	var	sent	grunsamlegur	pakki	3	4	28
president.the.DAT	was.3SG	sent.DEF	suspicious.M.NOM	package.M.NOM			
frá	útlöndum						
from	abroad						
"A suspicious package was sent to the president from abroad."							

Thus, our results do not support Árnadóttir and E. F. Sigurðsson's (2008) claim.

The results for *sýna* "show" in (29) are the same as for *senda* "send" in (27) and (28): DAT-ACC passive with *sýna* was less accepted than some of the DAT-ACC sentences in the active (see subsection 2.2 above). Also, the same was true for the DAT-NOM passive with nonagreeing passive participle, which none of the speakers accepted. This is shown in (29). (29a) is an instance of a nonagreeing passive participle with a nominative object; (29b) shows agreement; (29c) shows DAT-ACC; and, finally, (29d) has agreement with an accusative object.

(29)   Results for *sýna* "show"   *accepted by*

a. | Mér | var | sýnt | tveir | jeppar | á | bílasölunni | 0 |
|-----|-----|------|-------|--------|---|-------------|---|
| me.DAT | was.3SG | shown.DEF | two.M.PL.NOM | jeeps.M.PL.NOM | at | car.dealer.the | |

   "I was shown two jeeps at the car dealer's."

b. | Mér | voru | sýndir | tveir | jeppar | | | 33 |
|-----|------|--------|-------|--------|---|---|----|
| me.DAT | were.3PL | shown.M.PL.NOM | two.M.PL.NOM | jeeps.M.PL.NOM | | | |
| á | bílasölunni | | | | | | |
| at | car.dealer.the | | | | | | |

c. | Mér | var | sýnt | tvo | jeppa | á | bílasölunni | 2 |
|-----|-----|------|-----|-------|---|-------------|---|
| me.DAT | was.3SG | shown.DEF | two.PL.ACC | jeeps.PL.ACC | at | car.dealer.the | |

d. | Mér | voru | sýndir | tvo | jeppa | á | bílasölunni | 2 |
|-----|------|--------|-----|-------|---|-------------|---|
| me.DAT | were.3PL | shown.M.PL.NOM | two.PL.ACC | jeeps.PL.ACC | at | car.dealer.the | |

                                                                    answered by: 34

Out of the thirty-four participants who answered which sentences of those four they could say, only one did not choose agreement in (29b) (remember that the speakers were allowed to choose more than one sentence). Our results thus indicate that agreement in the passive is much more robust than in the active (for comparison, see section 2.3).

The fact that the DAT-ACC construction in the ditransitive passive was less accepted in our survey than DAT-ACC might be of some surprise. Jónsson (2009a: 303) reports a study from the "Variation in syntax" project (cf. Thráinsson, Angantýsson, & E. F. Sigurðsson 2011) where 59 percent of fourteen- to fifteen-year-olds (born 1991 and 1992) accepted the ditransitive DAT-ACC construction in the passive (the total number of fourteen- to fifteen-year-old speakers who filled out that survey was a little less than two hundred according to Jónsson 2009a).[14] Most speakers in our survey were a little older, which might explain this difference to a certain degree.

14 The example Jónsson gives is the following:

(i) | Var | þeim | ekki | einu sinni | sýnt | íbúðina | fyrst? |
|-----|------|------|-----------|------|---------|--------|
| was | them.DAT | not | even | shown.DEF | apartment.ACC | first |

   "Were they not even shown the apartment first?"
   (Jónsson 2009a: 303)

Examples like these have been discussed in relation to the so-called New Passive, or the New Impersonal, in Icelandic. Jónsson (2009a: 303) says that the example above provides a very strong argument against Maling and Sigurjónsdóttir's (2002) analysis that the New Passive is, in fact, an impersonal active construction.

2.5 Summary

A change from DAT-NOM to DAT-ACC in the active seems to be under way. There is, however, variation between different verbs. The reason for this is not clear. This may have to do with the thematic role of the dative subject—verbs that take an experiencer subject (*líka* "like," *leiðast* "be bored by") are less likely to take an accusative object than verbs that take a recipient or a beneficiary subject (*nægja* "suffice," *áskotnast* "acquire," *hlotnast* "acquire"). This does not, however, apply to the verb *berast* "receive," which also takes a recipient subject but was in general rejected with the DAT-ACC pattern in our questionnaire.

When we conducted our questionnaire, we expected pure DAT-NOM verbs to be accepted more readily with an accusative object than alternating verbs. This was not borne out, although *áskotnast* with DAT-ACC was accepted to some extent: accusative case object with *nægja* (alternating verb) was produced by almost half of the speakers, whereas accusative object with *líka* and *leiðast* (nonalternating verbs) was rejected by almost everyone. On the other hand, the alternating verbs *berast* and *henta* were rejected with an accusative object by most speakers, which means we cannot state that alternating DAT-NOM verbs are in general more acceptable with an accusative object than nonalternating verbs.

We believe that our small survey shows that there is a change under way in Icelandic, although we cannot draw conclusions about what the biggest factors are (e.g., regarding thematic roles, alternating verbs versus nonalternating verbs). The results from REAL support our claim. However, we want to emphasize that a bigger survey is needed.

In the next section we compare the development in Icelandic to a similar development in related languages.

3. COMPARISON WITH OTHER GERMANIC LANGUAGES

In this section we look at what seems to be oblique subjects in the history of English, Faroese, and Swedish—in each language we discuss the development of oblique subjects with monadic and dyadic verbs in the active and monotransitives and ditransitives in the passive. The changes in Icelandic, discussed in sections 1 and 2, are in many respects comparable to changes in case marking in English, Faroese, and Swedish.

The development of DAT-NOM constructions seems to be similar in all these languages; we follow Hrafnbjargarson (2004) in that DAT-NOM constructions were reanalyzed as NOM-ACC in English and Swedish (and other Mainland Scandinavian languages) in three steps:

(30)   DAT-NOM   >   DAT-ACC   >   NOM-ACC

This seems to apply to Faroese (Hrafnbjargarson 2004), as we discuss below, and also to Icelandic.

3.1 The Development in Faroese

Faroese, like Icelandic, has a rich case system, although verbs no longer assign genitive case to their arguments (Thráinsson et al. 2004). Furthermore, as first shown by Barnes (1986), Faroese exhibits oblique subjects, but the use is far more limited than in Icelandic. This indicates that the decline of oblique subjects, discussed in this section, is not driven by loss of morphology.

3.1.1 Loss of Oblique Subjects

In Faroese, oblique theme subjects of monadic verbs have been replaced by nominative (e.g., Eythórsson & Jónsson 2003: 209). In this respect, Icelandic and Faroese follow the same path (cf. (8) above):

(31) Bátarnir   róku   á   land   *Faroese*
     boats.the.PL.NOM drifted.3PL to shore
     "The boats drifted to the shore."
     (Thráinsson et al. 2004: 228)

In addition to this, dative experiencer subjects of most monadic verbs seem to have been substituted as well, with nominative (see (32)).[15] These verbs usually still take dative experiencer subjects in Icelandic (see (33)):

(32) Eg   kólnaði,   sum   eg   stóð   *Faroese*
     I.NOM   got.cold   as   I   stood
     "I got cold as I stood."
     (*Føroysk orðabók* 1998: 626)
(33) Mér   kólnaði   *Icelandic*
     me.DAT   got.cold
     "I got cold."

The same goes for oblique subjects of monotransitives in the passive in Faroese: they barely exist anymore. Whether this is changing in Modern Icelandic needs to be studied. In any case, the passive of monotransitives

---

15 According to a few Faroese informants, verbs like *kólna* are preferred with a theme subject (e.g., *veðrið kólnaði* "weather.the.NOM got cold"). There, the subject is originally nominative, both in Faroese and Icelandic. However, if an experiencer subject is used, it must be in the nominative case in Faroese, not the dative case.

has changed a lot more in Faroese than Icelandic (e.g., Thráinsson et al. 2004). Compare (34) to (9) above.

(34) a. Eg   hjálpti   honum   *Faroese*
       I   helped him.DAT
       "I helped him."

    b. *Honum varð   hjálpt
       him.DAT   was   helped.DEF
       "He was helped."

    c. Hann   varð   hjálptur
       he.M.NOM was   helped.M.NOM

There are, though, a few verbs that, according to Thráinsson et al. (2004: 267), preserve the dative case marking in the passive of monotransitives in Faroese: *bíða* "wait," *dugna* "help," *takka* "thank," and *trúgva* "believe."

3.1.2 DAT-ACC *in the Active,* DAT-NOM *in the Passive*

Dative subjects of DAT-NOM verbs are rather well preserved, although they are clearly losing ground among monadic verbs. However, most DAT-NOM verbs assign accusative case to their object (e.g., Barnes 1986, Thráinsson et al. 2004)—in this respect the new variety in Icelandic, discussed in section 2, resembles Faroese.

(35)   Mær   dámar   væl   hasa   bókina
        me.DAT   likes.3SG   well   that.ACC   book.the.ACC
        "I like that book."
        (Barnes 1986: 33)

There are, though, clear signs of dative subjects developing toward nominative (e.g., Barnes 1986; Eythórsson & Jónsson 2003; Thráinsson et al. 2004).

(36)   Eg   dámi   væl   hasa   bókina
        I.NOM   like.1SG   well   that.ACC   book.the.ACC
        "I like that book."
        (Barnes 1986: 33)

Jónsson (2009b) argues that dative subjects in Faroese have covert nominative Case which is not morphologically realized. He refers to this as the Covert Nominative Hypothesis, where the dative subject is assigned nominative Case by T in Spec,T. Empirical evidence he gives for this is number agreement with dative subjects:

(37) Vit   vóna   at   teimum   dáma   hugskotið
      we   hope   that them.DAT like.3PL idea.the.ACC
      "We hope that they like the idea."
      (Jónsson 2009b: 156)

In (37) the verb *dáma* "like" agrees with the dative subject *teimum* "them." There is, however, only agreement in number but not in person as seen by the fact that (38) is ungrammatical.

(38) *Mær   dámi   hasa   bókina
       me.DAT   like.1SG that.ACC book.the.ACC
      "I like that book."
      (Jónsson 2009b: 159)

The next step in the development might however be person agreement but that might not sound plausible since many speakers already use morphological nominative case with *dáma*.[16]

Jónsson (2009b) gives an additional argument for dative subjects being established as nominative Case. That involves the use of the anaphoric element *sjálvur* "self," which is coindexed with the dative subject (*honum* "him" in (39)) and should receive the same case (see (39a)). For many speakers it does not: that is, in (39b) the anaphoric element is not in the dative case even though the subject is. Instead it bears nominative case, which is a manifestation of covert nominative Case of the subject.

(39) a. Sjálvum dámar   honum   ikki at lurta   eftir tónleiki
        self.DAT likes.3SG him.DAT   not   to listen   to   music
        "He himself does not like to listen to music."

     b. Sjálvur dámar   honum   ikki at lurta   eftir tónleiki
        self.NOM likes.3SG him.DAT   not   to listen   to   music
        (Jónsson 2009b: 159)

Jónsson (2009b) claims that only in Faroese, and not in Icelandic, does the dative subject get covert nominative Case, since examples corresponding to (37) and (39b) are ungrammatical in Icelandic. While this is true for most speakers of Icelandic, we argue that some speakers (Icelandic C speakers, to be precise) have covert nominative on oblique subjects (see section 4).

16 According to Jónsson (2009b: 158–159) the reason for the lack of person agreement may be that nominative Case is assigned in Spec,T rather than checked.

Dative subjects in the DAT-NOM ditransitive passive in Faroese, however, do not show signs of developing toward nominative case. In addition to this, the argument corresponding to a direct object in the active is usually in the nominative case and not accusative (e.g., Thráinsson et al. 2004). Thus, the DAT-NOM pattern is rather well preserved in the passive, unlike the active.

Number agreement with dative subjects is less accepted in the ditransitive passive (Jónsson 2009b). Since the DAT-NOM pattern is so well preserved in the passive, this might not be surprising. Note, however, that in the following example the second argument is not a DP in nominative case, but an infinitival clause.[17]

(40) ?Teimum   verða   eggjað   at koyra   saman
       them.DAT   will.be.3PL encouraged.DEF   to drive   together
      "They will be encouraged to drive together."
      (Jónsson 2009b: 151)

There is, though, an indication of a change in the DAT-NOM passive. Barnes (1986) discusses the DAT-ACC pattern in the passive voice in Faroese and shows the following DAT-ACC example (*var **honum** ætlað **somu viðferð***) from a 1939 text:

(41) Og   var   honum   óivað   ætlað   somu
      and   was   him.DAT   doubtless   intended.DEF same.ACC
      viðferð   og   Øgmundi
      treatment.ACC   and   Øgmundur.DAT
      "And he was doubtless going to be given the same treatment
      as Øgmundur."
      (Dahl 1939: 119; Barnes 1986: 35)

In addition to this, Eythórsson (2009) conducted a study in the Faroe Islands in 2008 where he asked if the following sentences were acceptable:[18]

17 Still, many speakers accept *eggja* "encourage" in the passive with a nominative subject (see Jónsson's (2009b:149) example (9)). The reason that none of Jónsson's (2009b) informants accepted the plural agreement with a dative subject of *eggja* might thus be that they preferred nominative case on the subject.

18 It should be noted that Thórhallur Eythórsson tested the DAT-ACC passive in (42b) with the passive participle *givin* "given," which shows masculine/feminine morphology instead of the default third-person singular *givið*, which is the form to expect, since agreement with an accusative case object is unexpected. However, it is also possible to interpret *givin* as agreeing with the dative subject *gentuni*, since verbal agreement with dative subjects is possible in the active voice in Faroese (see (37); Jónsson 2009b). It should be noted that Eythórsson also tested a sentence equivalent to (42b) with the default third-person singular *givið* and the definite accusative object *telduna* "the computer." That was, however, accepted by only four speakers. The same applies to a sentence equivalent to (42a) with the definite nominative case argument *teldan* "the computer," which was accepted by one speaker.

(42) Results for *giva* "give" in ditransitive passive in Faroese   *yes* *?* *no*

a.	Gentuni	bleiv	givin	ein	telda	11	13	38
	girl.the.DAT	was	given.F.SG.NOM	a.F.SG.NOM	computer.F.SG.NOM			
	"The girl was given a computer."							
b.	Gentuni	bleiv	givin	eina	teldu	16	13	31
	girl.the.DAT	was	given.F.SG.NOM	a.ACC	computer.ACC			

Few speakers accepted the DAT-NOM pattern in (42a), possibly because NOM-DAT is preferred (where the nominative subject corresponds to the direct object in the active). However, more speakers accepted the DAT-ACC pattern in (42b) than DAT-NOM. In this regard, Faroese might be different from Icelandic in that the change DAT-NOM > DAT-ACC is without a doubt more recent in the passive than in the active. In Icelandic, however, the changes might be from the same time period since they were discovered at a similar time.

3.2 The Development in Swedish

In Modern Swedish, as in other Mainland Scandinavian languages, morphological case marking is lost on full DPs.[19] Old Swedish, however, had case distinction and preposed oblique DPs. We follow Barðdal (2000) and Hrafnbjargarson (2004), who argue that Old Swedish, as well as other Old Scandinavian languages, exhibited oblique subjects. Falk (1995, 1997) gives the chronological order for the morphological changes of oblique case (dative) to nominative of preposed DPs in earlier Swedish. The parallels to the changes in Faroese and Icelandic are obvious.

The first step of these changes is within monadic verbs in the active and monotransitives in the passive. The examples in (43) show how a dative subject–like argument, (43a) *wardh honom forgifwit*, changes to a nominative subject, (43b) *han wart förgiffwen*, of a monotransitive verb in the passive. This happened before 1500 (Falk 1995: 208):

(43) a. Llangt   ther   æpter   wardh   honom   forgifwit
        long   there   after   was   him.DAT   poisoned
        "A long time after that, he was poisoned."
        (ST: 102; Falk 1995: 208)

     b. han   wart   förgiffwen
        he.NOM   was   poisoned
        "He was poisoned."
        (PK: 234; Falk 1995: 208)

19 This is in general true for Mainland Scandinavian dialects, although morphological distinction is found to a certain degree in some of the dialects.

The next step, according to Falk, is when case marking of dyadic verbs in the active changes (see the dative argument *henni* in (44a) versus the nominative *du* in (44b)). This happened mostly between 1500 and 1600.

(44) a. Henni   likar   thätta
       her.DAT   like   this
       "She likes this."
       (Falk 1997: 10)

    b. Du   likar   mig
       you.NOM   like   me.ACC

The third and last step is a change in the case marking of oblique arguments of ditransitives in the passive (see the nominative subject *han* in (45)). Recipient subjects (corresponding to indirect object in the active), infrequently occurred in the nominative case before 1800 (Falk 1995: 210).

(45) Han   bleeff   ...   mycken   ähre   bewijst
      he.NOM   was   much   honor   shown
      "He was shown a great honor."
      (Tegel, G 1 2: 65, 1622; Falk 1995: 210)

Interestingly, these steps have parallels in Faroese with respect to diachrony. As we have already discussed, oblique subjects of intransitive verbs in the active and monotransitives in the passive are nearly nonexistent in Modern Faroese (the first step). Oblique subjects of dyadic verbs are still retained with most verbs—although there is a tendency to use a nominative subject with some of them (the second step). However, the use of oblique subjects in the passive of ditransitives is robust, although there are some hints of a change (nominative objects becoming accusative). There are no clear signs in the morphology, yet, of the dative subject changing to nominative in Faroese (the third step).

3.3 The Development in English

3.3.1 Oblique Subjects of Monadic Verbs

At earlier stages of English, arguments were case marked. Oblique experiencers were sometimes preposed in Old English (OE) and thus look like oblique subjects, similar to oblique subjects in Icelandic. Allen (1995: 442–443) argues that these non-nominative NPs were, in fact, subjects in earlier

English (see also Barðdal 2000 and Hrafnbjargarson 2004).[20] In this sub-section, we discuss how English follows the same path as Faroese, Swedish and—presumably—Icelandic, with regard to the DAT > NOM change.

Falk showed for Swedish that the DAT > NOM change affected monadic oblique verbs first. This seems to be the case for English as well: monadic oblique subject verbs already at the OE stage could be found with nominative subjects (Allen 1995: 72).

(46) forþam   þe   ge   hingriað
      for.that that   you.NOM   hunger.PL
      "Because you will hunger."
      (Lk [WSCp] 6.25; Allen 1995: 72)

Although Allen does not describe this in detail, it is obvious that this change happened long before the change in DAT-NOM verbs. As we will discuss below, the DAT > NOM change with dyadic verbs mainly occurred in the fifteenth century.

3.3.2 DAT-NOM Verbs

Examples of DAT-NOM in the active are found in OE. Hrafnbjargarson (2004: 50) considers the following example to show a dative subject and a nominative object:

(47) ðam   wife   þa   word   wel   licodon
      the.DAT   woman.DAT   the.PL.NOM   words.PL.NOM   well   liked.3PL
      "The woman liked the words well."
      (cobeowul 639.538; Hrafnbjargarson 2004: 50)

As seen from the data for Faroese, the case of the object of DAT-NOM verbs changes into accusative before the case of the subject can become nominative. In Early Middle English (EME), examples like (48) are found (Allen 1995: 236–238):

(48) swetest   him   ðuncheð   ham
      sweetest   him   thinks   them
      "They seem the sweetest to him."
      or: "He thinks them the sweetest."
      (AW 101.7; Allen 1995: 237)

20 However, Allen (1995) argues that preposed dative recipients in passive ditransitive constructions did not behave like subjects, unlike in Icelandic.

In examples like these, both the subject and the object appear to be in the dative case. However, at this stage there was no longer a distinction between accusative and dative in pronouns, so the object (and the subject for that matter) might really be accusative. In light of the development in other languages, we assume that the construction shown in (48) really is DAT-ACC. At least it is important to notice that the case of the object no longer is nominative. And the data is clear according to Allen: she finds no examples in which a postposed pronominal theme of DAT-NOM verbs is a nominative pronoun.[21] Nevertheless, if the theme is a preposed pronoun, it always appears in the nominative case.[22]

In a similar time period (EME), there are examples of a possible number agreement with the dative subject (see *ham likieð* in (49)) (Allen 1995: 235):

(49) swuðe wel   ham   likieð   biuoren þe   to beon
      very well   them   like.PL   before thee   to be
      ("Cristes milde moder"; Allen 1995: 235)

Examples of this sort, however, are very rare in EME but become more common in later Middle English (ME) and in Early Modern English (Allen 1995: 235–236). Allen (1995: 241–243) also doubts that in EME there was any agreement with the postposed theme.

The DAT > NOM change for pronominal subjects of DAT-NOM verbs starts to occur in the fourteenth century (Allen 1995: 250). In the fourteenth century, the first examples of *like* appear with the experiencer subject in the nominative case (Allen 1995: 251). In the earliest examples, like (50a) which is from around 1330, *like* takes a sentential complement, but in later examples, like (50b) which is from late fourteenth century, *like* with a nominative subject can also take a DP complement (notice that the theme object is in the dative/accusative case and not the nominative).

(50) a. And bot þou like we seruen þe we will ʒern fram þe te
       "and unless you.NOM would like us to serve you, we will make our way from you."
       (A&M 5529; Allen 1995: 251)

21 Studying the development of the experiencer verbs in EME, Allen (1995: 221–249) looked at texts written in the dialects in which the systematic distinction between accusative and dative pronouns had broken down. She only uses examples where the theme is pronominal, since nominative/dative distinction for nouns had also been lost in these dialects.

22 One could argue that these verbs are alternating verbs, as found in Icelandic, since either the theme or the experiencer could be the subject.

b. ...somehat she likede hym the bet
    "She liked him better."
    (Ch.LGW. 1076; Allen 1995: 251)

In the late fourteenth century, dative experiencers were still more common than nominative experiencers. At the same time, however, there is an increase in examples with number agreement with dative subjects (see *hem oughten* in (51)) (Allen 1995: 263):

(51) how   that hem   oughten   have greet repentaunce
      how   that them.DAT   ought.PL have great repentance
      "How they should have great repentance."
      (Ch.B.Mel. 1731 (2920–2925); Allen 1995: 263)

In short, the use of dative subjects started to decrease in the fourteenth century, and, in the fifteenth century, dative subjects were still a structural possibility, but the dative was clearly losing ground. In the sixteenth century dative subjects became structurally impossible (limited to fixed expressions) (Allen 1995: 286–287). The end result is, of course, Modern English with NOM-ACC pattern:

(52) He   likes   her/*she

3.3.3 Passive of Monotransitives

In Old English, dative case in passives of monotransitives was retained in subject position (see (53a) *him bið gedemed*). However, this case marking was lost in Middle English, as seen in (53b), where the subject *he* is in nominative case:

(53) a. hi   ne   demað nanum men, ac   him   bið gedemed
        they not judge no   men but them.DAT   is   judged
        "They will not judge any men, but they will be judged."
        (Ælc.P.XI.369; Allen 1995: 27)
     b. for he   nes   þeo   noht iquemed
        for he.NOM not.was then not   pleased
        "For he was not then pleased."
        (BrutC 1529; Allen 1995: 349)

Although the data is not very clear, Allen (1995: 366) assumes that the dative passive of monotransitive verbs "disappeared as a productive process by the early thirteenth century." This is a little later than the DAT > NOM change in monadic verbs in the active.

3.3.4 Passive of Ditransitives

Until around the middle of the fourteenth century, preposed dative passives of ditransitives were possible in English (54), but it was more common to have the theme preposed (55):

(54) and him   wearð geseald an   snæd   flæsces
      and him.DAT was   sold   a   piece.NOM flesh.GEN
      "and he was given a piece of flesh"
      (ÆLS (Basil) 158; Allen 2001: 45)

(55) þatt heffness ȝate uss oppnedd be
      that heaven's gate us   opened   be
      "That heaven's gate should be opened to us."
      (Orm 13988; Allen 1995: 382)

Between the use of examples like (54), with a preposed dative recipient, and until the use of a nominative experiencer passive, there is a gap: the nominative recipient passive does not directly replace the dative experiencer passive (Allen 1995: 386). Nominative recipients with ditransitive verbs in the passive voice are not found until the late fourteenth century (see *she* in (56)).[23] In the fifteenth century they became more common.

(56) Item as for the Parke, she is alowyd Every yere a dere and xx
      Coupull of Conyes and all fewell Wode to her necessarye...
      "Item: as for the park, she is allowed a deer every year and 20
      pairs of rabbits and all firewood necessary to her..."
      (Award Blount, p. 207; Allen 2001: 51)

Just like in the active, originally DAT-NOM pattern in the passive—later DAT-ACC—is now NOM-ACC (for a short discussion on the similarity between English examples like (57) below and the Faroese DAT-ACC passive, see Barnes 1986: 35):

(57) I was given them/*they for Christmas
      (Maling & Sprouse 1995: 177)

---

23 However, earlier examples appear with verbs that have a PP or a clausal second in addition to the indirect object. We have left such verbs out of the discussion, since we have not fully studied such constructions, i.e., whether they should be considered monotransitives or ditransitives, or possibly neither.

The short overview given above is intended to show that some of the Germanic languages have undergone, or are undergoing, the same changes—in the same chronological order. It shows, then, that the change in the DAT-NOM construction to DAT-ACC is not unexpected at all. However, not all Germanic languages have gone through that change; some do not show any signs of it. German is one such language.

Whether German has oblique subjects is debated. The standard view has been that it does not exhibit oblique subjects, as seen by the fact that PRO subjects, corresponding to oblique arguments, have been considered ungrammatical:

(58) a. Ihm   wurde   geholfen
     him.DAT   was   helped
     "He was helped."
     (Zaenen, Maling, & Thráinsson 1985: 476)

     b. *Er   hofft   _____   geholfen   zu   werden
     he   hopes   PRO.DAT   helped   to   be.INF
     "He hopes to be helped."
     (Zaenen, Maling, & Thráinsson 1985: 477)

(59) a. Mir   gefällt   der   Mann
     me.DAT   likes.3SG   the.NOM   man
     "I like the man."

     b. *Ich   hoffe   _____   der   Mann   zu   gefallen
     I   hope   PRO.DAT   the.NOM   man   to   like.INF
     "I hope to like the man."

     c. Ich   hoffe   _____   dem   Mann   zu   gefallen
     I   hope   PRO.NOM   the.DAT   man   to   like.INF
     "I hope to please the man."

Although the dative arguments in (58a) and (59a) look like they might be subjects, they are not if PRO subjects in control infinitives cannot correspond to oblique case arguments (see (58b) and (59b)). Eythórsson & Barðdal (2005) argue against the standard view and give interesting evidence for their claim that German exhibits oblique subjects and, furthermore, that oblique subjects are a Germanic inheritance.[24]

---

24 Examples equivalent to the German examples in (58b) and (59b), marked with "*," are grammatical in Modern Icelandic. In these examples the subject is PRO, corresponding to a dative subject. However, a PRO subject corresponding to a nominative argument is ungrammatical (remember that *líka* is a pure DAT-NOM verb):

If German does not have oblique subjects, then it does not have nominative objects either. A change in the case of an argument from structural nominative to structural accusative is expected only if the argument is the object of the verb; thus, the change equivalent to the DAT-NOM > DAT-ACC in English, Faroese, Icelandic, and Swedish would be unexpected in German unless it exhibits nominative objects.

Why, then, is the change from DAT-NOM to DAT-ACC only at its beginning stages in Icelandic? Why has Icelandic not already undergone the same changes as, e.g., English and Swedish? Why does German not exhibit oblique subjects (according to the standard view)? We do not know the answer to these questions. For the last question, however, the obvious direction to look, as an anonymous reviewer points out, is that all the languages discussed here have changed word order from OV to VO, except German. Rögnvaldsson (1996), Barðdal & Eythórsson (2003) and Ingason, E. F. Sigurðsson, & Wallenberg (2011) give compelling evidence that oblique subjects existed in Old Icelandic (Old Norse).[25] This suggests that oblique subjects were not a consequence of the OV-to-VO change, since the change

---

(i) a. Strákarnir   vonast til   að   _____   verða hjálpað
     boys.the.M.PL.NOM   hope   for   to   PRO.DAT   be.INF   helped.DEF
     "The boys hope to be helped."

   b. *Strákarnir   vonast til   að   _____   verða hjálpaðir
     boys.the.M.PL.NOM   hope   for   to   PRO.NOM   be.INF   helped.M.PL.NOM
     (H. Á. Sigurðsson 1991: 336)

(ii) a. Ég   vonast   til   að   _____   líka   maðurinn
     I.NOM   hope   for   to   PRO.DAT   like.INF   man.the.NOM
     "I hope to like the man."

   b. *Ég   vonast   til   að   _____   líka   manninum
     I.NOM   hope   for   to   PRO.NOM   like.INF   man.the.DAT
     "I hope to please the man."

Interestingly, in Old Norse *líka* "like" was like *gefallen* "like" in the German example (59c), i.e., the subject of *líka* is found in the nominative case as shown in the following example from the Old Norwegian Book of Homilies; here the subject is PRO, corresponding to a nominative argument (and the object is then the dative argument):

(iii)   ef   *hann*   girnifc   at   _____   líca   guði   þæim   er...
     if   he   desires   to   PRO.NOM   like.INF   God.DAT   that.DAT   who
     "If he desires to be liked by God who..."
     or: 'If he desires to please God who...'
     (Indrebø 1931: 24.10–14, AM 619 4to)

In Old Norse *líka* was either a pure NOM-DAT verb or an alternating verb (like, e.g., Barðdal 2001 proposes). Given compelling evidence in favor of the hypothesis that Old Icelandic (Old Norse) exhibited oblique subjects, it is likely, at the very least possible, that *líka* was an alternating verb where either the dative or nominative argument could raise to the subject position.

25 Whether Old Icelandic had oblique subjects has been debated. Faarlund (1999, 2004), for example, argues that oblique subjects are not found in Old Icelandic texts. For a recent discussion, see Viðarsson (2009).

was in progress during the time period of Old Icelandic (see Ingason, E. F. Sigurðsson, & Wallenberg 2011).

3.5 Summary

There are striking similarities in the development of the changes discussed above, in English, Faroese, Icelandic, and Swedish, although they happen at different time periods (the changes occurring first in Old English, and last in Modern Icelandic). The status of the case system is also different at the time of the changes: English was undergoing a drastic change in the case system, which partly seems to precede the DAT > NOM change, while Icelandic and Faroese still have a rich case system.

The steps of the development, outlined by Falk (1995, 1997) for Swedish, seem to apply for the other languages as well, namely that monadic (active) and monotransitive (passive) verbs undergo the DAT > NOM change before dyadic (active) and ditransitive (passive) verbs do. In each language the changes in the DAT-NOM constructions in the active and the passive appear to be intertwined and all of them also have intermediate stages, which are expected under our analysis (see section 4). These include nonagreement with nominative object, NOM > ACC change of the object of dyadic and ditransitive verbs, and plural agreement with dative subjects.

In (60) we show the development for the languages discussed in this section, English, Faroese, and Swedish. We use Icelandic examples, even though Icelandic has undergone only some of these changes. We expect Icelandic to follow the same path as the other languages.

(60) Step 1: DAT > NOM ((a) the active: monadic verbs, (b) the passive: monotransitives)

a.	Mér	kólnar	>	Ég	kólna	see (8), (32), (33), (46)
	me.DAT	gets.cold.3SG		I.NOM	get.cold.1SG	
	"I get cold."					
b.	Þeim	var	hjálpað	>	Þeir	voru	see (9), (34), (43)
	them.DAT	was.3SG	helped.DEF		they.M.PL.NOM	were.3PL	
					hjálpaðir		
					helped.M.PL.NOM		
	"They were helped."						

Step 2: DAT-NOM > NOM-ACC ((a) the active: dyadic verbs, (b) the passive: ditransitives)

1: DAT-nom > DAT-ACC[26]

a.	Mér	líkar	hún	>	Mér	líkar	hana	see (3), (35), (48)
	me.DAT	likes.3SG	she.NOM		me.DAT	likes.3SG	her.ACC	
	"I like her."							

26 We assume that before or at the beginning of this stage one can find occurrences of nonagreement with the nominative object. This can be seen in Modern Icelandic (see example (2)).

b.

Þeim	var	gefin	>	Þeim	var	see (7), (41), (42)
them.DAT	was.3SG	given.F.SG.NOM		them.DAT	was.3SG	
hún				gefið	hana	
she.F.SG.NOM				given.DEF	her.ACC	

"They were given her."

2: DAT-ACC > NOM-ACC[27]

a.

Mér	líkar	hana	>	Ég	líka	hana	see (36), (44), (50), (52)
me.DAT	likes.3SG	her.ACC		I.NOM	like.1SG	her.ACC	

b.

Þeim	var	gefið	hana	>	Þeir	voru	see (45), (57)
them.DAT	was.3SG	given.DEF	her.ACC		they.M.PL.NOM	were.3PL	(i) fn. 32
					gefnir	hana	
					given.M.PL.NOM	her.ACC	

4. ANALYSIS

Legate (2008) proposes that Case is established in the syntax but that it is realized in the morphology. We agree with that view and argue that such an approach is needed to account for Nominative Substitution (NS) with monadic verbs and the change of DAT-NOM case > DAT-ACC. In this section we limit the discussion to the active voice and leave the passive mostly aside. We propose that (a) NS is expected if accusative and dative case arguments of monadic verbs are a morphological realization of nominative Case and (b) that for Icelandic C speakers DAT-NOM case is a morphological realization of abstract NOM-ACC Case.

Our view is that usually there is a one-to-one correspondence between abstract Case and morphological case, but a distinction is possible while a change is under way.[28] Under those circumstances a speaker may use the "pre-change" morphological case while showing syntactic signs of the "post-change" abstract Case. Only if these signs are found do we assume there may be a distinction between abstract Case and morphological

---

27 Before or at the beginning of this stage we assume that there may be found instances of number agreement with the dative subject. This has been observed for Faroese (see (37) (Jónsson 2009b:151)) and English (see (49) (Allen 1995: 235)).

28 This goes against Legate's (2008: 90) claim that "[o]nly when a morphological realization of a particular abstract Case is not available do we find a distinction between abstract Case and morphological case." We believe that we can find a distinction between abstract Case and morphological case, even though a morphological realization of the Case in question does exist, for example with DAT-NOM verbs (abstract NOM-ACC) in Icelandic C. We claim that nominative case is not available for the subject of DAT-NOM verbs, not in the sense that the morphology does not exist, but in the sense that it cannot apply because another nominative already exists in the sentence (on the object). This is further discussed in footnote 32.

case.[29] A sign of an abstract nominative Case subject on a verb with morphological dative case is, for example, number agreement with the dative case subject (see section 4.2).

4.1 Nominative Substitution

For languages where morphological default case is absolutive, such as Warlpiri, Niuean, Enga, and Hindi, Legate (2008) proposes that even though the morphological case of subjects of intransitives and objects of transitives is realized as absolutive, they don't have the same abstract Case: the former has abstract nominative Case, and the latter abstract accusative Case. A similar claim can be made for NS in Icelandic (discussed in section 1). Most verbs described in the literature as showing NS are intransitives. Some of these verbs have transitive counterparts that take a nominative subject and an accusative or a dative object. In such cases the intransitive and the transitive often have a similar meaning, but not exactly the same, and the subject of the intransitive verb corresponds to the object of the transitive verb. In the following examples, we show the verbs *reka* and *hvolfa* used transitively and intransitively. In the intransitive use, see (61a), the meaning of *reka* is "drift," but the transitive can have several meanings. In the context given in (61b) it means "order (someone to go away)." *Hvolfa*, however, has the meaning "capsize" whether it is used intransitively or transitively, see (62).

(61) a. Bátinn   rak   á   land   intransitive of *reka*
     boat.the.ACC   drifted   to   land
     "The boat drifted to the shore."
     (Jónsson 2003: 154)

     b. Hann   rak   manninn   burt   transitive of *reka*
       he.NOM   drove   man.the.ACC   away
       "He ordered the man to go away."

(62) a. Bátunum   hvolfdi   á   miðju   vatninu   intransitive of *hvolfa*
     boats.the.PL.DAT   capsized.3SG   in   middle   water.the
     "The boats capsized in the middle of the water."
     (Eythórsson 2000: 188)

29 To give a concrete example of this one might ask whether it is possible to claim that the nominative case subject of the unergative verb *dansa* "dance" in (i) has, say, dative Case. The answer is no because there are no signs of that. If the nominative case subject *við* "we" in (i) had abstract dative Case, we would expect examples where the subject does not agree in number and person with the finite verb:

     (i) Við   dönsum/*dansar   í kvöld
        we.NOM   dance.1PL/3SG   tonight
        "We dance tonight."
Such examples are ungrammatical to all speakers as far as we know.

b. Við   hvolfdum   bátunum   transitive of *hvolfa*
    we.PL.NOM   capsized.1PL   boats.the.PL.DAT
    "We capsized the boats."

The case of the subjects in the intransitive clauses in (61a) and (62a) is originally accusative and dative, respectively, but for some speakers the abstract Case is sometimes realized as nominative (hence Nominative Substitution; see (63) below).

(63) a. Báturinn   rak   á   land   NS with *reka*
        boat.the.NOM   drifted   to   land
        "The boat drifted to the shore."
        (Jónsson 2003: 154)

    b. Bátarnir   hvolfdu   á   miðju   vatninu NS with *hvolfa*
        boats.the.PL.NOM capsized.3PL in   middle   water.the
        "The boats capsized in the middle of the water."
        (Eythórsson 2000: 188)

To our knowledge, the case of the object of transitive *reka* and *hvolfa* (or any other transitive counterpart of an intransitive NS verb for that matter), see (61b) and (62b), is always accusative and dative, respectively, and never realized otherwise.

We take these facts to show that although the morphological case of the subject of intransitive *reka* and *hvolfa* and the object of the corresponding transitive verbs is identical, the abstract Case is not one and the same—the subject of the intransitive bearing abstract nominative Case but the object of the transitive bearing abstract accusative Case. Therefore, only the oblique subject of the intransitive verb may change to nominative, and not the oblique object of the transitive counterpart. We argue that for those who show intraspeaker variation regarding the case of the subject of the monadic verbs in question, the abstract Case is nominative (this goes also for speakers who always use nominative subjects with these verbs). For others, who consistently use accusative or dative with the NS verbs, we do not propose that the abstract Case of the subject is nominative.

A part of our proposal is that Icelandic C speakers, who accept DAT-ACC with nonalternating DAT-NOM verbs or alternating verbs, also accept NS of monadic verbs. Also, we propose that Icelandic A and B speakers (who prefer or allow number agreement with nominative objects) are less likely to accept NS. However, we didn't include NS sentences in our study (reported in section 2 above). We leave the correlation between these two phenomena for future research, but now we turn to discussion on DAT-NOM verbs established in the syntax as NOM-ACC.

4.2 Nominative Case Realized as Dative Case

In Icelandic, some speakers seem to have number agreement with the dative subject of DAT-NOM verbs. In examples like (64) *þeim líkuðu*, where the verb agrees in number with a third-person subject, it is impossible to tell whether this is also person agreement. Note that the singular object in (64) is in the nominative case:

(64) ...þar sem þeim   líkuðu   ekki þessi   mikla   aukning

        since them.PL.DAT liked.3PL not this.SG.NOM much.SG.NOM increase.SG.NOM

    á   fylgi

    on   support

    "Since they did not like this big increase in support..."

    http://tiger.blog.is/blog/tiger/entry/110811/, posted January 28, 2007

For these speakers, we argue that the subject is realized morphologically as dative case but established in the syntax as nominative Case.

However, not only have we discovered examples of number agreement, but also of person agreement with oblique subjects. These are not, though, examples of DAT-NOM verbs; *leiðast* in (65a) means "be bored" and is used as a monadic verb, and *dreyma* "dream" in (65b) is used with an oblique subject (accusative or dative) and a prepositional phrase:

(65) a. Hitt   skiptið   var   þegar   mér   og   Helgunni   minni

      other   time   was   when   me.DAT   and   Helga.the.DAT   mine.DAT

      leiddumst   geggjað

      were.bored.1PL   crazy

      "The other time was when I and Helga were very bored..."

      http://hallla.blogspot.com/2007_07_01_archive.html, posted July 19, 2007

    b. Þarna   voru   stelpurnar   sem   okkur   dreymum   um

      there   were   girls.the.PL.NOM   who   us.PL.ACC/DAT   dream.1PL   of

      að missa   sveindóminn   með

      to lose.INF   virginity   with

      "The girls, with whom we dream about losing our virginity, were there..."

      http://hreinirsveinar.blogcentral.is/blog/2005/9/5/pjallantk-a-leid-til-glotunnar/, posted September 5, 2005

The subject in (65a) is *mér og Helgunni minni* "me and my Helga." This coordinated DP then agrees with the verb *leiðast* "be bored" in person and number (1PL). Similarly, the accusative or dative subject *okkur* "us" in (65b) agrees in person and number (1PL) with the verb *dreyma* "dream." The first-person plural forms of these verbs are *leiddumst* and *dreymum*, respectively, but what would be expected are the third-person singular forms, *leiddist* and *dreymir*.

We have also found examples where the anaphoric element *sjálfur* "self" receives nominative case, even though it is coindexed with an oblique subject (similar to Jónsson's (2009b: 159) Faroese example, shown in (39b) above). In (66) *sjálfur* bears nominative case even though the subject *mér* "me" is in the dative case.

(66) a. Sjálfur líkar mér ekkert vel við nasista
self.NOM likes.3SG me.DAT not well to Nazis
"I do not like Nazis myself..."
www.hugi.is/ljod/providers.php?page=view&contentId=3180131, posted March 7, 2006

b. ...sjálfur langar mér í hund
self.NOM wants.3SG me.DAT in dog
"I want a dog myself..."
www.hugi.is/kettir/threads.php?page=view&contentId=6986464#i tem6986560, posted December 6, 2009

For the two speakers in (66) we might conjecture, as Jónsson (2009b) does for Faroese, that the nominative *sjálfur* shows that the dative case subject is really abstract nominative Case.

The following example is interesting, since it not only has number agreement with a dative subject, but also a nominative case floating quantifier modifying the dative subject. Note that the quantifier cannot modify the object; that is ruled out morphologically. (*Aðgerðarleysið* "the inaction" is a neuter singular noun, whereas *öll* "all" is the form of either feminine singular or neuter plural; here it is the latter form, modifying the neuter plural pronoun *þeim* "them.")

(67) Þeim leiddust öll aðgerðarleysið
them.PL.DAT were.bored.by.3PL all.PL.NOM inaction.the.NOM/ACC
"They were all bored of doing nothing."
http://ernah-761436.blogcentral.is/?page=5, posted December 13, 2006

These examples, taken from the Internet, must be regarded with care. They seem to be used mostly by younger speakers, which—presumably—have oblique subjects established in the syntax in nominative Case.

In our questionnaire we tested number agreement with a plural dative subject.

(68) Results for number agreement with dative subject of *líka* "like"

					yes	?	no
Kennurunum	líkuðu	ekki	þessi	hegðun	8	5	23
teachers.the.DAT	liked.3PL	not	this.NOM	behavior.NOM			
nemendanna							
students.the.GEN							

"The teachers did not like the students' behavior."

Note that the object is in the nominative case and that it is in the singular, as in (64) above. The plural form of the verb, which is in the past tense, thus agrees with the plural dative subject. Those speakers who rejected the sentence in (68) presumably did so because in order to be grammatical for them the verb would have to be in the third-person singular, *líkaði*, instead of plural *líkuðu*. More speakers accepted this sentence than the DAT-ACC version in (13) above, suggesting that those speakers have covert nominative Case on the subject, although the object is in the nominative case (we argue that the nominative object in (68) actually bears accusative Case; see next subsection). None of the speakers who accepted (68) accepted number agreement with a nominative object of *líka* in (25b): six of them rejected that sentence, and two found it questionable. These speakers are thus Icelandic C speakers, at least with respect to the verb *líka*.

We argue that for those who find (68) acceptable, the dative case argument really is an abstract nominative Case subject that triggers agreement. Legate (2008: 95) argues that agreement is "triggered by the highest DP bearing structural abstract Case." For Icelandic A and B speakers, dative subjects with DAT-NOM verbs bear inherent abstract Case. For those speakers the nominative object is the highest (and the only) DP bearing structural abstract Case and thus it can trigger agreement. For Icelandic C speakers, however, both the dative case subject and the nominative object bear structural abstract Case, nominative and accusative, respectively. The dative case subject is then the highest DP bearing structural abstract Case and that DP can trigger agreement, not the lower one (the nominative case object).

In this article we focus on analyzing the Icelandic C variety, and in order to do so we adopt Jónsson's (2009b) Covert Nominative Hypothesis for Faroese, where nominative Case on dative subjects is assigned in Spec,T, by T. Although Jónsson (2009b) doesn't explicitly say it, dative case is possibly checked in Spec,Appl (within the *v*P) but then, as mentioned, assigned nominative Case in Spec,T. This approach might be too simplistic, though.

Cardinaletti (2004) argues that different types of subjects occupy different subject positions. It might be possible to account for the difference between Icelandic C (nonagreement) and Icelandic A (number agreement) in such a way. Then an IP might consist of NumberP, PersonP, and TP (see H. Á. Sigurðsson & Holmberg 2008; see also H. Á. Sigurðsson 2000, 2006). For

Faroese (Jónsson 2009b) and Icelandic C the dative subject might move to Spec,Number, rendering number agreement with the dative case subject. In cases like (65) where the verb agrees with the dative subject not only in number but also in person, the subject presumably occupies a higher position, namely Spec,Person. For Icelandic A, on the other hand, the dative subject might occupy a lower subject position, for example Spec,T.

4.3 Accusative Case Realized as Nominative Case

Nominative on subjects and objects is standardly said to be connected to T, and accusative is then connected to v (see, though, e.g., Alexiadou 2003, who argues against this). However, Eythórsson & Jónsson (2009), who build on H. Á. Sigurðsson (2000), claim that for speakers who do not allow number agreement with nominative objects in DAT-NOM constructions (Icelandic C speakers), v always assigns nominative case to the object. Under that approach no link can be established between T and the nominative object, rendering obligatory nonagreement. We agree with their suggestion. Thus, for these speakers, the nominative object in (69b) is assigned its case in the same way as the structural accusative object in (69a).

(69) a. Konan   drap   manninn
        woman.the.NOM   killed man.the.ACC
        "The woman killed the man."

    b. Mér   líkar   bílarnir
       me.DAT   likes.3SG cars.the.PL.NOM
       "I like the cars."

Our interpretation of this is that the nominative case in (69b) is really abstract accusative Case.

As discussed above, for many speakers, number agreement (as in (70b)) with the nominative object is either preferred (the Icelandic A variety in H. Á. Sigurðsson & Holmberg 2008) or optional (Icelandic B) in the DAT-NOM construction in Icelandic, whereas for other speakers (Icelandic C) nonagreement (as in (70a)) is required.

(70) a. Mér   líkar   bílarnir
        me.DAT   likes.3SG cars.the.PL.NOM

    b. Mér   líka   bílarnir
       me.DAT   like.3PL   cars.the.PL.NOM

However, this is restricted to number. Thus, person agreement is excluded (H. Á. Sigurðsson 1996, 2006) in all varieties—this includes number agreement with nominative objects that are first- and second-person pronouns (H. Á. Sigurðsson & Holmberg 2008).

(71) a. Henni   *leiddumst   /?*leiddust   við
       her.DAT   were.bored.by.1PL / were.bored.by.3PL we.PL.NOM
       "We bored her."
       (H. Á. Sigurðsson 1996: 28)

    b. Mér   *líkið   /?*líka   þið
       me.DAT like.2PL   / like.3PL   you.PL.NOM
       "I like you."

The Person Restriction (H. Á. Sigurðsson 2006; H. Á. Sigurðsson & Holmberg 2008) captures this: quirky dative blocks first- and second-person agreement in Icelandic A, B, and C. Only in Icelandic C, though, is a personal pronoun "not sharply unacceptable" (H. Á. Sigurðsson & Holmberg 2008: 256) as a nominative object. It follows, then, that the verb does not agree in number with the object (as in the following example; we don't mark (72a–b) with "?" even though "not sharply unacceptable" probably entails that many Icelandic C speakers don't find these examples particularly good):

(72) a. Henni   leiddist   við   *Icelandic C*
       her.DAT   was.bored.by.3SG   we.NOM
       "We bored her."

    b. Mér   líkar   þið
       me.DAT likes.3SG   you.PL.NOM
       "I like you."

This is not surprising if the nominative is assigned by *v* in Icelandic C, because then the object cannot agree with the verb (objects assigned by *v* in Icelandic don't agree with finite verbs).[30]

---

30 A consequence of the change from DAT-NOM to DAT-ACC should be that there is no restriction on the accusative object, i.e., it can be a first- or second-person pronoun (thanks to Rajesh Bhatt for pointing this out to us originally). In our survey for Icelandic, four speakers accepted accusative object, which was a second-person pronoun, with the verb *leiðast* "be bored by" (compare this to the results for *leiðast* in (18) above, where three accepted an accusative object):

(i) Results for a second-person plural object with *hundleiðast*   yes ? no
    "be very bored by"
    Mér   hundleiðist   ykkur!   4   7   25
    me.DAT is.very.bored.by.3SG you.PL.ACC
    "You bore me to death."

Now take a look at the following ECM constructions:

(73) a. Ég   lét   hana   verða   *reið/reiða
       I   let   her.F.ACC   become.INF   angry.F.NOM/ACC
       "I made her become angry."

    b. Ég   lét   hana   slá   manninn
       I   let   her.ACC   hit.INF   man.the.ACC
       "I made her hit the man."

    c. Ég   lét   hana   ýta   *manninn/manninum
       I   let   her.ACC   push.INF   man.the.ACC/DAT
       "I made her push the man."

The ECM verb *láta* "let" takes a bare infinitive complement. *Láta* licenses the accusative case on the subject and the adjectival predicate in the embedded clause in (73a). However, only the accusative on the subject is licensed by *láta* in (73b), since the main verb in the embedded clause assigns the object its case. This is further confirmed in (73c), where the object in the embedded clause gets not accusative case from *láta* but lexical dative from *ýta* "push."

But what about nominative objects in DAT-NOM constructions with the ECM verb *láta* "let"? According to Wood (2011), nominative is ungrammatical with the DAT-NOM verb *nægja* "suffice" under the ECM verb *láta*.

(74) a. *Ég   lét   mér   nægja   tveir   miðar
       I   let   me.DAT   suffice.INF   two.PL.NOM   tickets.PL.NOM
    b. Ég   lét   mér   nægja   tvo   miða
       I   let   me.DAT   suffice.INF   two.PL.ACC   tickets.PL.ACC
       "I let myself make do with two tickets."
       (Wood 2011: 2)

If this is true for all speakers, including those Icelandic C speakers who do not accept accusative case object but still always prefer nonagreement with the verb, then nominative case is probably not assigned by *v*. This, however, remains to be studied. For now, we can only predict that for those speakers who do not have number agreement with nominative case object (Icelandic C), only (74a) is grammatical, since *v* assigns the object its case (like it does in (73b–c))—then the paradigm in (74) is borne out for Icelandic A and B speakers and also for those Icelandic C speakers who accept accusative objects with DAT-NOM verbs; for Icelandic A and B speakers the accusative on "two tickets" in (74b) is assigned by *láta* "let" but for Icelandic C speakers it is assigned by *v*.[31]

---

31 The pattern of DAT-NOM verbs in ECM constructions is more complicated than shown in (74). Not all DAT-NOM verbs take an accusative object in an ECM

Finally, agreement with dative subjects of DAT-NOM verbs in Icelandic may uncover the Case of the object. In Faroese, the object of DAT-NOM verbs is usually in the accusative case, including when there is number agreement with the dative subject (see (37) above). In Icelandic, however, we have seen examples of number agreement with dative subjects where the object is, surprisingly, assigned not accusative case (see (64) and (68)) but nominative. These examples suggest that, for some speakers, covert nominative Case on the morphologically dative subject is possible even if the object is morphologically nominative. Now, two possibilities arise concerning the syntactic Case of the two arguments: either the subject and the object both have nominative Case, or only the dative case subject gets covert nominative Case and the nominative case object gets accusative Case. We find it highly unlikely that two arguments can be assigned nominative Case.[32] Thus, we propose that the object gets covert accusative Case, assigned by v.

---

construction with *láta* (those Icelandic C speakers who accept DAT-ACC would be an exception from this). For example, nominative object with *líka* "like" in such a construction is usually preferred to acccusative.

(i) Ég   læt   mér   ekki   líka   svona dónaskapur /??dónaskap
    I   let   me.DAT not   like.INF such rudeness.NOM /??ACC
    "I don't let myself like such rudeness."
    (Wood 2011: 2)

Also, which ECM verb is used matters. Accusative case objects (with DAT-NOM verbs) under *telja* "believe" are less acceptable than under *láta* (Wood 2011; see, however, Jónsson's (1996: 170) examples with *telja*).

32 This is expected, since only one nominative c/Case is assigned (Yip et al. 1987, H. Á. Sigurðsson 2003) in other than predicate constructions, contra Barðdal's (2009) analysis of the change, which states that the reason for the dative subjects of DAT-NOM verbs resisting morphological change longer than the objects is that dative subjects are higher in type frequency than nominative objects. According to such an analysis, two nominative arguments of the same verb could be grammatical.

Eythórsson's (2009) results on the DAT-NOM ditransitive passive in Faroese confirm that two nominative cases at once are ruled out. In his acceptability judgment task none of the sixty-two informants found the NOM-NOM case pattern in (i-a) grammatical. However, nine speakers found the NOM-ACC pattern in (i-b) grammatical, showing that the DAT-NOM passive is more likely to develop into NOM-ACC than NOM-NOM.

(i)	Results for *giva* "give" in ditransitive passive in Faroese			*yes*	*?*	*no*
a.	Gentan	bleiv	givin	teldan	0	0	62
	girl.the.F.SG.NOM	was	given.F.SG.NOM	computer.the.F.SG.NOM			
	"The girl was given the computer."						
b.	Gentan	bleiv	givin	telduna	9	5	47
	girl.the.F.SG.NOM	was	given.F.SG.NOM	computer.the.F.SG.ACC			

It should be noted that two nominatives show up in predicate constructions in many languages, such as Icelandic, Faroese, German, and Swedish—the predicate is then arguably not assigned the nominative case but agrees in case with the subject (e.g., Maling & Sprouse 1995). In Icelandic the copula verbs *vera* "be" and *verða* "become" take a

For the DAT-NOM pattern examples in (64) and (68), the dative subject is assigned covert nominative Case. However, nominative case is unavailable to it, since the object receives nominative case, and two nominatives are ruled out. Accusative case, on the other hand, is available to the object, and this results in morphological realization of the accusative Case. Only then is the nominative case available to the subject.

4.4 Explaining the Diachrony

For the languages discussed above, we have seen that oblique subjects are replaced by the nominative. In general, oblique subjects of monadic verbs

---

nominative predicate (and a nominative subject), and so do a few others, such as *heita* "be called." In addition to these verbs some verbs take two accusative case arguments that form a small clause (where the relationship between the two arguments is predicational, *x* ("the dog") is *y* ("Guðmundur")):

(ii) Ég   kalla   hundinn   Guðmund
     I   call   dog.the.ACC   Guðmundur.ACC
     "I call the dog Guðmundur."

When those verbs are passivized or take the affix *-st*, they take two arguments, a subject and a predicate. When some of these verbs don't end with the affix *-st*, like *kalla* "call" and *gera* "do, make," and are passivized, they also take two nominative arguments, a subject and a predicate (see a discussion in Yip, Maling, & Jackendoff 1987):

(iii) a. Hundurinn   er   kallaður Guðmundur
         dog.the.NOM   is   called   Guðmundur.NOM
         "The dog is called Guðmundur."
      b. Hundurinn   kalla-st   Guðmundur
         dog.the.NOM   calls-st   Guðmundur.NOM
         "The dog is called Guðmundur."

Some other verbs take either an infinitival clause with a copula or a small clause. An example of this is the ECM verb *telja* "believe," which governs the accusative case on both the subejct and the predicate. When passivized, both the subject and the predicate become nominative:

(iv) a. Ég   tel   Maríu   (vera)   snilling
        I   believe   Mary.ACC   (be.INF)   genius.ACC
        "I believe Mary to be a genius."
     b. María   er   talin   (vera)   snillingur
        Mary.NOM   is   believed   (be.INF)   genius.NOM
        "Mary is believed to be a genius."
        (Thráinsson 2007: 158)

For a deeper discussion on predicates in Icelandic we refer the reader to Thráinsson (2007).

Although we predict that two nominatives in Germanic languages at different diachronic stages are ruled out in other than predicate constructions, we don't make the claim that this is universally true in all languages that show case morphology because, as an anonymous reviewer points out, two nominatives are possible in, e.g., Korean (see Maling 2000).

in the active and monotransitives in the passive change before subjects of dyadic verbs and ditransitives.

The change of oblique subjects of monadic verbs and monotransitives needs only one step, that is, the substitution by the nominative case. In the case of oblique subjects of dyadic verbs and ditransitives, however, the oblique subject cannot be substituted with the nominative since that would result in the sentence having two nominatives, which is ruled out (in the examples in this subsection we use Icelandic, even though Icelandic has not undergone the changes discussed here):

(75) Mér   > *Ég   líkaði   bílarnir
      me.DAT   I.NOM   liked.1SG   cars.the.PL.NOM
      "I liked the cars."

Even though the same change is going on for monadic and monotransitive verbs, on the one hand, and dyadic and ditransitive verbs, on the other hand, that is, oblique subjects having abstract nominative Case, the nominative object blocks the oblique subject from receiving morphological nominative case.

Before the dative subject of dyadic and ditransitive verbs can change to nominative, there must be some changes to the nominative object. We assume that first the object gets abstract accusative Case, even though it may be realized morphologically as nominative. An indication of this is the Icelandic C variety, where nonagreement is obligatory (see results in our questionnaire for *líka* "like" in (25) above). We assume this happens after (or possibly at the same time as) the subject gets nominative Case. If the subject was still in dative Case, the sentence would have no nominative. That would go against, for example, H. Á. Sigurðsson's (2003)) Sibling Correlation, which states that structural accusative Case is not assigned in the absence of nominative Case (for similar accounts see, among others, Yip, Maling, & Jackendoff 1987, Marantz 1991/2000, Woolford 2003).

The next step, then, is for the object to get morphological accusative case:

(76) Mér   líkaði   bílana
      me.DAT   liked.3SG   cars.the.PL.ACC

As our examples in section 2.2 show, some Icelandic speakers seem to be at this stage.

It is predicted that next the subject receives nominative case, since nothing is holding back the change of the subject. These changes in the dyadic DAT-NOM construction in the active correspond to the steps outlined in Hrafnbjargarson (2004) for English and Mainland Scandinavian.

(77) Ég   líkaði   bílana
      I.NOM   liked.1SG   cars.the.PL.ACC

Icelandic has not reached this stage, but Faroese seems to be in the middle of these stages, while English and the Scandinavian languages have completed the change. As we can see, this explains the chronological order of the change of oblique subjects as outlined by Falk (1995, 1997), for the first two steps.

As mentioned above, in Swedish the passive of ditransitives resists the change the longest (Falk 1995, 1997), and this also seems to be the case for Faroese and English. In Icelandic, this is less clear: it seems that either the change from DAT-NOM to DAT-ACC in the passive happens at the same time as in the active, or even earlier. The reason this is the last step in some languages but not in others remains unclear. We want to point out that a possible factor might be which DP is usually moved in the ditransitive passive: the DP corresponding to the indirect object in the active, or the one corresponding to the direct object. In at least earlier English and Modern Faroese, the DP corresponding to the direct object in the active is preferred as the subject in the ditransitive passive. In Icelandic, however, the DP corresponding to the indirect object is usually moved to subject position in the ditransitive passive.

This means that the third step, which Falk (1995, 1997) gives, does not have to be the third step in all languages. It seems to be true for English, Faroese, and Swedish, but probably not for Icelandic. The conclusion is that monadic verbs in the active voice change before the dyadic verbs do, and monotransitives in the passive voice change before the ditransitives do.

5. CONCLUSION

In this article, we have argued that a change from DAT-NOM to DAT-ACC is under way in Icelandic. To show this, we reported results from a small survey we conducted. However, we believe this change is currently only at its beginning stage. We would like to emphasize the necessity to investigate this further. The thematic role of the dative subject appears to be an important factor. Also, what types of verbs are involved, that is, whether they are pure DAT-NOM verbs or alternating verbs, might be relevant. By comparing Icelandic to related languages—English, Faroese, and Swedish—we have shown that this change is, in fact, expected.

Furthermore, we agree with Legate (2008) in that Case is established in the syntax but then case is realized in a postsyntactic morphology. We have argued along the lines that NOM-ACC Case is disguised in the Icelandic C variety, first as DAT-NOM case, and then as DAT-ACC, before becoming NOM-ACC case, eventually.

We have shown that the chronological development of the change of dative subjects is very similar between the languages listed above: dative case subjects of monadic verbs in the active change before dative subjects of dyadic verbs do, and, similarly, dative subjects of monotransitives in the passive change before dative subjects of ditransitives do. Our account of Case in disguise explains this development: the abstract Case of dative case subjects becomes nominative, but the nominative object of DAT-NOM verbs prevents the subject from becoming morphologically nominative until the morphological case of the object has changed from nominative to accusative. Nothing, however, prevents nominative Case subjects of monadic and monotransitive verbs from being realized in the morphology as nominative case. Therefore, they are the first to show up with nominative subjects.

TEXTS CITED

Here we list the texts we cite in the examples above. We do not, however, list blogs and newspaper texts for Modern Icelandic. Linguistic texts from which examples are taken are, of course, found in the References.

ENGLISH

Examples from earlier English are taken from Allen (1995, 2001) and Hrafnbjargarson (2004). We cite them like they do. The comments on the texts are taken from Allen (1995). However, Allen's examples from ÆLS (Basil) and Lk (WSCp) are taken from *COE* (Antoinette Healey and Richard Venezky, *A Microfiche Concordance to Old English* [Toronto: Centre for Medieval Studies, University of Toronto, 1980]), and the example from "Cristes milde moder" is taken from *MED* (*Middle English Dictionary*, edited by Hans Kurath and Sherman Kuhn [Ann Arbor: University of Michigan Press, 1956]). We cite those examples like *COE* and *MED* do.

Old English

Ælc.P. = *Homilies of Ælfric: A Supplementary Collection*. Edited by John Pope, EETS 259 and 260, 1967. Cited by homily and line number.

ÆLS (Basil) = Saint Basil: Skeat, 1881–1900 I, 50–90; W. W. Skeat, *Ælfric's Lives of Saints*, 4 vols., EETS 76, 82, 94, 114 (London; rpt. in 2 vols., Oxford: Oxford University Press, 1966). Citation is by line no. assigned by DOE, following the lineation of the edition.

cobeowul = *Beowulf*. From the York Poetry Corpus. Source: *Beowulf and Judith: The Anglo-Saxon Poetic Records*, vol. 4, 3.1–98.3182. Edited by E. V. K. Dobbie. New York: Columbia University Press, 1953.

Lk (WSCp) = Luke (Cambridge, Corpus Christi College, MS 140): Skeat, 1871–1887, 14–238; W. W. Skeat, *The Four Gospels in Anglo-Saxon, Northumbrian, and Old Mercian Versions* (Cambridge; rpt., Darmstadt, 1970). Cited by chapter and verse numbers following edition.

The Thirteenth Century

AW = *The English Text of the Ancrene Riwle: Ancrene Wisse.* Edited by J. R. R. Tolkien. EETS 249, 1962. MS Cambridge, Corpus Christi College 402. Date: c. 1230, composition somewhat earlier. Cited by page and line number.

BrutC = *Laȝamon: Brut.* Edited by G. L. Brook and R. F. Leslie, EETS 250 and 277, 1963 and 1978. MS Cotton Caligula A. ix. Date: MS date is probably thirteenth century, but composition is considerably earlier, although post-1189.

"Cristes milde moder." In *English Lyrics of the XIIIth Century,* ed. C. Brown (1932). 3–8. Date: c. 1250. (Nero A.14)

Orm = *The Ormulum: With the Notes and Glossary of Dr. R. M. White.* 2 vols. Edited by Robert Holt. Rpt. New York: AMS Press, 1974. MS Oxford University, Junius I, Bodleian Library 5113. Date: usually dated c. 1200. Cited by line number.

The Fourteenth Century

A&M = *Of Arthour and of Merlin.* Edited by O. D. Macrae-Gibson, EETS 268, 1973. The longest of the poems found in the Auchinleck Manuscript (= *The Auchinleck Manuscript. National Library of Scotland Advocates' MS 19.2.1.* With an introduction by Derek Pearsall and I. C. Cunningham. [London: Scholar Press, 1977]).

Award Blount = *Award of Dower by Sir Thomas Blount.* In "The Early History of Mapledurham," by A. H. Cooke, *Oxfordshire Record Society* 7 (1925), 204–206. This document is dated 1375.

Ch. = *The Riverside Chaucer.* 3rd ed. Larry D. Benson, general editor. Boston: Houghton Mifflin, 1987. The abbreviations are those used in TK [= Tatlock and Kennedy's concordance to Chaucer's work and the *Romant of the Rose*] preceded by "Ch."; however, when the TK system of numbering differs from the Riverside system, the Riverside line reference is given first, and the TK reference is given in parentheses.

FAROESE

Dahl, Sverri. 1939. "Jón Arason biskupur." *Varðin* 19: 113–126.

OLD NORSE

Indrebø = *Gamal norsk homiliebok.* 1931. Cod. AM. 619 4°. Utgjevi for Kjeldeskriftfondet ved Gustav Indrebø. Oslo: Universitetsforlaget.

SWEDISH

The examples from earlier Swedish are taken from Falk (1995). We cite them like she does.

PK = *Sveriges krönika. Små stycken på forn svenska,* 219–248. Edited by G. E. Klemming. Stockholm, 1868–1881. Written c. 1452–1456.

ST = *Siælinna Thröst.* SFSS 59. Edited by S. Henning. Uppsala, 1954. Translated c. 1420.

ACKNOWLEDGMENTS

We wish to thank the editors and two anonymous reviewers, whose comments greatly improved the paper. Thanks to Anton Karl Ingason and Katrina Nicholas for reading an earlier draft of the paper. We also want to thank Joan Maling, Heimir Freyr Viðarsson, Joel C. Wallenberg and Matthew Whelpton for discussions and helpful comments. Special thanks go to Thórhallur Eythórsson, Jóhannes Gísli Jónsson, Halldór Ármann Sigurðsson, Höskuldur Thráinsson and Jim Wood.

REFERENCES

Alexiadou, Artemis. 2003. "On nominative case features and split agreement." In Ellen Brandner and Heike Zinsmeister (eds.), *New perspectives on case theory,* 23–52. Stanford, CA: Center for the Study of Language and Information.

Allen, Cynthia. 1995. *Case marking and reanalysis: Grammatical relations from Old to Early Modern English.* Oxford: Oxford University Press.

Allen, Cynthia. 2001. "The development of a new passive in English." In Miriam Butt and Tracy Holloway King (eds.), *Time over matter: Diachronic perspectives on morphosyntax,* 43–72. Stanford, CA: Stanford, Center for the Study of Language and Information.

Andrews, Avery. 1976. "The VP-complement analysis in Modern Icelandic." *North Eastern Linguistic Society* 6: 1–21.

Árnadóttir, Hlíf, and Einar Freyr Sigurðsson. 2008. "The glory of non-agreement: The rise of a new passive." Unpublished ms.

Barðdal, Jóhanna. 2000. "Oblique subjects in Old Scandinavian." *North-Western European Language Evolution* 37: 25–51.

Barðdal, Jóhanna. 2001. "The perplexity of Dat-Nom verbs in Icelandic." *Nordic Journal of Linguistics* 24: 47–70.

Barðdal, Jóhanna. 2009. "The development of case in Germanic." In Jóhanna Barðdal and Shobhana Chelliah (eds.), *The role of semantic, pragmatic and discourse factors in the development of case*, 123–159. Amsterdam: John Benjamins.

Barðdal, Jóhanna, and Thórhallur Eythórsson. 2003. "The change that never happened: The story of oblique subjects." *Journal of Linguistics* 39(3): 439–472.

Barnes, Michael P. 1986. "Subject, nominative and oblique case in Faroese." *Scripta Islandica* 37: 13–46.

Cardinaletti, Anna. 2004. "Towards a cartography of subject positions." In Luigi Rizzi (ed.), *The structure of IP and CP: The cartography of syntactic structures*, vol. 2, 115–165. New York: Oxford University Press.

Eythórsson, Thórhallur. 2000. "Fall á fallanda fæti? Um breytingar á frumlagsfalli í íslensku [Case in danger? On changes in subject case in Icelandic]." *Íslenskt mál* 22: 185–204.

Eythórsson, Thórhallur. 2002. "Changes in subject case-marking in Icelandic." In David W. Lightfoot (ed.), *Syntactic effects of morphological change*, 196–212. Oxford: Oxford University Press.

Eythórsson, Thórhallur. 2009. "Passive and case in Faroese." Unpublished ms.

Eythórsson, Thórhallur, and Jóhanna Barðdal. 2005. "Oblique subjects: A common Germanic inheritance." *Language* 81: 824–881.

Eythórsson, Thórhallur, and Jóhannes Gísli Jónsson. 2003. "The case of subject in Faroese." *Working Papers in Scandinavian Syntax* 72: 207–231.

Eythórsson, Thórhallur, and Jóhannes Gísli Jónsson. 2009. "Variation in Icelandic morphosyntax." In Andreas Dufter, Jürg Fleischer, and Guido Seiler (eds.), *Describing and modelling variation in grammar*, 83–96. Berlin: Mouton de Gruyter.

Faarlund, Jan Terje. 1999. "The notion of oblique subjects and its status in the history of Icelandic." *Working Papers in Scandinavian Syntax* 63: 1–44.

Faarlund, Jan Terje. 2004. *The syntax of Old Norse*. Oxford: Oxford University Press.

Falk, Cecilia. 1995. "Lexikalt kasus i svenska [Lexical case in Swedish]." *Arkiv för nordisk filologi* 110: 199–226.

Falk, Cecilia. 1997. *Fornsvenska upplevarverb [Experiencer verbs in Old Swedish]*. Lund: Lund University Press.

Føroysk orðabók. 1998. [*Faroese dictionary*]. Edited by Jóhan Hendrik W. Poulsen et al. Tórshavn: Føroya Fróðskaparfelag.

Hrafnbjargarson, Gunnar Hrafn. 2004. "Oblique subjects and stylistic fronting in the history of Scandinavian and English: The role of IP-Spec." PhD diss., University of Aarhus.

Ingason, Anton Karl. 2010. "Productivity of non-default case." *Working Papers in Scandinavian Syntax* 85: 65–117.

Ingason, Anton Karl, Einar Freyr Sigurðsson, and Joel Wallenberg. 2011. "Distinguishing change and stability: A quantitative study of Icelandic oblique subjects." A talk given at DiGS 13, University of Pennsylvania, Philadelphia, June 2–5.

Jónsson, Jóhannes Gísli. 1996. "Clausal architecture and case in Icelandic." PhD diss., University of Massachusetts, Amherst.

Jónsson, Jóhannes Gísli. 1997–1998. "Sagnir með aukafallsfrumlagi [Verbs with oblique subjects]." *Íslenskt mál* 19–20: 11–43.

Jónsson, Jóhannes Gísli. 2003. "Not so quirky: On subject case in Icelandic." In Ellen Brandner and Heike Zinsmeister (eds.), *New perspectives on case theory*, 127–163. Stanford, CA: Center for the Study of Language and Information.

Jónsson, Jóhannes Gísli. 2009a. "The new impersonal as a true passive." In Artemis Alexiadou, Jorge Hankamer, Thomas McFadden, Justin Nuger, and Florian Schäfer (eds.), *Advances in comparative Germanic syntax*, 281–306. Amsterdam: John Benjamins.

Jónsson, Jóhannes Gísli. 2009b. "Covert nominative and dative subjects in Faroese." *Nordlyd* 36(2): 142–164.

Legate, Julie Anne. 2008. "Morphological and abstract case." *Linguistic Inquiry* 39: 55–101.

Maling, Joan. 2000. "Whether to agree or not: The syntax of inalienable possession." In Akio Kamio, Ken-ichi Takami, and John Whitman (eds.), *Syntactic and functional explanations: A festschrift for Susumu Kuno*, 345–370. Tokyo: Kuroshio Press.

Maling, Joan, and Sigríður Sigurjónsdóttir. 2002. "The 'new impersonal' construction in Icelandic." *Journal of Comparative Germanic Linguistics* 5: 97–142.

Maling, Joan, and Rex A. Sprouse. 1995. "Structural case, specifier-head relations, and the case of predicate NPs." In Hubert Haider, Susan Olsen, and Sten Vikner (eds.), *Studies in comparative Germanic syntax*, 167–186. Dordrecht: Kluwer.

Marantz, Alec. 1991/2000. "Case and licensing." In Eric Reuland (ed.), *Arguments and case: Explaining Burzio's Generalization*, 11–30. Philadelphia: John Benjamins.

Rögnvaldsson, Eiríkur. 1996. "Frumlag og fall að fornu [Subject and case in Old Icelandic]." *Íslenskt mál* 18: 37–69.

Sigurðsson, Halldór Ármann. 1991. "Icelandic case-marked PRO and the licensing of lexical arguments." *Natural Language and Linguistic Theory* 9: 327–363.

Sigurðsson, Halldór Ármann. 1996. "Icelandic finite verb agreement." *Working Papers in Scandinavian Syntax* 57: 1–46.

Sigurðsson, Halldór Ármann. 2000. "The locus of case and agreement." *Working Papers in Scandinavian Syntax* 65: 65–108.

Sigurðsson, Halldór Ármann. 2003. "Case: Abstract vs. morphological." In Ellen Brandner and Heike Zinsmeister (eds.), *New perspectives on case theory*, 223–267. Stanford, CA: Center for the Study of Language and Information.

Sigurðsson, Halldór Ármann. 2006. "Agree in syntax, agreement in signs." In Cedric Boeckx (ed.), *Agreement systems*, 201–237. Amsterdam: John Benjamins.

Sigurðsson, Halldór Ármann, and Anders Holmberg. 2008. "Icelandic dative intervention." In Roberta D'Alessandro, Susann Fischer, and Gunnar Hrafn Hrafnbjargarson (eds.), *Agreement restrictions*, 251–279. Berlin: Mouton de Gruyter.

Svavarsdóttir, Ásta. 1982. "Þágufallssýki [Dative sickness]." *Íslenskt mál* 4: 19–62.

Thráinsson, Höskuldur. 1979. *On complementation in Icelandic*. New York: Garland.

Thráinsson, Höskuldur. 2005. *Setningar: Handbók um setningafræði* [Sentences: Handbook of syntax]. Íslensk tunga 3. Reykjavík: Almenna bókafélagið.

Thráinsson, Höskuldur. 2007. *The syntax of Icelandic*. Cambridge Syntax Guides. Cambridge: Cambridge University Press.

Thráinsson, Höskuldur, Ásgrímur Angantýsson, and Einar Freyr Sigurðsson, eds. 2011. "Tilbrigði í íslenskri setningagerð [Variation in Icelandic syntax]." Unpublished ms., University of Iceland.

Thráinsson, Höskuldur, Hjalmar P. Petersen, Jógvan í Lon Jacobsen, and Zakaris S. Hansen. 2004. *Faroese: An overview and reference grammar*. Tórshavn: Føroya Fróðskaparfelag.

Viðarsson, Heimir Freyr. 2009. "Tilbrigði í fallmörkun aukafallsfrumlaga: Þágufallshneigð í forníslensku? [Variation in case marking of oblique subjects: Dative substitution in Old Norse?]." *Íslenskt mál* 31: 15–66.

Wood, Jim. 2011. "Icelandic *let*-causatives and case." *Working Papers in Scandinavian Syntax* 87: 1–52.

Woolford, Ellen. 2003. "Burzio's Generalization, markedness, and locality constraints on nominative objects." In Ellen Brandner and Heike Zinsmeister (eds.), *New perspectives on case theory*, 301–329. Stanford, CA: Center for the Study of Language and Information.

Yip, Moira, Joan Maling, and Ray Jackendoff. 1987. "Case in tiers." *Language* 63(2): 217–250.

Zaenen, Annie, Joan Maling, and Höskuldur Thráinsson. 1985. "Case and grammatical functions: The Icelandic passive." *Natural Language and Linguistic Theory* 3(4): 441–483.

CHAPTER 5

Dative versus Accusative and the Nature of Inherent Case

JÓHANNES GÍSLI JÓNSSON

1. INTRODUCTION

Woolford (2006) argues that there are two kinds of oblique case cross-linguistically:[1] (a) inherent case licensed by various light/little v heads, and (b) lexical case licensed by lexical heads, such as V or P. This means that inherent case and lexical case are in complementary distribution with respect to licensing heads. According to Woolford (2006), inherent case is relatively predictable semantically and occurs on external arguments and goal arguments, but not on theme/internal arguments. Inherent case is exemplified by ergative case in ergative languages and dative goal arguments in languages like Icelandic, Latin, and German. By contrast, lexical case is idiosyncratic and may only occur on theme/internal arguments.

Although a division between two kinds of oblique case has often been proposed for Icelandic on semantic grounds (see Yip, Maling, & Jackendoff 1987, Maling 2002, Jónsson 2000, 2003), Woolford's (2006) analysis has never been tested against Icelandic data. In this article, I will do so and argue that her dichotomy is not empirically viable for Icelandic, where a third kind of oblique case must be recognized: semantically predictable case with theme arguments. Building on important insights by Maling (2002) and Svenonius (2002), I will show that a sizable and well-defined subclass of motion verbs only allows dative objects in Icelandic. On the standard assumption that arguments undergoing motion are themes, this shows that theme objects with inherent case are possible, contrary to Woolford's claims.

---

[1] Woolford (2006) uses the term "nonstructural case," but I prefer the shorter term "oblique case."

Of particular importance for my discussion below will be verbs that vary between accusative and dative object. Typically, these verbs denote some kind of motion: for example, *skalla* "head" and *hnoða* "knead," as shown in (1):

(1) a. *Messi* *skallaði* *boltann/boltanum* *í* *netið*
      Messi headed the.ball.ACC/DAT in the.net

   b. *Anna* *hnoðaði* *saman* *rúgbrauð/rúgbrauði*
      Ann kneaded together rye.bread.ACC/DAT

If examples of this kind involved formal variation without any semantic significance, they would surely be indicative of irregularity in the use of accusative and dative objects in Icelandic. However, as I will argue in section 3 below, this variation is based on semantic factors that also play a role in object case marking with verbs that do not show any variation. Thus, examples like (1a) and (1b) provide further evidence that dative themes in Icelandic can have inherent case.

Despite the variation illustrated in (1), there is an important difference between accusative and dative objects in that the accusative is structural case, whereas the dative is oblique case. This is shown by the standard test for this dichotomy, case preservation in passives, as dative is preserved in passives but accusative is not. For instance, there are two passive counterparts of (1a) and (1b) in Icelandic; the passives corresponding to (1a) are shown in (2):

(2) a. *Boltinn* *var* *skallaður* *í* *netið*
      the.ball.NOM was headed in the.net

   b. *Boltanum* *var* *skallað* *í* *netið*
      the.ball.DAT was headed in the.net

This shows that the dative objects of verbs like *skalla* and *hnoða*, or any other two-place verb in Icelandic, instantiate oblique case. The same is also true of dative indirect objects. Thus, we can safely assume that the dative objects under discussion here are relevant for the evaluation of Woolford's (2006) theory of oblique case.

It seems that lexical semantics play an important role for case marking in all languages that have a rich case system distinguishing between structural and oblique case. For instance, it is a well-known cross-linguistic generalization that dative arguments typically denote sentient but nonagent participants in events, such as recipients, benefactives, experiencers, and possessives (cf. the various contributions in Belle & Langendonck 1996). It is also well established within accusative languages that oblique subjects are typically experiencers and cannot be agents.

2. OBJECT CASE IN ICELANDIC

Accusative is the most common object case with two-place verbs in Icelandic, but the number of verbs taking direct dative objects is quite high, compared to, for example, German or Faroese.[2] According to Maling (2002), verbs with direct dative objects in Icelandic number almost five hundred. (For information about the token frequency of accusative and dative objects in Icelandic, see Barðdal 2008.) This high number combined with the fact that dative is readily used with many new transitive verbs (Barðdal 2001, 2008) suggests that dative is at least partly determined by the semantic properties of the verbs in question. Still, it has proven very difficult to delimit dative objects in Icelandic by precise semantic generalizations; the most ambitious effort to date is Svenonius (2002) (but see also Maling 2002, Sigurðsson 2009).

2.1 Some Verb Classes

Since accusative case is structural, and therefore assigned under syntactic conditions that are independent of theta-marking, there should be no semantic restrictions on accusative objects. This is indeed borne out, as transitive verbs with accusative objects are found in most classes of transitive verbs in Icelandic. However, as exemplified in (3) below, there are some verb classes that take dative objects exclusively.[3,4]

(3) a. Emission verbs: *blikka* "blink," *blæða* "bleed," *endurvarpa* "relay," *gjósa* "erupt, spew," *gubba* "vomit," *hringja* "ring," *hrækja* "spit," *leka* "leak," *míga* "urinate," *pissa* "urinate," *rigna* "rain," *skíta* "shit," *slefa* "drool," *sprauta* "spray, inject," *spúa* "spout," *stafa* "shine," *útvarpa* "broadcast," *æla* "vomit"

   b. Verbs of ballistic motion: *bomba* "hit hard, blast," *dúndra* "hit hard, blast," *fleygja* "toss," *henda* "throw away," *kasta* "throw," *skjóta* "shoot," *sparka* "kick," *varpa* "throw," *þeyta* "fling," *þruma* "hit hard, blast," *þrusa* "hit hard, blast," *þrykkja* "hit hard, blast"

   c. Pour verbs: *ausa* "scoop, ladle," *demba* "spill, pour out," *hella* "pour," *skvetta* "splash," *sletta* "splash," *sulla* "splash (around)"

---

2 As discussed by Jónsson (2009), there are only about one hundred verbs in Faroese that still select for dative direct objects.

3 The term "emission verb" is intended to cover not only those verbs that Maling (2002) labels "verbs of heavenly and bodily emission" but also various other verbs describing the emission of substance, light, or sound. Most of the verbs in this class are basically intransitive but are occasionally found with objects denoting the substance, light, or sound being emitted.

4 For a definition of "pour verbs," see Levin (1993: 115–166).

These lists are not exhaustive but still fairly representative, since all these verb classes are rather small (but see Jóhannsdóttir 1996 for more complete lists of these and other verbs discussed in this article). Two examples from each of these three classes are shown in (4).

(4) a. *Nautið meig þá öllu vatninu*
the.bull urinated then all.DAT the.water.DAT

b. *Eldfjallið gaus mikilli ösku*
the.volcano spewed much.DAT ash.DAT
"The volcano spewed a lot of ashes."

c. *Einar kastaði spjótinu 70 metra*
Einar threw the.javelin.DAT 70 meters

d. *Ég henti þessari bók í fyrra*
I threw this.DAT book.DAT in last.year
"I threw this book away last year."

e. *Óskar jós vatni úr brunninum*
Oscar scooped water.DAT off the.fountain

f. *Barnið hellti mjólkinni á gólfið*
the.child spilled the.milk.DAT on the.floor

If we take emission to be a kind of motion, the dative with these verbs can be subsumed under the generalization that verbs of translational motion always take dative objects. As discussed by Maling (2002), most transitive motion verbs in Icelandic take dative objects, and Svenonius (2002) makes the important observation that all motion verbs taking accusative objects denote accompanied or directed motion.[5] These verbs include the following:

(5) Motion verbs with accusative object: *bera* "carry," *ferja* "ferry," *flytja* "move, transport," *færa* "move," *draga* "pull, drag," *hefja* "raise, lift," *hífa* "lift, pull," *hreyfa* "move," *hrista* "shake," *keyra* "drive," *leggja* "place" put,' *reiða* "transport" (on horseback or bike), *setja* "put," *toga* "pull," *tosa* "pull, tug"

As far as I know, verbs of translational motion constitute the only class of two-place verbs in Icelandic that require dative objects. There are verb classes where dative objects are very common—for example, verbs of social interaction (cf. the verbs *hjálpa* "help," *fagna* "rejoice," *fylgja* "accompany,"

---

5 Interestingly, most of the English counterparts of the verbs listed in (5) are classified by Levin (1993) not as motion verbs but rather as verbs of sending and carrying, verbs of exerting force, or verbs of putting.

and *hlýða* "obey")—but accusative objects are also found with such verbs (cf. *aðstoða* "assist" and *elta* "chase"). This is unsurprising, since verbs of social interaction tend to take dative objects cross-linguistically (Blume 1998), a tendency that is presumably due to the fact that objects of such verbs denote animate participants with few proto-patient properties.

Turning to accusative objects, there are some well-defined verb classes in Icelandic that take accusative objects exclusively. Some of these classes are exemplified in (6):[6]

(6) a. Verbs of creation, preparation, and transformation: *baka* "bake," *byggja* "build, erect," *elda* "cook," *grilla* "grill," *hanna* "design," *hita* "heat," *laga* "make," *mála* "paint," *prjóna* "knit," *reisa* "erect," *rista* "toast," *sauma* "sew," *semja* "write," *sjóða* "cook," *skapa* "create," *smíða* "build," *spæla* "fry (an egg)," *steikja* "fry," *tálga* "carve," *teikna* "draw," *vefa* "weave"

   b. Verbs of forceful contact:[7] *berja* "hit," *biddslappa* "punch, bitch-slap," *buffa* "beat the crap out of," *flengja* "spank," *hnífa* "stab with a knife," *hýða* "flog," *kjöta* "attack (in football)," *kýla* "punch," *lemja* "hit," *ljósta* "strike," *löðrunga* "slap," *rassskella* "spank," *rota* "knock out," *stanga* "butt," *stinga* "stab," *tækla* "tackle, foul"

   c. Change-of-state verbs (degree achievements): *auðga* "make richer," *bleyta* "wet," *dýpka* "make deeper," *frysta* "freeze," *fylla* "fill," *herða* "tighten," *kæla* "cool," *lengja* "lengthen, extend," *minnka* "make smaller, diminish," *óhreinka* "make dirty," *skerpa* "sharpen," *styrkja* "strengthen," *stytta* "shorten," *tæma* "empty," *veikja* "weaken," *víkka* "widen," *þrengja* "tighten," *þynna* "dilute," *þýða* "defrost"

   d. Butter verbs: *bronsa* "bronze," *girða* "fence," *innramma* "frame," *króma* "chrome," *krydda* "spice," *merkja* "label," *múra* "plaster," *salta* "salt," *söðla* "saddle," *tjarga* "tar," *varalita* "lipstick," *veggfóðra* "wallpaper"

Examples from each of these verb classes are provided in (7), but note that the first two classes here will be particularly relevant for the discussion of the variation between accusative and dative objects in section 3.

---

6 The term "butter verbs" is taken from Levin (1993: 120–121). As she explains, these verbs mean "to put X in or on something," where X refers to the thing specified by the verb.

7 Note that some of these verbs are fairly recent slang verbs: e.g., *biddslappa* "punch, bitch-slap," *buffa* "beat the crap out of," and *hnífa* "stab with a knife." That these verbs consistently take accusative objects underlines the fact that the connection between accusative case and forceful contact is still operative and is not an artifact of language history.

(7) a. *Eiríkur*   *bakaði*   *kökuna*
       Eric   baked   the.cake.ACC

   b. *Einhver*   *barði*   *þjóninn*
      someone   hit   the.waiter.ACC

   c. *Halldór*   *kældi*   *bjórinn*
      Halldór   cooled   the.beer.ACC

   d. *Sigga*   *innrammaði*   *myndina*
      Sigga   framed   the.picture.ACC

As we will discuss shortly, there are various change-of-state verbs that select for dative objects in Icelandic but none of them are degree achievements.

Intuitively, what all the verbs listed in (6) have in common is that they lexicalize some kind of result. This is fairly clear with creation, preparation, and transformation verbs as well as with change-of-state verbs; contact can be seen as a result (Erteschik-Shir & Rapoport 2010), and with butter verbs the result is an entity or substance being attached to the locatum argument. Still, it not the case that all result verbs take accusative objects in Icelandic. Some verbs denoting change of state select dative objects. This is exemplified in (8) with the verbs *fresta* "postpone," *fjölga* "increase in number," *eyða* "spend, annihiliate," *breyta* "change," and *ljúka* "finish":

(8) a. *Foreldrarnir*   *vildu*   *fresta*   *brúðkaupinu*
       the.parents   wanted   postpone the.wedding.DAT
       "The parents wanted to postpone the wedding."

   b. *Fyrirtækið*   *fjölgaði*   *starfsfólkinu*
      the.company   increased   the.staff.DAT
      "The company increased the number of employees."

   c. *Sigga*   *eyddi*   *öllum*   *skjölunum*
      Sigga   destroyed   all.DAT   the.documents.DAT

   d. *Þessi*   *tækni*   *breytir*   *miklu*   *fyrir*   *patients*
      this   technology   changes   much.DAT   for   sjúklinga

   e. *Enginn*   *lauk*   *ritgerðinni*   *á*   *réttum*   *tíma*
      nobody   finished   the.paper.DAT   on   right   time
      "Nobody finished the paper on time."

Accusative-taking change-of-state verbs in Icelandic correspond quite closely to the so-called degree achievements, the deadjectival change-of-state verbs of variable telicity that have been so widely discussed in the lexical semantics literature (see, e.g., Kearns 2007, Kennedy & Levin 2008). The dative-taking change-of-state verbs, like those exemplified above, are of a different kind. Apparently, these verbs are always telic in the presence of a quantized object, and only a handful of them are deadjectival.

2.2 Datives and Event Structure

The importance of lexical semantics for object case in Icelandic is probably most evident with verbs that alternate between accusative and dative objects. For many of these verbs, the accusative is used for physically affected objects, but the dative is used for objects undergoing motion (Svenonius 2002, Barðdal 1993). One of these verbs is *sópa* "sweep":

(9) a. *Jón   sópaði   gólfið*
        Jón   swept   the.floor.ACC

     b. *Jón   sópaði   snjónum   burt*
        Jón   swept   the.snow.DAT   away

This alternation is fully expected given the data we have examined so far, as (9a) involves a locatum object and all such objects bear accusative case (cf. the butter verbs in (6d)), whereas (9b) describes translational motion and all objects undergoing such motion have dative case.

To account for alternations like the one exemplified in (9) and the distribution of dative objects more generally, Svenonius (2002) makes crucial use of the idea that events associated with verbs divide into smaller events where each subevent is linked to a particular participant in the whole event. He claims that dative case in Icelandic is assigned to objects if the verb denotes two subevents that do not overlap temporally. This is explicitly stated in the following biconditional (from Svenonius 2002: 209):

(10)   In a syntactic context α representing an event x composed of subevents y and z, dative case is licensed in α iff the temporal relationship of y and z is not total overlap.

This derives the alternation in (9a–b) because the two subevents in (9a) are temporally indistinguishable: the action of the agent cannot be teased apart from the effects on the object. As a result, the object can only be accusative in (9a). In (9b), the subevent associated with the agent need not last for the duration of the movement subevent, since the agent does not completely determine the outcome of the second subevent. Hence, the object in (9b) is assigned dative case.

The biconditional in (10) seems to be correct for dyadic verbs involving two subevents that do not completely overlap temporally. However, (10) is too strong for examples where the two subevents are temporally nondistinct, as it incorrectly rules out dative objects in such cases. This is shown most clearly by verbs of accompanied or directed motion that take dative objects in Icelandic (e.g., *mjaka* "budge, move slowly," *lauma* "sneak," *lyfta* "raise," and *smeygja* "slip, slide"). Presumably, it is also shown by various other dative-taking verbs such as *áfrýja* "appeal," *gleyma* "forget," *lýsa* "describe," *trúa* "believe," *treysta* "trust," and *vorkenna* "pity." With all these verbs, it is hard to see how the whole event can be divided into two temporally distinct two subevents.

The conclusion is that although the generalization in (10) is stated as a biconditional, it only works in one direction, by correctly excluding accusative objects with verbs denoting two temporally separable events. Still, the important point is that the systematic exclusion of accusative objects from verbs of this kind means that the dative with these verbs is semantically predictable, and this is exemplified by the three verb classes shown in (3). This runs counter to Woolford's (2006) analysis which does not allow for inherently case-marked themes or internal arguments.

2.3 Themes versus Goals

At this point, it is worthwhile to ask if semantically predictable dative objects of motion verbs can be analyzed as some kinds of goals so that they would be compatible with Woolford's (2006) analysis. Prima facie, this is not implausible in view of the fact that motion verbs can sometimes be paraphrased as ditransitives, as in English examples like *kick the ball* vs. *give the ball a kick*. In this particular case, the theme object of *kick* seems to correspond semantically to the goal object of *give* (*a kick*). Icelandic has some pairs like these but most of them have nothing to do with motion and they do not distinguish between accusative and dative direct objects. Thus, along with expected cases like *hjálpa e-m* "help somebody (dat)" versus *veita e-m hjálp* "give somebody (dat) help" we also find *heiðra e-n* "honor somebody (acc)" versus *veita e-m heiður* "give somebody (dat) honor."

I am not aware of any evidence independent of case marking to suggest that dative objects of motion verbs in Icelandic are more like goals than themes. By contrast, there are many good reasons to reject any proposed parallels between goals and dative objects of motion verbs. Goals are clearly different from such objects in that they necessarily denote sentient beings. In that respect, goals are very similar to experiencers, a point often made in discussions of dative case marking. This contrast between goals and themes is also reflected in Faroese, where goals are typically marked dative but objects of motion verbs are (nearly) always accusative (Jónsson 2009).

There is also an important contrast in Icelandic that shows up in middle formation with the suffix *–st* in Icelandic. As exemplified below, such middles preserve dative with goals but not with themes (see Jónsson 2003, Svenonius forthcoming):

(11) a. *Einhver   bauð   henni   að fara til Ítalíu*
    somebody invited her.DAT to go to Italy

 b. *Henni   bauðst   að fara til Ítalíu*
    her.DAT invited.ST to go to Italy
    "She got an invitation to go to Italy."

(12) a. *Bílstjórinn   kastaði   farþeganum   út   úr   bílnum*
    the.driver threw the.passenger.DAT out off the.car

 b. *Farþeginn   kastaðist   út   úr   bílnum*
    the.passenger.NOM thrown.ST out off the.car
    "The passenger was thrown out of the car (in an accident)."

These facts are important because they suggest yet another difference between goals and themes, namely that dative case assignment to goals involves a different case-assigning head than dative case assignment to themes. This fits nicely with the view that dative goals are case-licensed by a designated functional head in the vP-shell, for example, an applicative head (Cuervo 2003), whereas dative themes are assigned case by V. Moreover, goals in Icelandic get dative case by virtue of being goals,[8] whereas theme objects can get both accusative and dative case, depending on the semantic factors that we have already discussed in 2.1 and 2.2.

3. VARIATION BETWEEN DATIVE AND ACCUSATIVE OBJECTS

It should be clear from the data we have seen so far that the object case assigned by a two-place verb in Icelandic is often predictable from its meaning, as some verb classes only allow accusative objects, whereas other classes only select for dative objects. This is summarized in (13):

---

8 As discussed by Jónsson (2000), all indirect objects that are recipients or benefactives (subclasses of goals) get dative case in Icelandic.

	Accusative	Dative
(13) a. Verbs of creation, preparation, and transformation	+	−
b. Verbs of forceful contact	+	−
c. Change-of-state verbs (degree achievements)	+	−
d. Butter verbs	+	−
e. Emission verbs	−	+
f. Verbs of ballistic motion	−	+
g. Pour verbs	−	+

In this section, we will examine two-place verbs that can express semantic features that call for accusative case as well as features that trigger dative case, and these features relate to the verb classes in (13a), (13b), and (13f). The result is that these verbs vary between accusative and dative object.[9] Variation of this kind provides further evidence for the semantic predictability of dative theme objects in Icelandic, thereby contradicting the analysis of Woolford (2006).

To my knowledge, there are at least fifty to sixty verbs in Icelandic that vary between accusative and dative objects. These verbs have received very little attention in the linguistic literature so far (but see Maling 2000, 2002, for some examples). We will focus here on what seem to be the two biggest classes of such verbs, "ball verbs" and verbs of mixing or creating. The term "ball verb" is used here for verbs that describe the control of a ball or how a ball is put in motion (see 3.1 below). I have not done a detailed study of the diachrony of verbs varying between accusative and dative object, but it seems that the dative is usually the innovative case, at least with ball verbs, and it is gradually being extended at the expense of the original/standard accusative. Such extension is clearly the hallmark of inherent case, since lexical case only rarely spreads to replace other cases (see Jónsson & Eyþórsson 2011).

Since there are semantic differences between the accusative and the dative variant with the verbs discussed below, it is perhaps more accurate to talk about an "alternation" between dative and accusative objects rather than "variation." The term "variation" is justified by the fact that native speakers differ with respect to the acceptability of each variant. In the discussion below, I will abstract away from these differences, but the native speakers I have consulted are in broad agreement with my judgments about case assignment with these verbs.

---

9 As we will discuss shortly, the term "alternation" might be more appropriate here than "variation."

3.1 Ball Verbs

The variation discussed in this section concerns ball verbs. Some examples of ball verbs varying between accusative and dative object are shown in (14):

(14) a. *Markmaðurinn   sló   boltann/boltanum   yfir   markið*
the.goal.keeper   punched the.ball.ACC/DAT   over   the.goal

    b. *Messi   skallaði   boltann/boltanum   í   netið*
Messi   headed   the.ball.ACC/DAT   in   the.net

    c. *Albert   negldi   boltann/boltanum   fram*
Albert   nailed   the.ball.ACC/DAT   forward

I am aware of fourteen transitive ball verbs that show accusative/dative variation in Icelandic. These verbs are listed in (15):

(15)   Ball verbs showing ACC/DAT variation: *flengja* "spank, kick," *flikka* "flick," *framlengja* "extend," *hamra* "hammer," *hitta* "meet," *hreinsa* "clear away," *klína* "stick," *krossa* "cross," *negla* "nail, hit hard," *skalla* "head," *skrúfa* "screw, put a spin on," *slá* "hit," *snúa* "turn," *smyrja* "butter"

As the translations indicate, some of these verbs are basically verbs of forceful contact and when they are used as such only accusative is possible. This is shown in (16):

(16) a. *María   sló   mig/*mér*
Mary   hit   me.ACC/DAT

    b. *Zidane   skallaði   varnarmanninn/*varnarmanninum*
Zidane   headbutted   the.defender.ACC/DAT

    c. *Hann   vildi   ekki   flengja   börnin/*börnunum*
he   wanted   not   spank   the.children.ACC/DAT
"He did not want to spank the children."

Although this is difficult to see when ball verbs are accompanied by PPs or particles that indicate the direction of the motion as in (14), there is a subtle semantic difference between the two variants with ball verbs. While both the accusative and the dative variant assert contact with the object, only the latter variant asserts motion of the object. For instance, *skalla* + accusative means something like "make forceful contact with some entity using the forehead," whereas *skalla* + dative means something like "make forceful contact with some entity using the forehead and thereby cause that entity to move."[10] It should be clear from these paraphrases that the dative variant entails the accusative variant but not the other way around. This is shown by the fact that (17b) below is a contradiction but (17a) is not.

(17) a. *Jón   skallaði boltann   án þess að skalla honum   (neitt)*
      John headed the.ball.ACC without to head him.DAT anywhere

   b.**Jón skallaði boltanum   (burt) án þess að skalla hann*
      John headed the.ball.DAT away without to head him.ACC

One can utter (17a) if John makes contact with the ball with his forehead but still fails to cause the ball to move. This can happen, for example, if a player in the opposite team also manages to head the ball and his contact is stronger than John's so that he gets the ball moving. However, (17b) is a contradiction because it asserts that John got the ball moving by making contact with it by his forehead and yet failed to make contact with the ball.

The contrast between accusative and dative with verbs like *skalla* also shows up when the object denotes something that is necessarily moving, for example, *fyrirgjöf* "pass," in which case only accusative sounds natural:

(18) *Katrín skallaði fyrirgjöfina/??fyrirgjöfinni í   slána*
     Katrin headed the.pass.ACC/DAT   into the.bar

The dative is very odd here because it is tautological to assert that a moving ball is put into motion by heading it. An accusative object is fine here because in that case (18) states that the forehead was used to make contact with the moving ball. Note that (18) is different from examples where the object is a concrete entity like a ball because a ball is not necessarily moving when it is headed by someone, although this will nearly always be the case in a real game of football. Thus, one can imagine a scenario where someone is practicing his football skills by heading a ball that is not moving.

The ball verbs listed in (15) are verbs where many speakers can use both accusative and dative. For other ball verbs, accusative is clearly preferred, as in (19), or only dative is possible, as in (20). In all those cases, it can be argued that the crucial factors for case marking are forceful contact and ballistic motion, as before.

---

10 One may ask why only dative is possible here, since forceful contact is also involved, but this is what the generalization in (10) leads us to expect, since the subevents associated with the subject and object do not completely coincide temporally in this case.

(19) a. *Hún   sneiddi   boltann/??boltanum   fram   hjá   markmanninum*
       she   sliced   the.ball.ACC/DAT   past   the.goal.keeper

   b. *Jón   kreisti   boltann/?boltanum   í   netið*
      John   squeezed   the.ball.ACC/DAT   in   the.net

   c. *Hann   kiksaði   boltann/?boltanum   út   af*
      he   mishit   the.ball.ACC/DAT   out   off
      "He mishit the ball out of play."

(20) a. *Hann   mokaði   *boltann/boltanum   út   af*
        he   shovelled   the.ball.ACC/DAT   out   off

   b. *Bolton   dældi   *sendingar/sendingum   inn í   teiginn*
      Bolton   pumped   passes.ACC/DAT   into   the.penalty.box

   c. *Gunnar   þrusaði   *boltann/boltanum   í   stöngina*
      Gunnar   blasted   the.ball.ACC/DAT   in   the.post

The verbs in (19a–b) and (20a–b) are used in a metaphoric sense, and the preferred case in all these examples is the same that would be employed in a more literal sense of these verbs, accusative in (19a–b) and dative in (20a–b). There is a difference, though, in that dative is more acceptable in (19a–b) than accusative in (20a–b). The reason is that the verbs *sneyða* "slice" and *kreista* "squeeze" are not motion verbs in their basic sense, but when used in a football context they can be understood (at least by some speakers) as asserting caused motion, thereby licensing a dative object. By contrast, the verbs *moka* "shovel" and *dæla* "pump" are motion verbs in their basic sense, so nothing relevant to case marking is added by using them to describe getting a ball in motion.

The difference between (19c) and (20c) seems to be due to the fact that *kiksa* "mishit" is very specific about the kind of contact made with the ball. Hence, accusative is clearly preferred to dative. By contrast, *þrusa* "blast" does not assert any forceful contact. This is shown by the fact that *þrusa* can easily be used in handball, where the ball is usually put in motion without any forceful contact with the ball.

3.2 Verbs of Mixing or Creating

Some verbs have a dual status as verbs of mixing or verbs of creation in the presence of the particle *saman* "together," and this ambiguity is reflected in variation in object case marking. This is illustrated below with the verb *hnoða* "knead," but other verbs in this class include *flétta* "twist," *hræra* "mix, stir," and *tvinna* "twist, twine."

(21) a. *Anna   hnoðaði   saman   sykur,   hveiti   og   smjör*
      Ann   kneaded   together sugar.ACC wheat.ACC and butter.ACC

   b. *Anna   hnoðaði   saman   sykri,   hveiti   og   smjöri*
      Ann   kneaded   together sugar.DAT wheat.DAT and butter.DAT

There is a subtle semantic difference between (21a) and (21b) in that the accusative variant asserts that something is created but the dative variant indicates only mixing. Since creation involves a natural endpoint, that is the created object, the accusative variant with *hnoða saman* is clearly telic. This is shown by traditional tests for telicity such as compatibility with temporal phrases such as *in ten minutes* and incompatibility with phrases like *for ten minutes*:

(22) a. *Anna   hnoðaði   saman   sykur   og   smjör   á   tíu   mínútum*
        Ann   kneaded   together sugar.ACC and butter.ACC in ten minutes

   b. *Anna   hnoðaði   saman   sykur   og   smjör   í   tíu   mínútur*
      Ann   kneaded   together sugar.ACC and butter.ACC for ten minutes

My judgments about the dative variant are somewhat less clear, but they seem to point in the opposite direction, namely that the dative signals mixing without any natural endpoint:

(23) a.? *Anna   hnoðaði   saman   sykri   og   smjöri   á   tíu   mínútum*
         Ann   kneaded   together sugar.DAT and butter.DAT in ten minutes

   b. *Anna   hnoðaði   saman   sykri   og   smjöri   í   tíu   mínútur*
      Ann   kneaded   together sugar.DAT and butter.DAT for ten minutes

This contrast between accusative and dative objects is consistent with the fact that all verbs of creation, preparation, and transformation in Icelandic take accusative objects. This can also be seen when the verb *hnoða* is used without the particle *saman* to describe the preparation of food, in which case only accusative is possible:

(23) *Anna   hnoðaði   deigið/*deiginu*
      Ann   kneaded   the.dough.ACC/DAT

The verb *blanda* "mix" provides a nice illustration of the fact that creating calls for an accusative object whereas mixing triggers a dative object. This is shown by the following examples (see also Maling 2002):

(24) a. *Magga*   *blandaði*   *góðan*   *drykk*   *fyrir*   *mig*
       Magga   fixed   good.ACC   drink.ACC   for   me

    b.*Magga   *blandaði*   *góðum*   *drykk*   *fyrir*   *mig*
       Magga   fixed   good.DAT   drink.DAT   for   me

(25) a. *Hann*   *blandar*   *saman*   *óskyldum*   *hlutum*
       he   mixes   together   unrelated.DAT   things.DAT

    b.*Hann   *blandar*   *saman*   *óskylda*   *hluti*
       he   mixes   together   unrelated.ACC   things.ACC

Since mixing a drink is unambiguously an example of the preparation of food, only accusative is possible, as in (24). By contrast, mixing unrelated things—for example, in debates or argumentation—creates nothing, and as a result only dative can be used, as shown in (25).

There is one complication here that should be noted when verbs like *hnoða* take an object that names the created thing. (In (21), the object names the ingredients of the mixture.) This can be seen, for example, when *hnoða* is used metaphorically to describe the composition of poems, as in (26). Interestingly, dative is possible here as an alternative to accusative even though the interpretation is necessarily telic, as shown by the usual tests for telicity.

(26) a. *Róbert*   *hnoðaði*   *saman*   *eina*   *vísu*   **í/á*   *klukkutíma*
       Robert   kneaded   together   one.ACC   poem.ACC   for/in   an.hour

    b. *Róbert*   *hnoðaði*   *saman*   *einni*   *vísu*   **í/á*   *klukkutíma*
       Robert   kneaded   together   one.DAT   poem.DAT   for/in   an.hour

I have not been able to find any semantic difference between examples like (26a) and (26b), but the dative is presumably licensed by the fact that all particle verbs denoting hurried, clumsy, or imperfect creation only take dative objects in Icelandic. This is exemplified in (27):

(27) a. *Nemandinn*   *rubbaði*   *upp/saman*   *þessari*   *ritgerð*
       the.student   hurried   up/together   this.DAT   essay.DAT

    b. *Ég*   *klambraði*   *saman*   *einu*   *borði*
       I   patched   together   one.DAT   table.DAT

    c. *Fólkið*   *hrófar*   *upp*   *kofum*   *úr*   *timbri*
       the.people   knocks   up   huts.DAT   of   timber

(28) a.* *Nemandinn*   *rubbaði*   *upp/saman*   *eina*   *ritgerð*
       the.student   hurried   up/together   one.ACC   essay.ACC

b.* *Ég klambraði saman eitt   borð*
   I   patched together one.ACC table.ACC

c.* *Fólkið hrófar upp kofa   úr   timbri*
   the.people knocks up huts.ACC of timber

This verb class is indeed very small, but every single verb in this class that I know of takes a dative object. There is no obvious reason why this is so in the general context of dative case assignment in Icelandic.

4. CONCLUSIONS

In this article, I have argued that semantically predictable datives (inherent datives) in Icelandic are found with at least three classes of two-place verbs: emission verbs, verbs of ballistic motion, and pour verbs. If emission verbs are taken to be verbs of motion, this can be subsumed under the generalization, due to Svenonius (2002), that all motion verbs that express neither accompanied nor directed motion take dative objects in Icelandic. Since the object of a motion verb is a theme, this kind of inherent dative is predicted not to occur in Woolford's (2006) theory of possible case types across languages.

I have also shown that themes with inherent dative are found among verbs displaying variation between accusative and dative objects, ball verbs, and verbs of mixing or creating. With these verbs, the dative expresses ballistic motion or mixing, as opposed to forceful contact or creation/preparation, and this is fully consistent with the case-marking properties of verbs showing no variation in object case.

REFERENCES

Barðdal, Jóhanna. 1993. "Accusative and dative case of objects of some transitive verbs in Icelandic and the semantic distinction between them." In *Flyktförsök: Kalasbok till Christer Platzack på femtioårsdagen 18 november 1993, från doktorander och dylika*, 1–13. Lund.

Barðdal, Jóhanna. 2001. "Case in Icelandic—A synchronic, diachronic and comparative approach." PhD diss., Lund University, Department of Scandinavian Languages. [Lundastudier i nordisk språkvetenskap A57.]

Barðdal, Jóhanna. 2008. *Productivity. Evidence from case and argument structure in Icelandic*. Amsterdam: John Benjamins.

Belle, William van, and Willy Van Langendonck (eds). 1996. *The dative*. Vol. 1, *Descriptive studies*. Amsterdam: John Benjamins.

Blume, Kerstin. 1998. "A contrastive analysis of interaction verbs with dative complements." *Linguistics* 36: 253–280.

Cuervo, Maria Cristina. 2003. "Datives at large." PhD diss., MIT.

Erteschik-Shir, Nomi, and Tova Rapoport. 2010. "Contact and other results." In Malka Rappaport Hovav, Edit Doron, and Ivy Sichel (eds.), *Lexical semantics, syntax, and event structure*, 59–75. Oxford: Oxford University Press.

Jóhannsdóttir, Kristín M. 1996. "Á sögnum verður sjaldnast skortur. Afleiðslusagnir og innlimunarsagnir í íslensku. [Verbs are rarely in short supply. Derivational and incorporating verbs in Icelandic.]" MA thesis, University of Iceland, Reykjavík.

Jónsson, Jóhannes Gísli. 2000. "Case and double objects in Icelandic." In Diane Nelson and Paul Foulkes (eds.), *Leeds Working Papers in Linguistics and Phonetics*, 71–94. Also available at www.leeds.ac.uk/linguistics/index1.htm.

Jónsson, Jóhannes Gísli. 2003. "Not so quirky: On subject case in Icelandic." In Ellen Brandner and Heike Zinsmeister (eds.), *New perspectives on case theory*, 127–164. Stanford, CA: Center for the Study of Language and Information.

Jónsson, Jóhannes Gísli. 2009. "Verb classes and dative objects in Insular Scandinavian." In Jóhanna Barðdal and Shobhana Chelliah (eds.), *The role of semantic, pragmatic and discourse factors in the development of case*, 203–224. Amsterdam: John Benjamins.

Jónsson, Jóhannes Gísli, and Þórhallur Eyþórsson. 2011. "Structured exceptions and case selection in Insular Scandinavian." In Horst Simon and Heike Wiese (eds.), *Expecting the unexpected: Exceptions in the grammar*, 213–242. Berlin: Mouton de Gruyter.

Kearns, Kate. 2007. "Telic sense of deadjectival verbs." *Lingua* 117: 26–66.

Kennedy, Christopher, and Beth Levin. 2008. "Measure of change: The adjectival core of verbs of variable telicity." In Louise McNally and Christopher Kennedy (eds.), *Adjectives and adverbs. Syntax, semantics and discourse*, 156–182. Oxford: Oxford University Press.

Levin, Beth. 1993. *Verb classes and alternations. A preliminary investigation*. Chicago: University of Chicago Press.

Maling, Joan. 2000. "Modern Icelandic verbs governing dative objects." Unpublished ms., Brandeis University.

Maling, Joan. 2002. "Það rignir þágufalli á Íslandi: Verbs with dative objects in Icelandic." *Íslenskt mál og almenn málfræði* 24: 31–105.

Sigurðsson, Halldór Ármann. 2009. "The no case generalization." In Artemis Alexiadou, Jorge Hankamer, Thomas McFadden, Justin Nuger, and Florian Schäfer (eds.), *Advances in comparative Germanic syntax*, 249–279. Amsterdam: John Benjamins.

Svenonius, Peter. 2002. "Icelandic case and the structure of events." *Journal of Comparative Germanic Linguistics* 6: 197–225.

Svenonius, Peter. Forthcoming. "Case alternations in the Icelandic passive." In Satu Manninen, Diane Nelson, Katrin Hiietam, Elsi Kaiser, and Virve Vihman (eds.), *Passives and impersonals in European languages*. Amsterdam: John Benjamins.

Woolford, Ellen. 2006. "Lexical case, inherent case, and argument structure." *Linguistic Inquiry* 37: 111–130.

Yip, Moira, Joan Maling, and Ray Jackendoff. 1987. "Case in tiers." *Language* 63: 217–250.

CHAPTER 6

Ideal Speakers and Other Speakers: The Case of Dative and Some Other Cases

HÖSKULDUR THRÁINSSON

1. INTRODUCTION

In this article I would like to discuss the nature of linguistic variation, basing my discussion on variation in Icelandic and Faroese datives, among other things. The specific questions I will address are the following:

(1) a. What is the nature of linguistic variation in general and intraspeaker variation in particular?

b. What can we learn about internal grammars (the nature of I-language) by studying intraspeaker variation?

c. What can we learn about the nature of linguistic change by studying intraspeaker variation?

The data come from three major variation studies:

(2) a. Syntactic variation in Icelandic (IceDiaSyn) 2005–

b. Syntactic variation in Faroese (FarDiaSyn) 2008–

c. Phonological variation in Icelandic (RÍN) 1980s

The data from the first two surveys will center around variation in case marking in general and dative variation in particular. A major point will be the pervasiveness of intraspeaker variation in case marking. Data from the phonological variation study will then be presented to show that the extensive intraspeaker variation observed in the syntactic overview projects is not just some sort of an artifact of the research methods used, since very similar variation was also found in a phonological study that used very different methods of data elicitation. I will then argue that as linguists we need to take intraspeaker variation seriously when we develop models of speakers' internal grammars. Intraspeaker variation reflects an important aspect of the grammars of normal speakers, especially when there is an "ongoing change." More particularly, I will maintain that the kinds of results reported on are predicted by the approach to intraspeaker variation advocated by Tony Kroch (1989, 2001) and Charles Yang (e.g., 2004, 2010).

2. DIFFERENT APPROACHES TO INTRASPEAKER VARIATION

As is well known, linguists of different theoretical persuasions tend to have widely diverging ideas about the nature of intraspeaker variation. Thus many sociolinguists tend to believe that extensive intraspeaker variation is a normal state of affairs. They claim that speakers often alternate between forms that have the same meaning or function and their choice is then typically governed by various factors depending on the linguistic context or social situation. This concept goes back to the work of Labov (see, e.g., Labov 1972) and also to the influential article by Cedergren and D. Sankoff where it is maintained (1974: 333) that optional rules can be "assigned application probabilities as functions of the structure of the input strings, possibly depending on the extralinguistic environment."

While linguistic variation of all kinds can be said to be the "bread and butter" of sociolinguistics ("the more the merrier"), the generative approach to linguistic variation is often rather different. Generative linguists are typically more concerned with the *limits* of linguistic variation, namely the question why languages are not more different than they are. They (we) thus completely reject the famous statement attributed to American structuralists by Martin Joos (1957: 96) "that languages can differ from each other without limit and in unpredictable ways." An extremely influential and productive approach to linguistic variation is the so-called Principles and Parameters approach of Chomsky (1981) and much later work. As is well known, this approach assumes that all languages follow certain fundamental principles and that linguistic (or at least syntactic) variability between languages (and dialects) is determined by a finite set of parameters, typically (or ideally) binary. Under this approach, variation between languages, dialects and speakers (*interspeaker variation*) is to be expected to the extent it can be accounted for in terms of different parameter setting. The so-called *intraspeaker variation* (variation within the language of a single speaker) is less straightforwardly accounted under a parametric account, as we shall see below. Similarly, if one equates intraspeaker variation with some sort of optionality and believes in the principle of economy of derivations, which is, for example, basic to Chomsky's 1995 Minimalist Program, then it is not immediately obvious how to deal with intraspeaker variation. One way to do so is to argue that certain instances of variability should be possible under economy because the variants could be equally economical and hence "the grammar doesn't mind" (see Biberauer and Richards 2006). Another minimalistic approach maintains that intraspeaker variation may result from underspecified functional categories and different "lexical choices" (see Adger and Smith 2010).

An alternative approach has been proposed by Kroch and his associates (see, e.g., Kroch 1989, 2001 and references cited there). One of Kroch's main points is that the linguistic competence of speakers is often best characterized by assuming that they have acquired two grammars (i.e., as a case of diglossia) and that these grammars are in competition, both in the linguistic community in general (where one grammar might represent a more conservative and the other a more innovative variant) and in the language of individual speakers. Thus the speakers' output may at times be more consistent with one grammar than the other and "competing forms may differ in social register" (Kroch 2001: 702).[1] In such cases we might then expect to find evidence for dialect accommodation in the sense of Trudgill (1986) and others.

In a similar spirit, Yang has in recent work (e.g., 2004, 2010) argued that parameter setting in language acquisition is not "triggered" once and for all by some crucial evidence but, rather, proceeds in a probabilistic fashion. He has summarized the main points as follows (2004: 455):

> [T]he learning model extends to a model of language change (Yang 2000), which agrees well with the findings in historical linguistics (Kroch 2001) that language change is generally (i) gradual, and (ii) exhibits a mixture of different grammatical options. But these are possible only if one adopts an SL [statistical learning] model where parameter setting is probabilistic.

Yang's work can thus be seen as a further development of the idea of "competing grammars" usually attributed to Kroch (1989), as described above. Yang puts this as follows (2000: 248):

> The model formalizes historical linguists' intuition of grammar competition and directly relates the statistical properties of historical texts (hence, acquisition

---

1 Speaking of "two grammars" in this context is in fact an idealization of sorts. What is meant is that that with respect to a given phenomenon that is changing, there will be a grammar that is consistent with the earlier stage (say, OV word order, to pick a phenomenon that has been much discussed by Kroch and his associates) and a grammar that is consistent with the later stage (VO word order in this case). The idea is that the linguistic situation in the speech community can be described as the result of a competition between these "two grammars," and also that the competence of certain speakers can profitably be so described. There is no claim being made to the effect that speakers cannot have more than two internalized grammars nor that there cannot be multilingual speakers.

evidence) to the direction of language change. It is important to recognize that, while sociological and other external forces clearly affect the composition of linguistic evidence, grammar competition as language acquisition (the locus of language change) is internal to the individual learner's mind/brain.

I shall argue in some detail below that data from the variation surveys mentioned above provide support for this way of looking at variation while at the same time shedding a new light on the way in which linguistic judgments and linguistic output can vary between speakers under the same conditions. As mentioned above, the data come from a number of rather extensive linguistic surveys, both syntactic and phonological, which have made it possible to study linguistic change in progress and the properties of the synchronic grammars of a large number of speakers.

3. THE METHODOLOGY OF THE SYNTACTIC SURVEYS

3.1 The Main Method and Some Precautionary Measures

In the syntactic surveys (IceDiaSyn and FarDiaSyn) we used written questionnaires and then interviewed a (rather small) subset of the participants in the surveys. In a separate pilot study we experimented with a few different methods of questioning the subjects and then ended up with questionnaires with three separate tasks. The main task involved evaluation of sentences where the subjects were given three choices, as shown in Table 6.1:[2]

Settu X í viðeigandi dálk:
   Já = **Eðlileg** setning. Svona get ég vel sagt.
   ?   = **Vafasöm** setning. Ég myndi varla segja svona.
   Nei = **Ótæk** setning. Svona get ég ekki sagt.

There were typically over one hundred examples of this kind in each questionnaire, broken up by different tasks, as will be illustrated below. The grading was explained and illustrated at the beginning of the session and

---

2 Although the glosses of the sentences in Table 6.1 are irrelevant for our present purposes, the curious linguist might want to know what they are anyway:

Þingmaðurinn	heimsótti	kjósendur.							
the parlamentarian	visited	voters							
Hann	spurði	hvort	að	þeir	alltaf	hefðu	búið	í	kjördæminu.
he	asked	whether	that	they	always	had	lived	in	the district

Table 6.1. AN EXAMPLE FROM AN ICEDIASYN QUESTIONNAIRE.

		já	?	nei	Athugasemdir
T2100	Þingmaðurinn heimsótti kjósendur. Hann spurði hvort að þeir alltaf hefðu búið í kjördæminu.				

the basic instructions were then repeated at the top of each page as shown here. These instructions read as follows in English translation:

(3) Yes = A **natural** sentence. I could easily say this.

  ?   = A **questionable** sentence. I would hardly say this.

  No = An **unacceptable** sentence. I could not say this.

As explained and illustrated at the beginning of each session, the purpose of the italicized sentence (see Table 6.1) was just to give an appropriate context and the subjects were asked to evaluate the second (the nonitalicized) sentence only. At the end of each line some space for optional remarks (*athugasemdir*) was provided.

In order to maximize the likelihood of getting reliable answers we took a number of precautions, partly following methodological suggestions found in the literature (see, e.g., Schütze 1996: chap. 5, Cornips & Poletto 2005). Thus we would, for example,

(4) a. **explain the grading scale** by giving illustrative examples

  b. **vary the order** of the test sentences (e.g., reverse for half of the subjects)

  c. **test different constructions** in each overview and **include fillers**

  d. **vary the tasks** (absolute judgments, relative judgments, fill-ins...(see below))

  e. **include a break** in long sessions to prevent excessive fatigue and boredom

  f. **include context sentences** to get all subjects thinking of similar contexts

  g. **try to use natural sounding examples** (short, plausible, lexically neutral...)

  h. test **multiple examples** of each construction to minimize unwanted effects

  i. try to make the contrasting variants maximally close to **minimal pairs**

j. test **different types of speakers** (age groups, locations…)

k. throw out data from **"unreliable speakers"** (e.g., "language specialists")

l. get speakers to **report on their own intuition** (see Henry 1995, 2005a, b)

The reason for most of these should be obvious but the last one may warrant an explanation. It is sometimes maintained that investigators should ask their subjects *indirect* rather than *direct* questions, for example, "What do people around here say?" or "What is most common in your (local) dialect?" rather than "Could you say this yourself?" The idea behind this is the belief that speakers might not want to admit that they use a particular variant themselves. In our kind of study it would not have made any sense to use the indirect method. The main reason is that we wanted to compare groups of speakers so we had to try to make sure that the speakers were in fact reporting on their own intuition. We were not interested in their beliefs about the language of others. Besides, asking about such beliefs is actually a question of a very different nature as it is in fact not a question about linguistic intuition at all but rather a metalinguistic one. As will be argued in the following subsection, there is every reason to believe that most speakers answered honestly to questions about their intuitions and were in general not influenced by prescriptive ideas.

3.2 Indicators of Reliability

Before presenting relevant results from our syntactic surveys, it is useful to give some thought to the question how one can tell whether the results are reliable. Some of the indicators of reliability are listed in (5):

(5) a. The observed **systematic** (e.g., differences between age groups and (in a few cases) regions, etc.) and not random.

b. Answers from **all generations seem reliable,** e.g. it is not the case that the youngest generation "accepts everything."

c. The **subjects answer honestly** in general and don't seem worried by any kind of prescriptivism or the like (see below).

d. Comparison of **different tasks** confirms reliability of judgments.

e. Comparison with **corpora** confirms reliability of judgments.

f. Comparison with **interviews** confirms reliability of judgments.

g. Comparison of results from IceDiaSyn and FarDiaSyn with results of the **phonological interviews** in RÍN shows interesting parallels strengthening the conclusion.

By the first point we basically mean that *the proof is in the pudding*: If there had been something seriously wrong with the methodology we would not have expected the results to be systematic. Instead, we should have observed cases of random variation, which we did not find.

The second point is also worth emphasizing. We were among other things interested in detecting ongoing changes and also variants that are on their way out. Hence there was a rather large spread in the age of our subjects, the youngest group typically being around fifteen years of age and the oldest one sixty-five to seventy. Now it had been suggested to us that it might be difficult to get reliable judgments from the youngest group, for example because the youngest speakers might accept everything. As illustrated by Figures 6.1–6.2, however, some variants were accepted most readily by the youngest generation, whereas others were favored by the oldest one, which is obviously what we had hoped for (these are figures from IceDiaSyn):[3]

The third point has to do with possible reluctance of the subjects to admit that they find stigmatized variants acceptable. Fortunately, very few of the variants we were interested in had figured at all in the prescriptive discussion. One notable exception, however, was the so-called Dative Sickness,

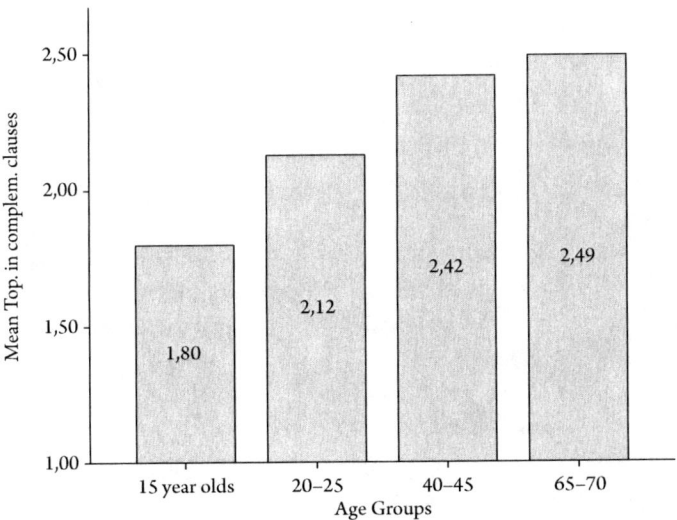

Figure 6.1
Mean evaluation of topicalization in complement clauses ($N > 700$). Correlation with age: $r = .466$. Statistical significance: $p < .001$.

3 We made three different surveys using written questionnaires in IceDiaSyn with the number of participants in each ranging from 714 to 772. The means in the graphs are "mean grades" from the evaluation (see Table 6.1), where 3 = "all examples found to be natural" and 1 = "no examples found to be natural."

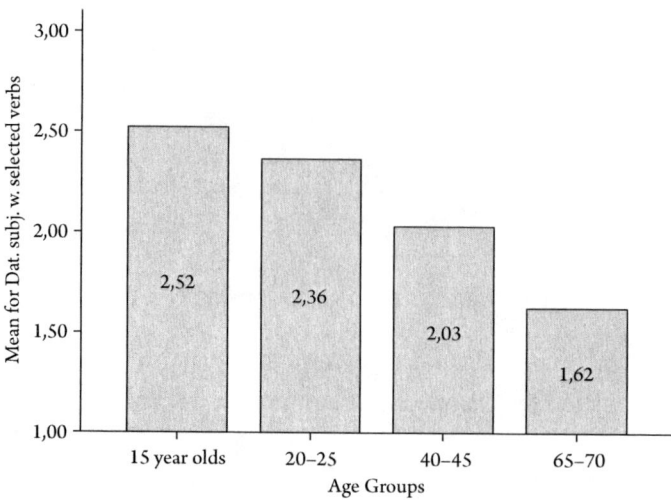

Figure 6.2
Mean evaluation of dative subjects with typical Dative Sickness verbs ($N > 740$). Correlation with age: $r = -.511$. Statistical significance: $p < .001$.

namely the tendency to replace accusative subjects with dative subjects for a particular class of ("impersonal") verbs (see Figure 6.2). This particular variant has been frowned upon in schools for a few decades at least, although there is very little evidence that this prescriptivism has slowed the change down, as Figure 6.2 indicates. As mentioned above, the questionnaires in IceDiaSyn typically involved different tasks. One of the tasks was the absolute evaluation of sentences explained in the discussion around Table 6.1 above. Another was a fill-in task where the subjects were asked to fill in blanks in a short passage by using the pronouns "I, he, she" as appropriate for the context. Some of the blanks were for subjects of typical Dative Sickness (DS) verbs. This method for investigating subject case marking with this particular class of verbs was originally developed by Svavarsdóttir (1982). It was found to work well and has been used several times since then (see, e.g., Jónsson & Eythórsson 2003, 2005). These studies have suggested that the speakers were generally unaware of the fact that they were providing information about case-marking preferences by filling the blanks with pronominal forms. Given this, one might have expected that the acceptance rate of sentences with dative subjects of the relevant verbs would have been lower than the relative frequency of dative subjects selected for these verbs in the (disguised) fill-ins and in spontaneous speech. But this is not what we found. The acceptance rate of sentences with dative subjects for typical DS verbs was consistently higher in the judgment tasks than the selection rate of dative subject pronominal forms in the fill-in tasks. This is illustrated in the first row of Table 6.2 with numbers from IceDiaSyn for the verb *langa* "want," which is one of the most common DS verbs. The other rows show figures from a couple of other studies, as will be explained below:

Table 6.2. ACCEPTANCE, SELECTION, AND USAGE OF DATIVE SUBJECTS WITH *LANGA* "WANT" IN VARIOUS STUDIES.

Study	All age groups			Youngest age group	
	Judgments	Fill-ins	Corpora	Judgments	Fill-ins
IceDiaSyn	68% accept	19% select	7%/25% use	77% accept	35% select
Jónsson & Eythórsson 2003					40% select
Svavarsdóttir 1982					32% select
Friðriksson 2008			15% use		

The figure 68 percent in the first row shows the acceptance rate by all age groups combined in IceDiaSyn for sentences with a dative subject with *langa* "want" and the figure 19 percent indicates how many of these subjects actually selected a dative pronominal subject in a fill-in task in the same survey. Corresponding figures for the youngest age group separately are 77 percent and 35 percent, respectively. In a spoken language corpus considered for comparative purposes the corresponding figure is 25 percent, as shown in the middle column, but in a corpus that is mostly based on written (published) material the figure is only 7 percent, as dative subjects of *langa* are typically weeded out by proofreaders.

The remaining numbers in Table 6.2 are also of some comparative interest. First, note that some 40 percent of the youngsters tested on a fill-in task by Jónsson and Eythórsson (2003) selected dative form of the subject. A corresponding figure from Svavarsdóttir's original study (1982) was 32 percent. Since the tasks and the age groups were comparable (twelve-year-olds mostly, i.e., somewhat younger than the youngest group in IceDiaSyn), this indicates a slow but steady increase in Dative Sickness among Icelandic teenagers during the twenty years that had passed between the studies. Finally, spontaneous speech recordings made by Friðriksson (2008) showed only 15 percent usage of dative (as opposed to accusative) subjects. This is lower than the 25 percent usage rate reported for a spontaneous speech corpus by Svavarsdóttir (2006, 2011) in connection with IceDiaSyn and closer to the 19 percent selection rate for the fill-ins in IceDiaSyn. The observed differences might be due to a number of reasons, one being difference in the age of the speakers involved in the different studies, another the topic of the conversation, as it has often been observed that speakers are more likely to use third-person dative subjects than first-person (see, e.g., Svavarsdóttir 1982).

The most important aspect of these results is the fact that they show very clearly that the speakers have no problem with accepting dative subjects of a DS verb like *langa* "want" in a judgment task (the acceptance rate ranges from 68 percent for the group as a whole to 77 percent for the youngest age group). But this does not necessarily mean that all of the speakers who accept the dative variant will actually select a dative subject form in a fill-in task. As it turns out, many of the speakers actually prefer an accusative subject with *langa* even if they find the dative subject natural. This is what the selection figures show: 19 percent of the whole group select the dative subject in the fill-in task, and 35 percent of the youngest group. This is consistent with the finding that the accusative subject variant with *langa* actually gets an even higher acceptance rate than the dative subject variant in the judgment task (88 percent of the whole group accepted the accusative variant and 68 percent the dative one).

These results suggest, then, that the subjects in IceDiaSyn were largely unaffected by prescriptivism since Dative Sickness was actually our main concern from that point of view and here the subjects had no problem admitting that they found the (stigmatized?) dative subjects with the DS verbs natural.[4] In addition, although the acceptance rate was considerably higher than the selection rate, there was a *strong and highly significant correlation* between the judgments and the selection: $r = .570$, $p < .001$. This is obviously encouraging and lends further support to our belief that the judgments were reliable.

As a final indicator that the subjects' judgments are generally reliable consider the following: As mentioned above, a subset of those who had filled in the written questionnaires were interviewed later. In these interviews we wanted among other things to try to elicit production data to compare to the judgment data that we had obtained. The so-called New Passive Construction (or the New Impersonal, see Maling & Sigurjónsdóttir 2002, Thráinsson 2007: 273ff.) seemed to offer an opportunity to do this, since here there was a great difference between the age groups: The youngest speakers would typically accept the NewPass examples, whereas the older ones would virtually all reject them. A typical NewPass example is given in (6c):

---

4 Although prescriptivists often talk about Dative Sickness and school teachers have tried to eradicate it for decades, it seems that there is very little awareness of the phenomenon among the general public. In interviews conducted in connection with IceDiaSyn we sometimes asked the subjects if they had heard about Dative Sickness. While many of them said that they had, and knew that it had something to do with the use of Dative, they were usually unable to give relevant examples.

(6) a. Krakkarnir hrintu **mér** í frímínútunum. (active)
the kids   pushed me(D) in break
"The kids pushed me during the break."

   b. **Mér**   var hrint   í frímínútunum. (regular passive)
me(D) was pushed in break
"I was pushed during the break."

   c. Það   var hrint   **mér** í frímínútunum.   (new passive)
there was pushed me(D) in break
"I was pushed during the break."

The regular passive in (6b) is characterized by the auxiliary "be" and the past participle of the main verb "push" and the theme (or patient) of the predicate occurs in subject position.[5] In the NewPass we also get the auxiliary "be" and the past participle of the main verb, but the theme (patient) stays in situ (in apparent object position) and the subject position is typically filled by an expletive það "there" (or some other element occurs in initial position).

In the interview the subjects were first presented with a model pair of sentences like (7a, b) and it was pointed out to them that a sentence like (7a) could be paraphrased by starting with (the expletive) það "there" as in (7b) (a natural expletive passive for all speakers):

(7) a. Einhverjir   köstuðu tómötum í   söngvarann.
some people threw   tomatoes in the singer
"Some people threw tomatoes at the singer."

   b. Það   var kastað tómötum í   söngvarann.
there was thrown tomatoes in the singer
"Tomatoes were thrown at the singer."

The subjects were then presented with an example like (8a) and asked to paraphrase it by a sentence beginning with það "there" and they typically had no problem coming up with a paraphrase like (8b), which is a natural expletive sentence for all speakers of Icelandic:

(8) a. Einhverjir   fóru   að   syngja í rútunni.
some people began to   sing   in the bus

   b. Það   fóru einhverjir   að syngja í   rútunni.
there began some people to sing   in   the bus

---

5 Since Dat. objects have a lexically assigned case, they keep their case in the passive construction. Acc. objects do not in the regular passive, as is well known, but in the NewPass the theme/patient argument would retain an Acc. case (see, e.g., Maling and Sigurjónsdóttir 2002, Thráinsson 2007: 273ff.).

But when the subjects were presented with (9a), only the youngest speakers could paraphrase it as (9b), which is a NewPass example as explained above, whereas the older speakers were at a loss:

(9) a. Krakkarnir hrintu **mér** í frímínútunum.
      the kids   pushed me   in break

     b. **Það**   var   hrint   **mér** í frímínútunum.
        there   was   pushed me   in break

Here there was almost a perfect correlation between the judgments of the speakers and their production: $r = .989$, $p < .001$. This means that virtually all of the speakers who had accepted NewPass sentences in the questionnaires could produce such sentences under these circumstances, whereas the ones who had rejected NewPass examples could not produce them either. One could not really ask for a stronger confirmation of reliability of the judgments.

4. OBSERVED VARIATION IN DATIVE CASE MARKING—AND ELSEWHERE

In this section I will first present evidence for interspeaker variation in datives and then turn to the extensive intraspeaker variation. At the end of the section I will then present some data from phonology to show that the observed intraspeaker variation in case marking is by no means an isolated phenomenon.

Before we turn to the examples it should be pointed out that variation in case marking is arguably more "pure" from a syntactic point of view than many other instances of variation, as it typically seems devoid of any semantic or pragmatic nuances (the same is probably true of agreement but not necessarily of word order variation, use of reflexives/nonreflexives, etc.).[6] Hence case alternations are useful for determining the nature of variation. But before we continuing our discussion of variation in case marking, it should be emphasized that for most verbs in Icelandic there is no variation in subject nor object case marking. The same is true of Faroese. So variation in case marking is the exception and not the rule. Nevertheless, these exceptions are important in the present context.

---

6 Note that this implies that (morphological) dative does not in such instances express a particular meaning different from the meaning conveyed by accusative, for instance. More specifically, there is no reason to believe that speakers who use a dative subject (or object) with a given verb have a particular lexical meaning in mind for this verb different from the meaning that it has for speakers who use an accusative subject (or object) with it. This semantic neutrality of case marking variation is particularly obvious when we have intraspeaker variation in the case marking with a given verb, as we shall see below.

4.1 Interspeaker Variation in Case Marking

Dative case variation in Icelandic is mainly of two kinds: variation in subject case and object case. Some speakers accept (and use) dative subjects with experiencer-type verbs that used to take accusative or even nominative subjects. The acceptance rate for selected verbs of this kind in IceDiaSyn is shown in Table 6.3:

Table 6.3. ACCEPTANCE RATE OF DIFFERENT CASES IN SUBJECT POSITION FOR SELECTED VERBS (N > 740).

Verb	Nom. subject	Acc. subject	Dat. subject	(N+)A+D
hlakka til "look forward to"	48.6%	**59.7%**	44.2%	152.5
langa "want, long for"		**88.3%**	68.2%	148.7
vanta "need, lack"		**92.1%**	56.6%	156.5

As the reader will note, the figures in Table 6.3 indicate not only interspeaker variation but also intraspeaker variation. If there was no intraspeaker variation, the figures in each row (acceptance of Nom. + Acc. + Dat. subjects) would add up to 100 percent but they add up to around 150 in each case. We will return to this issue in section 4.2 below.

Originally, the verb *hlakka til* "look forward to" took a nominative subject, whereas *vanta* "need, lack" and *langa* "want, long for" took an accusative subject. As Table 6.3 shows, accusative is (still) the most widely accepted subject case for all of these verbs, although it represents an innovation for *hlakka til* and has been corrected in schools. Two-thirds of the oldest generation (66.0 percent) accepted (the original) nominative subject with *hlakka til*, but only one-third of the youngest generation did (32.5 percent). But if we compare the acceptance by different age groups of accusative subjects and dative subjects for the typical DS verbs *vanta* and *langa*, we see that the dative subject is most widely accepted by the youngest generation, but there is very little difference between age groups in the acceptance of accusative subjects with these verbs. This is illustrated in Table 6.4.

Table 6.4. ACCEPTANCE RATE OF ACCUSATIVE AND DATIVE SUBJECTS WITH SELECTED DS VERBS (N > 740).

Verb	15-year-olds	20–25	40–45	65–70
langa acc.	85.2%	88.2%	**90.8%**	89.3%
langa dat.	**79.6%**	78.0%	66.7%	43.8%
vanta acc.	86.7%	**96.1%**	93.8%	91.7%
vanta dat.	**46.9%**	35.1%	15.4%	7.5%

This becomes even clearer on the bar chart in Figure 6.3, where the mean evaluation of accusative subjects for examples with the verbs *langa* and *vanta* is broken up according to age groups. Figure 6.4 shows comparable results for dative subjects with the same verbs.

These figures show that the younger age groups are more "bidialectal" than the older ones in the sense that they typically accept both the innovative case marking (Dat.) and the traditional one (Acc.), whereas the older generations (especially the oldest one) only accept the traditional value. This is an interesting result from a theoretical point of view, since it gives an idea of how linguistic change may spread and suggests that intraspeaker variation may be a more common state of affairs under such circumstances than often assumed. But before we look more closely at intraspeaker variation, it is useful to look at an instance of variation in object case for comparison.

While it is standardly assumed that accusative is the default (or structural) object case in Icelandic and dative is a lexically assigned case, it is also well known that dative object case shows some regularities (see, e.g., Barðdal 2001, Maling 2002, Svenonius 2002, Woolford 2006, Thráinsson 2007: 156ff.). What has been less well documented in the literature is the fact that for some verbs there is a variation between dative and accusative on objects. This is obviously of interest for theories that attempt to relate dative object case marking to semantic or thematic notions, since there is no reason to assume that this variation correlates with differences of interpretation by the speakers involved. First, consider the figures in Table 6.5.

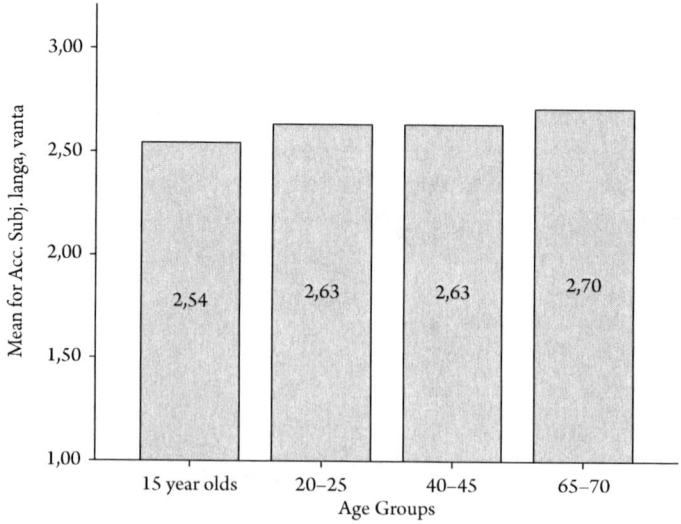

Figure 6.3
Mean evaluation of accusative subjects with *langa* "want" and *vanta* "need." Correlation with age: $r = .133$.

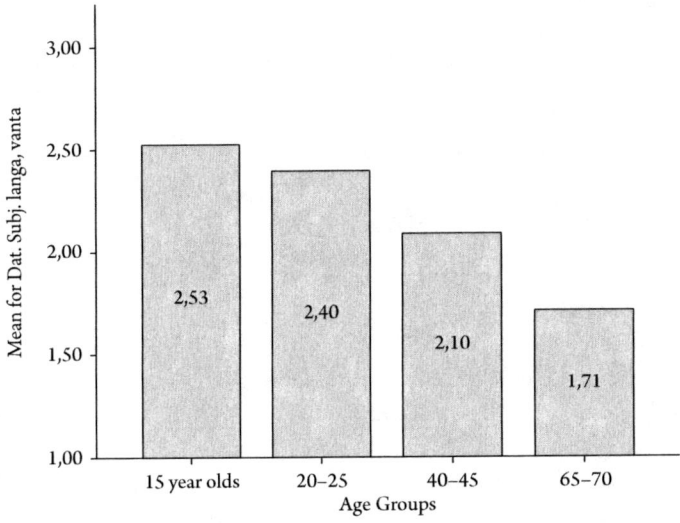

Figure 6.4
Mean evaluation of dative subjects with *langa* "want" and *vanta* "need." Correlation with age:
r = −.459.

Table 6.5. ACCEPTANCE OF ACCUSATIVE AND DATIVE OBJECTS
WITH SELECTED VERBS.

Verb	Acc. object	Dat. object	Total Acc.+Dat.
faxa "faxa"	91.3%	23.8%	115.1
framlengja "extend"	82.7%	61.0%	143.7
negla "nail (a ball into a goal)"	66.5%	72.6%	139.1
rústa "demolish" (lit. and fig.)	22.3%	82.4%	104.1

As pointed out in connection with Table 6.3, the combined acceptance of the different cases indicates intraspeaker variation, namely that many speakers accept both accusative and dative objects with these verbs. It is interesting to note, however, that there is a considerable difference between the verbs involved. Thus there is hardly any intraspeaker variation in object case selection of *rústa* "demolish" but large variation in the case of *framlengja* "extend," for instance.

It is also important to note in this connection that we were able to discover another important difference in case variation by combining the methods of elicitation we used. Recall that we collected information about case marking preferences in two different ways: The speakers were both asked to evaluate sentences and to fill in blanks in short narratives. As discussed in connection with Table 6.2 above, this combination of methods showed in

Table 6.6. SELECTION AND ACCEPTANCE OF DATIVE OBJECT WITH
RÚSTA "DEMOLISH" AND DATIVE SUBJECT WITH *LANGA* "WANT."

Verb	Dat. selected	Dat. accepted
Object case with *rústa* "demolish"	88.1%	83.6%
Subject case with *langa* "want"	19.2%	68.2%

some instances that speakers who accepted a dative subject with a given verb might nevertheless select an accusative subject when filling in the blanks. Table 6.6 shows an interesting difference between the subject case of *langa* "want" and object case of *rústa* "demolish" in this respect.

As Table 6.6 shows, there is hardly any difference between the selection rate and acceptance rate of dative objects with *rústa* "demolish" whereas there is considerable difference between corresponding figures for the subject case of *langa* "want." This means, then, that a speaker who accepts dative object case with *rústa* will also use it, but a speaker who accepts dative subject case with *langa* may not use it. The other side of the coin is that a speaker who does not select dative subject case with *langa* may nevertheless accept it. The reason for this difference is that speakers are much less likely to be bidialectal with respect to object case of *rústa* (see also the figures in Table 6.5), but they may very well be with respect to subject case of *langa*, as already discussed. Assuming that the selection task under discussion mirrors production (you select the form that you would use), this clearly shows that production data do not necessarily tell us the whole story about the internalized grammar of speakers. Facts of this sort should thus help dispel the myth that it would be best if we could rely on "natural data" in syntactic studies ("real examples" found in spontaneous speech).

With this in mind, we can now turn to a more detailed investigation of intraspeaker variation in case marking.

4.2 Intraspeaker Variation in Case Marking

The differences in intraspeaker variation between *langa* "want" and *rústa* "demolish" can be visualized in histograms like the following (here we are only considering two examples with dative arguments for each verb).

If there was no intraspeaker variation, the only bars that would show up on these histograms would be the ones for 1 (= no dative examples found natural) and 3 (= all dative examples found natural). Thus the values in between show how many speakers accepted some but not all of the examples under consideration, that is, for how many speakers some sort of intraspeaker variation was found. By adding up the numbers we can see that this holds for 171 (out of 747) speakers for dative objects of *rústa* and for 252 (out of 746) speakers for dative subjects of *langa*.

Now the intraspeaker variation observed in Figures 6.5–6.6 may not look all that impressive. After all, the majority of the speakers found all of the dative examples natural, both for objects of *rústa* "demolish" and subjects of *langa* "want." But if we add more examples and include the verb *vanta* "need" in the picture, the other most typical DS verb in Icelandic, we see that the intraspeaker variation is actually more pervasive. This is shown in Figure 6.7. In Figure 6.8 I have added comparable information for corresponding verbs in Faroese.

What these figures reveal is that there is much more intraspeaker variation in subject case marking of *langa* "want" and *vanta* "need" in Icelandic than there is for the comparable verbs *dáma* "like," *mangla* "lack," *nýtast* "need," and *tørva* "need" in Faroese. As Figure 6.8 shows, about 43 percent of the Faroese speakers tested (135 out of a total of 316 in this instance) accepted all examples of dative subjects with the verbs in question, whereas only about 19 percent of the Icelandic speakers accepted all of the dative subject examples with *langa* and *vanta*.

It is important to note in this connection, however, that the historical development has been rather different in the two languages in this area. The Icelandic verbs *langa* and *vanta* originally took accusative subjects, and the dative subjects are an innovation still frowned upon in schools. This is the so-called Dative Sickness, a change in progress, as we have seen. In Faroese, on the other hand, the accusative subjects have virtually

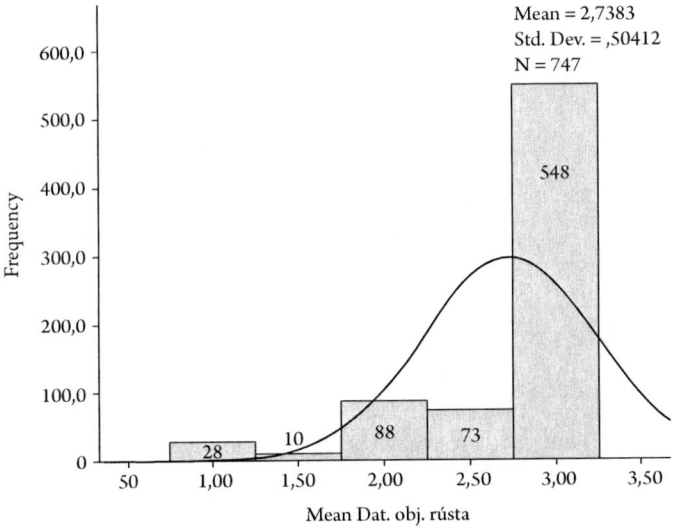

Figure 6.5
Distribution of means for dative objects of *rústa* "demolish."

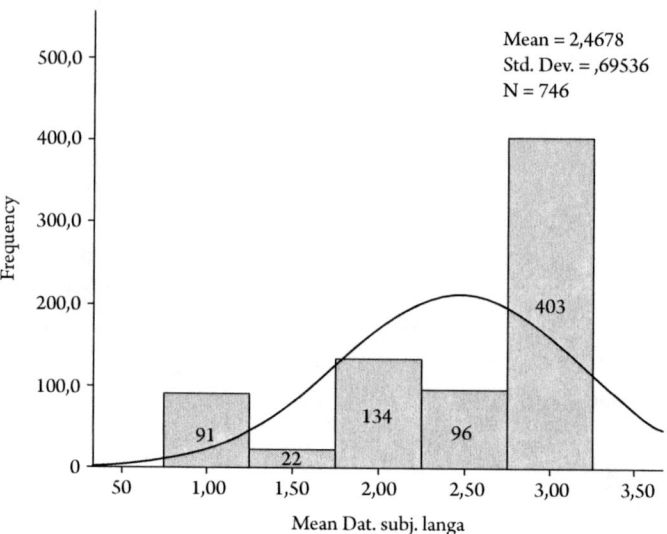

Figure 6.6
Distribution of means for dative subjects of *langa* "want."

disappeared (see, e.g., Thráinsson et al. 2004: 252ff., Jónsson and Eythórsson 2005). Here, too, many verbs that originally took accusative subjects now take dative subjects (including *vanta*; the verb *langa* is not used anymore in Faroese). But a further development is now taking place in Faroese as nominative subjects are replacing dative ones for many verbs. Now the

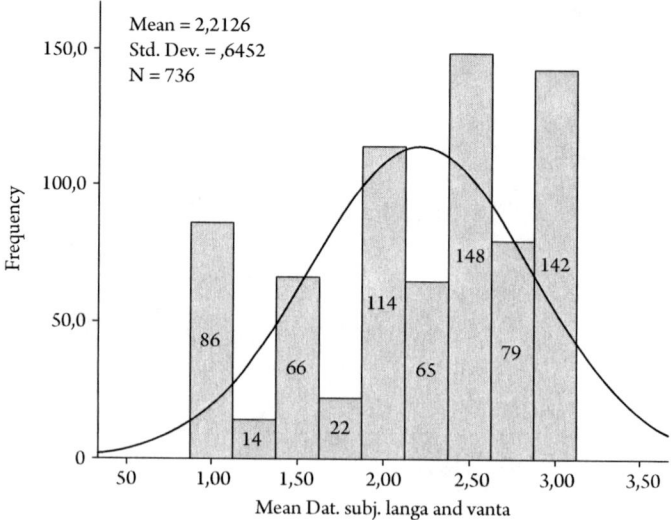

Figure 6.7
Distribution of means for dative subjects of Icelandic *langa* and *vanta*.

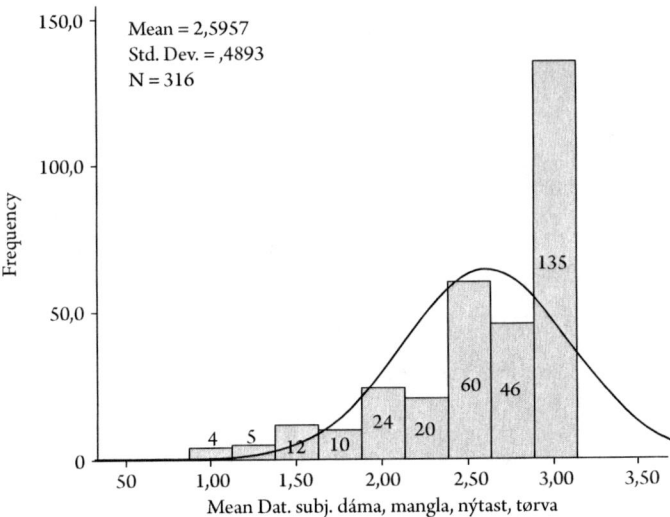

Figure 6.8
Distribution of means for dative subjects of Faroese *dáma*, *mangla*, *nýtast*, and *tørva*.

Faroese verbs *dáma* "like" and *nýtast* "need" presumably took dative from early on (as their Icelandic counterparts still do). The verb *tørva* "need," on the other hand, corresponds to Old Norse (and Icelandic) *þurfa*, which took a nominative subject, so here the dative subject is an innovation. The same is presumably true for *mangla* "lack," which is apparently a loanword from Danish (d. *mangle*). Thus the dative case marking of the subject of the last two verbs indicates a strong tendency to regularize thematic case marking of a subclass of experiencer verbs in earlier stages of Faroese, although it is now beginning to give way to structural nominative case.[7]

As a final illustration of intraspeaker variation in case marking, consider the following: there is a strong correlation between Dative Sickness and age in Icelandic. The prediction is, then, that this should be reflected in different intraspeaker variation patterns for different generations. As Figures 6.9 and 6.10 show, this prediction is borne out.

As these figures show, the means cluster to the left (very little Dative Sickness, 46 subjects with none at all) for the oldest group, whereas they cluster to the right (more Dative Sickness, 63 subjects who found all of the examples natural) for the youngest group.

We have now seen considerable evidence for the existence of widespread intraspeaker variation in case marking. Since the data reported on

---

7 A similar development has happened in English. Thus the verb *like*, for instance, used to take a non-nominative argument (e.g., **him** *liketh*) which now occurs in the nominative (**he** *likes*). The controversy about the details of this development need not concern us here (see, e.g., Allen 1986, Eythórsson and Barðdal 2005).

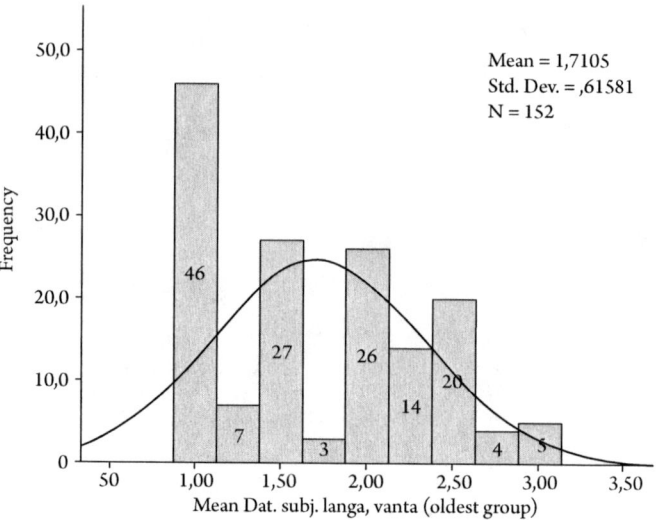

Figure 6.9
Distribution of means for dative subjects of *langa* and *vanta* for the oldest group.

are based on the judgments of speakers for the most part, one might think that the extensive intraspeaker variation observed is somehow an artifact of the research method used. Hence it is important to point out that variation between accusative and dative subjects is also found in the production of speakers, although it should be less common there for the reason described

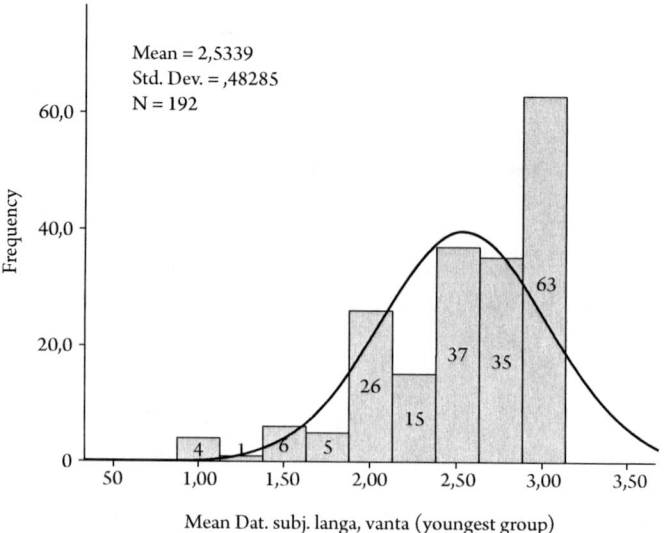

Figure 6.10
Distribution of means for dative subjects of *langa* and *vanta* for the youngest group.

in connection with Table 6.2 above. This has been pointed out by (for example) Jónsson (2007), citing examples like (10a) from the Internet. The additional examples in (10) have similar sources, as indicated:

(10) a. **mig**   langar   að eiga   endalausa   innistæðu
    me(Acc) wants   to have   endless   money-in-the-bank
    og   kaupa   allt sem   **mér**   langar í
    and   buy   everything me(Dat)   wants in
    "I want to have a truckload of money and buy everything I want."

   b. **Mér**   langar   til þess   að komast   í þetta   fit form...
    me(Dat) wants to it   to get   to this   fit form
    Mig   langar   að breyta   fitu   ...   í vöðva.
    me(Acc.) wants to   change   fat   to muscles
    "I want to get fit. I want to change fat to muscles."
    (www.eas.is/einkathjalfarinn/personuleg-radgjof/169-eg-er-alveg-lost,   accessed June 15, 2012)

   c. **mér**   langar   að vita   mjög   mikið   um   rafmagn og   tækni...
    me(Dat.) wants to know very   much   about electricity and technology
    mig   langar að vita   kvort   þú   vitir   um   einhverja búð...
    me(Acc.) wants to   know   whether you   know about any   store
    "I want to know a lot about electricity and technology.
    I'd like to know if you know of any store..."
    (www.totalradgjof.is/new/faq/index.php?action=artikel&cat=13&id=830&artlan g=en, accessed June 15, 2012)

   d. **mér**   langar   að verða   miklu þyngri   en ég er í dag...
    me(Dat.) wants to become much heavier   than I am today
    Mig   langar   að keppa   í vaxtarrækt...
    me(Acc.) wants to compete in bodybuilding
    "I want to become much heavier than I am today. I'd like to compete in bodybuilding."
    (www.fitnesssport.is/index.php?option=com_content&view=article&id=108:la ngar-ae-keppa-i-vaxtarraekt-&catid=46:starfsfolk-fitnesssport-svarar-spurningum, accessed June 15, 2012)

   e. **mig**   langar að fá   hjá   þér þarna plattana sem...
    me(Acc.) wants to get from you there plates   that
       t.d langar **mér**   í einn sem...
       e.g. wants me(Dat.) in one that
    "I would like to get from you those plates that...I'd for instance like the one that..."
    (http://erwin.barnaland.is/gestabok/, accessed June 15, 2012)

Similarly, Svavarsdóttir (2011) reports that in a corpus of spontaneous speech, the verb *langa* was found in the sample for ten speakers (out of twelve). Although there were usually very few examples with *langa* for each speaker, some intraspeaker variation was observed in the use of subject case. This is summarized in Table 6.7 (actual numbers and percentages are only given for the speakers showing intraspeaker variation):[8]

Table 6.7. THE USE OF SUBJECT CASES WITH *LANGA* "WANT" BY TEN SPEAKERS IN A SMALL CORPUS OF SPONTANEOUS SPEECH

Speaker	Nom. subject		Acc. subject		Dat. subject	
	N	%	*N*	%	*N*	%
Sp. 1	1	20%	3	60%	1	20%
Sp. 2	0	0%	19	95%	1	5%
Sp. 3	1	16.7%	5	83.3%	0	0%
Sp. 4					x	
Sp. 5					x	
Sp. 6			x			
Sp. 7			x			
Sp. 8			x			
Sp. 9			x			
Sp. 10			x			

As shown here, three of these speakers show signs of intraspeaker variation, whereas the remaining seven do not (there was only one example for each of the speakers using a dative subject). Although the numbers are quite low (except for speaker 2), they show that intraspeaker variation also occurs in the use of subject case in spontaneous speech, not only in the judgments of these or on the Internet.

Now intraspeaker variation is, of course, not at all restricted to case marking nor to syntactic phenomena. To illustrate this we will next consider phonological production data that show intraspeaker variation which is very similar to the kind observed above: While some of the speakers stick pretty much to one variant of a given phonological variable, others use two variants interchangeably but to different degrees.

4.3 Intraspeaker Variation in Phonology

One of the rather unexpected results of the survey of phonological variation in Icelandic mentioned above (RÍN, see, e.g., Thráinsson & Árnason 1992,

8 The numbering of the speakers is mine. Speakers 1, 2, and 3 are labeled A2, A3, and A4 in Svavarsdóttir's paper (2011).

Árnason & Thráinsson 2003) was the extensive intraspeaker variation found for many of the phonological variables investigated.[9] It should be emphasized here that this variation was found even when the situation and social context was held constant so it does not have anything to do with socially conditioned dialects. The extent to which it shows up depends, however, on the nature of the phonological variables in question. It would take us too far afield to go into this in any detail, but a demonstration of two cases should suffice to show the similarities to the intraspeaker variation observed in case marking.

Although it has proved to be very difficult to find any geographical variation in Icelandic syntax, such variation can still be found in Icelandic phonology. Two phonological features that basically characterize Northeastern Icelandic are voiced sonorants (i.e., /l,m,n/) and voiced/ð/ before/p,t,k/ (the so-called voiced pronunciation) and aspirated stops after long vowels (the so-called hard pronunciation). The intraspeaker variation of these features can be seen in Figures 6.11 and 6.12 (note that here the means range from 100 (= does not occur at all) to 200 (= occurs in every possible instance)):

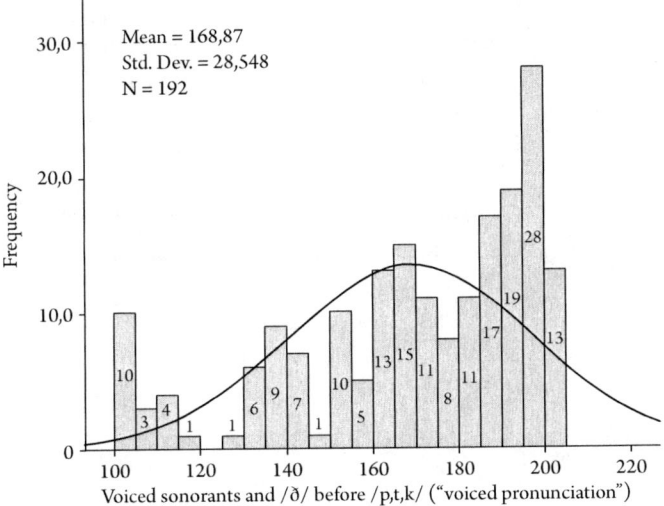

Figure 6.11
Distribution of means for voiced sonorants and /ð/ before /p,t,k/ in an area in NE Iceland (*N* = 192).

9 Actually, if one asks Google to search for "intraspeaker variation," it seems that the majority of hits have to do with variation in phonetic detail. The examples to be discussed below are of a different nature, however, since they involve variation in phonological variables that have standardly been believed to define different phonological dialects (or variants) of Icelandic.

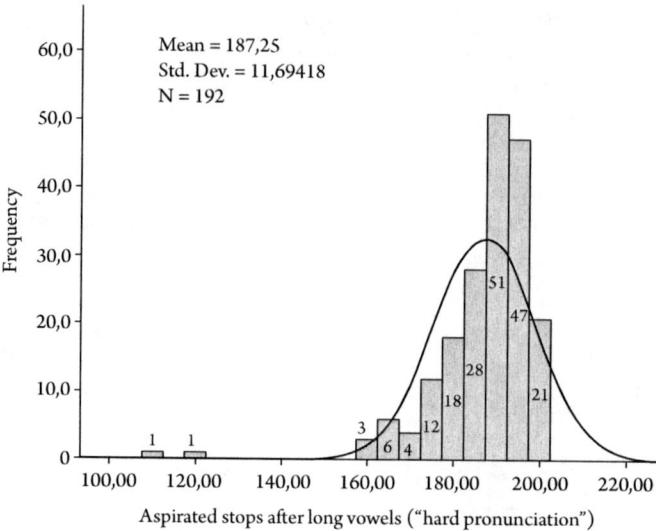

Figure 6.12
Distribution of means for aspirated stops after long vowels in an area in NE Iceland
(N = 192).

These figures show that there is much greater intraspeaker variation in the voiced pronunciation than there is in the hard pronunciation. This reflects the fact that the former is on the way out, whereas the latter is relatively stable. The pattern observed here is remarkably like the one found in the syntax, although the data come from very different parts of the grammar and the method of elicitation was radically different (the results from the phonological survey are all based on production data elicited in structured interviews). Hence it is clear that the intraspeaker variation observed in the syntax is neither an artifact of the elicitation method used nor a special characteristic of case marking.

5. CONCLUSION

I would now like to summarize the main results and claims of this article as follows:

(11) a. Intraspeaker variation is common and pervasive in those aspects of grammar that are undergoing change.
b. Intraspeaker variation can be observed in (spontaneous) speech production but sometimes even more clearly in (syntactic) judgments.

c. Intraspeaker variation is probably by nature a transitional stage, caused by inconsistent and conflicting input. Under such circumstances it typically shows up on a scale with a number of speakers at either end of the scale showing very little or no intraspeaker variation (these are the "ideal speakers") and the rest of the speakers showing varying degrees of intraspeaker variation. This phenomenon needs to be taken seriously in models of grammar.

By the last point I want to claim that when the input (or the primary linguistic data) is relatively consistent and uniform, as it may very well be, there is no reason to expect extensive intraspeaker variation. Hence we should find areas of grammar without any significant intraspeaker variation. But when the input is inconsistent and even conflicting, as it typically is when a change is ongoing, be it a spreading Dative Sickness, spreading devoicing of sonorants before /p,t,k/, or whatever, intraspeaker variation will be a natural outcome. But since most changes eventually reach an endpoint, the relevant inconsistency in the input should disappear in the end and so should the related intraspeaker variation, at least in theory.

With this in mind, we can now go back to the different ideas about variation discussed in section 2 above and try to determine which ones seem most suitable to deal with facts of the sort discussed in this article. The concept of variable rules along the lines suggested by Labov (1972) and his followers seems too performance-oriented, on the one hand, as it can make reference to extralinguistic contextual or situational features. On the other, it does not really seem to be an adequate model of the situation found here, where there is a clear difference between speakers in the "amount" of intraspeaker variation characteristic of their grammars under the same circumstances. The same can be said about the proposals of Biberauer and Richards (2006), on the one hand ("the grammar doesn't mind"), and Adger and Smith (2010), on the other ("underspecified functional categories"). It seems more promising to seek an account along the lines proposed by Yang (2000, 2004, 2010), which can partly be seen as an extension or further development of the original idea about "competing grammars" proposed by Kroch (1989). Contrary to ideas argued for by Lightfoot (1999) and Hale (2007), for instance, it does not seem that speakers settle relatively early on a grammar that is consistent and uniform in all respects. Rather, it seems that certain areas of their grammar may remain incompletely specified for a long time, even their whole lifetime. But they are not completely unspecified, either. Some speakers are more likely than others to use voiced sonorants although they do not do so all the time, and some speakers are more likely than others to accept and use dative subjects with experiencer-type verbs although they do not do so all the time.

This is an important fact, and it is not just a matter of random performance or performance influenced by some social situation or context. It is a part of these speakers' competence and can be reflected in their (syntactic or phonological) performance and also in their evaluation or judgments of sentences. Hence it needs to be taken into account in our models of linguistic competence, even if it means that we cannot allow ourselves to deal only with ideal speakers but will have to consider other speakers as well.

Finally, there are probably several ways of modeling this aspect of our competence. One question is whether or to what extent this can be related to parameter settings (see the discussions in Yang's work, e.g., 2004, 2010). I find it likely that this may vary from case to case (no pun intended). One way to find out is to investigate whether there is any relationship between variations in different areas, so to speak. If there is such a relationship or correlation, then one might want to look for a suitable parameter, at least if one assumes a fairly standard concept of parameters, such as the ones suggested to account for observed variation within Scandinavian by Holmberg & Platzack (1995) and Bobaljik & Thráinsson (1998), for instance (for somewhat different notions of parameters see, for example, the discussions in Kayne 2005 and in Manzini & Savoia 2011). At present I do not know if there is any correlation between variation in case marking of the sort reported on here and anything else in the grammars of the speakers involved. But I do know that although there is considerable interspeaker and intraspeaker variation in verb placement in Faroese, this variation correlates to some extent with available subject position, availability of transitive expletives and probably also Stylistic Fronting. This suggests that some sort of parametric variation is involved, but it would take us too far afield to go into this here (see Thráinsson 2010).

ACKNOWLEDGMENTS

The generous support of The Icelandic Research Fund to all of these projects is gratefully acknowledged. IceDiaSyn and FarDiaSyn (principal investigator Höskuldur Thráinsson) were connected to the Scandinavian research networks Scandinavian Dialect Syntax (ScanDiaSyn) and Nordic Center of Excellence in Microcomparative Syntax (NORMS). Höskuldur Thráinsson and Kristján Árnason were principal investigators of RÍN. I am grateful to all my collaborators in these projects, both Icelandic, Faroese and Mainland Scandinavian ones, too numerous to mention here.

Thanks are also due to two anonymous reviewers and the editors of this volume, who helped me improve the article. It is not their fault it the article is still less than ideal. Ideal linguists are probably even more rare than ideal speakers.

REFERENCES

Adger, David, and Jennifer Smith. 2010. "Variation in agreement: A lexical feature-based approach." *Lingua* 120: 1109–1134.

Allen, Cynthia L. 1986. "Reconsidering the history of *like*." *Journal of Linguistics* 22: 375–409.

Árnason, Kristján, and Höskuldur Thráinsson. 2003. "Fonologiske dialekttræk på Island: Generationer og geografiske områder." In Gunnstein Akselberg, Anne Marit Bødal, and Helge Sandøy (eds.), *Nordisk dialektologi*, 151–196. Oslo: Novus.

Barðdal, Jóhanna. 2001. "Case in Icelandic—a synchronic, diachronic and comparative approach." PhD diss., University of Lund.

Biberauer, Theresa, and Marc Richards. 2006. "True optionality: When the grammar doesn't mind." In Cedric Boeckx (ed.), *Minimalist essays*, 35–66. Amsterdam: Benjamins.

Bobaljik, Jonathan D., and Höskuldur Thráinsson. 1998. "Two heads aren't always better than one." *Syntax* 1: 37–71.

Cedergren, Henrietta, and David Sankoff. 1974. "Variable rules: Performance as a statistical reflection of competence." *Language* 50: 333–355.

Chomsky, Noam. 1981. *Lectures on government and binding*. Dordrecht: Foris.

Chomsky, Noam. 1995. *The minimalist program*. Cambridge, MA: MIT Press.

Cornips, Leonie, and Cecilia Poletto. 2005. "On standardizing syntactic elicitation techniques (part 1)." *Lingua* 115: 939–957.

Eythórsson, Thórhallur, and Jóhanna Barðdal. 2005. "Oblique subjects: A common Germanic inheritance." *Language* 81: 824–881.

Friðriksson, Finnur. 2008. "Language change vs. stability in conservative language communities: A case study of Icelandic." PhD diss., University of Gothenburg.

Hale, Mark. 2007. *Historical linguistics: Theory and method*. Oxford: Blackwell.

Henry, Alison. 1995. *Belfast English and Standard English: Dialect variation and parameter setting*. Oxford: Oxford University Press.

Henry, Alison. 2005a. "Idiolectal variation and syntactic theory." In Leonie Cornips and Karen P. Corrigan (eds.), *Syntax and variation: Reconciling the biological and the social*, 109–122. Amsterdam: John Benjamins.

Henry, Alison. 2005b. "Non-standard dialects and linguistic data." *Lingua* 115: 1599–1617.

Holmberg, Anders, and Christer Platzack. 1995. *The role of inflection in Scandinavian syntax*. Oxford: Oxford University Press.

Joos, Martin, ed. 1957. *Readings in linguistics*. The Development of Descriptive Linguistics in America since 1925. Washington, DC: American Council of Learned Societies.

Jónsson, Jóhannes Gísli. 2007. "Variation in morphosytax: Some lessons from Insular Scandinavian." Paper presented at the conference "Formal Approaches to Variation in Syntax," May 10–12, University of York, UK.

Jónsson, Jóhannes Gísli, and Thórhallur Eythórsson. 2003. "Breytingar á frumlagsfalli í íslensku [Changes in subject case in Icelandic.]" *Íslenskt mál* 25: 7–40.

Jónsson, Jóhannes Gísli, and Thórhallur Eythórsson. 2005. "Variation and change in subject case marking in Insular Scandinavian." *Nordic Journal of Linguistics* 28(2): 223–245.

Kayne, Richard S. 2005. "On parameters and on principles of pronunciation." In Hans Broekhuis, Norbert Corver, Riny Huybregts, Ursula Kleinhenz, and Jan Koster (eds.), *Organizing grammar*. Linguistic Studies in Honor of Henk van Riemsdijk, 289–299. Berlin: Mouton de Gruyter.

Kroch, Anthony S. 1989. "Reflexes of grammar in patterns of language change." *Language Variation and Change* 1: 199–244.

Kroch, Anthony S. 2001. "Syntactic change." In Mark Baltin and Chris Collins (eds.), *The handbook of contemporary syntactic theory*, 699–729. Oxford: Blackwell.

Labov, William. 1972. *Sociolinguistic patterns*. Philadelphia: University of Pennsylvania Press.

Lightfoot, David. 1999. *The development of language*. Oxford: Blackwell.

Maling, Joan. 2002. "Það rignir þágufalli á Íslandi: Verbs with dative objects in Icelandic." *Íslenskt mál* 24: 31–105.

Maling, Joan, and Sigríður Sigurjónsdóttir. 2002. "The 'New Impersonal' construction in Icelandic." *Journal of Comparative Germanic Linguistics* 5: 97–142.

Manzini, M. Rita, and Leonardo M. Savoia. 2011. *Grammatical categories*. Variation in Romance Languages. Cambridge: Cambridge University Press.

Schütze, Carson T. 1996. *The empirical base of linguistics: Grammatical judgments and linguistic methodology*. Chicago: University of Chicago Press.

Svavarsdóttir, Ásta. 1982. "Þágufallssýki: Breytingar á fallnotkun í frumlagssæti ópersónulegra setninga [Dative Sickness. Changes in the subject case of impersonal sentences]." *Íslenskt mál* 4: 19–62.

Svavarsdóttir, Ásta. 2006. "Texti, tal og tilraunir. Um efnivið og aðferðir í tilbrigðarannsóknum [Text, spoken language and experiments. About data and methodology in variation research]." Paper presented at Hugvísindaþing, University of Iceland, November 3.

Svavarsdóttir, Ásta. 2011. "Þágufallshneigð í sjón og raun [Dative Sickness in appearance and in reality]." In Thráinsson et al. (eds.) 2011: chap. 4.

Svenonius, Peter. 2002. "Icelandic Case and the structure of events." *Journal of Comparative Germanic Linguistics* 5: 197–225.

Thráinsson, Höskuldur. 2007. *The syntax of Icelandic*. Cambridge: Cambridge University Press.

Thráinsson, Höskuldur. 2010. "Variation and parametric correlations in Faroese." Unpublished ms. University of Iceland, Reykjavík. (Under review.)

Thráinsson, Höskuldur, Ásgrímur Angantýsson, and Einar Freyr Sigurðsson (eds.) 2011. *Tilbrigði í íslenskri setningagerð [Variation in Icelandic syntax]*. Unpublished ms., University of Iceland.

Thráinsson, Höskuldur, and Kristján Árnason. 1992. "Phonological variation in 20th century Icelandic." *Íslenskt mál* 14: 89–128.

Thráinsson, Höskuldur, Hjalmar P. Petersen, Jógvan í Lon Jacobsen, and Zakaris Svabo Hansen. 2004. *Faroese: An overview and reference grammar*. Tórshavn: Føroya Fróðskaparfelag.

Trudgill, Peter. 1986. *Dialects in contact*. Oxford: Blackwell.

Woolford, Ellen. 2006. "Lexical case, inherent case and argument structure." *Linguistic Inquiry* 37: 111–130.

Yang, Charles. 2000. "Internal and external forces in language change." *Language Variation and Change* 12: 231–250.

Yang, Charles. 2004. "Universal Grammar, statistics or both?" *Trends in Cognitive Sciences* 8(10): 451–456.

Yang, Charles. 2010. "Three factors in language variation." *Lingua* 120(5): 1160–1177.

CHAPTER 7

Feminine Bleeds Dative: The Syntax of a Syncretism Pattern

THOMAS LEU

In this article I present a novel view of the German dative and genitive morphs *m*, *r*, and *s* as contextual allomorphs of a single morpheme I call OK (Oblique Kase). OK, I claim, is categorially distinct from nominative and accusative determiner/adjective agreement. I discuss six syntactic contrasts supporting this claim. The consequences are important: (i) the superficial syncretism pattern in German oblique case marking is epiphenomenal and hence resolved without reference to morphological means such as underspecification, and (ii) the distribution of dative and genitive morphology does not inform an analysis of the German weak/strong adjectival declension alternation, the two being separate phenomena.

1. INTRODUCTION

Case is a noun phrase internal reflex of (aspects of) the noun phrase's external environment (i.e., of its syntactic position). The reflex may consist (among other things) of a morphological cue. In German, the main (though not the only) reflex of case is typically visible as a suffix on the definite article (if present). Consider (1). These examples illustrate the German four-way case distinction between nominative, accusative, dative, and genitive.

(1) a. Nominative:
   Der   **Fisch**   schwimmt   davon.
   the.NOM fish   swims   away

   b. Accusative:
   Nico   hat   **den**   **Fisch**   gesehen.
   Nico   has   the.ACC   fish   seen

c. Dative:

Nico	hat	mit	**dem**	**Fisch**	gespielt.
Nico	has	with	the.DAT	fish	played

d. Genitive:

Nico	hat	**des**	**Fisches**	wegen	die	Schule	geschwänzt.
Nico	has	the.GEN	fish.GEN	because.of	the	school	skipped

The bold-faced definite article has distinct inflectional endings in the (tensed) subject position, the direct object position, as the complement of the preposition *mit*, and as the complement of the postposition *wegen*.

The shape of the case morpheme is not only sensitive to the external environment, but also to other factors, including the grammatical gender of the head noun.[1] The four-way case contrast of German is overt only with masculine nouns. With neuter nouns and with feminine nouns, there is some degree of syncretism and possibly accidental homophony.

The singular (main) case/agreement markers, that is, those that are suffixed to the definite article in plain definite noun phrases, are given in the table in (2) (Vocalic material is not represented.).

(2)   Singular case marker exponents of German determiners (the traditional picture):

	MASCULINE	NEUTER	FEMININE
NOM	r	s	Ø
ACC	n	s	Ø
DAT	m	m	r
GEN	s	s	r

This table is traditionally thought to represent a morphological paradigm, that is, a featurally diverse collection of categorially identical elements. The criticism I will put forward applies independently of whether the paradigm is taken to be part of the grammar (as, e.g., in Zwicky 1985, Williams 1994) or epiphenomenal, as in Distributed Morphology (Halle & Marantz 1993, Bobaljik 2002). For concreteness, let me illustrate the backdrop of my criticism in the DM analysis of (2) from McFadden (2004). McFadden (2004: chap. 6.4) proposes that the syncretisms in (2) be captured in terms of underspecification of the relevant Vocabulary Items (VI) as in (3). Note that the cases are decomposed into features:[2]

1 It is also sensitive to number. I will set plural noun phrases aside for this discussion, focusing on singulars.

2 (3) is a simplified representation of McFadden's proposal, ignoring vocalic material.

(3) Upper half of (2):

    a. [+case ; -fem, -neu] $\Rightarrow$ /-r/

    b. [+case, +inferior ; -fem, -neu] $\Rightarrow$ /-n/

    c. [+case ; -fem, +neu] $\Rightarrow$ /-s/

    d. [+case ; +fem, -neu] $\Rightarrow$ /ø/

Lower half of (2):

    e. [+case, + oblique, +inferior ; -fem] $\Rightarrow$ /-m/

    f. [+case, +oblique, +inferior, +genitive ; -fem] $\Rightarrow$ /-s/

    g. [+case, +oblique, +inferior ; +fem, -neu] $\Rightarrow$ /-r/

(3e) derives the masculine-neuter syncretic *m* in datives, and (3f) derives the masculine-neuter syncretic *s* in genitives. But there is nothing in the system that would relate these two syncretisms and thus capture the metasyncretism of masculine-neuter in oblique environments.

(3g) derives the dative-genitive syncretic *r* for feminines. But there is not nor could there be anything in the system that relates the syncretism captured by (3g) to the above-mentioned metasyncretism.

The two halves of the table in (2) are distinguished by means of a feature [+oblique], a stipulation that is necessary, but lies largely fallow, being tied to the postsyntactic component.

Let me, in part following Bayer et al. (2001), locate this necessary stipulation in the syntax, by hypothesizing that the node in which nominative and accusative case (and agreement) are realized is categorially distinct from the node in which dative and genitive are realized, that is, they are not simply featural variants of one another.

The lack of any syncretism spanning across (parts of) both halves is an initial motivation for this idea. But the crucial evidence for the categorial contrast is syntactic. The elements in the upper half of the table and those in the lower half have a distinct (noun phrase internal) syntactic distribution. An initial piece of syntactic evidence is visible once we shift from plain definite noun phrases to modified indefinite (singular count) noun phrases. Consider (4). In noun phrases like (4), the dative and genitive exponents *m*, *s*, and *r* (4b) systematically appear in a higher position than the nominative and accusative exponents *r* and *s* (4a). The former are suffixed to the indefinite article, the latter to the adjective, in (4).

(4)   a. ein gut-**er**   Wein / ein   gut-**es**   Müsli

         a   good-NOM wine / a   good-NOM/ACC muesli

    b. ein-**em** gut-en   Wein / ein-**es** gut-en   Wein**s** / ein-**er**   gut-en   Suppe

         a-DAT good-INFL wine / a-GEN   good-INFL wine/ a-FEM.DAT good-INFL soup

This fundamental distributional discrepancy between nominative and accusative morphology, on the one hand, and dative and genitive morphology, on the other, is usually dealt with by dramatically complicating the analysis of adjectival and determiner agreement (cf. Zwicky 1986, Roehrs 2006, among many others). I take it, instead, to reveal, syntactically, the categorial distinction between the elements in the upper half of table (2) and the ones in the lower half.

In agreement with the proposal by Bayer (2002: 1) that "inherent Cases must supply their own functional structure [...] the exponent of the dative's functional structure is its overt Case morphology KASE," I propose that dative (and genitive) morphology corresponds to pieces of syntactic structure beyond what we find in a nonoblique noun phrase, and hence that dative morphology and the category on which structural case is realized, namely adjectival/determiner inflection AGRA, do not belong in one and the same paradigm.[3] I will refer to the class of principal dative and genitive case marker morphs (m, r, and s) as OK, for "Oblique Kase marker." The reason it sometimes looks as if dative and genitive OK (1c,d) were in complementary distribution with nominative and accusative AGRA[4] (1a,b) is, I claim, that in the context [OK], AGRA remains unpronounced (cf. also Pesetsky 2010 on Russian).

In the remainder of the article, sections 2–6, I will discuss the following five contexts in which the oblique case markers s, m, and r contrast syntactically both with adjectival agreement and among each other. I conclude that the morphological divisions are syntactically grounded.

A) **Inflectional Parallelism** violation by m German

B) **Indefinite article** distinct positions for m and r Swiss German

C) **Possessive determiners** distinct positions for m German/Swiss
   and r German

D) **PD-contraction** with m but not r German/Swiss

E) **Genitive s** failure to occur on adjectives   German

In each of these contexts, one OK exponent contrasts syntactically both with another OK exponent and with AGRA. I will suggest that the five a priori surprising observations (A–E) are a unified phenomenon, and that, especially given the nature of (C), the phenomenon is syntactic. Hence there is a principled form-syntax correspondence $s > m > r$ which suggests a treatment of the OK exponents s, m, and r as contextual allomorphs.[5] In

---

3 See Caha (2009) for detailed discussion of the idea that some cases contain others, in a nanosyntactic framework.

4 Strong adjectival/determiner agreement

5 See Parrott (2009) for a recent proposal of English and Danish pronominal case variation in terms of contextual allomorphy (based, in part, on Emonds 1986).

fact, the additional functional oblique case structure consists of elements that are merged discontinuously, in a way reminiscent of a *wh*-morpheme in a *wh*-noun phrase and the [+wh] in C^0 that licenses it.

2. VIOLATION OF "PARALLEL INFLECTION"

Let us start with a contrast that has recently been discussed in some detail by Roehrs (2009b). Dative *m* disrespects a most fundamental constraint on adjectival agreement, which I interpret as suggesting that dative *m* is not an instance of adjectival agreement.

2.1 The Problem

In German, adjectives inflect according to one of two paradigms ("weak" and "strong," so named after the degree of paradigmatic contrasts). The choice of declension paradigm is correlated with the choice of determiner. For example, in (5a), after the demonstrative *dieser* "this," the adjectives exhibit weak inflection. In (5b), after the indefinite article, the adjectives exhibit strong inflection (cf. Bierwisch 1967, Milner and Milner 1972, Zwicky 1986, Gallmann 1996, 2004, Schlenker 1999, Müller 2002, Roehrs 2006, 2009a, Leu 2008, Schoorlemmer 2009, among others).

(5) a. dieser gut-**e**   frisch-**e**   Wein
        this   good-WK   fresh-WK   wine

    b. (ein) gut-**er**   frisch-**er**   Wein
       (a)   good-STR fresh-STR   wine

In a sequence of two (or more) adjectives that modify the same noun within a DP, the adjectives carry identical inflection, that is, either both are weak or both are strong, but no mixing. This is well known. Milner and Milner (1972: 42) consider such a generalization a plausible universal. The generalization has different names in the literature. Müller (2002) calls it the "Adjective Correspondence" constraint; Gallmann (2004) the "Parallel (NP, A-Infl)" constraint; and Roehrs (2009b) the "Inflectional parallelism generalization." I will call it *Parallel Inflection*.

Crucially, there should be (according to Parallel Inflection) no possible choice of noun and/or determiner and/or external environment such that the two adjectives would exhibit an inflection distinct from one another.[6] However, there are two environments, which have been discussed in the

---

6 Setting aside instances of modifiers that do not exhibit any inflection in the first place.

literature, in which Parallel Inflection seems to be violated: masculine dative singular bare nominals and neuter dative singular bare nominals.

Consider the three examples of modified dative singular bare nominals in (6). Parallel Inflection is obligatorily respected in the feminine example in (6a). But in the masculine example (6b) and in the neuter example (6c) two variants are fairly acceptable, one of which violates Parallel Inflection.

(6) a. FEMININE:

    mit   [gut-**er**]   [frisch*-**en**/-**er**]   Milch
    with good-DAT.F fresh-WK/DAT.F milk

  b. MASCULINE:

    mit   [gut-**em**] [frisch-**en**/-**em**] Wein
    with good-DAT fresh-WK/DAT wine

  c. NEUTER:

    mit   [gut-**em**] [frisch-**en**/-**em**] Wasser
    with good-DAT fresh-WK/DAT water

The relative judgments reported in the literature for the two variants in (6b) and in (6c) vary (see Roehrs 2009b). But everybody prefers either variant in (6b) and (6c) to the nonparallel variant in (6a).

Notice that the case (and agreement) morphology in the two contexts that allow a violation of Parallel Inflection is syncretic. Hence, the unruly behavior vis-à-vis Parallel Inflection should presumably not be allowed twice, once for masculine singular bare nominal datives and once for neuter singular bare nominal datives, but only once: for the dative element *m*. This seems uncontroversial in the literature. But where, in the grammar, the contrast between (6a) and (6b,c) is situated is debated.

2.2 Previous Proposals

There have been a number of reactions to the sort of surprising facts in (6). Let me mention three kinds.

2.2.1 Phonological Account

One kind of reaction is to try and mobilize phonology. Gallmann (2004: 156), for instance, proposes a phonological constraint "*SCHWA-m," which says that German word forms do not end in schwa + /m/. Since OT constraints can be violated, that does not mean that there are no German words ending in *əm*. But all else being equal, *ən#* would be preferable to *əm#*. No such restriction figures for words ending in ə r.[7] If this is combined with a requirement that (certain) features (e.g., dative) must be expressed at least once in a DP (in the relevant configuration), the contrast in (6) can be accounted for. Hence for Gallmann the contrast is phonologically grounded and bound to word-final position.

In a similar spirit Roehrs (2009b) formulates the phonological rule

(7) $m \rightarrow n/[...]^A + ə$ ___ #

which explicitly mentions adjectives. Roehrs hence also views the contrast in (6) as phonological and word-final, and furthermore as bound to the category of adjectives. Sensitivity to word-finality seems natural for a phonological constraint/rule, and so does substitution of a more marked phonetic feature by a less marked one. But if it turns out, as I will argue, that the relevant contrast is not restricted to word-final position, and that the contrast does not (need to) result in such substitution but may result in a contrast in linear order, the two phonological accounts are seriously challenged.

Independently of the line of argument I am developing in this article, a phonological proposal, such as Gallmann (2004) or Roehrs (2009b), must restrict the application of the relevant constraint or rule, in order to allow the obligatoriness of an *m* ending on the first adjective (8a) as well as on single adjectives (8b).

(8) a. mit gutem   roten   Wein
       with good.DAT red.INFL wine

    b. mit (rotem/*roten)   Wein
       with red.DAT/red.INFL wine

Roehrs (2009b) addresses the issue in terms of processing efficiency. He notes that *m* unlike *n* is unambiguously dative, and hence, Roehrs proposes, its appearance (on the first adjective in (8)) is due to an early disambiguation strategy.

However, notice that in (8) there is no risk of ambiguity in the relevant sense.[8] The preposition *mit* can only embed dative complements and hence precludes indeterminacy on that level. Second, in the absence of an adjective, the example is acceptable without any overt case marking.[9]

---

7 Perhaps rather than saying no such restriction exists for ə r, I should say, no such restriction against ə r seems to ever play a role in choosing the winning candidate in the relevant contexts.

8 To be precise there is ambiguity at a very local level, namely within the adjective (phrase). But at that level ambiguity must be permissible, since it also occurs in the second adjective of the acceptable (8a) for instance.

9 The puzzle of the obligatory absence in German of morphological dative marking in bare noun phrases will not be resolved in this article. See Gallmann (1998) for discussion.

It seems, then, that these phonological proposals would need an additional constraint to the effect that in the presence of an adjective or determiner, dative case must be overtly expressed by a case suffix at least once. While this would appear to give the right result, there is a profound problem with the combination of such a constraint and a phonological constraint of the sort Gallmann and Roehrs propose. The phonological constraint is operative at a later, more superficial level than the morphosyntactic constraint which would assure retention of *m* in (8b). In fact, Roehrs explicitly states that his rule in (7) is a "post-lexical, that is, lower-level process" concluding that therefore "strong morpho-syntactic conclusions should not be based on these data."

2.2.2 Morphological Account

Schlenker (1999: 11–12) proposes an account framed in a top-down late insertion model by means of a morphological feature [+Fission]. In Schlenker's model, morpheme insertion proceeds top-down. The features of a node that is being spelled out are passed on to the lower node, except if the inserted morpheme is marked [+Fission]. In that case the features it expresses are deleted and will not be copied down onto the next relevant node. The effect is that fewer features are present on the lower node, giving rise to a different choice upon vocabulary insertion (i.e., to weak inflection). In the typical case, in German, determiner inflection is marked [+Fission] (cf. (5a)), and adjectival inflection is marked [-Fission] (cf. (5b)). In (6), *m* is marked [+Fission] (even though it occurs on an adjective), while *r* (along with all inflection on adjectives other than *m*) is marked [-Fission]. In other words, for Schlenker, the contrast between (6b,c) and (6a) consists in the value of the feature [αFission] associated with *m* and *r* respectively, and the way it affects vocabulary insertion in lower nodes. Thus Schlenker expects a contrast between *m* and *r* only in pairs in which *r* is possible more than once. Thereby his proposal is paralytic with regard to the other four contrasts discussed in this article, as we will see. Hence if the contrast in (6) and the other four contrasts are related, Schlenker's proposal for (6) is insufficient (at least).

The idea that the contrast in (6) is not a solitary phenomenon is (among other things) suggested from an acquisition perspective. Note that the acceptability judgments on (6b,c), though somewhat variable across speakers, are very sharp with regard to the contrast between *m* and *r* (6a).

From an explanatory adequacy point of view, the question arises of how this contrast is acquired. On Schlenker's (1999) view, the contrast is only ever manifested in examples like (6b,c), in modified bare nominals with two noncoordinated adjectives. It is not obvious that there is much evidence in that regard which every child is guaranteed to come across. But more importantly, there is a "no negative evidence" issue here. If the contrast between *m* and *r* in (6) is arbitrary and entirely disconnected from anything else, the absence, as far as I know, of any speaker accepting a nonparallel example with *r* would be surprising. This is especially acute for speakers who allow both variants with *m* (which seem to be numerous; cf. Roehrs 2009b). Hence, it seems to me that if the only observable evidence that the child has access to comes from that rare kind of example, the sharp contrast between *m* and *r* in (6) is unexpected.

2.2.3 Questioning the Seriousness of the Issue

A third kind of reaction is that of Müller (2002: 24), who notes, "[I]t seems preferable to classify [the nonparallel variant of (6b,c)] as not resulting from the core system of nominal inflection in present-day German."

The status of such unexpected yet subtle contrasts as in (6) may indeed be up for discussion, as is the status of notions such as "core system." It seems clear that grammatical peripheralization of the (6b,c) phenomenon is (possibly) plausible to the extent that it is an isolated phenomenon. If, on the other hand, further contexts can be identified (ideally, high-frequency cases) in which a syntactic *m>r* contrast is easily observable, from which deeper grammatical properties associated with *m* and *r* are inferable, the acquisition problem will be solvable, but the theory will, of course, have to step up and take the contrast seriously.

In what follows I will show that a contrast between *m* and *r*, such that *r* occurs further to the right than *m*, is also observed in environments to which the rules and mechanisms mentioned above cannot apply (or where an application thereof would not have the desired effect). To the extent that the contrast in (6) and the ones discussed below are likely to be related, the proposals for (6) mentioned above are strongly misguided.[10]

3. SWISS GERMAN INDEFINITE ARTICLE

A simpler, though less widely known case in which dative *m* and feminine *r* contrast in their positional distribution is in the context of the indefinite

---

10 I will, unfortunately, not present a complete counterproposal for (6b,c). Accounting for (6b,c) would involve a number of unknown analytic variables to do with the syntactic representation of multiple adjectives, which is likely more complex than is usually assumed. I hope though that the arguments for the need of a syntactic account are nevertheless convincing.

article in Swiss German. The "indefinite article" in Swiss German dative DPs is (at least) trimorphemic.

(9) uf   əm   ən   ä   bärg   (Swiss German)
     on   DAT   STEM INFL mountain
     "on a mountain"

The element *ən*, which I gloss STEM, can sometimes remain unpronounced, especially in feminine contexts.[11] In addition to the STEM there is an invariant ending *ä*, and an OK (dative case) marker, *m* in the context of masculine and neuter nouns (9); *r* in the context of feminine nouns. I take the invariant ending *ä* to be an inflectional element, presently without discussion.

Interesting in the present context is the fact that the choice of OK (*m* versus *r*) correlates with a positional contrast of OK. Whereas *m* precedes the STEM, the feminine OK *r* surfaces between the STEM and the invariant ending *a*.[12,13]

(10) a. uf **əm**   [-ən   ]-ä   bärg$_{mas}$ (*on a mountain*)
      b. uf   [-ən   **-ər**]-ä   blüamä$_{fem}$ (*on a flower*)
              on DAT.M/N STEM DAT.F AGR   N

Notice that none of the proposals mentioned in section 2.2 extends to (10). Schlenker's (1999) morphological approach, first of all, cannot displace *m* or *r*, and second, it only effects a contrast at a possible second occurrence of the relevant feature(s). But since there is only one occurrence in (10), no contrast is expected.

The phonological proposals by Gallmann (2004) and Roehrs (2009b) are limited to word-final elements, but *r* and *m* in (10) do not qualify as such, nor is it, in (10), a matter of pronouncing an original *m* as *n* where an original *r* remains untouched. Hence the proposals in the literature that were designed to capture the contrast between *m* and *r* in (6) are profoundly ill

11 Cf. Weber (1964: 105) for Zürich German, Fischer (1960: 187ff.) for Lucerne German, Marti (1985: 79) for Bern German, and Bossard (1962: 45) for Zug German.

12 For Basel German, Suter (1976: 75) notes the additional possibility of leaving *m* in post-stem position. But pre-stem *r* remains excluded. This may be related to the note in Marti (1985: 75) that the *n*, which I call STEM, is historically related to the Middle High German cognate of the German indefinite article *ein*, which (still in contemporary Standard German) precedes both dative *m* and feminine *r*.

13 Fischer (1960: 187–188) notes (in footnotes and in addition to the variants above, which he gives in the main text) the possibility in Lucerne German of *r* preceding *n*, as in *of er(n)e Matte* "on a mat," as well as forms with two instances of *r*, as in *met erere Chue* "with a cow."

suited for an explanation of the contrast between m and r in (10). Finally, regarding the position that the nonparallel variant of (6b,c) is not part of the core grammar, it is not clear what that would mean for (10).

It is, of course, logically possible that (10) is due to yet another phonological rule (Studler 2001), a sort of metathesis, and hence (10) and (6) are unrelated. A more interesting hypothesis, however, is that (10) and (6) are related, and that hence any account of one must, at least in principle, be able to extend to the other. I conclude that to the extent that (10) and (6) are related, the proposals in 2.2 are incorrect.

As an alternative to the morphological and phonological proposals for (6), and importantly taking into account (10), I suspect that the contrast is syntactic. Concretely, I propose that the dative exponent m is in a different syntactic position from the feminine oblique case marker r. More specifically, the syntactic position of m is higher than that of r.[14]

(11) [...m... [...r...]]

It is this structural contrast that should be cashed out in an account of (6). I will, however, not propose an explicit account of (6), but focus instead on the syntactic contrast between m and r per se, which is epistemologically prior.

As a segue to the next section, let me state the second important aspect of my proposal. On the grounds of the relative syntactic independence of m, and given the fact that it violates an (otherwise) valid constraint on adjectival inflection (cf. section 2), I propose, following Bayer (2002), that m is not on a par with adjectival/determiner agreement (AGRA); instead it is the realization of a chunk of syntax that constitutes "oblique case." This chunk of syntax is, as we will see instantly, to an astonishing degree analogous to that involved in possessive determiners.

4. POSSESSIVE PRONOUNS/DETERMINERS

The syntactic contrast between dative m and feminine oblique r, which is sometimes surface apparent, also marks a morphosyntactic contrast in the domain of possessive determiners/pronouns in German and Swiss German. In this domain the surface effect is so blatant that it is traditionally understood as a lexical contrast, and is, hence, typically being set aside as idiosyncratic. I break with this tradition, proposing that it is an instantiation of (11).

---

14 (11) is not a partial representation of an actual example, but rather an abstract juxtaposition of the members of a minimal pair contrasting on the feminine/nonfeminine dimension.

4.1 Swiss German

To begin, consider the Swiss German singular possessive determiners.

(12) mis / dis / (im)   sis / irəs   piär
　　　 my   your (him)   self's   her   beer

With a first or second person possessor (13), the overt elements are three in number, from left to right: a possessor person morpheme, a vocalic element *i*, which I gloss as STEM, and an agreement ending *s*, reflecting the grammatical gender of the possessee. This agreement *s* corresponds to strong adjectival agreement (AGRA).[15]

(13) m-   i   -s   piär   ("my beer")
　　　 d-   i   -s   piär   ("your beer")
　　　 PERS STEM AGRA beer

Given the possessor marking in (13), *m* and *d*, the Indo-European *m-t-s* paradigm (Benveniste 1966, Kayne 2000b) raises the correct expectation that the corresponding third-person possessor determiner is *sis*.

(14) s-   i   -s   piär   ("his beer")
　　　 PERS STEM AGRA   beer

There are two extremely interesting caveats to (14). First of all, the possessor is "optionally" doubled, in that a pronominal *im* "him" (or full dative DP) possessor optionally precedes *sis* "his."

(15) im   sis   piär   ("his beer")
　　　 him   his   beer

And second, while the first and second person possessor forms (13) have no restrictions on the grammatical gender of the possessor, (14) is incompatible with a grammatically feminine gender possessor. For feminine possessors the corresponding determiner is *ires* "her."

(16) irəs   piär   ("her beer")
　　　 her   beer

---

15 There are a number of complications here, which I am setting aside. These include dialectal variation and some amount of paradigmatic "irregularity" with regard to the overt expression of AGRA with possessive determiners.

This is entirely unexpected. Note that it is not the "third person" *s* that is incompatible with feminine.

(17) a. Sie / er/ es hat sich umgedreht.   German
       She / he/ it has S.self around.turned
     b. Elle s' est   retournée.   French
        she S   is   around.turned

So what is it about (14) that makes it incompatible with a feminine possessor?

In order to answer this important question, let us contrast the feminine and the nonfeminine possessor determiners in more detail, including the pronominal possessor double *im* "him."

(18) a. **im**   s-[-i-   ]-s   piär   ("his beer")

     b.   [-i-   -**r**   ]-əs piär   ("her beer")

         DAT   STEM   FEM   AGRA beer

The right edge morpheme is the same in (18a) and (18b): strong adjectival agreement AGRA. In the nonfeminine variant (18a), the AGRA morpheme is immediately preceded by the stem *i*. This contrasts with the feminine possessor variant (18b), in which the feminine oblique case marker *r* intervenes. But even though in (18a) the nonfeminine dative morph *m* does not intervene between the suffixal AGRA and the STEM *i*, it is ("optionally") present in a left peripheral position, as part of the possessor doubling element *im* "him." The fact, now, that *sis piär* "his beer" is incompatible with a feminine possessor even without overt possessor doubling suggests that (*i*)*m* is syntactically present also when it is not pronounced, in a way that recalls topic drop (at least loosely, though cf. Haegeman 2004).[16]

---

16 Note that *r* is obligatory in (18b). This very fact as well as the interpretive restrictions on *sis* "his" strongly suggest that *m* is syntactically present in (14). What ever it is that makes the syntactic expression of the possessor by means of *r* and (optionally unpronounced) *m* obligatory in (18a,b) should, ceteris paribus, be expected to also require an analogous possessor marker in (13). We can, without pursuing this line further here, follow an idea by Gisbert Fanselow (noted as personal communication in Olsen 1989) that first and second person possessor determiners syntactically involve an initial possessor element. Note in this context also the Northwestern Norwegian innovation of first-person and second-person possessor doubling, reported in Vangsnes (2006).

i. mitt sitt hus
    "my house"
ii. ditt sitt hus
    "your house"

The function of *m* in (18a) and that of *r* in (18b) are identical in marking the possessor. Furthermore, it is impossible to substitute *r* for *m* in (18a) or vice versa in (18b). Furthermore (and as we have already seen; cf. (2)), nonfeminine dative *m* and feminine dative *r* are paradigmatic variants of the OK (oblique case) marker elsewhere (too). Given these considerations, I propose that the left peripheral *m* and the post-STEM *r* in (18) originate in the same position and that their contrasting in surface position is due to syntactic movement. That is, the two morphs are affected by partly distinct sets of displacement operations. Let me, at this point, bring in Hungarian.

4.2 Hungarian

The proposal of two distinct (noun phrase internal) positions for the possessor is strongly reminiscent of Hungarian, as discussed in Szabolcsi (1983/84, 1994). Hungarian has more than one possessor position. Possessors either surface in a low position, to the right of the definite article (19a), or in a higher position, to the left of the definite article (19b). In the high position, the possessor is marked for dative. In the lower position it is not dative-marked.

(19) a. (a) Mari   kalap-ja
         the Mary.NOM   hat-POSS.3SG

     b. Mari-nak   a   t   kalap-ja
        Mary-DAT the   hat-POSS.3SG

Szabolcsi argues that the position of the possessor in (19b) is the result of syntactic movement.[17] She notes that dative-marked possessors can extract from their noun phrase, while ones that are not dative-marked cannot. This leads her to analyze the left-peripheral position of *Marinak* in (19b) as escape hatch, analogous to Spec,CP in the clause.

It is worth noting that the parallel between Hungarian and Germanic extends to possessor extraction in that some Germanic languages, including Swiss German (20a), allow possessor extraction to a limited degree. Interestingly, the extracted (pronominal) possessor must contain an *m* dative marker. Related is the fact that a noun phrase internal pronominal *wh*-possessor pronoun also is obligatorily *m* dative-marked and

---

17 In German, (overt) first and second person possessor doubling is strongly degraded (but cf. note 16). This could now be related to the fact that in Hungarian pronominal possessors are hardly acceptable in the dative position (Szabolcsi 1994: 188), raising the question of why *ihm* "him" is different.

necessarily occurs at the left edge (20b), rather than to the right of the STEM (20c).[18]

(20) a. We-m   isch das sini Schrift?   Swiss German
       who-DAT is   this his handwriting

   b. We-m   sis piär isch das?
       who-DAT his beer is   this

   c. *I-we-r-əs   piär isch das?
       STEM-who.FEM-AGRA beer is   this

4.3 A Short Stopover

Let me briefly stop here and propose that we think of the similarity of (18) and (10) as not accidental, and that the unified underlying contrast is the result of phrasal movement of *m*. Both the parallel with Hungarian as well as the case syncretism of *r* across dative/genitive suggests that *m* is the true dative marker, where dative marking is the morphological interpretation of the combined properties of having certain features (those of OK) and being in a certain position. Note furthermore that in the case of the Swiss German possessive determiners, (13) and (14), it is immediately obvious that the OK elements *m* and *r* co-occur with strong adjectival/determiner agreement AGRA, implying that they are of distinct categories.

    Second, let me point out that the proposals discussed in section 2.2 are entirely impotent vis-à-vis the contrast in (18) (and the one in (10)). Of course, the authors never intended their proposals to be applicable to this contrast, but only to the one in (6). However, their viability even for (6) hinges on this being unrelated to (18) and (10). Recalling my remarks in sections 2.2.2 and 2.2.3, however, we do expect the contrast in (6) to be related to some surface contrast with a higher profile. Notice that possessive determiners (18) and indefinite articles (10) are high-frequency expressions, and are hence likely to be abundantly present in the child's input.[19] Given that in both cases we are concerned with a syntactic(-looking) contrast between the nonfeminine dative marker *m* and the feminine dative marker

---

18 This is plausibly close to the fact that *wh*-possessive pronouns cannot express feminine gender of the possessor.
19 While the considerations from acquisition argue in favor of the idea that the different surface contrasts in question are related, the relation cannot be trivial, given that Swiss German does not have the contrast in (6), whereas German does not have the one in (10). Both sets of varieties of Germanic have the contrast in (18), however, as well as the one concerning PD-contraction discussed in the next section.

r, it is likely that those surface contrasts are related and are connected to properties of the functional sequence of heads in the syntactic spine.

5. P-D CONTRACTION

Another set of high-frequency cases which expose a syntactic(-looking) contrast between dative *m* and feminine *r* are the so-called P-D-contraction (or "clipping") contexts. Descriptively speaking, when a definite DP is embedded under certain dative prepositions the masculine/neuter dative marker *m* amalgamates with the preposition and the definite article *d* remains unpronounced (21).

(21) a. vo-m   Baum
       from-DAT   tree
       "from the tree"

    b. a-m   Baum
       on-DAT   tree
       "on the tree"

In the feminine counterparts of (21), the feminine OK *r*, in contrast, does not amalgamate with the preposition, and the definite marker *d* is overt, linearly intervening between the preposition and the case marker *r* (22).[20]

(22) a. von   d-er   Blume
       from   the-FEM   flower

    b. an d-er   Blume
       on the-FEM   flower

Van Riemsdijk (1998) proposes a basically phonological analysis. However, thinking of the previous discussion, specifically the fact that in Hungarian the dative possessor (cf. German *m*) precedes the definite article associated with the possessed noun (Szabolcsi 1994: 200) while the nominative possessor (cf. German *r*) follows it, it seems plausible that the contrast between (21) and (22) is syntactic.

I propose that in (21) the OK *m* has moved to a left peripheral position within its containing DP, a position that precedes that of the definite article. Perhaps somewhat simplified, we can think of *m* as having moved to Spec,DP.[21] The feminine OK *r*, on the other hand, has not moved to

---

20 There is one exceptional preposition, *zu* "to," which also *r* contracts with, and the definite marker remains silent: *zu-r Blume* "to the flower." This is puzzling.

21 Let us assume that *m* in that higher position licenses the nonpronunciation of the definite article *d*-to its immediate right.

the DP-left periphery, but remains in a lower position, to the right of the definite article.

6. GENITIVE *S*

Let us, finally, turn to the *s* exponent in the OK paradigm. Just like dative *m*, genitive *s* is oblivious to the masculine/neuter distinction; and just like dative *m*, genitive *s* contrasts with feminine *r* (morphologically and syntactically); and just like dative *m*, genitive *s* has a morphosyntactic property that militates against its being of the same category as strong adjectival agreement AGRA, which is this: OK *s* never occurs on adjectives. Consider (23).

(23)   Masculine/Neuter

    a. wegen   d-**es**   gut-**en**   Wetter-s   German
       because.of   the-GEN   good-WK   weather-GEN

    b. wegen   gut   ***-es / -en**   Wetter-s
       because.of   good   -GEN/-WK   weather-GEN

When a definite article is present, OK *s* suffixes to the article, as do dative *m*, feminine *r*, and AGRA. In addition, *s* suffixes to the noun (except with the so-called masculine weak nouns), or perhaps more accurately to the entire projection, as a phrasal affix (on English *s*, cf. Anderson 2005: chap. 4). But when the leftmost element in the noun phrase is a (modifying) adjective, OK *s* refuses to suffix to that adjective (23b), contrary to OK *m* and *r*, and also contrary to adjectival agreement AGRA. This strongly suggests that it is not an instance of adjectival agreement. In other words, it is categorially distinct from AGRA.

If it is correct that genitive *s* is categorially identical to the feminine oblique case marker *r*, and to dative *m*, it follows that the latter two are also distinct from AGRA, as I have been arguing above on independent grounds.[22]

OK *s* is an unambiguous marker of genitive (with masculine nouns), and it is the only case marker that can occur on determiners but not on adjectives.[23] This contrasts with the feminine OK *r*, which can occur on both

---

22 NB: On my account, the fact that OK *m* and *r* have the same overt suffix-host as AGRA in bare modified noun phrases is in some sense accidental and does not imply categorial identity.

23 This property of genitive *s* raises nontrivial questions with regard to the idea that determiners, other than the articles, are adjectival phrases (Leu 2008). I will set this question aside for the present discussion.

determiners and adjectives and which is ambiguous between dative and genitive with regard to both its form and its position.

(24) FEMININE (Dative = Genitive)

a. wegen	d-**er**	gut-**en**	Sicht	German
because.of	the-GEN/DAT	good-WK	sight	
b. wegen	gut	**-er**	/ *-**en**	Sicht
because.of	good	-GEN/DAT/-WK		sight

This is important. OK *r* is keyed to a feminine gender, and it is oblivious to the dative/genitive contrast, while OK *s* is keyed to genitive, and oblivious to the masculine/neuter contrast, and OK *m* is keyed to dative and oblivious to the masculine/neuter contrast.

7. A GRAMMATICAL SKETCH

We are now in a position to state some important properties an adequate analysis of German case morphology must have.

7.1 Genitive *s*

We observed that both OK *s* and OK *m* exhibit gender syncretism, spanning across neuter and masculine, in contrast to feminine *r*. Genitive *s* contrasts with dative *m* in the following respects.

I OK *s* and OK *m* occur in different sets of DPs relative to the DP's external distribution (i.e., *s*, unlike *m*, occurs in DPs that are "assigned genitive case").
II OK *s* and OK *m* have different phonological/phonetic properties.
III OK *s* and OK *m* have a distinct positional distribution inside their containing DPs.

While usually property (I) is said to be related to a featural contrast in the DP, which is directly exploited by the morphology delivering property (II), this traditional view fails to take property (III) into account. In distinction to this, I propose that property (I) is due to a syntactic contrast in the DP. I.e. genitive DPs and dative DPs are syntactically distinct. Let us think of the notion of "oblique case assignment" in terms of categorial selection, such that a genitive environment (e.g., a genitive preposition) selects a

GenP, while a dative environment (e.g., a dative preposition) selects a DatP. Hence we can represent the contrast by postulating a Gen^0 head versus no Gen^0 head.[24]

The presence of Gen^0 in genitive environments is now responsible for property (III), assuming Gen^0 is an attractor and hence effects a movement operation, relocating a phrase, call it PoP, which (by stipulation) contains OK (or a trace thereof). The position of OK in(side) Spec,GenP (25a) is exploited by the morphology as in (25b), delivering property (II), that is, *s*.

(25) a.

GenP
PoP   Gen ...
OK

b. OK $\Rightarrow$ /-s/ /[____Gen^0]

7.2 Dative *m* and Feminine *r*

There are two scenarios on which an OK in a DP does not end up in Spec,GenP: one derives OK *m*, the other one OK *r*.

On the first such scenario, Gen^0 is not merged, in which case the relevant DP is not a possible genitive DP but must be a dative DP.[25] Let us assume that dative DPs are DatPs, with a Dat^0 head at their left-periphery into whose Spec PoP moves (26a). The position of OK in(side) Spec,DatP is exploited by the morphology as in (26b), delivering property (II), that is, *m*.

(26) a.

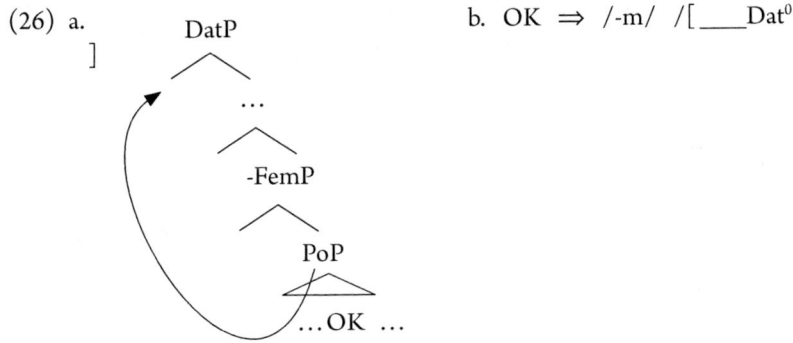

b. OK $\Rightarrow$ /-m/ /[____Dat^0

24 Possibly Gen^0 immediately embeds DatP.
25 PoP requires the presence of either Gen^0 or Dat^0, in a way that is comparable to *wh*-requiring C^0, or nominative requiring finite T.

On the second scenario, OK extracts from PoP prior to PoP-movement to Spec,GenP (or Spec,DatP). Since this is correlated with feminine nouns, let me stipulate a Fem⁰ attractor of OK. This second scenario, I claim, describes the case of feminine *r*. Note that extraction of OK out of PoP prevents OK from participating in PoP movement both to Spec,GenP and to Spec,DatP, correctly predicting that the *s-r* contrast and the *m-r* contrast are parallel. That is, *r* is correctly predicted to be oblivious to the contrast between dative and genitive, both in its morphology (27b) and in its syntax (27a).

(27) a.　DatP or GenP　　　　　　　　b. OK ⇒ /-r/

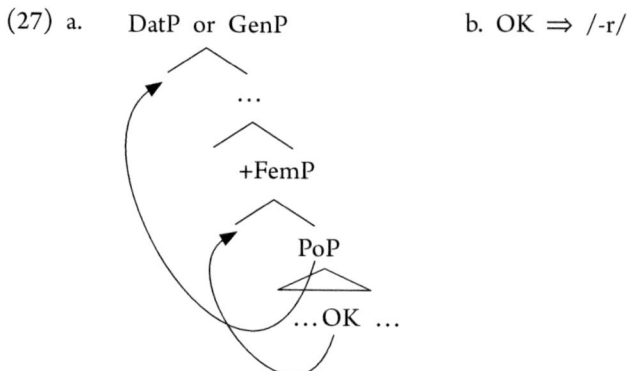

This proposal also correctly derives the fact that the positions of OK *m* and of OK *s* are syntactically higher than that of OK *r*. In order to account for the syntactic contrast between OK *m* and OK *s* something more will have to be said, presumably relating to the fact that genitive *s* also occurs at the very right edge of a genitive noun phrase, unlike dative *m*, which in turn should be related to its incapability of occurring at the level of embedding at which it could attach to an adjective in German.

8. CONCLUSION

I have discussed a fundamental split right through the middle of the traditional German determiner/adjective agreement paradigm, arguing that dative and genitive morphology is categorially distinct from nominative and accusative morphology. I adduced six syntactic contexts in which the dative/genitive morphs *m*, *r*, and *s* contrast syntactically with strong adjectival agreement and/or with one another.

The literature on German determiner and adjective inflection typically takes as the baseline for an analysis sets of examples in which the syntactic contrasts between the different morphs happen to be invisible, such as (1), and subsequently attempts to fit increasingly more deviant patterns into the picture. I suggest that we should, instead, start from generalizations based on visible systematic contrasts between the morphs, and worry later about the cases in which the contrasts are not surface apparent.

While I have not given detailed explicit analyses of the phenomena I discussed, I have, I hope convincingly, shown that an adequate analysis of German dative and genitive morphology must relate the syncretism pattern (2) to the syntactic distribution of the morphs in question (sections 2–6), along the lines of the proposal sketched in section 7.

An important consequence of this conclusion is that dative and genitive morphology is categorially distinct from (nominative and accusative) strong adjectival and determiner agreement; and that therefore the correct analysis of adjectival agreement, notably of the so-called weak/strong adjectival declension alternation, can and must be investigated independently of the distribution of dative and genitive morphology (cf. Leu 2008, 2009).

REFERENCES

Anderson, Stephen R. 2005. *Aspects of the theory of clitics*. Oxford Studies in Theoretical Linguistics. Oxford: Oxford University Press.

Bayer, Josef. 2002. "Dative pertinacity (or yet another morpheme that would not get away)." Handout from Workshop on Pertinacity, Freudental, July 11–14.

Bayer, Josef, Markus Bader, and Michael Meng. 2001. "Morphological underspecification meets oblique case: Syntactic and processing effects in German." *Lingua* 111: 465–514.

Benveniste, Emile. 1966. *Problèmes de linguistique générale*. Paris: Gallimard.

Bierwisch, Manfred. 1967. "Syntactic features in morphology: General problems of so-called pronominal inflection in German." In *To Honour Roman Jakobson*, 239–270. The Hague: Mouton.

Bobaljik, Jonathan. 2002. "Syncretism without paradigms: Remarks on Williams 1981, 1994." In Geert Booij and Jaap van Marle (eds.), *Yearbook of Morphology 2001*. Dordrecht: Kluwer.

Bossard, Hans. 1962. *Zuger Mundartbuch: Grammatik und Wörterverzeichnis*. Zürich: Schweizer Spiegel Verlag.

Caha, Pavel. 2009. "The nanosyntax of case." PhD diss., University of Tromsø.

Emonds, Joseph E. 1986. "Grammatically deviant prestige constructions." In Michael Brame, Heles Contrera, and Frederick J. Newmeyer (eds.), *A Festschrift for Sol Saporta*, 93–129. Seattle, WA: Noit Amrofer.

Fischer, Ludwig. 1989 [1960]. *Luzerndeutsche Grammatik*. Hitzkirch: Comenius Verlag..

Gallmann, Peter. 1996. "Die Steuerung der Flexion in der DP." *Linguistische Berichte* 164:283–314.

Gallmann, Peter. 1998. "Case underspecification in morphology, syntax and the lexicon." In Artemis Alexiadou and Chris Wilder (eds.), *Possessors, predicates and movement in the determiner phrase*, number 22 in Linguistik Aktuell, 141–176. Amsterdam: John Benjamins.

Gallmann, Peter. 2004. "Feature sharing in DPs." In Gereon Müller, Lutz Funkel, and Gisela Zifonun (eds.), *Explorations in Nominal Inflection*, 121–160. Berlin: Mouton de Gruyter.

Haegeman, Liliane. 2004. "A DP-internal anaphor agreement effect." *Linguistic Inquiry* 35: 704–712.

Halle, Morris, and Alec Marantz. 1993. "Distributed Morphology and the pieces of inflection." In Ken Hale and Samuel Jay Keyser (eds.), *The view from building 20: Essays in linguistics in honor of Sylvain Bromberger*, 111–176. Cambridge, MA: MIT Press.

Kayne, Richard S. 2000a. *Parameters and universals*. Oxford: Oxford University Press.

Kayne, Richard S. 2000b. "Person morphemes and reflexives in Italian, French, and related languages." In Kayne 2000a, 131–162.

Leu, Thomas. 2008. "The internal syntax of determiners." PhD diss., New York University.

Leu, Thomas. 2009. "From Greek to Germanic: Poly-(*in)-definiteness and weak/strong adjectival declension." In José M. Brucart, Anna Gavarró, and Jaume Solà (eds.), *Merging features: Computation, interpretation and acquisition*, 293–309. Oxford: Oxford University Press.

Marti, Werner. 1985. *Bern-Deutsch-Grammatik*. Muri-Bern: Cosmos Verlag.

McFadden, Thomas. 2004. "On the pronominal origins of the Germanic strong adjective inflection." Unpublished ms.

Milner, Judith, and Jean-Claude Milner. 1972. *La morphologie du groupe nominal en allemand*. DRLAV 2. Université de Paris VIII.

Müller, Gereon. 2002. "Remarks on nominal inflection in German." In Ingrid Kaufmann and Barbara Stiebels (eds.), *More than words: A festschrift for Dieter Wunderlich*, 113–145. Berlin: Akademie Verlag.

Olsen, Susan. 1989. Das Possessivum: Pronomen, Determinans oder Adjektiv? *Linguistische Berichte* 120: 133–153.

Parrott, Jeffrey K. 2009. "Danish vestigial case and the acquisition of vocabulary in distributed morphology." *Biolinguistics* 3: 270–304.

Pesetsky, David. 2010. "Russian case morphology and the syntactic categories." Unpublished ms., MIT.

Roehrs, Dorian. 2006. "The morpho-syntax of the Germanic noun phrase: Determiners MOVE into the determiner phrase." PhD diss., Indiana University.

Roehrs, Dorian. 2009a. *Demonstratives and definite articles as nominal auxiliaries*. Amsterdam: John Benjamins.

Roehrs, Dorian. 2009b. "Inflectional parallelism with German adjectives." *Interdisciplinary Journal of Germanic Linguistics and Semiotic Analysis* 14: 289–326.

Schlenker, Philippe. 1999. "La flexion de l'adjectif en allemand: La morphologie de haut en bas." *Recherches Linguistiques de Vincennes*,

Schoorlemmer, Erik. 2009. "Agreement, dominance and doubling: The morphosyntax of DP." PhD diss., Universiteit Leiden.

Studler, Rebekka. 2001. "Zur Syntax und Semantik der DP im Schweizerdeutschen." Master's thesis, University of Vienna.

Suter, Rudolf. 1976. *Baseldeutsch-Grammatik*. 2nd ed. Basel: Christoph Merian Verlag.

Szabolcsi, Anna. 1983–1984. "The possessor that ran away from home." *Linguistic Review* 3: 89–102.

Szabolcsi, Anna. 1994. "The noun phrase." In Ference Kiefer and Katalin Kiss (eds.), *Syntax and semantics 27: The syntactic structure of Hungarian*, 179–274. San Diego: Academic Press.

Van Riemsdijk, Henk. 1998. "Head movement and adjacency." *Natural Language and Linguistic Theory* 16: 633–678.

Vangsnes, Øystein A. 2006. "Syntactic doubling phenomena in Scandinavian." Handout from Workshop Syntactic Doubling in European Dialects, Amsterdam, March 16–18.

Weber, Albert. 1964. *Zürichdeutsche Grammatik*. 2nd rev. ed. Zürich: Schweizer Spiegel Verlag.

Williams, Edwin. 1994. "Remarks on lexical knowledge." *Lingua* 92: 7–34.

Zwicky, Arnold. 1985. "How to describe inflection." In *Proceedings of the Eleventh Annual Meeting of the Berkeley Linguistics Society*, 372–386.

Zwicky, Arnold. 1986. "German adjective agreement in GPSG." *Linguistics* 24: 957–990.

CHAPTER 8

Syntactic Microvariation: Dative Constructions in Greek

DIMITRIS MICHELIOUDAKIS AND IOANNA SITARIDOU

1. SCOPE AND STRUCTURE OF THE ARTICLE

This article is a first attempt at a syntactic analysis of dative constructions across a number of Greek varieties—a fairly understudied and inad-
equately explored area in the study of Greek dialects, in general (but see
Manolessou & Beis 2006 for a general overview). Drawing data from three
different varieties of Pontic Greek, namely Romeyka of Of (ROf), Romeyka
of Sürmene (RSür)—both spoken in Turkey—and Pontic Greek as spoken
in Thessaloniki (TPG), as well as Medieval and Modern Cypriot Greek
(MedCG and ModCG, respectively) and Standard Modern Greek (SMG),
we set out to explore all the possible patterns in the syntax of the substitutes of the Ancient Greek (AG) dative.

The main aspects of cross-dialectal variation in Greek with respect to
datives are (i) the availability of dative alternations, that is, PP alternants;
(ii) the structural position of indirect object DPs relative to direct objects
(and, mainly as a consequence of this, the passivisability of the direct
object); (iii) the presence or not of minimality/intervention effects in rais-
ing/Agree across datives; and (iv) the presence and the "strength" of person restrictions on the direct object in the presence of datives, both clitics
and full DPs. Of these four potential dimensions of variation, (iii) and (iv)
clearly depend on the status of (i) and (ii), that is, intervention effects of
the sort implied in (iii) and the strong PCC are available only when high
indirect DPs alternate with low (usually prepositional) indirect objects (but
the implication is certainly not bidirectional). For our purposes, "dative" is a
cover term for DPs and clitics serving as Goal/Recipient or Ablative arguments of ditransitives, Benefactives/Malefactives, External Possessors, Ethical

Datives, and Experiencers of *piacere*-type psych predicates (following Belletti & Rizzi's 1988 typology).

The article is organized as follows. In section 2, we outline our proposal. In section 3 we present an overview of the syntactic isoglosses across the varieties under discussion, which interact with the parameterization we propose and yield further apparent variation. In section 4, we discuss the structural representation of dative arguments in SMG in order to establish a comparative platform for the dialectal data to be examined in sections 5–7, in each of which we group our findings, depending on the availability of the relevant data, under the following broad categories: (i) ditransitive constructions; (ii) benefactives; (iii) datives with unaccusatives. In section 8 we discuss our analysis and its theoretical implications. Finally, we conclude in section 9.

2. AN OVERVIEW OF THE PROPOSAL

On the basis of how the above-mentioned properties (i–iii) correlate and (some of them) cluster together, we suggest a bipartite syntactic distinction, with the distinctive feature being the accessibility/visibility of the "dative" DP to Agree/Move. Following Chomsky (2000, 2001), we assume that the value and the "timing" of the valuation of the (abstract) Case feature of a DP determines whether or not it is an active goal, and following Michelioudakis (2010a, 2011), we put forward the proposal that minimality in φ-Agree must be relativized to Case features, basically interpreting Chomsky (2000, 2001) as follows: (a) DPs with unvalued, uninterpretable Case features are active goals; (b) DPs with uninterpretable Case features that have already been valued by a lower φ-head H_1 when probed by a higher φ-head H_2 are "defective interveners," in the sense that they cannot value H_2's $[u\varphi]$ while preventing it from probing further down; (c) DPs with fully interpretable and lexically valued theta-related Case do not induce any minimality effects because φ-heads only look for (and can only "see") DPs with [uCase]. What is particularly puzzling, then, in this respect, is the fact that, putting aside the variation in intervention effects and possibly A-movability, all Greek datives both diatopically and diachronically apparently bear inherent Case, which cannot be suppressed in either ECM or passivization.[1] This forces us to postulate (cf. McGinnis 1998, Michelioudakis 2010a, 2011) (at least) two types of inherent Case: one that only allows a dative DP to behave as described in (c) above; and a hybrid type that allows a dative to behave as in (a) or (b), while retaining its PF- and LF-interpretable part intact.

---

1 But see Anagnostopoulou & Sevdali (2010) for datives becoming nominative in a restricted number of passive constructions in Classical Greek, which we do not consider here. Crucially, in all the varieties we examine here, abstract dative (whatever its morphological exponent be) is never absorbed.

The latter may either be construed as a quirky Case feature in the sense of Chomsky (2000: 127), that is, as a "(theta-related) inherent Case with a [parasitic] structural Case feature" or, possibly, as a cluster of theta-features (in the spirit of Reinhart 2002), a part of which is inserted/valued in the derivation, while the rest of it is unvalued (or simply absent, making the theta-cluster incomplete) and awaits valuation (or supplementation) by some head carrying the corresponding LF-interpretable information (e.g., Appl, which may come in different semantic flavors). If the latter is on the right track, then inherent Case in its purest (i.e., *inactive*) form is a theta-cluster that is inserted fully valued/specified from the Lexicon. However, in this article, we do not discuss which (or whether only) one of these two conceptions is right, and for this reason we do not try to relate our cases with other cases that have been claimed to involve quirky Case, for example, Icelandic quirky datives (but see Svenonius 2006, 2010, who argues that quirky datives are actually structural). Furthermore, the way in which the availability of structurally "high/low" indirect object DPs correlates with animacy and person/agreement restrictions is argued to provide evidence for a movement analysis of the double object construction (DOC), compatible in fact with Kayne's (2010: 1) radical approach: "No dative is externally merged into its visible position," which we modify/relativize by construing "dative" in this context as any dative DP/pronoun in a language which also has prepositional alternants. That said, our analysis allows for "low" datives, possibly spelt out in their first-merged positions, in systems without dative alternations (e.g., Romeyka and, partly, MedCG), which overtly realize and therefore provide direct empirical evidence for a low first-merged position of these arguments. Also, in the context of our approach to Case, the "high/low" variation relates to whether or not the Case of the dative argument also originates low (see also Michelioudakis 2010a, 2011a, 2011b, forthcoming).

Our investigation clearly provides evidence for a radical dissociation between the morphological exponence and the syntactic properties of dative expressions; exploiting all possible combinations resulting from the existence of two morphological cases realizing abstract dative and the dichotomy between two flavors of inherent Case, the diachrony of Greek is such that all the syntactic patterns that logically follow from the above are actually attested and are apparently compatible with any of the two morphological exponents available in Greek dialects. Therefore, our findings essentially point toward a four-way typology of these expressions (see Table 8.8). All syntactic variation can then be shown to derive from factors other than morphological case, while even from a diachronic perspective it can be argued that there is only an indirect, but certainly not causal, relation between morphological and syntactic change with respect to datives (cf. Michelioudakis 2011, forthcoming).

3. SYNTACTIC ISOGLOSSES RELATING TO DATIVE CONSTRUCTIONS ACROSS GREEK DIALECTS

The goal of this section is twofold: (a) to provide some necessary information on the classification of the varieties under discussion; and (b) to introduce the facts which are pertinent to a discussion of dative constructions across the following diatopic and diachronic varieties of Greek—(i) SMG; (ii) TPG; (iii) Romeyka (ROf and RSür); (iv) MedCG; and (v) ModCG.

3.1 Morphosyntactic Distribution of "Dative" and Dialectal Variation in Greek

Once morphological dative was lost in Greek, almost all of its argumental functions were taken up by (see Manolessou & Beis 2006) (a) accusative: Constantinople Greek, Northern Greek, Pontic, etc.; (b) genitive: ModCG, Peloponnesian, Dodecanesian, etc.; (c) prepositional phrases (alongside (a) or (b)): *almost* all dialects (with cross-categorial variation).

The morphological substitution of ancient Greek "dative" yields the typology in Table 8.1.

Table 8.1. CLASSIFICATION OF MODERN GREEK DIALECTS ACCORDING TO M-SUBSTITUTION OF ANCIENT GREEK DATIVE.

mCase	Varieties			
mACC	Pontic[2]	TPG		
		Romeyka	Of	
			Sürmene	
mGEN	(Peloponnesian)	SMG		
	MedCG	ModCG		

3.2 Head Directionality and Dialectal Variation in Greek

SMG, MedCG, and ModCG are all head-first varieties both within the VP (1) and the DP (2):

(1) a. O   Janis   efaje   to   milo. (SMG)
       the.NOM   John.NOM   ate.3SG   the.ACC   apple.ACC
       "John ate the apple."

---

2 For a discussion of the classification of Romeyka and other Pontic Greek varieties within the Asia Minor Greek group, see Sitaridou (forthcoming/b).

b. Edžerasa   tu   xtisti   kafen. (ModCG)
treated.1SG   the.GEN   builder.GEN   coffee.ACC
"I made coffee to the builder."
(Terkourafi & Sitaridou, in progress)

c. Kai   afinei   kanenan   pragman   katinos. (MedCG)
and   leave.3SG anything.ACC anyone.GEN
"And (if) he leaves anything to anyone."
(*Assizes* f.137, 190 in Michelioudakis 2010b:4)

(2) a. I   katastrofi   tu   kambu. (SMG & ModCG)
the.NOM   destruction.NOM   the.GEN   valley.GEN
"The destruction of the valley"
(Terkourafi & Sitaridou, in progress)

b. Is   tin   filakin   tus   kleptes.[3] (MedCG)
to   the.ACC   prison.ACC   the.ACC   thieves.ACC.PL
"To the prison of the thieves"
(*Assizes* f.2, §268 in Sitaridou & Terkourafi, in progress: 54)

Interestingly, although the VP in TPG is head-first (3a), genitive preposing within the DP is the only grammatical option (3b):

(3) a. Iða   tin   Parthena. (TPG)
saw.1SG   the.ACC   Parthena.ACC
"I saw Parthena."

b. T'armen   to   spaksimon. (TPG)
the.GEN.PL Armenian.GEN.PL   the.NOM   massacre.NOM
"The massacre of the Armenians"
(Drettas 1997: 122)

On the other hand, in Romeyka, apart from the DP which is head-final (4c), as in TPG, there is clear indication that the VP is predominantly head-final as well (4a–b) without however excluding VO orders:

(4) a. škilon   exo. (ROf)
dog.ACC   have.1SG
"I have a dog."

b. O   Mehmetis   tin   Aiše   psomin   eðotšen.
the.NOM   Mehmet.NOM   the.ACC Aise.ACC bread.ACC   gave.3SG
"Mehmet gave bread to Aise."

3 On the genitive/accusative syncretism with plural masculines, see Sitaridou & Terkourafi (2009, in progress).

c. To   zo   to   γlitsi.
    the.GEN   animal.GEN   the   milk.NOM
    "The milk of the animal"

Although the discussion of linear OV and its interaction with information structure falls outside the remit of the present article (but see Sitaridou & Kaltsa 2010), it is important to point out that (4a) is the preferred and unmarked option, that is, not the result of discourse-related movement, unlike OV in TPG, which is a more marked option.

3.3 Clitics and Dialectal Variation in Greek

The distribution of clitics alone is, according to Condoravdi & Kiparsky (2001: 1–3), a sufficient criterion for the cartography of Greek varieties. It is well known that SMG has clitics that are mostly proclitics (5a) (enclitics appear only after gerunds and imperatives; see (5b)).

(5) a. To   ipe. (SMG)
         it.ACC.CL   said.3SG
         "He told him."

      b. Leγondas   to/pes to.
         saying   it.ACC.CL/say.IMP it.ACC.CL
         "Saying it / say it!"

On the other hand, ModCG allows enclitics (6a), with proclitics triggered only when preceded by a NEG marker (6b), a mood marker, a focused XP, or a complementizer (6c):

(6) a. Ethkiavasa   to. (ModCG)
         read.1SG   it.ACC.CL
         "I read it."

      b. En   ton   iksero.
         not   him.ACC.CL know.1SG
         "I don't know him."

      c. Ksero   oti   i   Maria   to   ethkiavasen.
         know.1SG that   the.NOM Maria.NOM it.ACC.CL read.3SG
         "I know that Mary read it."

As for MedCG, the clitic placement pattern is not radically different from that of ModCG, and by no means different to what we find in other Medieval Greek varieties (7c), namely object clitic pronouns may appear either before or after the verb (cf. Pappas 2001, Vassiliou 2002), as shown in (7a–b):

(7) a. Oti ekinos o iatros didi tu pragmata
that that the doctor give.3SG him.GEN.CL things
kinitika i pragmata therma (MedCG)
mobile or things hot
"that that doctor gives him unblocking or hot things (for the intestines)"
(*Assizes*, f. 179, 9)

b. Ke ekinos endexete na tu
and that one may.3SG PRT.SUBJ him.GEN.CL
dosi pragmata stifthika
give.3SG things laxative
"And he may give him laxatives."
(*Assizes*, f. 189, 12)

c. To diadima perni to (Medieval Mainland Greek)
the crown.ACC takes it.ACC.CL
"The crown, he takes it."
(*Belisarios*, 42 in Pappas 2001: 82)

A third clitic placement pattern among Greek dialects is exemplified by TPG and Romeyka, which have enclisis to the verb form across the board:

(8) a. {as/ondas/eɣo/ki} telion'-ato (TPG)
MOOD.OPT/When/I.FOC/not finish.1SGCl.3SG.ACC
"{Let me / When I / I / I don't} finish it"
(adapted from Drettas 1997)

b. O Mehmetis emenan/EMENAN eðotšen-æ. (ROf)
The Mehmet me.ACC/ME.ACC.FOC gave.3SG-Cl.3SG.ACC
"Mehmet gave it to me /ME."

However, Romeyka and TPG do not seem to behave identically when it comes to clitic clusters. In Romeyka the clitic/æ/ (9a) cannot combine with any other clitic in any person to form clitic clusters (9b), whereas in TPG this is possible (9c–d):

(9) a. O Mehmetis emenan eðotšen-æ. (ROf)
the.NOM Mehmet.NOM me.ACC gave.3SG-Cl.3SG.ACC
"Mehmet gave it to me."

b. *O Mehmetis eðotše-m-æ.
the.NOM Mehmet gave.3SG-me.ACC.CL-3SG.ACC.CL
"Mehmet gave him/her/it to me."

c. O   Mehmetis   eðoke-m(e)-æ. (TPG)
the.NOM   Mehmet   gave.3SG-me.ACC.CL-3SG.ACC.CL
"Mehmet gave it to me."

d. Leγo-s-ata.
tell.1SG-you.ACC.CL-them.ACC.CL
"I am telling you these."

In Romeyka, /æ/ appears to be the only third-person clitic (with neutralized gender and possibly number), whereas the Romeyka counterpart of the TPG third-person clitic "aton.MASC/NEUT- atin.FEM," etc., that is, "ato(n(a))" or "ado(n(a))" for the masculine and the neuter, "ati(n(a))" for the feminine, does not appear to be a clitic; apart from not being able to cluster with clitics such as /æ/ (10c), it can also follow words other than verbs, having roughly the same distribution as full DPs (10b), while it can also carry independent stress when appearing as trisyllabic (10b–c).[4] The syntactic status of first- and second-person pronominal forms is more dubious, however, as they cannot easily occur in a nonadverbial position (see (10a, 10d)).[5]

(10) a. Eðotšen-eme(n)   o   Mehmet   ato(n). (ROf)
gave.3SG me.ACC.CL   the   Mehmet.NOM   him/it.ACC
"Mehmet gave me this/it."

b. Eðiksane   to   Mehmet   atona. (RSür)
showed.3PL   the   Mehmet.NOM   him.ACC
"They showed Mehmet to him."

c. O   Mehmetis   adona   etšino   fanerose. (RSür)
the.NOM Mehmet.NOM   him.ACC this.ACC   showed.3SG
"Mehmet showed this to him."

d. Eðotšen   eme(n(an))   o   Mehmet   aton. (ROf)
gave.3SG   me.ACC   the   Mehmet.NOM him/it
"Mehmet gave him/it to me."

It is also worth pointing out that in both Romeyka varieties, namely ROf and RSür,[6] there is no evidence that tonic object pronouns are only used for emphatic or other discourse-related reasons; rather, they seem to constitute an unmarked option, clearly owing also to the restricted distribution of

4 When trisyllabic, it cannot be neuter.
5 The full cartography of the Pontic pronominal system awaits further study.
6 It should be noted that there is a third Romeyka variety still spoken in Turkey, namely the variety of Tonya, for which, however, we do not have any data at this stage.

clitics (cf. English stressed pronouns that are not used emphatically).[7] Thus the behavior of the Romeyka pronominal system contrasts with the other Greek varieties, notably SMG (cf. Kayne 1975, Bianchi 2006 for Italian), where strong pronouns are always a marked option and focused(either contrastively or informationally) when appearing undoubled in an A-position (see also Cardinaletti & Starke 1999 for an overview of the process that allows tonic pronouns to occur only when focalized or topicalized). On the basis of this description, it follows that in Romeyka even when object pronouns precede the verb, the resulting OV lacks the interpretive effects it has in most other varieties (e.g., SMG); therefore, Romeyka pronouns can still have a neutral reading. Furthermore, given the general unavailability for clitics, PCC-like restrictions in Romeyka seem to apply to strong pronouns, unlike SMG.

3.4 Wh-Formation and Dialectal Variation in Greek

It is well known that SMG does not allow multiple wh-fronting, as shown in (11b):

(11) a. Pjos eðose   ti   se   pjon? (SMG)
     who   gave.3SG   what   to   whom
     "Who gave what to whom?"

   b. *Pjos   ti   (se pjon)   eðose?
      who   what   to whom   gave.3SG

ModCG is by no means different from SMG:

(12) a. Pcos   iðen   pcon   pothe? (ModCG)
     who   saw.3SG   whom   where
     "Who saw whom where?"

   b. *Pcos   pcon   (pothe)   iðen?
      who   whom   where   saw.3SG
      "Who saw whom where?"
      (Stavroula Tsiplakou, p.c.)

Interestingly, however, TPG, like Romeyka, seems to allow multiple-wh fronting:

---

7 Overall, there seems to be an interesting correlation between lack of clitics, pronouns used nonemphatically, predicate duplication for affirmation, null objects, and the OV status in languages such as Latin, Portuguese to a certain extent, and Romeyka (for a discussion see Sitaridou 2012).

(13) a. Tinan   pion   ospit   eðiksises? (TPG)
        whom   which   house   showed.2SG
        "Which house did you show to whom?"

   b. *Pion   ospit   eðiksises   tinan?
       which   house   showed.2SG   whom

   c. O   Mehmetis   tinan   doɣnan   eðotše? (ROf)
       the.NOM   Mehmet.NOM   whom   what+PRT.SUBJ   gave.3SG
       "Mehmet gave what to whom?"

Crucially, Romeyka seems to exhibit Superiority effects (14a–b), which show that multiple wh-fronting is strictly order-preserving, as in Bulgarian (14c–d) albeit not otherwise identical (see Bošković 1997, Michelioudakis & Sitaridou 2012):

(14) a. Pios   tinan   aɣapai? (ROf)
        who   whom   love.3SG
        "Who loves whom?"

   b. *Tinan   pios   aɣapai?
       whom   who   love.3SG

   c. Koj   kogo   obia? (Bulgarian)
       who   whom   love.3SG
       "Who loves whom?"

   d. *Kogo   koj   obia?
       whom   who   love.3SG

3.5 Passives and Dialectal Variation in Greek

Unlike SMG, in which passives are fairly productive (15a), especially in "high" (written) register, passives in TPG and Romeyka are systematically dispreferred, despite the availability of verbs with mediopassive morphology (e.g., deponents). From all three Pontic varieties, TPG allows more passives, probably because of contact with SMG, but not so readily with ditransitives (15b); RSür more or less marginally tolerates passives even in the presence of indirect objects and benefactive DPs (15c–d), while ROf apparently allows very little passivization(15e).

(15) a. I   Maria   filithike   apo   ton   Jani. (SMG)
        the   Maria.NOM   kissed.PASS.3SG   from   the.ACC   John.ACC
        "Mary was kissed by John."

   b. Ta   paraðas   eðothan   (?sin Anastan). (TPG)
       the   money.NOM.PL given.PASS.3PL   to+the Anastasia.ACC
       "The money was given to Anastasia."

c. I para   tin   Aiše   eðoste. (RSür)

money.NOM   the.ACC   Anastasia.ACC   given.PASS.3SG

"Money was given to Aise."

d. To   xarti   eɣrafte   tin   Aiše. (RSür)

the   letter.NOM   the.ACC   written.PASS.3SG   Anastasia.ACC

"The letter was written for Aise."

e. *Ena   kitap   eɣrafte/eðothe(n)   (to Mehmet). (ROf)

a   book/letter.NOM   written.PASS.3SG   (the Mehmet.ACC)

"A book/letter was written/given (for/to Mehmet)."

As for MedCG and ModCG, although in general passives are usually not spontaneously produced, they are tolerated with both monotransitive and ditransitive predicates, which pattern with SMG in most respects (but cf. clefting in (16b)):

(16) a. Ta   rialia   eðothikasin/eðothisan   *(-tis)   tis Marias. (ModCG)

the   money.PL   were-given.3PL   her.GEN.CL   the Maria.GEN

"The book was given to Mary."

b. En TIS MARIAS₍ᵢ₎   pu   eðothikasin/eðothisan ta   rialia t₍ᵢ₎

is.3SG the Maria.GEN   that   given.PASS.3PL   the   money.3PL

"It was Mary that the money was given to."

(Theoni Neokleous, p.c.)

4. DATIVE CONSTRUCTIONS IN STANDARD MODERN GREEK

In SMG, the morphological exponent of abstract dative for DPs and clitics is the genitive. With the exception of some nonrecipient benefactives and ethical datives, the m-GEN datives alternate with PPs headed by "se"—a preposition roughly equivalent to "to," used in both motion-locative and stative-locative expressions.

4.1 Ditransitives in SMG

In SMG goal/recipient ditransitives, there are clearly two structural patterns (*pace* Dimitriadis 1999; see also Anagnostopoulou 2003, among others): one in which the indirect object (IO) asymmetrically c-commands the direct object (DO), which has often been likened to the English double object construction (DOC), and one in which DO asymmetrically c-commands IO. The former can be instantiated by either genitive DPs or PPs functioning as IOs, while the latter can only be instantiated by prepositional IOs, as is evident by the behavior of each type with respect to Barss & Lasnik's (1986) diagnostics[8] (17–19).

(i) Quantifier variable binding (SMG):

(17) a. O   Kesaras   eðikse   [(tu) kathe ðiikiti]$_i$
     the.NOM   Caesar.NOM   showed.3SG   the each governor.GEN
     [tin eparxia tu$_i$] (ston xarti). (IO$_{gen}$>DO)
     his province.ACC (on the map)
     "Caesar showed each governor his province."

   b. O   Kesaras   ʾ(tu)   eðikse   [tin eparxia tu$_i$]
     the.NOM   Caesar.NOM   ʾ(him.GEN.CL) showed.3SG   his province.ACC
     [tu kathe ðiikiti]$_i$ (underlying IO$_{gen}$ >DO in A-positions).
     each governor.GEN
     "Caesar showed each governor his province."

   c. ?*O   Kesaras   eðikse   [tu ðiikiti tis$_i$]
     the.NOM   Caesar.NOM   showed.3SG   the governor.GEN its
     [kathe eparxia]$_i$.(*underlying DO>IO$_{gen}$ in A-positions)
     every/each province.ACC
     "?*Caesar showed its governor every/each province."

   d. ?*O   Kesaras   eðikse   [kathe eparxia]$_i$
     the.NOM   Caesar.NOM   showed.3SG   [every province]
     [tu ðiikiti tis$_i$]. (*DO>IO$_{gen}$)
     [its governor.GEN]

   e. O   Kesaras   eðikse   [ston kathe ðiikiti]$_i$
     the.NOM   Caesar.NOM   showed.3SG   to-the each governor.ACC
     [tin eparxia tu$_i$] (ston xarti). (IO$_{pp}$>DO)
     his province.ACC (on the map)
     "Caesar showed each governor his province."

   f. O   Kesaras   eðikse   (?ston ðiikiti tis$_i$)
     the.NOM   Caesar.NOM   showed.3SG   (to-the governor.ACC its)
     [kathe eparxia]$_i$ (ston ðiikiti tis$_i$). (DO>IO$_{pp}$)
     each/every province (to-the governor its)
     "Caesar showed each/every province to its governor."

---

8 For expository reasons, we only make use of the three diagnostics shown in (17–19), as only these are applicable to all the Greek varieties under examination. See Catsimali (1990) and Anagnostopoulou (2003) for the full set of diagnostics. The asymmetric relation indicated by these tests is not necessarily reflected in the surface word order, which is relatively free, since any one of the two internal arguments can freely undergo A′-scrambling over the other.

(ii) Weak Crossover (SMG):

(18) a. [Pjanu ðiikiti]$_i$?(tu) eðikses
which governor.GEN (him.GEN.CL) showed.2SG
tin eparxia tu$_i$? (IO$_{gen}$>DO)
the province.ACC his
"(To) which governor did you show his province?"

b. (?)*[Pja eparxia]$_i$ eðikses tu ðiikiti tis$_i$? (*DO>IO$_{gen}$)
which province.ACC showed.2SG the governor.GEN its

c. [Se pjo(n) ðiikiti]$_i$ eðikses tin eparxia tu$_i$? (IO$_{PP}$>DO)
to which governor.ACC showed.2SG the province.ACC his
"(?*)Which governor did you show his province to?"

d. [Pja eparxia]$_i$ eðikses sto(n) ðiikiti tis$_i$? (DO>IO$_{PP}$)
which province.ACC showed.2SG to-the governor its
"Which province did you show to its governor?"

(iii) Superiority effects (SMG):

(19) a. (?)Pjanu eðikses ti/pjon? (IO$_{gen}$>DO)
who.GEN showed.2SG what.ACC/who.ACC

b. ?*Ti/pjon eðikses pjanu? (*DO>IO$_{gen}$)
what.ACC/who.ACC showed.2SG who.GEN

c. (?)Ti/Pjon eðikses se pjon? (DO>IO$_{PP}$)
what.ACC/who.ACC showed.2SG to who.ACC

d. (?)Se pjon eðikses ti/pjon? (IO$_{PP}$>DO)
to whom showed.2SG what.ACC/who.ACC
"What/whom did you show to whom?"

This pattern is partly replicated by benefactives in SMG, with the exception of prepositional beneficiaries—in particular, in those cases where prepositional realization is actually possible, especially when the beneficiary is a potential recipient or possible owner of DO. By applying Barss & Lasnik's paradigm again, we observe that benefactives, either realized as DPs or PPs, always have to asymmetrically c-command DO (20–22) (see also Anagnostopoulou 2005):

(20) a. O Kesaras zoɣrafise [ston kathe ðiikiti/tu kathe
the.NOM Caesar drew.3SG to-the each governor.ACC/every
ðiikiti]$_i$ [ena sxeðiaɣrama tis eparxias tu$_i$]/[tin eparxia tu]$_i$ (Benef$_{gen/PP}$>DO)
governor.GEN (a map of) the province his/his province
"Caesar drew every governor (a map of) their province."

b. ?*O Kesaras zoɣrafise [kathe eparxia]ᵢ

  Caesar drew.3SG [every province.ACC]

  [tu ðiikiti tis/ston ðiikiti tisᵢ] (*DO>Benef$_{gen/PP}$)

  [the governor.GEN its/to-the governor.ACC its]

  "Caesar drew every province for/to their governor."

(21) a. {Pjanu (tu)}/{Se pjon} zoɣrafises tin eparxia tuᵢ? (Benef$_{gen/PP}$>DO)

  Who.GEN (him.GEN.CL)/to whom.ACC drew.2SG the province.ACC his

  "?Who did you draw his province (for)?" (*DO>Benef$_{gen/PP}$)

  b. ?[Pja eparxia]ᵢ zoɣrafises tu ðiikiti tisᵢ/ston ðiikiti tisᵢ?

  which province.ACC drew.2SG the governor.GEN its/to-the governor.AC its

(22) a. Pjanu/se pjon zoɣrafises ti? (Benef$_{gen/PP}$>DO)

  who.GEN/to whom.ACC drew.2SG what.ACC

  b. ?*Ti zoɣrafises pjanu/se pjon? (*DO>Benef$_{gen/PP}$)

  what.ACC drew.2SG who.GEN/to whom.ACC

  "What did you draw for whom?"

The above tests are summarized in Tables 8.2 and 8.3, for (s-selected) IOs and benefactives, respectively.

Table 8.2. C-COMMAND RELATIONS IN GOAL DITRANSITIVES (SMG).

	IO>>DO	DO>>IO
DPgen	✓	*
se"to"-PP	✓	✓

Table 8.3. C-COMMAND RELATIONS IN BENEFACTIVES (SMG).

	Benef>>DO	DO>>Benef
DPgen	✓	*
se"to"-PP	✓	*

4.2 Passives in SMG

In SMG, IO$_{gen}$/Benef$_{gen}$ cannot be nominativized in passives (23a–b), as well as in middles and reflexives, which constitutes direct evidence that their

Case is inherent. On the other hand, DO can be passivized in the presence of an IO or even a Benef$_{gen}$ (*pace* Anagnostopoulou 2005), provided that its minimality effects (due to its intervention between T and DO) are obviated in some way, for example by clitic movement, or clitic doubling, which puts the head of IO$_{gen}$'s chain outside T's complement domain. Otherwise, direct passives are significantly degraded (23c–d). In accordance, then, with the assumptions sketched in section 2, this must be an instance of defective intervention, that is, IO$_{gen}$'s inherent Case feature must be active/visible for Agree. In the presence of a prepositional IO, on the other hand, DOs can passivize unproblematically (23e). Importantly, (23e) does not have a counterpart with benefactives (23f), as predicted by the observation (see Table 8.3) that Benef$_{pp}$s always intervene between T and DO.

(23) a. *I   Maria   epistrafike   ta lefta.
        the.NOM   Maria.NOM   returned.PASS.3SG   the money.NOM/ACC
        "Mary was given back the money."

      b. *O   Mara   ipsothike/xtistike   ena vomo   apo tus γalus.
        the.NOM   Marat   erected/built.PASS.3SG   an altar.ACC   by the French
        "?Marat was built an altar (by the French)."

      c. Ta   lefta ?*   (tis)   epistrafikan   tis   Marias.
        the.NOM   money.NOM   her.GEN   given.PASS.3PL   the.GEN   Maria.GEN
        "The money was returned to Mary."

      d. [...] opu ?*(tu)   ipsothike/xtistike   (tu Mara)   vomos apo tus γalus.
        where.REL   him.GEN.CL   erected/built.PASS.3SG   the.GEN Mara altar   by the French
        "where an altar was built for Marat by the French"
        (knol.google.com/k/ζαν-πωλ-μαρα)

      e. Ta   lefta   epistrafikan   sti Maria.
        the   money.NOM.PL   returned.PASS.3PL   to-the Maria.ACC
        "The money was returned to Mary."

      f. ?*Enas vomos   ipsothike/xtistike   sto   Mara.
        an altar.NOM   erected/built.PASS.3SG   to-the.ACC   Mara
        "An altar was built for Marat."

4.3 Unaccusatives (Psych and Motion) in SMG

In unaccusatives, genitive goals (with motion predicates) and genitive experiencers (with *piacere*-type psych verbs) appear to behave alike: (a) they alternate with "se"-PPs (thus contradicting Baker's (1996) generalization about the unavailability of dative alternations with unaccusatives), and allow every possible c-command/binding pattern (24a–d). Crucially, when realized as genitives, they always need to be cliticized or clitic-doubled, which again suggests that they always intervene and block the Agree relation between T and the nominative DO, that is, they always c-command DO when T is merged, thus deriving the well-known backward binding effects associated with these constructions. The availability of both binding patterns for both experiencers and goals is simply due to the fact that the nominative theme may be LF-interpreted in either its low (thematic) position or in a derived (subject) position. Note also that there is a number of contexts (e.g., control into absolutives, etc.; see Anagnostopoulou 1999) in which "dative" experiencers can have subjectlike behavior too, that is, they may occupy Spec-T, while this may also be the case for genitive goals with unaccusatives, middles, and passives (see Michelioudakis 2011 for discussion). Despite these similarities, however, a closer look at the cross-dialectal (see below) and cross-categorial variation (see Michelioudakis 2010b for syntactic asymmetries in datives with predicative deverbal APs) reveals that the first-merged positions of such datives cannot be quite the same.

(24) a. Kathe ðikeuxu$_i$ *(tu$_i$)   irthan/se   kathe
     every endorsee.GEN   him.GEN.CL came.3PL/to every
     ðikeuxo$_i$ irthan   i   epitajes   tu$_i$
     endorsee came.3PL   the   checks   his
     "Every endorsee$_i$ got/received his/their$_i$ checks."

    b. Kathe epitaji$_i$ pije/eftase   stus   ðikeuxus tis$_i$/*(tu)irthe
     Every check went/arrived.3SG to-the endorsees its/him.GEN.CL-
     tu   ðikeuxu   tis$_i$
     arrived.3SG   the endorsee.GEN   its
     "Every check went/arrived into the hands of its endorsees."

    c. Kathe miteras$_i$?*(tis)   aresun/se   kathe mitera$_i$
     every mother.GEN   her.GEN.CL appeal.3PL/to every mother
     aresun   ta peðja   tis$_i$
     appeal.3PL   the kids.NOM her
     "Every mother likes her (own) children."

    d. Kathe peði$_i$?*(tis)   aresi   tis   miteras
     every child   him.GEN.CL appeals.3SG   the   mother.GEN
     tu$_i$/aresi sti mitera   tu$_i$
     its/appeal.3SG to-the mother   its
     "Every child$_i$ appeals to her$_i$ mother."

4.4 Person Restrictions in SMG

In SMG, the strong version of the person case constraint (PCC) (Bonet 1991) appears to operate on clitic clusters with ditransitives (25a), as well as on DO clitics alone, in the presence of a genitive DP (25b). Crucially, it does not affect strong DO pronouns (25c). Also, interestingly enough, it does not block first- and second-person themes with dative experiencers[9] (25d).

(25) a. Mu/su/tu   ton/tin/*me/*se   eðiksan. (SMG)

       [me/you/him].GEN.CL   [him/her/me/you].ACC.CL   showed.3PL

       "They showed me/you/him him/her/*me/*you."

    b. To/(?)ton/?*me/?*se   eðiksan   tis   Marias.

       [it/him$_{[-animate]}$/$^{(?)}$him$_{[+animate]}$/me/you].ACC.CL   showed.3PL   the   Maria.GEN

       "They showed it/him/me/you to Mary."

    c. Tu/su eðiksan   emena.

       [him/you].GEN.CL   showed.3PL me.ACC

       "They showed *me* to him/you."

    d. Tu/tis/mu   *pro*   aresis.

       [him/her/me].GEN.CL   pro.2S   appeal.2SG

       "You appeal to him/her/me."

5. PONTIC VARIETIES OF NORTHERN GREECE (TPG)

The TPG data come from fieldwork in northern Greece—most speakers come from the Thessaloniki area. An important methodological caveat is attrition because of contact with SMG. Overall, TPG datives largely pattern with datives in SMG *modulo* the morphological exponence, which is accusative across the board (always within the vP).

5.1 Ditransitives in TPG

TPG employs morphologically accusative NPs for indirect objects, but those also alternate with PPs. What complicates the picture is the use of the fusional determiners *son/sin/so* [*se* + *ton/tin/to*]="to+the.MASC/FEM/NEUT": These are used (exclusively) for definite dative DPs across the board, making the use of the bare accusative article for these arguments hardly acceptable, even in the IO>>DO pattern, while "se" may be absent when this pattern is instantiated by quantified/wh- (bare accusative) IOs. This may mean that TPG has a specialized dative definite article. Also, TPG

---

9 The issue of the PCC with genitive goals in unaccusatives is more complicated and we do not address it here. At first sight, the varying tolerability of first-/second-person themes in such constructions seems to be coextensive with the variable tolerability of dative (nonprepositional) goals in nonactives in general (see Michelioudakis 2011)—cf. also Spanish, in which the strong blocking effects of datives, in, e.g., raising across them, even when cliticized/clitic-doubled, coexist with a strong ban on first-/second-person (or animate) theme-subjects co-occurring with dative clitics.

arguably has clitic clusters, with an IO-DO order (see 9c–d), subject to a weak version of the PCC (see the discussion on Romeyka in section 6).

(26) To peði   eðoke   fai   son aðelfo. (TPG)
      the child.NOM gave.3SG   food.ACC   to-the brother.ACC
      "The child gave food to the brother."

TPG patterns with SMG with respect to the hierarchical/c-command relations between IO and DO (27)–(29).

(i) Superiority effects (TPG):

(27) a. (Se) tinan   pion   ospit   eðiksises? (IO_{DP}>DO, IO_{PP}>DO)
        to who.ACC which   house.ACC   showed.2SG

    b. Pion   ospit   *(se) tinan   eðiksises? (*DO>IO_{DP}, DO>IO_{PP})
       which house.ACC   to whom.ACC   showed.2SG
       "Which house did you show to whom?"

(ii) WCO (TPG):

(28) a. (Se) tinan$_i$ eðiksises   t'ospitn-at$_i$? (IO_{DP}>DO, IO_{PP}>DO)
        to who.ACC   showed.2SG   the house.ACC-his
        "(to) whom did you show his house?"

    b. Pion   ospit$_i$ eðiksises   son   kirn-at$_i$ /*ton kirn-at$_i$? (DO>IO_{PP}, *DO>IO_{DP})
       which house.ACC showed.2SG to-the   owner.ACC-its/the owner.ACC-its
       "Which house did you show to his owner?"

(iii) Quantifier variable binding (TPG):

(29) a. [Enan enan ta   peðia]$_i$ eðiksan   ton
        one   one   the   children.ACC showed.3PL   the
        ðeskalon-at$_i$ (IO_{DP}>DO)
        teacher.ACC-its
        "They showed every child (one by one) his/her teacher."

    b. [Enan enan ta   peðia]$_i$ eðiksan-ato$_i$
       one   one the   children showed.3PL-Cl.3SG.ACC
       son ðeskalon-at$_i$ /*ton   ðeskalon-at$_i$ (DO>$IO_{PP/*DP}$)
       to-the teacher-its/the   teacher-its
       "They showed every child to his/her teacher."

Table 8.4 summarizes the c-command relations in goal ditransitives in TPG.

5.2 Benefactives in TPG

Benefactives in TPG appear to pattern with ROf, which we discuss collectively in section 6.2. However, one apparent difference is, as seen before, the realization of

Table 8.4. C-COMMAND RELATIONS IN GOAL DITRANSITIVES (TPG).

	IO>>DO	DO>>IO
DPacc	✓	*
se"to"-PP	✓	✓

definite benefactive arguments as *se*-PPs. This, in conjunction with the availability of "low" recipient-benefactives like in ROf (which do not intervene between DO and its probe), yields constructions that are unique to TPG (30b):

(30) a. Emairepsen   pita   son   Jorikan (TPG)
        cooked.3SG pie.ACC to-the Jorikas.ACC
        "(S)he baked a pie to/for Jorikas."

    b. I   pita   emaireften   son   Jorikan
       the pie   cooked.PASS.3SG   to-the Jorikas
       "The pie was baked for Jorikas."

5.3 Passives in TPG

TPG patterns with SMG with respect to the availability of direct passives: in the presence of hierarchically high IO DPs, direct passives are impossible (31a) unless the IO undergoes clitic movement (31b):

(31) a. *Para   eðothen   tin   Anastan. (TPG)
        money.NOM   given.PASS.3SG the   Anasta.ACC
        "The money was given (to) Anasta."

    b. (??Tin Anastan)   eɣraften-aten   to ɣraman.[10]
       the   Anasta.ACC written-PASS.Cl.ACC.3SG.FEM   the letter.NOM
       "Anasta was sent the letter."

5.4 Unaccusatives (Psych) in TPG

The use of unaccusatives with datives, especially *piacere*-type psych-predicates, is rather limited in Pontic, and mostly in the Romeyka varieties. To the extent that they are used, at least in TPG and ROf, they involve the same thematic hierarchy as their equivalents in SMG, Italian and so on, since, for instance, they allow for backward binding of the nominative theme by the dative experiencer (32).

10 Recall that bare definite IO_{DP}s are marginal anyway.

(32) O   eaftonats   ki   ares   sin/*tin   Aiše. (ROf)
      the self-her.NOM not   appeal.3SG   to-the   Aise.ACC
      "Aise does not like herself."

It is striking that TPG has suffered attrition, due to the influence of SMG, to such an extent that it has lost morphologically accusative Class III experiencers; instead, it has genitive—as well as PP (33)—"dative" experiencers, just like SMG does.

(33) Ti   Mehmet ke   ti   Aišes   aresi
      the.GEN   Mehmet and   the.GEN   Aise.GEN   appeal-to.3SG
      o enas   son/ton[11]   alon.(TPG)
      the one.NOM   (to-)the   other
      "Mehmet and Aise like each other."

6. ROMEYKA VARIETIES OF PONTUS (OF AND SÜRMENE)

Romeyka are Greek varieties still spoken in Pontus, Turkey. From a typological perspective, Romeyka are Pontic Greek varieties that, in turn, belong to the Asia Minor Greek dialectal group. From a glossonymic perspective, we use the term "Romeyka varieties of Pontus" to refer to what is previously known as "Muslim Pontic" (Mackridge 1987). When further specification is required—"Romeyka varieties of Pontus" is an umbrella term, after all (cf. Sitaridou forthcoming/a)—we specify it as "Romeyka of Of" or "Romeyka of Sürmene." The methodology we used entailed oral interviews based on structured questionnaires (cf. Sitaridou forthcoming/a). Overall, in the Romeyka varieties of Pontus, all datives are morphologically accusative DPs, which, however, behave as bearing genuinely inherent Case, inactive and inert for Agree/Move.

6.1 Ditransitives in Romeyka

IO DPs are accusative and do not alternate with PPs (34a), unlike TPG considered so far (34b):

(34) a. To   peði   eðotše   fai   ton   aðelfo/*son aðelfo. (RSür)
        the child gave-3SG food   the   brother.ACC/*to-the brother
        "The child gave food to the brother."

---

11 The possible use of a bare definite article in the accusative, which is not expected here, is probably a sign that in this variety the periphrasis "o enas ton alon" is becoming a *quasi* one-word reciprocal pronoun.

b. To peði eðose   fai   son   aðelfo. (TPG)
the child gave-3SG food to+the brother
"The child gave food to the brother."

Like other varieties, both surface orders (IO-DO and DO-IO) are licit, despite the morphological homonymy, although the most common order in our data was DO-V-IO:

(35) a. To peði eðotše   fai   ton aðelfo/ton aðelfo   fai. (RSür)
        the kid gave.3SG food the brother/the brother food
        "The kid gave food to the brother."

   b. Eγo eðoka   ton Mehmeti   ena kitap/ena kitap   ton Mehmeti. (ROf)
      I   gave.1SG the Mehmet   a letter/a letter   the Mehmet
      "I gave Mehmet a letter."

PP-realization is restricted to purely locative uses:

(36)   Epije   so   kulin. (ROf)
       went.3SG   to-the   school.ACC
       "He went to the school."

Crucially, Barss & Lasnik's (1986) diagnostics for c-command indicate that DP_{DO} asymmetrically c-commands DP_{IO}:

(i) Weak Crossover Effects (Romeyka):
(37) a. Pion   zon   ekloses   ton   tšopanonat? (RSür)
        which animal   sent.2SG   the   shepherd-its
        "Which animal did you send to its shepherd?"

   b. *Tinan   tšopan(i) ekloses   to zonat? (RSür)
      which   shepherd   sent.2SG   the animal-his
      "Which shepherd did you send his animal to?"

(ii) Superiority effects (Romeyka):
(38) a. Do   tinan   eðikses? (ROf)
        what   whom   showed.2SG

   b. *Tinan   do   eðikses? (ROf)
      whom   what   showed.2SG
      "What did you show to whom?"

   c. Pion   fa(j)in   tinan   eðotšen?
      which food   who-ACC   gave.3SG
      "Which food did she give to whom?"

(iii) Quantifier variable binding (Romeyka):

(39) Ta γarðelæ$_i$ xoræ xoræ$_i$ eðiksa   tši maγlimis'atun$_i$ (ROf)[12]
      the children each   each   showed.1SG   the teachers-their

      "I showed all the children, one by one, to their teachers (each child to her own
      teacher)."

      *"I showed every child his/her teacher."

Table 8.5 summarizes the c-command relations in goal ditransitives in Romeyka.

Table 8.5. C-COMMAND RELATIONS IN GOAL DITRANSITIVES (ROF, RSÜR).

	IO>>DO	DO>>IO
DPacc	*	✓
se"to"-PP	*	*

These data are rather important because it seems that the underlying DO>>IO in the double DP construction is not nonexistent or unique to German, for which the same diagnostics have led to the same conclusion (see Müller 1995, McGinnis 1999). In fact, the situation seems to be the same in some diachronic varieties of Greek as well, notably Medieval Cypriot Greek (as well as Hellenistic Greek; see Michelioudakis 2010b, 2011). This constitutes a serious challenge for the validity of any cross-linguistic generalization whereby IO DPs always merge higher than DOs. Furthermore, the observation that the IO is asymmetrically c-commanded by the DO also ties in well with the fact that direct passives are entirely unproblematic in such languages, since the low position of the IO cannot cause any locality effects.

6.2 Benefactives in Romeyka

As in the case of genuine (goal) ditransitives, both surface/linear orders (IO-DO and DO-IO) are attested in (almost) all varieties. Additionally, benefactives may alternate with PPs headed by ðæ "for" (in ROf) or ja "for" (in RSür and TPG). However, there is a dispreference for the $DP_{DO}>DP_{Benef}$ structure, when the beneficiary is not the potential/intended recipient—we shall call this subcase of benefactives "on behalf of/for someone's sake"—benefactives.

---

12 The speakers were presented with a context in which no more than one teacher corresponds to each pupil; therefore, the teachers necessarily covary with the children, i.e., a distributive interpretation of the plural is necessitated. Also, reversal of word order (with "their teachers" preceding "the children each") was deemed ungrammatical.

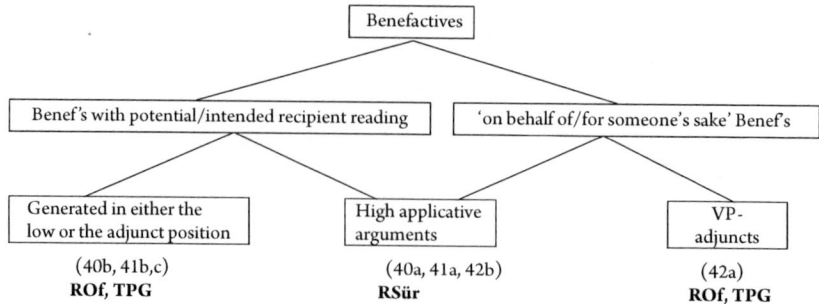

Figure 8.1
Benefactives in different Pontic varieties.

Although our data still do not give us conclusive indications, a first approximation about the c-command relations of benefactives would lead us to categorize them (see figure 8.1) on the basis of two main factors: (i) the distinction mentioned above, namely between "(potential/intended) recipient" benefactives (40–41) and "on behalf of" benefactives (42); this distinction is relevant for ROf and TPG, where beneficiaries may appear as adjuncts c-commanding [V DO], in which case they can neither bind the DO (because they are not in an A-position) nor be bound by it (since it does not c-command them), which is why the Quantifier Variable diagnostic is not applicable; "recipient" benefactives may either merge as adjuncts or in a low position (probably the one associated with goals/recipients), which is c-commanded by DO (41b–c), whereas "on behalf of" benefactives can apparently only merge with VP as adjuncts (42a); (ii) the availability of an A-position above VP for benefactives, possibly the specifier of a High Applicative head (Pylkkänen 2002)[13]: it appears that in RSür, all benefactives are being reanalyzed as high applicative arguments c-commanding DO and not vice versa (41a, 42b). This may also entail some change in the character/content of its [Case] feature, that is, the emergence of an "active" inherent Case feature, as in SMG, which is able to cause intervention effects; this would explain the unavailability of direct passives with benefactives in this variety (see 5.3) as the impossibility of raising DO to T across the dative (especially in the absence of clitic doubling in Romeyka); direct passives are ruled out in ROf anyway, even when the dative is a genuine (low) IO, probably because of a general avoidance of passivization, as mentioned in 3.5.

13 As an anonymous reviewer points out, "*on behalf of*-benefactives have been noted to be located high in the structure of the IP in several languages. [...] This [also] explains why ["free"] benefactives can only be clitics in Romance" (see also Michelioudakis 2011 for an analysis of "free" benefactives as (very) high applicatives, merging between VoiceP and T, which derives both the Romance facts and the obligatoriness of clitic-doubling in SMG).

(40) a. Aiše   epitše   to Mehmet   pide/pide   to Mehmet. (RSür)
      Aise   made.3SG   the Mehmet.ACC   pie.ACC/pie.ACC   the Mehmet.ACC
      "Aise baked Mehmet a pie."

   b. I Aiše   epitšen   aton   enan pita/?enan pita   aton. (ROf)
      the Aise.NOM   made.3SG   him.ACC   a pie.ACC/a pie.ACC   him.ACC
      "Aise baked him a pie."

(41) a. (Ja)   tinan   d'   epitše?/*Do tinan epitšen? (RSür)
      (for)   whom.ACC   what.ACC   made.3SG/What.ACC whom.ACC made.3SG

   b. Tinan   doxna   epitšen?/   Pion   fa(j)in   tinan   epitšen? (ROf)
      whom.ACC   what.ACC   made.3SG/   which   food.ACC.   whom.ACC   made.3SG

   c. Tinan   ti   epiken?/   Ti   tinan   epiken? (TPG)
      whom.ACC   what.ACC   made.3SG/   What.ACC   whom.ACC   made.3SG
      "What did (s)he make for whom?"

(42) a. Tinan tšopan$_i$ efaises   to zon-at$_i$?/??Pion zon$_i$ efaises   ton tšopanin-at$_i$? (TPG/ROf)
      which shepherd fed.2SG his animal/which animal fed.2SG his shepherd.ACC

   b. (Ja) tina tšopano   ta provatat   efaises?/*Pio provat efaises ton tšopan-at? (RSür)
      (For) which shepherd the sheep-his fed.2SG/which sheep fed.2SG the shepherd its
      "For which shepherd did you feed his sheep? / Which sheep did you feed for its
      shepherd?"

According to Pylkkänen (2002), a tell-tale sign of high Applicatives is their compatibility with unergatives. In SMG, where a high A-position for benefactives is independently supported, benefactives are indeed compatible with unergatives; interestingly, this is also the case in RSür, but crucially not in ROf and TPG, which works *in tandem* with our assumptions above.

(43) a. *O   Mehmet   etreksen/jelase   tin   Aiše. (ROf, TPG)
      the   Mehmet   ran.3SG/smiled.3SG   the   Aise.ACC
      "Mehmet ran for Aise / smiled for/at Aise."

   b. O   Janis   ?*(tis)   etrekse/?*(tis)   xamojelase tis   Marias. (SMG)
      the John Cl.GEN.3SG.F   ran.3SG/Cl.GEN.3SG.F smiled.3SG the   Mary.GEN
      "John ran for Mary/smiled for/at Mary."

   c. O   Mehmetis   sin   Aiše/*tin Aiše   merea   etrexse. (RSür)
      the Mehmet.NOM   to-the   Aise.ACC/theAise.ACC   toward   ran.3SG
      "Mehmet ran to / *for Aise."

   d. O   Mehmetis   tin   Aiše   examojelase. (RSür)
      the   Mehmet.NOM   the   Aise.ACC   smiled.3SG
      "Mehmet smiled for/at Aise."

Table 8.6 summarizes the c-command relations in benefactives across all varieties of Pontic.

Table 8.6. C-COMMAND RELATIONS IN BENEFACTIVES (ALL VARIETIES OF PONTIC GREEK).

	Benef>>DO	DO>>Benef
DPacc	✓ (in all varieties, esp. with nonrecipients)	* (RSür), ?/*✓ (ROf, PG)
se"to"-PP	* (RSür, ROf), ✓ (TPG)	* (RSür, Rof), *✓ (TPG)
ja/ðæ"for"-PP	✓ (RSür, Rof)	✓ (RSür, ROf, only with potential recipients)

6.3 Passives in Romeyka

In RSür passives, the theme Agrees with T and becomes nominative (and, possibly, moves to a subject-position), without the requirement that the dative argument cliticize (44a), unlike SMG and TPG, as expected, given that IO DPs (and "recipient" benefactives) were found to be lower than DO, that is, in a position not intervening between the latter and T (44a, b). Passivization of IO is again ruled out (44c). ROf, on the other hand, as already said, appears to lack passives altogether.

(44) a. I   para   tin Aiše   eðoste. (RSür)
        the   money.NOM   the Aise.ACC   given.PASS.3SG
        "The money was given (to) Aise."

    b. To harti   eɣrafte   tin Aiše. (RSür)
        the letter.NOM   written.PASS.3SG   the Aise.ACC
        "The letter was written for (and sent to) Aise."

    c. *I   Aiše   eðoste   tin paran. (RSür)
        the   Aise.NOM   given.PASS.3SG   the money.ACC
        "Aise was given the money."

6.4 Unaccusatives (Psych and Motion) in Romeyka

In Romeyka, apart from direct passives, Agree of the (nominative) theme with T, possibly followed by movement, is unproblematic with unaccusatives, both psych and motion ones. In motion unaccusatives, it can be argued that goal DPs are again merged below themes, thus not intervening (45). The availability of psych constructions is, however, more limited—the lexeme involved in (46) is borrowed from SMG and thus only employed by attrited speakers. When elicited, it arguably involves the same thematic hierarchy as their counterparts in all other varieties, i.e., an experiencer above the nominative theme (prior to movement of any of the two to a pre-INFL position (46a-b)), suggesting that what is crucial here for the absence of intervention effects between T and NOM is probably the inactive inherent Case feature of the experiencer which does not render it active/visible for Agree. Also, unlike SMG, which allows PP- and DP-experiencers of such predicates to have subjectlike behavior, quirky experiencer subjects are clearly not possible in Romeyka (47).

(45) To xarti   to Meme   epidže. (RSür)
      the paper.NOM   the Mehmet.ACC   went.3SG
      "The letter arrived (to) Mehmet."

(46) a. ?I patši   to Hosni   aresi. (ROf)
       the girl.NOM   the Hosni.ACC   appeal.3SG
       "The girl appeals to Hosni."

    b. ?To Hosni$_i$ tši   ares   to kendinat$_i$
       the Hosni.ACC   not   appeal.3SG   the self-his
       "Hosni does not like himself."

(47) *Ton Abdula$_i$ i   Aiše   aresen ROf   ama   pro$_i$
      The Abdulah.ACC the   Aise.NOM   appealed-to.3SG, but   pro
      tin Eminen   epiren (Rof).
      the Emine.ACC   married.3SG
      "Abdulah liked Aise, but he married Emine."

6.5 Person Restrictions in Romeyka

Interestingly enough, Person-Case effects are not absent from Romeyka, despite the lack of clitic clusters. Combinations of strong pronouns or of clitics and strong pronouns, are subject to the PCC, though a weaker version of it: as is expected in both strong and weak PCC languages, a first- and second-person accusative pronoun cannot be interpreted as a direct object in the presence of a third-person pronoun (48) –irrespective of their relative order, since both orders are in principle acceptable; however, the sequences of a first-person clitic and a second-person pronoun (cf. 49) are acceptable for most of the speakers, and surprisingly the same pattern (as in 49a–49b) is attested in some Pontic varieties of northern Greece too (cf. Chatzikyriakidis 2010). Recall that SMG has the strong version of the PCC (49c).

(48) a. Eðiksane   m(e)/emenan   atona. (RSür)
         showed.3PL   me.ACC.CL/me.ACC   him.ACC

b. Eðiksan(e)   æ/aton(a)   emenan. (RSür/ROf)
   showed.3PL   him.ACC.CL/him.ACC   me.ACC
   "They showed him to me / *They showed me to him."

(49) a. Eðiksane-m-ese   /*eðiksane-s-eme   (RSür)
        showed.3PL-me.ACC.CL you.ACC /showed.3PL-you.ACC.CL   me.ACC

   b. Atos   esena   emen   eðiksen. (ROf)
      he   you.ACC   me.ACC   showed.3SG

   c. *Mu   se/su   me   eðiksan. (SMG)
      me.GEN.CL you.ACC.CL/you.GEN.CL   me.ACC.CL showed.3PL
      "They showed you to me."

It is worth noting that the equivalent of (48b) in SMG (50), with an
IO-clitic and a strong pronominal first-person DO, would be perfectly grammatical on the reading "They showed me to him"; this is probably attributable to the observation in section 3.3 about the inherently emphatic use of
the strong pronoun in this context, while in Romeyka, as already claimed,
this is the unmarked option.

(50)   Tu   eðiksan   emena. (SMG)
       him.GEN.CL   showed.3PL   me.ACC
       "They showed me to him."

7. MEDIEVAL AND MODERN CYPRIOT GREEK

MedCG is trivially considered to be the earliest attested Modern Greek
dialect in the historical record. ModCG on the other hand, is a nonstand-
ardized variety, a continuation of MedCG, but which also exhibits various
degrees of intradialectal variation. Overall, although in both MedCG and
ModCG all datives are morphologically genitive, the MedCG datives behave
as inactive inherent, whereas the ModCG ones behave as active inherent.

7.1 Morphological Exponence/Distribution in Cypriot Greek

In ModCG, genitive DPs and *se*-PPs alternate in ditransitives (51) and experiencer constructions (52), as in SMG, although there is a clear preference
for genitives in the latter constructions.

(51)   Eðiksa   se kathe jeneka$_i$/kathe jenekas$_i$
       showed.1SG   to each woman.ACC/each woman.GEN

ton andran   tis_j(/kathe jeneka ston andran tis) (ModCG)

the man.ACC her(/each woman to her man)

"I showed every woman her husband."

(52) Efanin(-tis)   tis Marias/Efanin

seemed.3SG-3FSGEN.CL   the Mary.GEN/seemed.3SG

(%??) sti Maria (na en)   eksipnos. (ModCG)

to Mary.ACC (that is.3SG)   smart

"He seemed to Mary (to be) smart."

In MedCG, on the other hand, indirect objects and (so-called *piacere*-type) dative experiencers are exclusively realized as genitive DPs, as in Romeyka, *modulo* the m-case. *Se/is*-PPs only occur in constructions with either purely locative uses, that is, with V(P)s in which the transfer of location reading is more or at least as prominent as the transfer of possession reading, or with inanimate recipients (e.g., collective nouns (53) and metonymies (54)).

(53) Na   to   ksighunde is ton kosmon (MedCG)

PRT.SUBJ it.ACC.CL   narrate.3PL to the people.ACC

"To narrate it to the people"

(Machairas 2.99.5)

(54) oti to   dhikon tou na   dhothi [...] is ta   cherja

that the own   his PRT.SUBJ be-given.3SG to the hands.ACC

tous pateres (MedCG)   tu San Tomeniku

the fathers.GEN   the.GEN Saint Dominique.GEN

"that his fortune be given to the hands of the monks of St. Dominique"

(Machairas 1.56.1–2)

7.2 MedCG versus ModCG: The syntax of dative arguments

The first striking property of genitive arguments in MedCG is that, like accusative "datives" in Romeyka, they clearly do not induce any minimality effect, since any Agree/Move relation between a probing head and a lower goal can be established across a structurally intervening genitive argument, with no apparent effect, as if the genitive were not there. This appears to be the case in constructions with raising predicates (55) and psych unaccusatives that take dative experiencers (cf. (56) and (57), which allows even long-distance Agree between the matrix T and the embedded subject), as well as in passivizations of the direct object (56) ("direct passives"), although the absence of blocking effects in this case can simply be attributed to the fact that the genitive indirect object in MedCG is lower than the direct object, as we will suggest below, that is, the genitive in ditransitives is not even structurally an intervener; this appears to be the case in Romeyka too, that is, the indirect object DP, being lower than DO, is not an intervener there either.

(55) ekinon, [$_{CP}$ to$_i$ [$_{TP}$ t$_i$ efanin-T tis vulis   mu [$_{TP}$ t$_i$ ine   kalon]]], fenete
     that   which seemed.3SG the senate/diet.GEN my   be.INF good   seems
     mu   ki   emenan (MedCG)
     me.GEN.Cl   and   me.GEN
     "What seemed to my senators/consultants to be good seems to me (to be good) too."
     (Boustr. *Chron.* A 52.13–15)

(56) [Toutos o logos]$_i$ polla   aresen   tou rigos t$_i$(MedCG)
     This the words   very-much   appealed.3SG   the king.GEN
     "The king liked these words very much."
     (Machairas 2.274.1)

(57) Den areskoun   tous archondes   tous Genouvisous[na eine oi las
     not appeal.3PL   the masters.ACC   the Genoans.ACC to be.3PL the people.NOM
     mas (MedCG)   kai   to dhikon
     our   and the fortune-NOM
     tous apokato eis tin eksousian sas]
     their under to the power your
     "The Genoan masters do not like the fact that our people and their fortunes are under your rule."
     (Machairas 3, 372)

(58) Pos estrafin   to righaton$_i$ ape tous Romeous ke   (pro$_i$)
     that was-returned.3SG   the kingdom.NOM   by   the   Greeks   and
     edothin   t$_i$ tous Latinous
     was-given.3SG   the Latins.GEN
     "That the kingdom was returned by the Greeks and was given to the Latins"
     (Machairas 2.99.1–2)

It should be pointed out that in (55), Spec-T in the relative clause is occupied by the trace of the embedded subject rather than by pro$_{expl}$[14] since *efanin* here is clearly not used as impersonal, taking into

---

14 If we are to follow Alexiadou & Anagnostopoulou (1998) in that pro$_{expl}$ does not exist anyway, then the discussion here simply amounts to whether the matrix T Agrees with the embedded subject or not; we argue that, given the contextual information and the properties of the SMG equivalent, it does.

consideration that its other occurrence (*fenete*) in the matrix clause has an overt referential subject, arguably raised out of an elided complement-TP; note that in SMG, in which *fenete* appears to have the same usage, the embedded subject of an elided complement clause cannot be (A')-moved (i.e., topicalized) into the matrix CP, unless *fenete* agrees with it, that is, if it gives rise to raising.[15] At any rate, in MedCG there are also quite a few other instances of raising predicates agreeing with embedded nominative DPs (regardless of their surface position) across genitive experiencers unproblematically, without evidence of any intervention effect, for example without obligatory cliticization/clitic doubling (CD) of the genitive as in SMG; interestingly, cliticization/CD of the genitive is obligatory in SMG even when the raising predicate is impersonal, that is, there still appears to be a need to establish some Agree relation with the embedded CP, for which the genitive would act as an intervener. As far as (57) is concerned, the plural marking on the matrix verb could not be the result of sympathetic agreement with the experiencer, as there is no indication of such a possibility in any other point in the text, or any other Greek text for that matter; in all other cases with plural experiencers, psych Vs display singular agreement. On another topic, it seems that raising/long-distance Agree is possible out of subjunctive complements, probably because *na*-clauses at this stage serve mostly as substitutes of the infinitive (there still seems to be free variation among infinitival and *na*-clauses in this period) and arguably have not yet developed a full CP-structure (see Roussou 2000), that is, they are not strong phases, which is why they are not subject to the Phase Impenetrability Condition (Chomsky 2000, 2001). It is also worth pointing out that there is no evidence that dative arguments at this stage can undergo any kind of A-movement, that is, there are no quirky subjects, nor indirect passives; all genitive experiencers in the extant medieval Cypriot texts occur postverbally and do not seem to pass any of Sigurðsson's (1989) diagnostics for subjecthood.[16] Furthermore, if we follow Boeckx (2000: 361),

15 Consider, for instance, the following SMG example, which is as close structurally to (55) as possible:

(i) Ekines i lisis pus su fenonde.3PL esena na ine kales, mu fenonde.3PL ki emena (na ine kales)
(ii) ?*Ekines i lisis pu su fenete.3SG esena na ine kales, mu fenonde.3PL ki emena (na ine kales)
(iii) *Ekines i lisis pu su fenonde.3PL esena na ine kales, mu fenete.3SG ki emena (na ine kales)
(iv) *Ekines i lisis pu su fenete.3SG esena na ine kales, mu fenete.3SG ki emena (na ine kales)

"Those solutions that seem to you to be good, (they) seem good to me as well."
16 See also Sevdali (2009) who makesV the case for quirky datives in Classical Greek based on different types of evidence (case transmission, control, reflexive binding), which are also not to be found in Medieval Cypriot.

"[q]uirky elements always block raising of nominative 'objects' [...] to the highest ('subject') position, irrespective of agreement pattern," which is not the case in MedCG, as already shown.

Turning now our attention to ditransitives, there is evidence that in MedCG, genitive indirect objects can stay structurally low, possibly in the same position as prepositional IOs in languages with dative shift/dative alternations, which is probably a survival of the Koine DO>>IO pattern (cf. (59), in which the DO binds the dative reciprocal anaphor). In around 70 percent of all the cases in which both internal arguments occur postverbally, DO precedes IO. More importantly, this can be argued to be the unmarked order on the basis of the fact that it occurs when there is no reason or way to suspect or justify either focus- or topic-movement, for example with existential quantifiers ((60); cf. Philippaki-Warburton (1982) for a similar argument for Modern Greek VSO as the unmarked order). (61) also provides a piece of evidence that DO>IO cannot be claimed to be the result of A'-scrambling applied to an IO>DO base-generated order; if this were the case, it should give rise to WCO in examples such as (61), that is, if the DO had to cross over an IO-DP containing a coindexed possessor. Therefore, DOs can occupy an A-position above IO, and the simplest assumption would be that IO is base-generated below DO. On the other hand, it seems possible that IO>DO may, at least sometimes, be the result of A'-scrambling, since it can be employed for defocusing purposes, as in (62). Also, interestingly, there is no evidence in any of the extant texts for "free" benefactive DPs, which are typically first merged above DO.

(59) po:s oun he: theos [...]   tous agnooumenous edeiksen alle:lois
      how so the goddess [...] the missing showed.3SG each-other.DAT
      lekso: (Koine Greek)
      tell.1SG.FUT
      "So now I'll tell you how the goddess (Venus) showed/revealed
      the two   missing heroes to each other."
      (Chariton, *Callirhoe*, 8.1.5.2)

(60) kai   afini   kanenan   pragman   katinos (MedCG)
      and   leave.£SG   any thing.ACC   anyone.GEN
      "and (if) he leaves anything to anyone"
      (*Assizes* f.137, 190)

(61) an   thelete   me   to kalon   na strepsete
      if   want.2P   with the good PRT.SUBJ   return.2PL
      [to kastron]ᵢ   [tu afendi   tuᵢ] (MedCG)
      the castle   the owner.GEN its
      "if you want to return the castle to its owner willingly"
      (Machairas 3.472.10–11)

(62)   ke anen ke pepsoun   i Genuvisi [...]   tote na
       and if and send.3P   the Genoans   then PRT.SUBJ
       dosoun tus Genuvisus   100 doukata   (MedCG)
       give.3P the Genoans.ACC/GEN   100 ducats
       "and in case the Genoans send (someone)...then they (must)
       give the Genoans 100 ducats"
       (Machairas §353.17)

The unique instance, in the latest text of the period, of a quantified IO binding a variable in the DO (61), clearly indicating that it c-commands it, may be
an early example of the emergent IO>>DO pattern, which is now prevalent in
ModCG or may constitute evidence that both patterns coexisted in that period.
Interestingly enough, clitic clusters in the earliest text from that period, appear
to have an unfixed order, while being comparatively very few anyway, allowing
both IO-DO and DO-IO orderings (64). Finally, recall that MedCG can form
perfectly acceptable direct passives, without obligatorily resorting to special
strategies to circumvent any intervening DP's minimality effects, for example
cliticization/clitic doubling of the genitive IO (see (58) above).

(63)   kai   edhoken pasanou$_i$ tin dhoulian tou$_i$(MedCG)
       and   gave.3SG everyone.GEN   the job.ACC his
       "and (he) gave everyone his job"
       (Machairas §174.7)

(64) a. oti to   tou   afikan ekeino to   zitaei   (MedCG)
        that it.Cl.ACC him.Cl.GEN left.3P that   rel-pron. asks.3SG
        "that they left him what he asks"
        (*Assizes* f.134,188)

     b. Ape   ta perpira   κ' (=20) ta   sou
        as for the perpers 20 them.NEUT.Cl.ACC   you.SG.Cl.GEN
        eparadhoka.
        handed-in.1SG
        "As for the perpers (=local currency) (that I owed to you), I
        did give you 20."
        (*Assizes* f.74,103).

     c. oti ekeinos   to   tou   epoulisen ekeinon to alogon
        that he.NOM it.Cl.ACC him.Cl.GEN sold.3SG that   the horse
        "that he sold him that horse"
        (*Assizes* f.191.30)

     d. oti   eteros   tou   to   epoulisen
        that someone-else him.Cl.GEN it.Cl.ACC sold.3SG
        "that someone else sold it to him"
        (*Assizes* f.191.30)

To sum up, genitive "dative" arguments in MedCG do not display any minimality effects in Agree/Move, they arguably cannot undergo A-movement, and genitive indirect objects in particular are (often) asymmetrically c-commanded by the direct object in an A-position.

Moving on to ModCG, the picture is the reverse in most respects. To begin with, in ditransitives, it is quite straightforward that genitive IOs, as well as benefactives, asymmetrically c-command DO (based again on Barss & Lasnik's (1986) diagnostics, e.g., quantifier variable binding (65)), rather than the reverse. Moreover, the dispreference Anagnostopoulou (2003) observed for direct passives, is equally or even more robust in ModCG, where direct passives are deemed as totally ungrammatical (66a), unless IO is cliticized/clitic doubled or clefted (66b).

(65) Eðiksa   kathe jenekas$_i$ ton andran   tis$_i$/?*kathe andran$_i$ tis
      showed.1S   each woman.GEN   the man.ACC   her/every   man.ACC
      jenekas   tu$_i$ (ModCG)
      the woman.GEN his
      "I showed every woman her husband / ?*his wife every man."

(66) a. Ta   rialia   eðothikasin/eðothisan   *(-tis) tis Marias (ModCG)
        the   money.PL   were-given.3PL her.GEN.CL the Maria.GEN
        "The book was given (to) Mary."
        (Theoni Neokleous, p.c.)

     b. En   TIS MARIAS$_i$ pu   eðothikasin/eðothisan   ta   rialia t$_i$
        be.3SG the Maria.GEN   that were-given.3PL   the   money.3PL
        The money was given (to) Mary."
        (Theoni Neokleous, p.c.)

As far as the PCC is concerned, ModCG has its strong version, while in MedCG texts there are quite a few indications that first- and second-person clitics in the presence of a third-person genitive goal are systematically avoided and some escape strategy is opted for (e.g., strong accusative pronouns, alternative morphological exponence of the goal). Combinations of first- and second-person internal arguments (which should be available, given the parallel with Romeyka) are hard to be tested, due to the narrative nature of the extant texts, however there is no *a priori* evidence that these were ungrammatical.

Finally, in the syntax of unaccusatives with genitives, there is an interesting split. In SMG, as we said, both genitive experiencers selected by *piacere*-type psych predicates and genitive goals selected by motion unaccusatives must undergo cliticization or clitic doubling, otherwise the construction is significantly degraded, thus indicating that genitives in SMG do induce minimality effects, by both intervening between T and the theme, and having an active inherent Case feature. In ModCG, however, only motion unaccusatives with genitive goals pattern with SMG—in fact, Cypriot speakers find them sharply ungrammatical, unless a genitive clitic is present (67)—while genitive experiencers are perfectly acceptable either with or without cliticization/clitic doubling (68). Also, while both varieties allow raising (more or less marginally), only in SMG does the genitive experiencer require cliticization/clitic doubling (69).

(67) [to epiðoman]   irte   (-tis)   tis Marias (ModCG)
      the allowance.NOM came.3SG   her.GEN.CL   the Maria.GEN
      "Mary got the allowance." (= "The allowance came to Mary.")

(68) O   Janis   areski   (-tis) tis Marias polla (ModCG)
      the John.NOM   appeals her.GEN.CL the Mary.GEN much
      "Mary likes John a lot."

(69) Ta peðja   (ð)en [$\sqrt{}_{\text{Mod CG}}$ /$*_{\text{SMG}}$(tis)] fenonde tis Marias   (na ine$_{\text{SMG}}$/en$_{\text{ModCG}}$)
      the kids   not her.GEN.CL   seem.3P   the Mary.GEN (PRT.SUBJ/are.3PL)
      kurasmena (ModCG)
      tired
      "The kids do not seem to Mary to be tired."

8. CORRELATIONS AND THEORETICAL IMPLICATIONS

Despite the considerable amount of cross-dialectal and cross-categorial microvariation that can be found in the varieties we considered so far, there are some very important correlations and generalizations that appear to hold across all diachronic and diatopic varieties of Greek. First, as already mentioned in section 2, the existence of minimality effects in Agree/raising across a dative (at least a goal DP) seems to depend on the availability of structurally high IO DPs, which, in turn, presupposes the existence of dative alternations. There also appears to be a strong correlation between the existence of dative alternations and the strong PCC. On the contrary, in systems with no dative alternations, only a weak PCC is operative and no minimality effects in Agree/raising across datives is observed. The first tentative conclusion drawn from these facts is that whatever makes a dative visible for Agree/Move (even as a defective intervener) must also be found in the double object/dative-shifted construction, and not in the one where the IO stays "low."

What differentiates the double DP frame from the prepositional ditransitive construction in all varieties is the animacy restriction on the IO. There are systems (like Spanish, according to Ormazabal 2000) in which the presence of a dative pronoun, which is by definition animate, excludes any other animate internal argument. Compared to this, the strong PCC appears to be a weaker restriction, and the weak PCC an even weaker one. Following

Michelioudakis (2010b, 2011) we propose that all these restrictions are due to a selectional uninterpretable feature in the double DP construction, which encodes (e.g., [+animate]) or entails (e.g., [±Participant], in Harley & Ritter's (2002) feature geometry) the aforementioned animacy requirement.

In weak PCC systems, which also happen to be systems in which only IO DPs (and not PPs) may be animate, the situation is as follows: (i) both internal arguments can be third-person, therefore an uninterpretable [Participant] feature is matched by IO alone and is valued as [-Prt] (third-person DOs are not specified for this feature at all, see Adger & Harbour 2007); (ii) first- and second-person pronouns can co-occur, which suggests that they can both simultaneously match a positively valued [Participant]; (iii) the two internal arguments cannot have different values of [±participant], that is, no third-person ([-Prt]) datives co-occurring with [+Prt] DOs, which means that there may not be a mismatch between [Participant], whatever its value, and any of the internal arguments. All three states are only compatible with a first-merged configuration where the two internal arguments are probed by a low probe and are equidistant from it, perhaps in the spirit of Kayne's (1984, 2010) suggestion that they originate, quite symmetrically, in the same DP. Perhaps the probe is the ditransitive V/Root itself, which s-selects only animate DPs. DO then Agrees with v*, which inherits Voice's phi-features (which we take to be the real low phase head), and is finally attracted by it to its Spec, following Chomsky (2006, 2008),[17] thus deriving the DO>IO$_{DP}$ order attested in Romeyka and MedCG:

(70) $[_{VoiceP}$ EA V-v*-Voice $[_{v*P}$ DO$_{acc}$<V-v*$_{[u\phi]}$> $[_{VP}$<V$_{[uParticipant]}$> [<DO> IO$_{[iCase]}$]]]]

In strong PCC systems, on the other hand, the animacy restriction only affects IO DPs, not PPs, so we may not say that [uParticipant] is an s-selectional feature of V, but rather a feature associated with a head that is present only in the double object construction, arguably the one that hosts the IO DP in its Spec. Following the literature on applicatives, we take this to be an Appl head c-commanding VP. Moreover, we assume that two v-heads are present in DOCs, assuming that this is the right minimalist update of Larson's (1988) original idea about the presence of two VP-shells in DOCs, especially if, as commonly assumed, v-heads are the real verb(alizer)s rather than Roots themselves, as well as others' suggestion about the lexical decomposition of verbs taking double objects. Both v-heads inherit Voice's phi-features and its EPP. Then the derivation proceeds as follows. After DO's Agree with and raising to v$_2$, Appl probes the IO DP, which must then have an active, even if inherent, Case feature,

17 Chomsky's original suggestion, of course, is about V, as the inheritor of v*'s features.

perhaps akin to what Chomsky (2000) terms "quirky Case," as we have already said. If the intervening DO is 1st/second-person, then its defective intervention blocks Agree with IO and the deactivation of its Case, which derives the strong PCC. Otherwise, the IO DP matches Appl's [uParticipant] and is attracted to its Spec, where it can be probed and matched by v* and have its Case deactivated. This derives the familiar IO>DO order in DOCs (in, e.g., SMG, TPG, and ModCG):

(71)

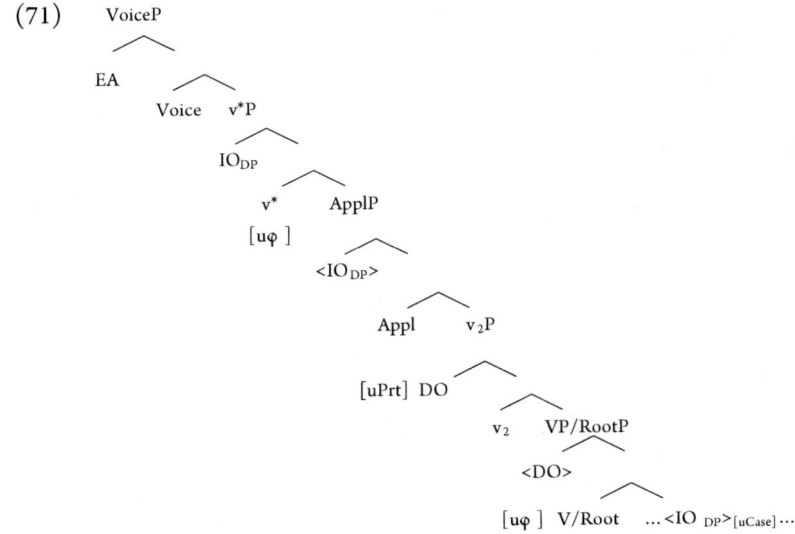

The schema in (71) may be generalized to all DOCs, even the ones that involve completely structurally Case-marked IO DPs, like English. Another implication of this is that the IO must have an active Case feature, whenever it c-commands DO from an A-position; this applies even to shifted IOs headed by a P (as e.g. in SMG, see Table 8.2), and of course *se*-PP benefactives (see Table 8.3). One then has to assume that P in this case is nothing more than a dative case marker; this must certainly be the case in benefactives, where *se* ("to") has none of its original locative (either directional or stative) meaning. A process of grammaticalization is probably still in progress in SMG, whereas *se* as a dative case marker has already become fully grammaticalized, hence the only option, in TPG definite dative DPs.

The postulation of two types of inherent Case for shifted and nonshifted "datives" also derives the correlation between dative-shift and intervention effects in Agree/raising across datives. As already assumed throughout the article, phi-probes, such as T and v*, probe for interpretable phi-features and consider an XP/DP as a possible/"active" goal if it carries an active, that is, uninterpretable Case feature (Chomsky 2000, 2001). Given that "datives" in all the varieties we considered arguably carry all the interpretable features required by any phi-probe, we are led to the conclusion that they must differ in their [Case] feature. More concretely, "dative" DPs in MedCG and Romeyka, despite their distinct morphological realization, are all assumed to carry a (fully) valued Case feature [iCase], associated with a series of theta-roles therefore, LF-interpretable, which makes the DP "invisible"/"transparent" for a phi-probe, which looks for [uCase] features. On the other hand, experiencers in SMG and TPG and genitive goals in both SMG/TPG and ModCG bear a partially interpretable and partially unvalued Case feature [uCase], which, while still inherent (i.e., still associated with a series of theta-roles and with a nonabsorbable PF-interpretable value),awaits valuation in the course of the derivation. This makes such DPs visible to phi-probes, either as active goals, or as defective interveners, if their [uCase] has already been valued and marked for deletion in the course of the derivation. So, for instance, when a dative intervenes between T and a nominative theme, its status as an intervener can be parameterized. Assuming "active" inherent Case is an instance of a [uCase] feature, while "pure" inherent Case is [iCase], the following three possibilities arise:

(72)   H[uφ]...DAT[iφ, uCase/ uCase/ iCase]...DP[iφ, uCase]
                        (i)   (ii)   (iii)

(i)   If DAT carries an unvalued [uCase] feature, then it is an active goal that can match and fully Agree with H, as long as it is its closest potential goal, deactivating its own [uCase], and preventing H from probing further down;

(ii) If DAT is the most local goal for H but it has already valued its [uCase] via Agree with a closer phi-head H<pr>, then DAT is a *defective* intervener, blocking Agree between H and any lower active goal. This defective intervention effect can be obviated if DAT undergoes some (movement-related)process which puts the head of DAT's chain outside H's Agree domain, following Chomsky (2000, 2001);

(iii) If DAT carries [iCase], it is transparent/invisible for Agree purposes, and H can unproblematically Agree with the next closest DP with [uCase].

As already implied, φ-probes such as T only probe for [uCase], hence the immunity of [iCase]. Blocking effects in DAT-above-NOM can then be parameterized, as necessary, if we treat them as defective intervention effects (case ii): in languages with [iCase], no intervention effects arise, while in languages with active inherent Case, they do and, being defective, they can be obviated via some movement process involving DATs with already valued [uCase] (clitic movement in SMG, perhaps scrambling in other languages (see Anagnostopoulou 2003), clefting in Modern Cypriot Greek, etc.). Finally, obligatory cliticization/clitic doubling in DAT-above-NOM contexts (e.g., in SMG) serves as a means of cancellation of defective intervention as follows:

(73) $[...*(\varphi P_{DAT})\text{-}T...[\ [DAT \ <\varphi P_{DAT}> \ [0/DP_{DAT[uCase]}]]...DP_{NOM}]]$

(a) T (which has an uninterpretable phi-set as well as [uD]) probes DAT first;
(b) if DAT is headed by a (φ-) clitic, it matches it, deletes the [uCase] of the clitic (and consequently DAT itself) and incorporates the clitic (see Roberts2010);
(c) the head of DAT's chain is now outside T's Agree domain(i.e., no longer visible);
(d) however, the dative clitic, being a $\varphi(P)$ (Cardinaletti & Starke 1999, Déchaine & Wiltschko 2002, Roberts 2010, as opposed perhaps to DO clitics, see Daskalaki & Mavrogiorgos 2010, Anagnostopoulou 2006), cannot satisfy T's [uD], so T (requiring full matching, see Chomsky 2001) has to probe all over again across the (now invisible) DAT in order to match [uD]; this enables T to fully match NOM and Agree with it.

The intervention then of a dative with active Case in unaccusative contexts (raising, *piacere*-type psych predicates, and motion unaccusatives) is an instance of defective intervention, as defined above, since in the configuration in which the dative intervenes between T and the theme, the dative's φ-features have already been matched and its Case deactivated by T itself. In (70–71), the dative appears to c-command the theme: this is the case with dative experiencers anyway, whether they are/need to be attracted by an Appl head or not, given the evidence we have about their thematic position (cf. backward binding, etc.); for goals, this is a derived position; in systems with inactive inherent Case and no dative alternations, goal DPs with unaccusatives may stay low causing no intervention effects (45, 67). However, given the uniform positioning of experiencers higher than nominative themes, the absence of intervention effects (68–69) in ModCG, which arguably has active inherent Case, is quite surprising. We are therefore led to one last factor that yields (cross-categorial, this time) microvariation, a split in Case features depending on theta-roles. Active inherent Case has apparently been spread to all IO-related theta-roles in both transitive and intransitive contexts, but crucially not to experiencers. In SMG (and TPG) this spread has been more pervasive and complete.

Therefore, as mentioned in section 2, there is only a one-way implication relating (i) the existence of "active" dative experiencers, giving rise to intervention effects, and (ii) the availability of "high" indirect object DPs (asymmetrically commanding DO): the former entails the latter but not vice versa. ModCG constitutes a counterexample explicable on these grounds, while experiencers with blocking effects also presuppose the availability of high IOs but do not in principle exclude the coexistence of low IO DPs asymmetrically c-commanded by DO (cf. Icelandic, where both high (i.e., "active") and low (i.e., "inactive") inherently Case-marked IOs are available (see Anagnostopoulou 2003)), as in Hebrew, although dative experiencers have active Case only, causing blocking effects, and arguably linked to quirkiness (Boeckx 2000, among others).

Finally, the apparent availability of high applicatives in RSür may be a first step for the emergence of quirky inherent Case in this variety too. On the other hand, TPG benefactives have the same properties as in ROf, which arguably do not involve Appl. Benefactives seem to develop quite independently from canonical ditransitives, especially when they do not involve a potential recipient interpretation.

Table 8.7 below summarizes our empirical findings in this article and Table 8.8 illustrates the four-way syntactic typology we have developed, based on our approach to inherent Case.

9. CONCLUDING REMARKS

This article has aimed to show that all cross-categorial and cross-dialectal (and possible diachronic) variation with regards to datives in Greek results from the interplay and the interaction of a limited number of variables: (i) the nature of the (inherent) Case feature, active (uCase) vs. nonactive (iCase), (ii) their position on the thematic hierarchy (goals, experiencers, or "free" benefactives behaving as semi-adjuncts), and (iii) their morphological exponence/m-case, which turned out to be the least crucial factor, as far as syntax is concerned. Furthermore, an important finding of this investigation is that the derivation of "dative" DPs, when these constitute the only realization of dative arguments, does not involve (high) Applicative heads, unlike SMG and TPG/ModCG goal constructions (with the only exception of some classes of benefactives in RSür, which in turn may have important diachronic implications). Indirect object DPs in Romeyka and ModCG are consistently structurally lower, asymmetrically c-commanded by the direct object, an observation that challenges any claims about universal IO>DO in the double DP frame. The central theoretical conclusion of this article, then, is that the thematic interpretation can be exclusively derived by the positioning of the arguments relative to V/Root, and that applicative heads, when/if present, simply attract DPs with active Case from their thematic positions to positions accessible to phi-probes/structural Case-assigners, rather than introducing/selecting them. Finally, our analysis predicts a number of correlations between person restrictions, agreement

Table 8.7. COMPARATIVE TABLE OF PROPERTIES ACROSS GREEK VARIETIES.

Properties	Active "inherent" Case			Nonactive Inherent Case		
Varieties	SMG	PG	ModCG	MedCG	ROf	RSür
Ditransitives						
c-command relations						
DP_{IO}	IO>DO			DO>IO		
DP_{Ben}	Ben>DO			n/a	Ben>DO (adjunct)	Ben>DO (argum)
Direct passives	yes			yes	yes	no
Cliticization/CD of the dative in passives	obligatory			optional	optional	n/a
Indirect passives	no			no		
Animacy restriction on dative "DPs"	yes			yes (all and only animate arguments)		
Person restrictions (PCC)	strong			n/a (cf. 7.2)	weak	
Clitic clusters	fixed IO-DO order (procl.)	fixed IO-DO order (encl.)	fixed IO-DO order (both)	Few; un-ordered	no	no
PP substitutes						
Goal	DO>PP PP>DO			no (but see 6.1)	no	no
Benef	PP>DO			no	only adjunct-PPs	only adjunct-PPs
"Datives" with unaccusatives						
Cliticization/Clitic doubling of the "dative"						
psych/raising	obligatory	optional		optional		n/a
Motion V's	oblig.	oblig.		n/a	n/a	optional

Table 8.8. M-CASE AND THE ACTIVE VS. NONACTIVE DISTINCTION ACROSS GREEK VARIETIES.

+/-active m-case	Active Inherent	Inactive Inherent
mACC	TPG	ROf, RSür
mGEN	SMG, ModCG	MedCG

restrictions across datives and the syntax of ditransitives, of which the following two also seem to hold cross-linguistically: (a) if a language has "active" dative experiencers, it also has high IO DPs; in other words, dative experiencers give rise to intervention effects in raising/unaccusative constructions, if IOs with the same form/Case have to escape VP/$\sqrt{P}$; and (b) The strong PCC in ditransitives presupposes the existence of high IOs, that is, the DOC frame (alongside prepositional low IOs).

ACKNOWLEDGMENTS

We are extremely grateful to our informants: T. & G. for ROf, Hakan Öz the kan for RSür, Lemonia Tsakiridou for TPG, and Theoni Neokleous for ModCG. All errors are our own. Dimitris Michelioudakis wishes to thank the Greek State Scholarships Foundation (IKY), the Alexander Onassis Foundation, and the A. Leventis Foundation for funding his graduate research at different stages. Ioanna Sitaridou wishes to acknowledge (i) for the Romeyka data, support from the British Academy (SRG #102639, 2011–2013, "Contact, continuity and change: The syntax of the Romeyka varieties in Pontus," PI: Ioanna Sitaridou); (ii) for the Medieval Cypriot Greek data, support from the British Academy (SRG #48312, 2007–2009, "Language contact in medieval Cyprus: The linguistic record," PI: Ioanna Sitaridou).

REFERENCES

Adger, Daniel, and Daniel Harbour. 2007. "The syntax and syncretisms of the person case constraint." *Syntax* 10: 2–37.

Alexiadou, Alexidou, and Elena Anagnostopoulou. 1998. "Parametrizing Agr: Word order, v-movement and EPP-checking." *Natural Language and Linguistic Theory* 16: 491–539.

Anagnostopoulou, Elena 1999. "On experiencers." In Artemis Alexiadou, Geoffrey Horrocks, and Melita Stavrou (eds.), *Studies in Greek Syntax*, 67–93. Dordrecht: Kluwer Academic.

Anagnostopoulou, Elena 2003. *The syntax of ditransitives: Evidence from clitics*. Berlin: Mouton de Gruyter.

Anagnostopoulou, Elena 2005. "Cross-linguistic and cross-categorial variation of datives." In Melita Stavrou and Arhonto Terzi (eds.), *Recent advances in Greek Generative Grammar: Festschrift for Dimitra Theophanopoulou Kontou*, 61–126. Amsterdam: John Benjamins.

Anagnostopoulou, Elena 2006. "Clitic doubling." In Martin Everaert and Henk van Riemsdijk (eds.), *The Blackwell companion of syntax*, 519–581. Oxford: Blackwell.

Anagnostopoulou, Elena, and Christina Sevdali. 2010. "Dative-Nominative alternations and voice: Ancient Greek vs. Icelandic." Paper presented at "MSM3," Athens, October 10.

Baker, Mark 1996. "On the structural positions of themes and goals." Unpublished ms., McGill University.

Barss, Andrew, and Howard Lasnik. 1986. "A note on anaphora and double objects." *Linguistic Inquiry* 17: 347–354.

Belletti, Adriana, and Luigi Rizzi.1988. "Psych-verbs and theta-theory." *Natural Language and Linguistic Theory* 6: 291–352.

Bianchi, Valentina 2006. "On the syntax of personal arguments." *Lingua* 116: 2023–2067.

Boeckx, Cedric 2000. "Quirky agreement." *Studia Linguistica* 54(3): 354–380.

Bonet, Eulalia 1991. "Morphology after syntax: Pronominal clitics in Romance." PhD diss., MIT.

Bošković. Željko. 1997. "Superiority effects with multiple wh-fronting in Serbo-Croatian." *Lingua* 102: 1–20.

Cardinaletti, Anna, and Michal Starke 1999. "The typology of structural deficiency." In Henk van Riemsdijk (ed.), *Clitics in the languages of Europe*, 145–233. Berlin: Mouton de Gruyter.

Catsimali, Georgia 1990. "Case in Modern Greek: Implications for clause structure." PhD diss., University of Reading.

Chatzikyriakidis, Stergios 2010. "Clitics in four dialects of Modern Greek: A dynamic account." PhD diss., King's College London.

Chomsky, Noam 2000. "Minimalist inquiries: The framework." In Roger Martin, David Michaels, and Juan Uriagereka (eds.), *Step by step: Essays on Minimalist syntax in honor of Howard Lasnik*, 89–156. Cambridge, MA: MIT Press.

Chomsky, Noam 2001. "Derivation by phase." In Michael Kenstowicz (ed.), *Ken Hale: A life in language*, 1–52. Cambridge, MA: MIT Press.

Chomsky, Noam 2006. "Approaching UG from below." Unpublished ms., MIT.

Chomsky, Noam 2008. "On phases." In Robert A. Friedin, Carlos Otero, and María Luisa Zubizarreta (eds.), *Foundational issues in linguistic theory: Essays in honor of Jean-Roger Vergnaud*, 133–165. Cambridge, MA: MIT Press.

Condoravdi, Clea, and Paul Kiparsky. 2001. "Clitics and clause structure." *Journal of Greek Linguistics* 2: 1–39.

Daskalaki, Evangelia and Marios Mavrogiorgos. 2010. "Clitic doubling and resumption of indirect objects in Greek." Ms./Paper presented at OnLI 2010, University of Ulster, December 2010.

Déchaine, Rose-Marie, and Martina Wiltschko. 2002. "Decomposing pronouns." *Linguistic Inquiry* 33: 409–442.

Dimitriadis, Alexis 1999. "On clitics, prepositions and case licensing in Standard and Macedonian Greek." In Artemis Alexiadou, Geoffrey Horrocks, and Melita Stavrou (eds.), *Studies in Greek Syntax*, 95–113. Dordrecht: Kluwer.

Drettas, Georges 1997. *Aspects pontiques.* Paris: Association de recherches pluridisciplinaires.

Harley, Heidi, and Elizabeth Ritter. 2002. "Person and number in pronouns: A feature-geometric analysis." *Language* 78(3): 482–526.

Kayne, Richard S. 1975. *French syntax: The transformational cycle.* Cambridge MA: MIT Press.

Kayne, Richard S. 1984. *Connectedness and binary branching.* Dordrecht: Foris.

Kayne, Richard 2010. "The DP-internal origin of datives." Paper presented at the 4th European Dialect Syntax Meeting, Donostia/San Sebastian, June 22.

Larson, Richard 1988. "On the double object construction." *Linguistic Inquiry* 19: 335–391.

Mackridge, Peter 1987. "Greek-speaking Moslems of north-east Turkey: Prolegomena to a study of the Ophitic sub-dialect of Pontic." *Byzantine and Modern Greek Studies* 11(1): 115–137.

Manolessou, I., and S. Beis. 2006. "Syntactic isoglosses in Modern Greek dialects: The case of the indirect object." In A. Ralli, M. Janse, and B. Joseph (eds.), *Proceedings of the 2nd International Conference on Modern Greek Dialects and Linguistic Theory* (Mytilene, September 2004), 220–235. Patras: University of Patras.

McGinnis, Martha 1998. "Locality and inert case." In Pius Tamanji and Kiyomi Kusumoto (eds.), *Proceedings of NELS 28*, 267–281. Amherst: GLSA, University of Massachusetts.

McGinnis, Martha 1999. "A-scrambling exists!" In Michelle Minnick and Na-Rae Han (eds.), *University of Pennsylvania Working Papers in Linguistics: Proceedings of the PLC 23*, 283–297. Philadelphia: University of Pennsylvania.

Michelioudakis, Dimitris 2010a. "Active vs. Inactive Inherent Case features: Evidence from three Greek varieties and diachronic implications." Paper presented at the Ninth *International Conference on Greek Linguistics,* Chicago, October 2009.

Michelioudakis, Dimitris 2010b. "The split identity of genitive in Modern Greek: Evidence from 'datives' in APs/NPs." In A. Karasimos et al. (eds.), *Proceedings of the Second Patras International Conference of Graduate Students of Linguistics,* June 8–10, University of Patras.

Michelioudakis, Dimitris 2011a. "All datives originate low: Direct and indirect evidence." Paper presented at the 34th *GLOW* Colloquium, April 30, University of Vienna.

Michelioudakis, Dimitris 2011b. "Dative arguments and abstract Case in Greek." PhD diss., University of Cambridge.

Michelioudakis, Dimitris (forthcoming/2013). "The evolution of Inherent Case in Greek." In T. Biberauer and G. Walkden (eds.), *Morphosyntax over time: The interaction of morphology, syntax and the lexicon. Proceedings of the Twelfth DiGS* (University of Cambridge, July 2011). Oxford: Oxford University Press.

Michelioudakis, Dimitris, and Ioanna Sitaridou. 2012. "Multiple wh-fronting in different varieties of Pontic Greek." Talk at EdiSyn VI, Cambridge, Queens College, Cambridge, March 31.

Müller, G. 1995. *A-bar syntax: A study of movement types.* New York: Mouton de Gruyter.

Ormazabal, Javier 2000. "A conspiracy theory of case and agreement." In Roger Martin, David Michaels, and Juan Uriagereka (eds.), *Step by step: Essays on minimalist syntax in honor of Howard Lasnik,* 89–155. Cambridge, MA: MIT Press.

Pappas, Panayiotis A. 2001. "Weak object pronoun placement in Later Medieval and Early Modern Greek." PhD diss., Ohio State University.

Philippaki-Warburton, Irene 1982. "Provlimata schetika me ti sira ton oron stis ellinikes protasis (Problems regarding word order in Greek sentences)." *Glossologia* 1: 99–107.

Pylkkänen, Liina 2002. *Introducing arguments*. PhD diss., MIT.

Reinhart, Tanya 2002. "The theta system: An overview." *Theoretical Linguistics* 2002: 1–60.

Roberts, Ian 2010. *Agreement and head movement: Clitics, incorporations and defective goals*. Cambridge, MA: MIT Press.

Roussou, Anna 2000. "On the Left Periphery: Modal particles and complementisers." *Journal of Greek Linguistics* 1: 65–94.

Sevdali, Christina 2009. "On the various verbs 'seem' in Ancient Greek and the role of datives." *Proceedings of the Third Mediterranean Syntax Meeting*, Istanbul, October 2008.

Sigurðsson, Halldór 1989. *Verbal syntax and case in Icelandic in a comparative GB approach*. PhD diss., Department of Scandinavian Languages, University of Lund.

Sitaridou, Ioanna Forthcoming/b. "The last Greek infinitive: Continuity, contact and change in the Hellenic varieties of Pontus (Romeyka)." *Diachronica*.

Sitaridou, Ioanna Forthcoming/a. "Documentation and revitalisation of Romeyka." In Mari Jones and S. Ogilvie (eds.), *Keeping languages alive: Language endangerment: Documentation, pedagogy and revitalisation*. Cambridge: Cambridge University Press.

Sitaridou, Ioanna 2012. "The null objects in Romeyka and the Turkish dialects of Trebizond: A case of reciprocal contact-induced change or internal conditioning?" Talk at the Second Workshop on Romeyka and Asia Minor Greek, Queens College, Cambridge, April 1.

Sitaridou, Ioanna, and Marina Terkourafi. 2009. "On the loss of the masculine genitive plural in Cypriot Greek: Language contact or internal evolution?" In Monique Dufresne, Fernande Dupuis, and Etleva Vocaj (eds.), *Historical Linguistics 2007: Selected Papers from the Eighteenth International Conference on Historical Linguistics* (Montréal, Québec, August 6–11, 2007), 161–173. Amsterdam: John Benjamins.

Sitaridou, Ioanna, and Marina Terkourafi. In progress. "Mutual reinforcement of external and internal factors in case syncretism in Cypriot Greek." Unpublished ms., University of Illinois at Urbana-Champaign and University of Cambridge, Queens College.

Sitaridou, I. and M. Kaltsa. 2010. "Information structure in Pontic Greek". Submitted.

Svenonius, Peter. 2006. "Case alternations and the Icelandic passive and middle." Unpublished ms., University of Tromsø, available at ling.auf.net/lingbuzz/000124.

Svenonius, Peter. 2010. "Boom and bust in North Germanic datives." Paper presented at the Fourth Edisyn Meeting, San Sebastian, June 21–23.

Terkourafi, Marina, and Ioanna Sitaridou. In progress. "The masculine genitive plural in contemporary Cypriot Greek." Unpublished ms., University of Illinois at Urbana-Champaign and University of Cambridge, Queens College.

Vassiliou, Emma 2002. *The word order of Medieval Cypriot*. PhD diss., La Trobe University.

CHAPTER 9

Dative Displacement in Basque

MILAN REZAC AND BEATRIZ FERNÁNDEZ

1. INTRODUCTION

In this article, we discuss differences across Basque dialects in the accessibility of datives to absolutive-type agreement. In most varieties, including Standard Basque, datives control a dedicated series of dative suffixes. In some varieties, however, their agreement "displaces" to take over agreement otherwise reserved for the absolutive. To this phenomenon we refer as *dative displacement*. It is a rich domain to explore the properties and parameters of dialectal variation: the basic morphology of more than fifty dative displacement varieties has been documented, and four have been examined in more detail for this work. Recent research on comparable agreement displacements reveals that sometimes they affect not only morphology, but also syntax. This appears to be true of Basque dative displacement as well, although much remains to be understood. We first describe the phenomenon and its parametrization across Basque dialects in section 2, then outline syntactic and morphological approaches to it and their different predictions in section 3, to conclude with hints of its syntactic character in section 4.

Dative displacement lies at the crossroads of two ways to treat an argument added to plain transitive and unaccusative structures. The argument structure of plain transitives consists of the *external argument EA* and the *internal argument O*, She_{EA} *boils* $water_O$, and that of plain unaccusatives of the internal argument S, $Water_S$ *boils*. To these may be added an argument that we will refer to as the *indirect object IO*, across a variety of structures and interpretations such as *send, bake, refuse, grudge* $someone_{IO}$ *a cake*. We will need to differentiate O and S according to whether they stand in a plain transitive or unaccusative, where we notate them O1, S1 as in *send a* $cake_{O1}$, or combine with an IO, in which case we notate them O2, S2 as in *send* $someone_{IO}$ *a* $cake_{O2}$.

The addition of an IO to a plain structure leads to two results cross-linguistically: *primary-IO* and *dative-IO* systems (Malchukov et al. 2010). In *primary-IO* systems, the IO behaves like the O1/S1 for case and agreement, while the remaining O2/S2 tends to behave differently.[1] In English (1), the IO is an accusative object in the active, but an agreeing nominative subject in the passive, like O1, while the remaining O2 is unaffected by passivization. In Inuit (2), the IO is an agreeing absolutive, like O1, and the remaining O2 is a nonagreeing instrumental. In Nahuatl (3), the IO controls the same agreement as O1, while the remaining O2 controls a special agreement restricted to 3SG/3PL.[2] In Mohawk, O2/S2 incorporates (Baker 1996), and in Southern Tiwa it both incorporates and contributes special 3SG/3PL agreement distinctions of the Nahuatl type (Allen et al. 1990). The IO of a primary IO system behaves like O1/S1 not only for case and agreement but also for A-movement, as seen in English passives (1), although it may differ from O1/S1 on other properties such as incorporability (Baker 1996: 7.3, Peterson 2007: 3.4, Ngonyani and Githinji 2006).[3]

(1) a. She baked/sent **us$_{IO}$** two cakes.
    b. **We$_{IO}$** were baked/sent two cakes (them) by Kate
    c. *Two cakes were baked/sent **us$_{IO}$** by Kate.
    (English)

(2)   Juuna-p   **Kaali$_{IO}$**   atuakka-nik   nassip-p-a-a.
    Juuna-ERG$_i$ Kaali[.ABS]$_k$ books-PL.INS send-INDIC-[+tr]-3s$_i$.3s$_k$
    "Juuna sent the books to Kaali."
    (Inuit, Bittner & Hale 1996: 18)

(3) Ni-**mitz$_{IO}$**-im-maca   in   huē-hue"xōlo-."
    1s.SU-2s.O-3P.O-give IN   RED-turkey-PL
    "I give you the turkeys."
    (Nahuatl, Baker 1996: 240 n. 12)

In *dative-IO* systems, O2/S2 has the same behavior as O1/S1, and it is the added IO that acts otherwise. In French (4), the IO is a nonagreeing

---

1 There are also *symmetric IO systems* where the IO and O2/S2 seem indistinguishable to Case/agreement system, sometimes participating in it simultaneously; see Baker (1988), Bresnan and Moshi (1990), MacKay and Trechsel (2008). A variant of primary-IO unaccusatives treats the IO as EA and the S2 as S1; see Baker (1996: 9.3.2), Rezac (2011: 5.6). For systems with multiple IOs, see McGinnis (2001).
2 This type of number-only agreement for O2/S2 will be important to us; for its occurrence in primary-IO systems, see further Baker (1996: 5.2.1., 2008: 3.3.3), Peterson (2007: 3.4.3).
3 We keep the glosses of the sources, save for person 1/2/3 number s[ingular]/P[lural] as in 1P; the abbreviations are FUT(ure), IMPERS(onal), IND(icative), INS(trumental), LOC(ative), OBJ(ect), RED(uplication), SU(bject).

dative in the active and passive, whereas O2 changes from an accusative in the active to an agreeing nominative subject in the passive, like O1. Among other systems that follow this pattern are Standard Spanish, Greek, as well as Inuit (5) beside the primary IO option in (2).

(4) a. Je   les   **lui**$_{IO}$ ai   cuits/envoyés.
        I.NOM them.ACC him.DAT have.1s cooked/sent.PL
        "I have baked them for him."

    b. Ils   **lui**$_{IO}$ ont   été   cuits/envoyés.
        they.NOM him.DAT are.3P been   cooked/sent.PL
        "They have been baked for him."
        (French)

(5) Juuna-p   atuakka-t   **Kaali-mut**$_{IO}$ nassi-up-p-a-i.
    Juuna-ERG$_i$ book-PL[.ABS]$_j$ Kaali-DAT   send-APPL-IND-[+tr]-3s$_i$,3P$_j$
    "Juuna sent the books to Kaali."
    (Inuit, Bittner & Hale 1996: 18)

Cross-linguistically, the different treatment of the IO in primary and dative systems is independent of the theta-role of the IO, such as goal or possessor, or the presence of applicative morphology, which signals the presence of (certain) IOs in some systems, although these properties may correlate with how an IO is treated within a given system, as in Inuit (2) with and (5) without applicative morphology (Baker 1988, 1996, Peterson 2007). The differences between primary and dative IO systems must lie either in other selectional properties or in higher functional architecture. We will return to these options in the analysis of Basque dative displacement.

2. DATIVE DISPLACEMENT

Most Basque varieties are dative-IO systems, including Standard Basque. Basque is an ergative-absolutive language. S and O participate in one case-agreement pattern, the *absolutive*, and EA in another, the *ergative*. The pattern of case and agreement is illustrated in (6). The absolutive controls the *prefix*, fusionally signaling the person and number of first- and second-person controllers, and the *PL* marker, which signals the plurality of 1/2/3.PL controllers. The ergative controls the *ergative suffix*, fusionally signaling person and number. The agreement controllers are also often detectable through root allomorphy: in (6), the root *u* is chosen when there is an ergative agreement controller, and hence we gloss it √EA for ergative-absolutive, while the root *iz* indicates that there is only an absolutive agreement controller, √A for absolutive.[4]

(6) a. zu-k   *gu*   ekarri   *ga-it*-u-zu
     you-ERG   us.ABS   brought   1P-PL-√EA-2sE
     "You invited us."

    b. *ni*   etorri   *na-iz*
       me.ABS   come   1s-√A
       "I came."
     (Standard Basque)

The addition of the IO in (7) adds a dative argument to the clause and a dative agreement suffix before the ergative suffix. It may also influence the form of the root, indicated as √EDA for an ergative-dative-absolutive root and √DA for a dative-absolutive one. The presence of an agreeing dative does not affect other arguments or their case and agreement, save in restricting the absolutive O2 and sometimes S2 to third person (the *Person Case Constraint*, Laka 1993, Albizu 1997, Rezac 2008c).

(7) a. zu-k   **gu-ri**   *sagarr-ak*   ekarri   d- **i**-   *zki*-**gu**- zu
     you-ERG   us-DAT   apple-PL.ABS   brought   D-√**EDA**-PL-**1sD**-2sE
     "You brought the apples to us."

4 For a detailed and perspicuous presentations of Basque agreement, see Laka (1993) and Albizu (2002). On nouns, we gloss plural as PL and case as ERG, ABS, DAT. Agreement is borne by an auxiliary root for most verbs. We use PL for the O/S pluralizer, PL2 for the O2/S2 pluralizer of dative displacement dialects; person 1/2/3 s[ingular]/P[lural], e.g. 1P, and furthermore case E[ergative]/[D]ative, e.g. 1PE, if the controller always has a unique case (suffixes but not the prefix); √EDA, √DA, √A, √EA for roots according to whether their form indicates the presence of E(rgative), D(ative), A(bsolutive) agreement controllers; and D for the default prefix varying by tense and mood. The agreement morphemes of Standard Basque and largely shared across the dialects are given below for reference. 2SG *zu* is historically 2PL and thus controls the PL as well as 2s, while 2PL is formed from it by the addition of a second pluralizer *(t)e*. Standard Basque agreement markers for the auxiliary (without dative and ergative displacement)

Case	ABS	DAT	ERG
PhiPosition	Prefix + PL	DAT suffix	ERG suffix
1SG	n-	-da-, -t	-da-/-t
1PL	g- + -it-	-gu-	-gu-
2SG	z- + -it-	-zu-	-zu-
2PL	z- + -it- (+ -te-)	-zue-	-zue-
3SG	-	-o-	-
3PL	- + -it-/-zki-	-e-	-te-

b. *gu*   **zu-ri**   *etorri*   *ga-* tzai- *zki-***zu**

    we.ABS   you-DAT   come   1P-√**DA**-PL-**2sD**

    "We came to you."

    (Standard Basque)

Some Basque dialects deviate from the foregoing system by *dative displacement DD* (Fernández 2001, 2002, 2004, Fernández and Ezeizabarrena 2003, Rezac 2006, 2008ab). The IO remains dative in case morphology, often continues to control dative suffixes, and often as well to trigger a form of the root indicating the presence of an agreeing dative. However, it usurps control of the prefix and PL morphology, otherwise reserved to O/S. This only occurs with first- and second-person IOs, and depends on other parameters that vary across dialects, such as the phi-features of the IO, tense, and transitivity.[5] Thus within one and the same dialect, the prefix and PL morphology is controlled by O1/S1, and by O2/S2 if dative displacement does not occur, but by IO if it does. When the IO takes over PL morphology, O2/S2 cannot control it, as it does in standard Basque, and often a second plural morpheme appears that is not found otherwise, PL2 (as in Standard Basque, O2/S2 can only be 3SG/PL in the presence of an agreeing IO).

We exemplify dative displacement from three varieties that illustrate these properties and the range of parametric variation. In (8) is shown dative displacement in Sara Basque (Lapurdian-Navarrese, Lapurdi).[6] Plain transitives are the same as in Standard Basque (6). All first and second datives undergo dative displacement, in the present and past, but only in transitives. Under dative displacement, the dative IO gains control of prefix and PL. Sometimes it continues to control the dative suffix as well, as in (8f), in a way that varies unpredictably across otherwise identical dialects.[7] The plurality of O2 is reflected by PL2. The dialect does not distinguish roots according to whether an agreeing dative is present or not.

(8)   a. **ni-ri**$_i$ *sagarr-a*$_k$ eman   **na**$_i$-u

      me-DAT   apple-ABS   given   1s-√E(D)A

      "She gave the apple to me." (Same form *nau* as for "She saw me," cf. (6))

---

5 The datives that can participate in dative displacement are thus those that could control the prefix, since it is reserved to first- and second-person controllers, but by undergoing dative displacement they control PL as well, which canonically has (1/2/)3PL.ABS controllers. Cf. the appendix.

6 We follow Zuazo's (2003) classification of Basque dialects.

7 For instance, in the Sara variety shown doubling only in ERG-2.IO.DAT-3PL.O2, but in the neighboring Ahetze Sara it also occurs in ERG-1.IO.DAT-3PL.O2 (*gaituzkigu* for *gaituzki* in (8)d; Yrizar 1997: 121).

b. **ni-ri**$_i$ *sagarr-ak*$_k$ eman   **na**$_i$**-u-***zki*$_k$
   me-DAT   apple-PL.ABS   given   1s-√E(D)A-PL2
   "She gave the apples to me."

c. **gu-ri**$_i$ *sagarr-a*$_k$ eman   **ga**$_i$**-it**$_i$**-u**
   us-DAT   apple-ABS   given   1p-PL-√E(D)A
   "She gave the apple to us." (Same form *gaitu* as for "She saw us," cf. (6))

d. **gu-ri**$_i$ *sagarr-ak*$_k$ eman   **ga**$_i$**-it**$_i$**-u-***zki*$_k$
   us-DAT   apple-PL.ABS   given   1p-PL-√E(D)A-PL2
   "She gave the apples to us."

e. **zu-ri**$_i$ *sagarr-a*$_k$ eman   **za**$_i$**-it**$_i$**-u**
   you-DAT   apple-ABS   given   2s-PL-√E(D)A
   "She gave the apple to you." (Same for *zaitu* as for "She saw you")

f. **zu-ri**$_i$ *sagarr-ak*$_k$ eman   **za**$_i$**-u-***zki*$_k$**-tzu**
   you-DAT   apple-PL.ABS   given   2s-√E(D)A-PL2–2sD
   "She gave the apples to you."
   (Dative displacement, Sara Basque, Fernández 2001)

Oñati Basque (Western Basque, Gipuzkoa) in (10) exhibits the same principles with different parameters. Plain transitives are again as in Standard Basque, save that first and second persons never control PL, so that for (6a) *gaitu* occurs *gau*. Dative displacement occurs only for first-person datives, only in the past, and only in transitives. The dative gains control of the prefix, but retains control of the dative suffix, and the root continues to indicate the presence of an agreeing dative. In this dialect S2/O2 never agrees for PL when an agreeing dative is present, whether the dative undergoes dative displacement as first person or not in other persons.

(9)   a. **ne-ri**$_i$ sagarr-a(k)$_k$ emun   **n**$_i$**-os-ta**$_i$**-n**
     me-DAT   apple-(PL.)ABS   given   1s-√EDA-1sD-PAST
     "She gave the apple(s) to me."

   b. **gu-ri**$_i$ sagarr-a(k)$_k$ emun   **g**$_i$**-os-ku**$_i$**-n**
     us-DAT   apple-(PL.)ABS   given   1p-√EDA-1pD-PAST
     "She gave the apple(s) to me."
     (Dative displacement, Oñati Basque, Yrizar 1992, Badihardugun 2005)

Oiartzun Basque (Central Basque, transitional variety, Gipuzkoa) completes the illustration of the range of variation. The system is shown in Table 9.1. For 1SG datives, dative displacement is obligatory. For the

Table 9.1. DATIVE DISPLACEMENT IN OIARTZUN PRESENT TENSE (CF. EX. (10)).

| | Transitive *eman* "give" | | | | Unaccusative *gustatzen* "liking" | | | |
| | SG *sagarra* "apple" | | PL *sagarrak* "apples" | | SG *sagarra* "apple" | | PL *sagarrak* "apples" | |
	Non-DD	DD	Non-DD	**DD**	Non-DD	DD	Non-DD	DD
1SG *nei*	–	nazu	–	**nazkizu**	–	nau	–	**nazki**
1PL *guri*	–	gattuzu	dizkizugu	(gattuzu)	digu	(gattu[8])	dizkigu	–
2SG *zuri*	–	zattut	dizkizut	(zattut)	dizu	zattu	dizkizu	–
2PL *zuei*	–	zattuztet	dizkizuet	(zattuz-tet)	dizute	zattuzte	dizkizute	–

Legend: bold = form has PL2; brackets = speakers other than our consultant

remaining first- and second-person datives, it is obligatory in transitives with a singular O2, but much more limited in transitives with a plural O2 or in unaccusatives with singular S2, and absent in unaccusatives with a plural S2. This pattern is characteristic of the area and reflects the diachronic spread of the phenomenon (Rezac 2008b).

In these three varieties, we have the following points of variation: the phi-features of the IO, the plurality of O2/S2, the transitivity of the construction, and tense.[9] The nature of the dative does not play a role in any of the five varieties in which we have examined it. The foregoing examples have illustrated dative displacement for the goal of the basic ditransitive *eman* "give," but other datives behave identically, as shown for Oiartzun in (10). In Standard Basque they would also behave uniformly, controlling only the dative suffix (illustrated by the forms in brackets, the suffix in bold).

8 But *gattuzu* only for the motion verb *etorri* "come" + dative; see section 4.

9 At present, correlations between these parameters seem due to the diachronic origin and spread of DD (see Rezac 2008b). Thus, Oñati DD differs from the other two in the absence of number agreement with both O2 (necessarily third-person) and datives (necessarily first- or second-person) (Richard S. Kayne, p.c.). It originates in a non-DD system where there already was no PL agreement (i) with 1/2 O1 and (ii) with 3 O2/S2. (i) and (ii) do not seem to correlate in Basque varieties and to have different causes (see the references in Rezac 2011: 294 note 16, 190 note 9 for parallels; the former is perhaps due to the associative nature of 1/2PL, the latter to dative intervention). Thanks to (ii), Oñati had no O2 PL agreement to appear under DD as PL2. In contrast, other DD systems recruit O2 PL as PL2: thus non-DD *(eman)* d-i-zki-gu D-√EDA-**PL**-1PD "she has (given) **them** to us" + DD gives Sara DD ga-it-u-zki 1P-PL-√E(D)A-**PL2**.

Nevertheless, we will see hints in section 4 that the nature of the dative may condition dative displacement.

(10) a. Zu-k   ne-i   sagarr-a   man   na-zu. [d-i-**da**-zu]
     you-ERG   me-DAT   apple-ABS   given   1s-2sE
     "You gave me an apple." (*goal of ditransitive*)

    b. Zu-k   ne-i   sagarr-a   man   arazi   na-zu. [d-i-**da**-zu]
     you-ERG   me-DAT   apple-ABS   given   cause   1s-2sE
     "You made me give an apple." (*causee of transitive*)

    c. Zu-k   ne-i   besu-a   hautsi   na-zu.   [d-i-**da**-zu]
     you-ERG   me-DAT   arm-ABS   broken   1s-2sE
     "You broke my arm." (*possessor in transitive*)

    d. Ne-i   txakurr-a   hil   na-u. [zai-**t**]
     me-DAT   dog-ABS   died   1s-√
     "My dog died/The dog died on me." (*dative of interest*)

    e. Ne-i   sagarr-ak   gustatzen   na-zki. [zai-zki-**t**]
     me-DAT   apple-PL.ABS   liking   1s-PL2
     "I like apples." (*psych-verb experiencer*)

    f. Ne-i   lagun-ak   torri   na-zki.   [zai-zki-**t**]
     me-DAT   friend-PL.ABS   come   1s-PL2
     "Friends came to me." (*goal of motion*)
     (Oiartzun Basque)

Dative displacement modifies the agreement of dative IOs in a specific way that is more abstract than simple allomorphy, such as that of the English past participle suffix in *heav-ed, lef-t, though-t, clov-en, spat, cast*. It does not introduce its own exponents, such as a prefix *p-* for 1PL.DAT, or arbitrarily recruit existing exponents, such as the prefix *n-* controlled by 1SG.ABS for agreement with 1PL.DAT. Rather, it maps the phi-features of the dative to existing positions of exponence, the prefix and PL, where they are realized by exponents that realize the same phi-features when they come from the absolutive, for instance 1SG *n-*. The result is a syncretism between the exponents controlled by absolutive O1/S1 and by dative IO under dative displacement, illustrated in Table 9.2. However, Table 9.2 also shows that the syncretism does not extend to entire words, because the dative may retain control of its own dative suffix, trigger a dative-indicating root, and co-occur with PL2 controlled by O2/S2. If any of this occurs, the agreement complex used by dative displacement is unique to it.[10]

10 Dative displacement may also affect allomorphy of elements not discussed here (Rezac 2006, 2008b).

Table 9.2. DATIVE DISPLACEMENT (DD) MORPHOLOGY
IN SARA BASQUE.[11]

O1/IO	3SG.EA-O1.ABS	3SG.EA-IO.DAT-3SG.O2		3SG.EA-IO.DAT-3PL.O2	
		DD	non-DD	DD	non-DD
3SG	d-u$_{\sqrt{EA}}$	–	d-i$_{\sqrt{EDA}}$-*o*	–	d-i$_{\sqrt{EDA}}$-*o*-**zka**
1SG	na-u$_{\sqrt{EA}}$	na-u$_{\sqrt{EA}}$	da-u$_{\sqrt{E(D)A}}$-*t*	na-a-$_{\sqrt{E(D)A}}$-*zki*	da-u$_{\sqrt{E(D)A}}$-**zki**-*t*
1PL	ga-it-u$_{\sqrt{EA}}$	ga-it-u$_{\sqrt{EA}}$	da-u$_{\sqrt{E(D)A}}$-*ku*	ga-it-$_{\sqrt{E(D)A}}$-*zki*	da-u$_{\sqrt{E(D)A}}$-**zki**-*gu*
2SG	za-it-u$_{\sqrt{EA}}$	za-it-u$_{\sqrt{EA}}$	da-u$_{\sqrt{E(D)A}}$-*tzu*	za-i-*zki-tzu*	da-u$_{\sqrt{E(D)A}}$-**zki**-*tzu*

Legend: **person-number prefix—PL, PL2,** *dative suffix.*

Dative displacement is descriptively at the crossroads of primary and dative IO systems. As in dative-IO systems such as Standard Basque, the IO is dative and may control dative agreement and root morphology. As in primary-IO systems such as Nahuatl, the dative control the prefix and PL morphology otherwise dedicated to O1/S1, and O2/S2 controls a special plural morpheme not found otherwise.

Phenomena similar to dative displacement exist outside Basque, but they seem rare, if we set aside syncretisms due to paucity of morphological distinctions. A clear parallel is found in Itelmen (11), analyzed in Bobaljik and Wurmbrand (2002) and related to Basque in Rezac (2008a, b). Under certain conditions, which as in Basque include the phi-features of the IO and transitivity and show variation, the IO beats O2/S2 for regular O1/S1 agreement. Section 4 adds Faroese, and perhaps Middle English and *laísta* Spanish. Other examples may be Hyow in Haspelmath (2005), Amharic in Malchukov et al. (2010), and participle agreement in Romance (Rezac 2011: 191 n. 10).

(11) a. isx-enk   n-zəl-ał-**in**$_i$ *kza*$_i$ **kəma-nk**?
        father-LOC   IMPRS-give-FUT-2s.O   you   me-DAT
        "Will Father give *you* to me?"

     b. isx-enk   n-zəl-ał-**um**$_k$ *kza*   **kəma-nk**$_k$?
        father-LOC   IMPRS-give-FUT-1s.O   you   me-DAT
        "Will Father give you *to me*?"
        (Itelmen, Bobaljik & Wurmbrand 2002: ex. 15, 14b)

---

11 The speaker of Sara Basque has access to both its dative displacement system and a minimally different one without it, permitting a contrast of two dialects with otherwise identical morphology (Fernández 2001).

3. MORPHOLOGY AND SYNTAX

Two broad classes of approaches to dative displacement may be distinguished: syntactic and morphological. They differ in the type of information to which it may refer, including its parameters; in the properties of the operations or structures that distinguish it from a regular dative IO system: and in its potential to interact with syntax and interpretation (Rezac 2011). Our understanding of the phenomenon does not yet permit a sure choice among these alternatives, still less a concrete theory. However, a syntactic approach seems best fitted both to the parametric variation, to which it is applied in this section, and to the hints of syntactic correlates, discussed in the next. We outline the range of syntactic theories and compare them with morphological ones.

A syntactic approach to dative displacement expects it to exhibit the properties of syntactic computation: manipulate syntactic rather than purely morphophonological information, obey constraints on syntactic dependencies such as locality and cyclicity, and have the potential to affect syntax and interpretation as well as realization. Two types of syntactic approaches to agreement displacements have been explored for Basque (specifically for ergative displacement, discussed in the appendix). One is through movement of syntactic constituents (i) (cf. Laka 1993, but see below). The other is through feature transmission (ii) (Fernández and Albizu 2000, Fernández 2001, 2004, Rezac 2003, 2006, 2008a, 2008c, Béjar & Rezac 2009). Both share the common core (iii).[12]

(i)   Positions of exponence, including the prefix and suffix, reflect constituents that double argument positions, for instance cliticized (clitic-doubling) D°s. Agreement displacement occurs when movement displaces such a constituent, say $D_{DAT}°$, to a position otherwise filled by another, say the v-adjoined position otherwise filled by $D_{ABS}°$ (perhaps leaving a copy that may also be realized).

(ii) Positions of exponence reflect phi-features on clausal functional heads valued by Agree from arguments. Agreement displacement occurs when a head, say v°, Agrees with a different argument than it typically does.

(iii) The conditions under which displacement occurs are determined by syntactic properties of the configurations or derivations involved, such as absence of the usual agreement controller, its underspecification, or movement that brings the de facto controller closer to the target of agreement than the usual controller.

---

12 The following proposals have been originally developed for *ergative displacement*; see the appendix.

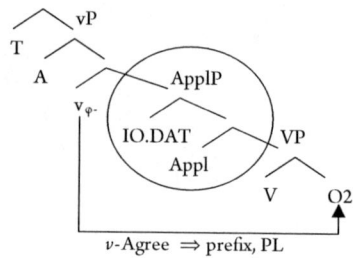

Figure 9.1
No dative displacement

To dative displacement, the second type of approach has been applied (Fernández 2001, 2004, Rezac 2006: chap. 3, 2008a, 2008b). Figures 9.1 and 9.2 sketch its essentials, keeping to transitives for simplicity. The point of departure is a theory of Basque-type ergativity where the absolutive locus v_{ABS} is below the ergative locus $T_{ERG,}$ so that the closest goal of v_{ABS} is the O/S and that of T_{ERG} the EA (cf. Ortiz de Urbina 1989, Laka 2000). The dative IO is base-generated in Spec,ApplP between v and O for transitives, resulting in the c-command EA > IO > O, which remains stable through A-movement (Elordieta 2001). Person and number phi-probes on v_{ABS} are the locus of prefix and PL agreement; the nature of dative and ergative suffixes as agreement or clitics may be left open for our purposes. In Figures 9.1 and 9.2, the IO is structurally higher than the O2 and so should be the closer goal for v, giving it control of v's phi-probes and thus the prefix and PL. The result is dative displacement, Figure 9.2, where the IO controls them if it is present, and the O1 does otherwise. When dative displacement does not occur, some factor renders the IO's phi-features inaccessible to v, indicated by the circle in Figure 9.1. The O2 is then the closest goal, behaving like O1 even in the presence of the IO. In dative displacement, v fails to Agree with the O2, which might be expected to lead to a Case licensing problem. Just in this situation, the special PL2 agreement for the O2 appears. We treat it as a number-only phi-probe on Appl°, the closest head above the O2, and so correctly limited to Agree with it (Rezac 2006: 3.7, 2008b: 722).

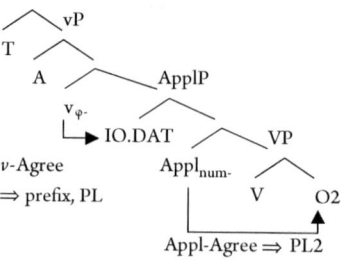

Figure 9.2
Dative displacement

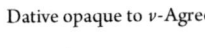

Dative opaque to *v*-Agree   Dative transparent to *v*-Agree

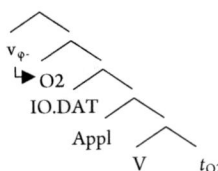   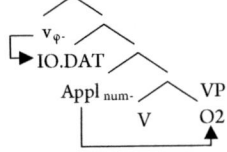

Figure 9.3
O2 parametrically bypasses dative IO

The nature of the parameter that differentiates between structures or derivations where dative displacement does or does not occur, between Figures 9.2 and 9.1, is unknown. Syntactic tests of the two structures currently reveal very little (section 4). The literature presents several options for why a dative IO might fail to control a phi-probe and let the O2 do so. One, in Figure 9.3, is that the O2 moves past the IO prior to Agree with v. If this occurs, the phi-Agree of v is with the O2, otherwise with the IO. McGinnis (1998) and Anagnostopoulou (2003) develop similar proposals to differentiate those primary IO systems in which the IO ends up highest from those where the O2 does.

Another option, illustrated in Figure 9.4, is for datives to have a richer structure than bare DPs, an added KP or PP, which parametrically hides the phi-features of DP that it contains, for instance when it is a phase. If the dative is transparent to Agree, v Agrees with it as the closest goal, otherwise past it with the O2 (Rezac 2006: chapter 3, 2008a, cf. Taraldsen 1995, Anagnostopoulou 2003 on the opacity of datives to some Agree). The parametric opacity of the dative KP/PP shell must reside in its structure or derivation. If the KP/PP is present around the DP upon base-generation, its opacity derives from the content of its functional architecture (Rezac 2008a, 2011). If the KP/PP is introduced around the DP by movement of the DP through the functional architecture of the clause, as Kayne (2004) proposes for French dative causees, its opacity to phi-Agree with v may be due to its introduction before rather than after v engages in phi-Agree.[13]

In either type of system, there is a difference between the syntactic structures or derivations with and without dative displacement, and it could be detectable through other syntactico-semantic phenomena. For instance, the different heights of the O2 in Figure 9.3 could be revealed through binding/obviation or accessibility to further A-movement, and the different functional architectures of the

---

13 Basque datives are less like PPs and more but not quite like ergatives and absolutives for such matters as anaphora licensing and adnominal marking (Albizu 2001, Fernández & Sarasola forthcoming). Cross-linguistically, these properties do not correlate with accessibility to agreement (Rezac 2008a).

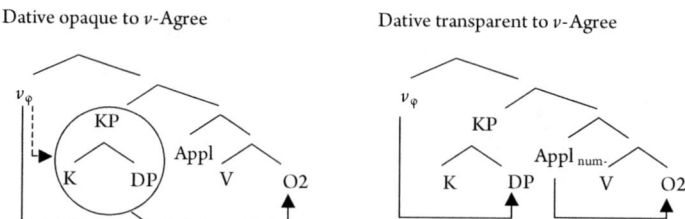

Figure 9.4
Dative IO is parametrically transparent to phi-Agree.

dative in Figure 9.4 through bare floating quantifiers that require bare DPs antecedents. At the moment, these tools are either unavailable or inconclusive, as will be seen in section 4. The simplest difference is whether the phi-features of v are valued by IO or O2; but it is also the most difficult to detect, for few or no clearly syntactico-semantic phenomena depend on the values of uninterpretable phi-features on clausal functional heads (Rezac 2010).

Simpler to examine are the predictions that syntactic approaches make about the parameters that modulate dative displacement. The differences between datives that do and do not undergo dative displacement reside in the region circled in Figure 9.1, which contains the dative, its selector Appl, and the material between them and v as the locus of phi-Agree for prefix and PL morphology. The information in this region includes the phi-features of the dative, the properties of Appl, and the properties of v. Outside information should not impinge on dative displacement. Specifically, the properties of C, T, or Spec,vP should not affect what occurs between v and Spec,ApplP, because they do not reach this region by selection or other mechanisms.[14]

These predictions are partly but not wholly borne out in the survey of the parameters that enter into dative displacement in Rezac (2006, 2008a, b). The database is the fifty varieties of Basque that have dative displacement in Pedro de Yrizar's exhaustive survey of agreement morphology of the Basque verb (e.g., Yrizar 1992, 1997), confirmed by our investigation of the phenomenon in Lekeitio (Western Basque, Bizkaia), Oiartzun, Hondarribia (both Central Basque, transitional variety, Gipuzkoa), and Ziburua (Coastal Basque, Lapurdi):

(12) a. Factors that systematically influence dative displacement (see section 2):
- The phi-features of the dative IO (Sara vs. Oñati, Oiartzun).
- The phi-features of O2/S2 (Oiartzun)

14 Thus in systems with clausal functional architecture comparable to Basque, we do not find the force or tense of a clause affecting object licensing or internal argument selection.

- Transitivity: unaccusatives only if transitives, and rarely (Oiartzun, Oñati).
- Tense: past tense only (Oñati), present only (Ainhoa), both (Sara).

b. Factors that have no systematic effect on dative displacement:
- The phi-features of the ergative.
- The phi-features of "allocutive" agreement in C (q.v. Oyharçabal 1993).
- The class of the dative such as goal vs. benefactive (see above).

By systematic factors, we mean properties that govern the availability of dative displacement, or of aspects of it such as doubling, independently of some other variable. For instance, in Oñati, transitivity determines the availability of dative displacement independently of the phi-features of the dative, and the phi-features of the dative do so independently of those of the ergative. Distinct from systematic factors are arbitrary gaps which correspond to no syntactico-semantic natural class (Baerman et al. 2010) and are invisible to syntax (Embick & Marantz 2008, Rezac 2011). They are common in morphological systems and arise in the realization of syntactic structures; an English example is the lack of a past participle for *stride* but not *ride*, *glide*, *hide*. Such seems to be the absence of dative displacement for 1PL. IO.DAT-3SG.O2.ABS in Oiartzun, or the limitation of prefix-suffix doubling to ERG-2.IO.DAT-3PL.O2 in Sara. Arbitrary gaps are common in agreement paradigms across Basque varieties, and may draw upon any information in the agreement complex (Fernández 2001, Rezac 2006, forthcoming, Arregi & Nevins 2006).

The syntactic approaches sketched above properly distinguish between the factors that do and do not parametrize dative displacement, save for tense and dative class. Tense restrictions have plausible diachronic explanations and may be construed as arbitrary gaps (Rezac 2008b). However, tense also conditions another Basque agreement displacement, discussed in the appendix, in which the ergative controls the prefix if there is no absolutive controller. The role of tense in it has been construed through a T-v relationship, and this may be adapted to the foregoing analyses (see further Laka 1993, Fernández & Albizu 2000, Rezac 2003, 2006: 2.3.5). Dative class, such as goal versus benefactive, is expected to have the potential to influence dative displacement to the extent that it reflects structural differences in the infra-v region, for instance different dative heights. Despite the symmetry observed above among all datives for participation in dative displacement, section 4 hints that dative class may matter to it after all.

Syntactic approaches to dative displacement define a hypothesis space of its potential parameters and correlates. With them in hand, we may more briefly contrast morphological approaches (developed for ergative displacement by Albizu 2002, Arregi & Nevins 2008).[15] A morphological approach attributes dative displacement to an extrasyntactic realizational morphology component, such as that of Bonet (1991, 1995), Noyer (1992), Halle & Marantz (1993). Its operations cannot affect the syntactic mapping from lexicon to interpretation, and may differ in the information accessed and the mechanisms used. For instance, datives in Basque and Romance fall into different classes according to their syntactic and interpretive properties, including ditransitive goals, causees, and possessors. However, morphology neutralizes them for the form of case and clitics or agreement affixes, thus accessing an impoverishment of syntactic information. It manipulates this information in a way that differs from syntax, by selecting and placing allomorphs according to the morphophonological context within but not outside the extended word. The resulting allomorph choice and placement have no consequences for syntax and interpretation, even when syncretic with the realization of other syntactic structures such as locatives (Rezac 2011: 2.2, 4.1).

We have seen that dative displacement is not the contextual selection of allomorphs, but the mapping of the phi-features of dative agreement to the prefix and PL positions of exponence, otherwise controlled by O/S. The theories of morphology cited above provide the mechanisms necessary for such morphosyntactic feature transfer, for instance feature (de/re)linking in Bonet (1991, 1995). Such an operation would take the phi-features of dative agreement linked by syntax to a terminal, say Appl° or v°-adjoined $D_{DAT}°$, and move or copy them to the terminal that otherwise hosts the phi-features of O/S agreement, say v°. It is expected to obey the impoverishment of syntactic information reflected in morphology elsewhere, including that of differences between dative classes in Basque. It is likewise expected to obey the constraints on morphological mechanisms, including restriction to phrase-structurally local domains like the extended word. Finally, it is expected to have no consequences for syntax or interpretation. The properties of dative displacement in Basque seen so far match these predictions, but we shall see potential counterexamples in the next section.

Like syntactic approaches, morphological approaches make predictions about the factors that can parametrize dative displacement. In a simple view, any morphological information in the agreement complex could matter. Different syntactic classes of datives should therefore be indistinguishable, while the phi-features of all agreeing arguments as well as tense should be equipollent conditioning factors. However, more articulated models of the interaction of different feature types with hierarchical and linear structure

---

15 In this work, we have not been able to take into account Arregi and Nevins (forthcoming), to which the reader is referred for a thoroughly worked-out morphological analysis of dative and ergative displacement.

in the syntax-to-realization mapping may nuance this prediction (Bonet & Harbour forthcoming: 3.5).

The categorical syntax-morphology dichotomy set out so far is only slightly weakened if the mapping of syntactic structures to realization makes use, wholly or in part, of the same computation as the mapping from lexicon to interpretation (Halle & Marantz 1993, Embick & Noyer 2007, Ackema & Neeleman 2007). Morphology so construed uses the same operations and principles as core syntax, such as movement, but their consequences are invisible to the lexicon-to-interpretation mapping because they occur outside it, and their outcome depends on the distinctive character of the information present in the syntax-to-realization mapping, such as morphophonological features. Laka's (1993) seminal analysis of ergative displacement develops precisely this proposal. Agreement displacement is Move-α, but it occurs in the mapping from S-structure to PF. In consequence, it cannot affect the mapping from D-structure to S-structure to LF and makes use of phonological features that are invisible to the latter (Laka 1993: 57–59).

4. THE SYNTACTIC EFFECTS OF DATIVE DISPLACEMENT

Cross-linguistically, there are agreement displacements similar to Basque dative and ergative displacement that affect syntax and so are syntactic (Rhodes 1994, Rezac 2011, Patel 2010). For dative displacement, Jónsson (2009) finds a syntactic analogue in Faroese. Faroese and Icelandic both have "quirky" dative subjects: external arguments with theta-related dative case but otherwise like nominative DPs for A-movement and subjecthood— save in agreement. In Icelandic, dative subjects cannot control verb agreement or agree in nominative case with dependents such as floating quantifiers. In contemporary Faroese, third-person dative subjects can, variably, control verb agreement and antecede nominative floating quantifiers, as shown in (13) (Jónsson 2009: 155–156, 159). This difference between the two systems may correlate another: unaccusatives with dative subjects typically assign nominative to their object in Icelandic, but in Faroese accusative, as if the nominative were used up. This has led Sigurðsson (2003: 250, 2004: 149) to suggest that in Faroese nominative is assigned to dative subjects in addition to their theta-related dative. The result is their partly nominative syntax.[16]

16 Agreement of datives with the verb, including nonadjacent ones, occurs in Middle English (Lightfoot 1977, Allen 1986). For an effect in Korean case stacking similar to Faroese, see Schütze (2001: 201, 207), and for an analysis in terms of structural on top of inherent case, Yoon (1996). See also Romero (this volume), who investigates a variety of laísta Spanish where a subset of third-person person IOs are doubled by clitics syncretic with accusative ones, and finds aspects of accusative/primary-IO syntax.

(13) a. **Nógvum kvinnum** *dámar/*dáma mannfólk við eitt sindur av búki.

many.DAT women.DAT like.3s/3P men.ACC with a bit of belly.

"Many women like men with a bit of belly."

b. **Mér** [*dámar*]/*dámi hasa bókina.

I.DAT like.3s/*1s this.ACC book.ACC

"I like this book."

c. *Sjálvum/*sjálvur dámar **honum** ikki at lurta eftir tónleiki.

self.DAT/NOM like.3s him.DAT not to listen to music

"He himself does not like to listen to music."

(Jónsson 2009: 157, 159)

Dative displacement in Basque resembles Faroese dative subjects in taking control of agreement that ordinarily falls to a controller with different, clearly structural case, the absolutive O/S. However, we have not yet found diagnostics that would let us see whether there are syntactic correlates, comparable to the licensing of nominative floating quantifiers in Faroese. As an example, consider *reflexive detransitization* (Etxepare 2003: 4.1.9.3, Artiagoitia 2003: 4.9.1.3, 4.9.2.3). In Basque, reflexives may be formed from plain transitives by eliminating the EA with its ergative case and agreement, resulting in a structure that is surface-identical to an unaccusative from the same stem (14).

(14) a. Ikasle-ek ikasle-ak aurkeztu d-it-u-zte.

student-PL.ERG student-PL.ABS introduced D-PL-√EA-3PE

"Students introduced (other) students."

b. **Ikasle-ak** aurkeztu **d-ira**.

student-PL.ABS introduced D-√A + PL

"The students introduced themselves/each other."

The dative IO is generally invisible to this process. The IO in transitive (15) cannot be interpreted as reflexive to the EA (or O), whether it continues to be dative (15b), or is changed to absolutive (15c).[17] Some speakers do in fact allow some analogues of the latter, but independently of dative displacement (Albizu 2000, Etxepare 2003: 4.1.6.2). Thus the dative IO's control of O-type agreement in dative displacement does not confer on it

---

17 The same is true in unergatives where there is no O candidate for EA = O reflexivization; *The girls.ERG looked [at] the boys.DAT* (*Neskek mutilei begiratu diete*) cannot be detransitivized to *The girls.ABS looked* and mean "The girls looked at each other, at themselves" (*Neskak begiratu dira*).

O-like behavior for reflexive detransitivization. Yet in the absence of a better understanding of reflexive detransitivization, this negative fact tells us little.[18]

(15) a. Ikasle-ek   nesk-ei   ikasle-ak   aurkeztu   d-i-zki-e-te.
        student-PL.ERG girl-PL.DAT student-PL.ABS   introduced D-√EDA-PL-3pD-3pE
        "Students introduced students to the girls."

   b. **Ikasle-ak**   nesk-ei   aurkeztu   **zai-zki-e**
        students-PL.ABS   girl-PL.DAT   introduced   √DA-PL-3pD
        "The students introduced themselves/each other to the girls."
        *The girls introduced the students to themselves/each other.

   c. ***Nesk-ak**   ikasle-ak   aurkeztu   **d-ira**.
        girl-PL.ABS   student-PL.ABS   introduced   D-√A + PL
        "The girls introduced students to themselves/each other."

We have found two hints of syntactic effects of dative displacement that further research may explore. The first is an effect on causativization described by Trask (1981). The relevant causative construction is illustrated in (18) (Ortiz de Urbina 2003: 4.8). The causative suffix *arazi* attaches to the participle/infinitive of the causativized verb, the causer is introduced as the ergative EA, the O of a causativized (di)transitive remains absolutive and agrees with the auxiliary as in a simple clause, and the EA of the causativized verb is interpreted as the causee and becomes a dative that likewise agrees with the auxiliary. The resulting case-agreement profile is identical to a ditransitive.

(16)   Eliza-k   **ni-ri**$_i$ diru-a   eman-arazi   d-i-t$_i$.
       church-ERG   me-DAT   money-ABS   give-cause   D-√EDA-1sD
       "The church made me give money (to people)."

When the causativized verb would itself take a dative IO, as is possible for *eman* in (16), its dative may remain present for some speakers, but it cannot itself agree with the matrix auxiliary, whose (unique) dative agreement suffix is obligatorily interpreted as the EA-causee (Ortiz de Urbina 2003: 4.8.2). This is the property that dative displacement seems to change. Trask reports this constraint in the dialect of Milafranga (Lapurdian-Navarrese, Lapurdi), so that (17a) only has the reading where the 1SG dative agreement suffix -ta- is interpreted as the causee. However, he also reports that under dative displacement (17b), where the 1SG dative suffix

18 Cross-linguistically, dative IOs in actives can correspond to nominatives in various detransitivizations, although it is not agreed whether the process is lexical or not (see, e.g., Feldman 1978 on Ancient Greek passives, Folli and Harley 2007 on Japanese causative passives, Svenonius forthcoming on Icelandic middles, Medová 2009: 6.3.2 on French reflexives).

-ta- is doubled by the person prefix n-, the 1SG agreement is interpreted as the IO of the causativized ditransitive, not the EA-causee.[19]

(17) a. Eman-a(r)azi   da-u-ta-k.
      given-cause   D-√E(D)A-1sD-2ME
      "You've made me give it away." (= Standard for Eastern varieties)

    b. Eman-a(r)azi   **na-u-ta-k.**
      given-cause   1s-√E(D)A-1sD-2ME
      "You've made him give it to **me**."
      (Trask 1981: 294)

There are two striking aspects to this pattern. One is that different datives agree differently. It seems from Trask's description that dative causees can only control the dative suffix, while the datives of causativized ditransitives can only control the prefix + suffix (dative displacement). Since morphology otherwise never differentiates the two dative classes, dative displacement appeals to a syntactic distinction.

Second, dative displacement lets agree a dative that is otherwise inaccessible to agreement. How it does so would be easier to understand if Trask's data were interpreted somewhat differently than he does. He translates the nonagreeing argument of (17b) as *him*, but that seems foreign to Basque, where the causee in *arazi* causatives is either an agreeing dative, overt or pro-dropped, or a nonagreeing and overt oblique, or a nonagreeing and silent impersonal causee.[20] The silent nonagreeing causee of (17) is thus most naturally taken as an impersonal causee. Such causatives behave as described above, save that the causee does not agree, and unlike agreeing datives does not restrict absolutives to first and second person (18) (Ortiz de Urbina 2003: 4.8.2, Albizu 2001).

(18) a. *(*Ni$_j$)   etxe-ra   eraman-arazi **na**$_i$-i-o   (anaia-ri)
      me.ABS   home-to   bring-cause 1s-√EDA-3sD   brother-DAT
      "She made him/brother bring **me** home."

---

19 The gloss 2M is the masculine of the 2SG familiar, which we have not so far used in our exposition. Trask's other example is parallel to (17) with *jan-a(r)azi* "feed," sc. "make eat," for *eman-a(r)azi*.

20 The situation seems parallel to French, corresponding respectively to *à*-causees of direct causation (*J'ai fait manger le gâteau au chien* "I made the dog eat the cake"), *par*-causees of indirect causation (*J'ai fait manger le gâteau par le chien* "I had the dog eat the cake"), and silent impersonal causees (*J'ai fait manger le gâteau* "I had the cake eaten"). We are grateful to Beñat Oyharçabal (p.c.) for discussion of Trask's data and for pointing out the oblique causatives of Basque.

b. **Ni**$_i$ etxe-ra   eraman-arazi **na**$_i$-u
    me.ABS   home-to   bring-cause 1s-√EA
    "She made *someone*/*him bring **me** home."
(Albizu 2001)

For some but not all speakers, an impersonal causee renders impossible agreement with the dative IO of the causativized verb, just as an agreeing causee does (19).[21] The restriction appears to be syntactic rather than morphological, since impersonal causees are not reflected in and do not otherwise constrain agreement morphology (18).

(19) a. Eliza-k   **ni-ri**$_i$ diru-a   eman-arazi *d-i-**t**$_i$ /d-u
      church-ERG   me-DAT   money-ABS   give-cause D-√EDA-1sD/D-√EA
      The church makes pro$_{arb}$ (=*someone, people*) give **me.DAT** money.
      (*dit* ok. as: The church makes *me* give money (to pro$_{arb}$))
      (Ortiz de Urbina 2003: 4.8.2, cf. Albizu 2001)

    b. Eman-arazi da-u-**ta**-k   (da-u-**t**).
       give-cause D-√E(D)A-1sD-2MD   (D-√E(D)A-1sD)
       You made **me** give it.   (He made me give it.)
       You made *someone* give it to **me**.   (He made some give it to me.)
       (Beñat Oyharçabal, p.c.)

If the causee in (17) is an impersonal causee, it blocks agreement with the IO of the causativized verb when it controls regular dative agreement (17a), but not when it also controls the prefix under dative displacement (17b). This can be related to the invisibility of the impersonal causee to person agreement of the absolutive O (18b), in contrast to dative-agreeing causees that restrict it to third person (18a) (cf. Rezac 2008a: 102). Dative displacement attributes to the dative IO control of the prefix, a morphological property of the absolutive O; in Trask's (17) it would also attribute to it a syntactic property, the ability to agree past an impersonal causee. Needless to say, we are far from understanding Trask's pattern, including its spread in other dative displacement dialects.

---

21 This variation recurs in French (i). It resembles restrictions on the movement of a DP past another with the same case, for instance wh-movement of a dative banned past a dative but not an accusative object controller discussed for French by Milner (1979); similar phenomena vary in strength from parsing difficulty to ungrammaticality (Rivas 1977, Milner 1979, Solà 2002, Dotlačil 2004, Rezac 2005).

(i)   L'église *m'*a fait donner de l'argent.
(a)   The church has made *me* give money.
(b)   %The church has made *someone* give *me* money.
((b) ok for M. Jouitteau, p.c., B. Oyharçabal, p.c., *for A. Dagnac, p.c.)

The second syntactic correlate of dative displacement also licenses an otherwise impossible agreeing dative. Basque unaccusatives combine with two
syntactically different classes of datives: high, applicative datives introduced
above S, including psych-experiencers, possessors, and datives of interest,
and low, prepositional datives introduced below S, including animate goals-
of-motion verbs (Rezac 2008c, 2011, forthcoming, Fernández and Ortiz de
Urbina 2010). In Standard Basque, both classes must agree, but in eastern
dialects, only high datives control agreement, and low ones appear as nonagreeing datives (Etxepare and Oyharçabal forthcoming, this volume, Etxepare
forthcoming, Fernández, Ortiz de Urbina & Landa 2010, Fernández and
Landa forthcoming, Fernández forthcoming). In many western dialects, low
datives not only fail to agree, but are replaced by alternatives such as allative
PPs (nonagreeing, as all PPs). Among them is Hondarribia Basque (Central
Basque, transitional variety, Gipuzkoa) in (20), where datives in unaccusatives
may be psych-experiencers but not goals of motion. However, dative displacement permits both classes of datives (21), reestablishing their symmetric behavior in Standard Basque. Since the morphology of Basque agreement
does not otherwise differentiate dative classes, the effect seems syntactic.

(20) a. Gu-ri   sagarr-a   gusta-tzen   d-i-gu.[22]
        us-DAT   apple-ABS   like-ing   D-√(E)D(A)-1ᴘD
        "We like apples."

     b. Gu-ri   Jon   etorri   —
        us-DAT   Jon-ABS   come
        "Jon came to us."
        (Hondarribia Basque, 1PL.DAT has no dative displacement)

(21) a. Ni-ri   sagarr-a   gusta-tzen   na-u.
        me-DAT   apple-ABS   like-ing   1s-√
        "I like apples."

     b. Ni-ri   Jon   etorri   **na-u**
        me-DAT   us-ABS   come
        "Jon came to me."
        (Hondarribia Basque, 1SG.DAT with dative displacement)

A similar effect is found in Oiartzun Basque (see Table 9.1). In unaccusatives with a singular absolutive, our consultant has the option of using
dative displacement for all psych-experiencer datives save 1PL (other speakers may have it here as well), but for dative goals of motion, she requires
dative displacement for even for 1PL.

---

22 In Hondarribia and Oiartzun, the √EDA *i* root has replaced √DA *(t)zai*, giving
digu, dit for Standard *zaigu, zait,* for which in turn dative displacement uses √EA *u*:
gattu, nau (Fernández 2004, Rezac 2008b).

(22) a. Guri sagarra gustatzen d-i-gu   /   (ga-tt-u)
        us.D apple.A liking   DFLT-$\sqrt{}$D-1pD   1p-PL-$\sqrt{}$
        "We like the apple."

    b. Guri Jon   etorri —   /   ga-tt-u
       us.D Jon.A come   1p-PL-$\sqrt{}$
       "Jon came to us."
       (Oiartzun Basque, no dative displacement/dative displacement)

It is not yet well understood how to properly differentiate high and low datives, apparently applicative versus prepositional, yet force both to agree in Standard Basque, unlike in eastern dialects where only high, applicative datives agree. Therefore, it is not clear how to construe the effect of dative displacement that permits low yet agreeing datives. One possibility is that agreeing datives always involve a high configuration, and that Standard Basque but not the eastern and western varieties in question have a way for low datives to participate in it, perhaps by movement from their low position (Rezac forthcoming, Rezac, Albizu, & Etxepare 2011). Dative displacement would enable this movement when not otherwise available, but the mechanics remain unclear.

5. CONCLUSION

The study of dative displacement is at its beginnings. The foregoing hints of the syntactic correlates do not bring us to a concrete theory of it. They do suggest that the mechanism is syntactic and section 3 outlines the hypothesis space of syntactic analyses that lie within current approaches to IOs, datives, agreement, and agreement displacement. These analyses also predict reasonably what properties should and should not parameterize dative displacement, namely the phi-features of the dative and the properties of Appl and v. A syntactic approach does not eliminate a role for morphology. The output of syntax must be realized, and morphological effects surface in arbitrary gaps in the realization of dative displacement as for other agreement. The two components of syntax and morphology are distinguishable sources of dialectal variation, each identifiable by its formal properties such as information accessed, nature of operations, and effects on syntax and interpretation.

6. APPENDIX: ERGATIVE DISPLACEMENT

Standard Basque and most Basque varieties have the phenomenon of *ergative displacement*, (23). In some varieties, the ergative EA only controls the ergative suffixes under all circumstances (Bermeo, Hualde 2002). In most, it controls the prefix but not the PL morphology if there is no absolutive O controller for it, that is when O is absent or 3rd person, in certain moods and tenses, sometimes also retaining control of the ergative suffix (Laka 1993, Fernández & Albizu 2000, Rezac 2003). In between these two extremes, there is a range of variation that depends on factors similar to dative displacement, for instance the phi-features of the ergative (Rezac 2006: chapter 2). However, there are two important differences: ergative displacement does not take control of prefix morphology away from O, because it only occurs when O as third person cannot agree, and that it never affects PL morphology, which remains controlled by O.

(23) **Zu-k**$_i$ ne-ri$_j$ sagarr-a$_k$/ak$_n$ eman **zen**$_i$-i- $\emptyset_k$/zki$_n$-da$_j$- (**zu**$_i$-) n.
   you-ERG me-DAT apple-SG.ABS given 2s- $\sqrt{\text{EDA}}$-$\emptyset$/PL- 1sD-(2sE-)PAST
   (*ergative displacement*)

Competition arises in systems that have both ergative and dative displacement whenever both could control the prefix. The winner seems unpredictable, although there is preference for the dative to decide the tendency of a given system (Rezac 2006: chap. 3). Thus both the options in (24) occur in dative displacement systems, and the choice of one or the other depends on apparently arbitrary factors.[23]

(24) **Gu-k**$_i$ **zu-ri**$_k$ sagarr-a eman **gen**$_i$-i-zu$_k$-n /**za**$_k$-**it**$_k$-u-gu$_i$-n
   we-ERG you-DAT apple-ABS given 1P-$\sqrt{\text{EDA}}$-2sD-PAST 2P-PL-$\sqrt{\text{EA}}$-1sE-PST
   (*ergative vs. dative displacement*)

ACKNOWLEDGMENTS

We thank Ane Barriola, Arantzazu Elordieta, Irantzu Epelde, Beñat Oyharçabal, Julen Manterola, Céline Mounole, and an anonymous informant from Oñati for answering our questionnaire on dative displacement or collecting data for us and for sharing their insights. We are also grateful to the participants of the workshop on *Variation in Datives* for discussion, to an anonymous reviewer and to Richard S. Kayne for insightful and helpful comments, and to Pablo Albizu for much debate over the years. This work has been partially supported by the following grants: Basque Government HM-2008–1-10, HM-2009–1-25 and IT4–14–10; Ministerio de Ciencia e Innovación FFI2008–00240/FILO and FFI2011–26906; Agence Nationale de la Recherche ANR-07-CORP-033.

23 Current descriptions give a single winner for combinations where the paradigm suggests both EL and DL should be available, but more investigation is needed to ascertain that this is indeed so. Conflicts between controllers in Italian participle agreement are sometimes resolved categorically, sometimes give rise to vaccilation (Burzio 1986: 60–62, 363, 405–406, drawn to our attention by Richard S. Kayne, p.c.).

REFERENCES

Ackema, Peter, and Ad Neeleman. 2007. "Morphology ≠ syntax." In Gillian Ramchand and Charles Reiss (eds.), *The Oxford handbook of linguistic interfaces*, 325–352. Oxford: Oxford University Press.

Albizu, Pablo. 1997. "Generalized PCC." In Myriam Uribe-Etxebarria and Amaya Mendikoetxea (eds.), *Theoretical issues on the morphology-syntax interface*, 1–33. Donostia: Euskal Herriko Unibertsitatea.

Albizu, Pablo. 2000. "Sobre la distribución sintáctica de las formas finitas del verbo vasco." Unpublished ms., Euskal Herriko Unibertsitatea.

Albizu, Pablo. 2001. "Datibo sintagmen izaera sintaktikoaren inguruan: Eztabaidarako oinarrizko zenbait datu." In Beatriz Fernández and Pablo Albizu (eds.), *On case and agreement*, 49–69. Bilbo: EHUko Argitalpen Zerbitzua.

Albizu, Pablo. 2002. "Basque verbal morphology: Redefining cases." In Patxi Goenaga and Joseba A. Lakarra (eds.), *Erramu Boneta: Festschrift for Rudolf P. G. de Rijk*, 1–19. Bilbo: EHUko Argitalpen Zerbitzua.

Allen, Barbara J., Donald Franz, D. B. Gardiner, and David Perlmutter. 1990. "Verb agreement multistratal representation in Southern Tiwa." In Paul Postal and Brian Joseph (eds.), *Studies in Relational Grammar 3*, 321–383. Chicago: University of Chicago Press.

Allen, Cynthia. 1986. "Reconsidering the history of 'like.'" *Journal of Linguistics* 22: 375–409.

Anagnostopoulou, Elena. 2003. *The syntax of ditransitives*. Berlin: Mouton.

Arregi, Karlos, and Andrew Nevins. 2006. "Obliteration vs. impoverishment in the Basque g-/z- constraint." In *Proceedings of the Penn Linguistics Colloquium 30, U Penn Working Papers in Linguistics 13*, 1–14. Philadelphia: University of Pennsylvania.

Arregi, Karlos, and Andrew Nevins. 2008. "A principled order to post-syntactic operations." Unpublished ms., University of Illinois at Urbana-Champaign and Harvard University. Online at ling.auf.net/lingbuzz/000646.

Arregi, Karlos, and Andrew Nevins. Forthcoming. *Morphotactics: Basque auxiliaries and the structure of spell-out*. Dordrecht: Springer.

Artiagoitia, Javier. 2003. "Reciprocal and reflexive constructions." In José Ignacio Hualde and Jon Ortiz de Urbina (eds.), *A grammar of Basque*, 607–631. Berlin: Walter de Gruyter.

Badihardugun. 2005. *Oñatiko aditz-taulak*. Oñati: Badihardugu Euskara Elkartea.

Baerman, Matthew, Greville G. Corbett, and Dunstan Brown. 2010. *Defective paradigms*. Oxford: Oxford University Press.

Baker, Mark. 1988. *Incorporation*. Chicago: University of Chicago Press.

Baker, Mark. 1996. *The polysynthesis parameter*. Oxford: Oxford University Press.

Béjar, Susana, and Milan Rezac. 2009. "Cyclic Agree." *Linguistic Inquiry* 40: 35–73.

Bobaljik, Jonathan David, and Susi Wurmbrand. 2002. "Notes on agreement in Itelmen." *Linguistic Discovery* 1, available at http://journals.dartmouth.edu/cgi-bin/WebObjects/Journals.woa/1/xmlpage/1/article/21?htmlOnce=yes, accessed June 25, 2012.

Bonet, Eulàlia. 1991. "Morphology after syntax: Pronominal clitics in Romance." Ph.D. diss., MIT.

Bonet, Eulàlia. 1995. "Feature structure of Romance clitics." *Natural Language and Linguistic Theory* 13(4): 607–647.

Bonet, Eulàlia, and Daniel Harbour. Forthcoming. "Contextual allomorphy." In Jochen Trommer (ed.), *The handbook of exponence*. Oxford: Oxford University Press.

Bresnan, Joan, and Lioba Moshi. 1990. "Object asymmetries in comparative Bantu syntax." *Linguistic Inquiry* 21: 147–185.

Burzio, Luigi. 1986. *Italian syntax: A government-binding approach.* Dordrecht: Reidel.

Dotlačil, Jakub. 2004. "The syntax of infinitives in Czech." MA thesis, University of Tromsø.

Elordieta, Arantzazu. 2001. "Verb movement and constituent permutation in Basque." PhD diss., University of Leiden.

Embick, David, and Alec Marantz. 2008. "Architecture and blocking." *Linguistic Inquiry* 39: 1–53.

Embick, David, and Rolf Noyer. 2007. "Distributed Morphology and the syntax-morphology interface." In Gillian Ramchand and Charles Reiss (eds.), *The handbook of linguistic interfaces,* 289–324. Oxford: Oxford University Press.

Etxepare, Ricardo. 2003a. "Valency and argument structure." In Hualde and Ortiz de Urbina (eds.), *A grammar of Basque,* 363–425. Berlin: Mouton de Gruyter.

Etxepare, Ricardo. Forthcoming. "Contact and change in a restrictive theory of parameters." In Carmen Picallo and José M. Brucart (eds.), *Linguistic variation and Minimalism.* Oxford: Oxford University Press.

Etxepare, Ricardo, and Bernat Oyharçabal. Forthcoming. "Hautazko datibo komunztadura ifarekialdeko euskalkietan." *Lapurdum* 13.

Feldman, Harry. 1978. "Passivizing on datives in Greek." *Linguistic Inquiry* 9: 499–502.

Fernández, Beatriz. 2001. "Absolutibo komunztaduradun ergatiboak, absolutibo komunztaduradun datiboak: Ergatiboaren Lekualdatzetik Datiboaren Lekualdatzera." In Beatriz Fernández and Pablo Albizu (eds.), *On case and agreement,* 147–165. Bilbo: EHUko Argitalpen Zerbitzua.

Fernández, Beatriz. 2002. "Komunztadura bikoitza eta lekualdatzea." In Xabier Artiagoitia, Patxi Goenaga, and Joseba Lakarra (eds.), *Erramu Boneta: Fetschrift for Rudolf P. G. de Rijk,* 247–260. Bilbo: UPV/EHUko Argitalpen Zerbitzua.

Fernández, Beatriz. 2004. "*Gustatzen nau gustatzen dizu*: Aditz laguntzaile eta komuntzadura bitxiak perpaus ez-akusatiboetan." In Pablo Albizu and Beatriz Fernández (eds.), *Euskal gramatika XXI. mendearen atarian: Arazo zaharark, azterbide berriak,* 89–112. Gazteiz: Arabako Foru Aldundia.

Fernández, Beatriz. Forthcoming. "Goi- eta behe-datiboak eta Datibo-Komunztaduraren Murriztapena: Ipar-ekialdeko hizkerak eta euskara estandarra." In Irantzu Epelde (ed.), *Euskal dialektologia: lehena eta oraina. Supplements of the International Journal of Basque Linguistics and Philology (ASJU),* 69. University of the Basque Country (UPV/EHU).

Fernández, Beatriz, and Pablo Albizu. 2000. "Ergative displacement in Basque and the division of labour between morphology and syntax." In Akira Okrent and John P. Boyle (eds.), *Proceedings of the Chicago Linguistic Society 36,* vol. 2, 103–118. Chicago: Chicago Linguistic Society.

Fernández, Beatriz, and Marijose Ezeizabarrena. 2003. "Itsasaldeko solezismoa, Datiboaren Lekualdatzearen argipean." In *Euskal gramatikari eta literaturari buruzko ikerketak XXI. mendearen atarian. Gramatika gaiak. Iker* 14(1): 255–278. Bilbo: Euskaltzaindia.

Fernández, Beatriz, and Josu Landa. Forthcoming. "Datibo komunztadura beti zaindu, inoiz zaindu ez eta batzuetan baino zaintzen ez demean. Hiru ahoko aldagaia, datu iturri bi eta erreminta bat: Corsintax." *Lapurdum* 13.

Fernández, Beatriz, and Jon Ortiz de Urbina. 2010. *Datiboa hiztegian.* Bilbo: UPV/EHU.

Fernández, Beatriz, Jon Ortiz de Urbina, and Josu Landa. 2010. "Komunztadurarik gabeko datiboen gakoez." In Ricardo Etxepare, Ricardo Gómez, and Joseba Lakarra (eds.), *Beñat Oihartzabali gorazarre. Festschrift for Bernard Oyharçabal,* 357–380. *International Journal of Basque Linguistics and Philology (ASJU)* 43: 1–2.

Fernández, Beatriz, and Ibon Sarasola. Forthcoming. "*Marinelei abisua*: Izen ondoko datibo sintagmak izenburuen sintaxian." *Lapurdum* 13.

Folli, Raffaella, and Heidi Harley. 2007. "Causation, obligation, and argument structure: On the nature of little v. " LI 38:197–238.

Halle, Morris, and Alec Marantz. 1993. "Distributed Morphology and the pieces of inflection." In Kenneth Hale and Samuel J. Keyser (eds.), *The view from Building 20*, 111–176. Cambridge, MA: MIT Press.

Haspelmath, Martin. 2005. "Ditransitive constructions: The verb 'give.'" In Martin Haspelmath, Matthew S. Dryer, D. Gil, and Bernard Comrie (eds.), *The world atlas of language structures*, 426–429. Oxford: Oxford University Press.

Hualde, José Ignacio. 2002. "On the loss of ergative displacement in Basque." In Fabrice Cavoto (ed.), *The linguist's linguist*, vol. 1, 219–230. Munich: Lincom Europa.

Jónsson, Jóhannes Gísli. 2009. "Covert nominative and dative subjects in Faroese." In *Nordlyd 36.2: NORMS Papers on Faroese*, 142–164.

Kayne, Richard. 2004. "Prepositions as probes." In Adriana Belletti (ed.), *Structures and beyond: The cartography of syntactic structures*, vol. 3, 192–212. Oxford: Oxford University Press.

Laka, Itziar. 1993. "The structure of inflection: A case study in X^0 syntax." In José Ignacio Hualde and Jon Ortiz de Urbina (eds.), *Generative studies in Basque linguistics*, 21–70. Amsterdam: John Benjamins.

Laka, Itziar. 2000. "Thetablind Case: Burzio's Generalisation and its image in the mirror." In Eric Reuland (ed.), *Arguments and case: Explaning Burzio's Generalisation*, 103–129. Amsterdam: John Benjamins.

Lightfoot, David. 1977. "Syntactic change and the autonomy thesis." *Journal of Linguistics* 13: 191–216.

MacKay, Carolyn, and Frank R. Trechsel. 2008. "Symmetrical objects in Misantla Totonac." *International Journal of American Linguistics* 74: 227–255.

Malchukov, Andrej L., Martin Haspelmath, and Bernard Comrie. 2010. "Ditransitive constructions: A typological overview." In Andrej L. Malchukov, Martin Haspelmath, and Bernard Comrie (eds.), *Studies in ditransitive constructions: A comparative handbook*, 1–64. Berlin: Mouton de Gruyter.

McGinnis, Martha. 1998. "Locality in A-movement." PhD diss., MIT.

McGinnis, Martha. 2001. "Variation in the phase structure of applicatives." *Linguistic Variation Yearbook* 1: 101–142.

Medová, Lucie. 2009. "Reflexive clitics in the Slavic and Romance languages." PhD diss., Princeton University.

Milner, Jean-Claude. 1979. "La redondance fonctionnelle." *Lingvisticæ Investigationes* 3: 87–145.

Ngonyani, Deo, and Peter Githinji. 2006. "The asymmetric nature of Bantu applicative constructions." *Lingua* 116: 31–63.

Noyer, Robert Rolf. 1992. "Features, positions and affixes in autonomous morphological structure." Ph.D. diss., MIT.

Ortiz de Urbina, Jon. 1989. *Parameters in the grammar of Basque*. Dordrecht: Foris.

Ortiz de Urbina, Jon. 2003. "Causatives." In José Ignacio Hualde and Jon Ortiz de Urbina (eds.), *A grammar of Basque*, 592–606. Berlin: Walter de Gruyter.

Oyharçabal, Bernard. 1993. "Verb agreement with non-arguments: On allocutive agreement." In José Ignacio Hualde and Jon Ortiz de Urbina (eds.), *Generative studies in Basque syntax*, 89–114. Amsterdam: John Benjamins.

Patel, Pritty. 2010. "Disagree to agree." Unpublished ms., MIT.

Peterson, David A. 2007. *Applicative constructions*. Oxford: Oxford University Press.

Rezac, Milan. 2003. "The fine structure of cyclic Agree." *Syntax* 6: 156–182.

Rezac, Milan. 2005. "The syntax of clitic climbing in Czech." In Lorie Heggie and Francisco Ordóñez (eds.), *Clitic and affix combinations*, 103–140. Amsterdam: John Benjamins.

Rezac, Milan. 2006. "Agreement displacement in Basque." Unpublished ms., University of the Basque Country, Vitoria-Gasteiz. Online at www.umr7023.cnrs.fr/spip.php?article675.

Rezac, Milan. 2008a. "Phi-Agree and theta-related Case." In Daniel Harbour, David Adger, and Susana Béjar (eds.), *Phi theory: Phi-features across interfaces and modules*, 83–129. Oxford: Oxford University Press.

Rezac, Milan. 2008b. "The forms of dative displacement: From Basauri to Itelmen." In Xabier Artiagoitia and Joseba A. Lakarra (eds.), *Gramatika jaietan*, 709–724. Bilbo: UPV/EHU.

Rezac, Milan. 2008c. "The syntax of eccentric agreement: The Person Case Constraint and Absolutive Displacement in Basque." *Natural Language and Linguistic Theory* 26: 61–106.

Rezac, Milan. 2010. "Phi-Agree vs. movement: Evidence from floating quantifiers." *Linguistic Inquiry* 41: 496–508.

Rezac, Milan. 2011. *Phi-features and the modular architecture of language.* Dordrecht: Springer.

Rezac, Milan. Forthcoming. "Person restrictions in Basque intransitives." *Lapurdum* 13.

Rezac, Milan, Pablo Albizu, and Ricardo Etxepare. 2011. "The structural ergative of Basque and the theory of case." Unpublished ms., UMR 7023 CNRS, University of the Basque Country, and UMR 5478 CNRS. Online at www.umr7023.cnrs.fr/Publications,675.html.

Rhodes, Richard. 1994. "Valency, inversion, and thematic alignment in Ojibwe." *Proceedings of BLS 20*, 431–446. Berkeley, CA: Berkeley Linguistics Society.

Rivas, Alberto. 1977. "Clitics in Spanish." PhD diss., MIT.

Schütze, Carson. 2001. On Korean "case-stacking." *Linguistic Review* 18: 193–232.

Sigurðsson, Halldór Ármann. 2003. "Case: Abstract vs. morphological." In Ellen Brandner and Heike Zinzmeister (eds.), *New perspectives on case theory*. Stanford: CSLI Publications.

Solà, Jaume. 2002. "Clitic climbing and null subject languages." *Catalan Journal of Linguistics* 1: 225–255.

Svenonius, Peter. Forthcoming. "Case alternations in the Icelandic passive and middle." In Satu Manninen, Katrin Hiietam, Elsi Kaiser, and Virve Vihman (eds.), *Passives and impersonals in European languages*. Oxford: Oxford University Press.

Taraldsen, Knut Tarald. 1995. "On agreement and nominative objects in Icelandic and Faroese." In Huberts Haider, Susan Olsen, and Sten Vikner (eds.), *Studies in comparative Germanic syntax*, 307–327. Dordrecht: Kluwer.

Trask, R. T. 1981. "Basque verbal morphology." *Iker* 1: 285–304.

Yoon, James Hye-Suk. 1996. "Ambiguity of government and the Chain Condition." *Natural Language and Linguistic Theory* 14: 105–162.

Yrizar, Pedro de. 1992. *Morfología del verbo auxiliar vizcaíno.* 2 vols. Zarautz: Euskaltzaindia.

Yrizar, Pedro de. 1997. *Morfología del verbo auxiliar labortano.* Pamplona: Euskaltzaindia.

Zuazo, Koldo. 2003. *Euskalkiak, herriaren lekukoak.* Donostia: Elkar.

CHAPTER 10

Accusative Datives in Spanish

JUAN ROMERO

As exemplified in (1), in Standard Spanish and most Spanish dialects, dative clitics, contrary to accusative ones, do not specify gender.[1]

(1) le   envié   un regalo (al niño/a la niña)
    3sD   sent.I   a gift; (to the boy/to the girl)
    "I sent the boy/the girl a gift."

There are, however, certain dialects in the northwest quadrant of Spain, the so-called *laísta* dialects, where a gender distinction regularly shows up by means of the clitic *le* for the masculine (2a) and the clitic *la* for the feminine (2b) (see Fernández Ordóñez 1994, 1999, and references therein).

(2) a. le envié el regalo (al niño/*a la niña)
       3smD sent.I the gift (to the boy/to the girl)
       "I sent him (the boy) a gift."

    b. la envié el regalo (*al niño/a la niña)
       3sfD sent.I the gift (to the boy/to the girl)
       "I sent her (the girl) a gift."

Traditionally, it is assumed that in these dialects dative gender motion reflects a bias in Spanish to replace Latin Case with gender distinctions similar to the ones found in the demonstrative paradigm.

---

1 The following abbreviations are used in the glosses: 1, 2, 3 = first, second, third person, respectively; s = singular; p = plural; f = feminine; m = masculine; a = animate; D = Indirect Object; O = Direct Object. Subject agreement in the verb is glossed by the corresponding English pronoun, and the animacy/Case marker *a* that appears with animate specific direct objects in Spanish has been left untranslated and is represented by the small capital A.

(3) Demonstrative paradigm:

	Masculine	Feminine	Neuter
This	Este	Esta	Esto
That	Ese	Esa	Eso

According to this description, examples in (2) merely reflect gender variation with no grammatical consequences whatsoever. Although this idea is weird for Spanish, since this language lacks neuter nouns, it has remained unchallenged since Lapesa (1968) proposed it. The first aim of this article is to show that this description is not accurate. In section 1 I will provide evidence that dative *la* (i) is actually accusative, (ii) it is restricted to animate arguments, and (iii) it only shows up when the dative stands up for an argument. In section 2, I will schematically present an analysis based in previous work by Uriagereka 1995, Roca 1992, Torrego 1998, Bleam 2000, and Ormazabal & Romero 2010, according to which accusative third-person clitics are actually determiners. In section 3, I derive the properties of *laísta* constructions from the peculiarities of object case in Spanish. Finally, in section 4 I will show that *laísmo* is not restricted to feminine arguments, masculine arguments also exhibit the effects described in section 1, but it is obscured by the fact that dative clitic has the same phonetic form than masculine person accusative one, namely, *le*.

A consideration is in order before proceeding. The properties described in this article are the ones found in what Fernández Ordóñez calls cult *laísta* dialect. There seems to be much more permissive dialects, but, for reasons that immediately become clear, descriptions are dubious, since they are based on the idea that *laísmo* is simply a feminine form for the dative. In consequence, dialects are broadly characterized as *laístas* independently of the syntactic contexts where the clitic actually appears. As long as the properties described in this article are correct, their proper characterization has to be completely reevaluated.

1. LAÍSMO RECONSIDERED

1.1 Feminine Datives Are Accusative

If *laísmo* were just gender motion, it would be expected to find feminine datives in any context where dative is assigned. However, this is not the case. Consider first passive constructions (4). The use of *la* is consistently barred in passives: we can passivize the sentence in (2a), deriving (4a); but when we try to do it in (2b), we are forced to change the feminine clitic *la* for the standard dative clitic *le* (4b).

(4) a. el regalo le fue enviado
    the gift 3sD was sent
    "The gift was sent to him/her."

b. *el regalo la fue enviado
    the gift 3sfD was sent
    "The gift was sent to her."

A natural way to explain the contrast between (2b) and (4b) is in terms of Case. Since the morphological shape of the feminine dative clitic *la* is identical to the accusative feminine clitic, the ungrammaticality of (4b) may be attributed to the fact that in passive sentences accusative case cannot be assigned. There are two reasons to think that this is the right approach. First, as extensively argued by several authors in the last twenty years (see, for instance, Uriagereka 1998, Demonte 1994, and Ormazabal & Romero 2007), dative constructions underlie the same processes than double object or applicative constructions, where the indirect object is accusative case marked. In this sense, the sentence in (2b) can be somehow best characterized as a double object construction, instead of a dative construction. And second, this explanation predicts that *laísmo* is incompatible with any context where accusative cannot be assigned, and this prediction is borne out.

Consider the case of unaccusative verbs. According to Burzio's Generalization, it is standardly assumed that these verbs are unable to assign accusative case. In consequence, this proposal predicts that the use of *la* in combination with an unaccusative verb will lead to an ungrammatical result, as it is confirmed by sentences in (5).

(5) a. la carta le/*la llegó tarde
    "The letter arrived late to her."

b. la piedra le/*la cayó encima
    "The stone fell on her."

c. la pregunta le/*la resultó extraña
    "The question sounds strange to her."

Furthermore, there are many adjectives that in combination with copular verbs may trigger the presence of a dative pronoun. Since accusative is not compatible with copular verbs, we expect, as it actually happens and it is shown in (6), not to find *laísmo* in these contexts.

(6) a. le/*la es fácil resolver esos problemas
    "It is easy for her to solve those problems."

b. le/*la parecía estúpido
    "He looks stupid to her."

Finally, another piece of evidence in this direction is found in the behavior of *la* with respect to doubling. In Spanish, clitic doubling is allowed for dative clitics, but in most peninsular dialects accusative clitics do not tolerate doubling except for personal pronouns and floating quantifiers. Sentences in (7) shows that when the clitic is doubled, *laísta* dialects resort to the unmarked form instead of the feminine dative clitic *la*.

(7) le/??la envié un regalo a la niña
"I sent the girl a gift."

Therefore, we can safely assert that *laísmo* may only arise in those contexts where accusative is or can be assigned.

1.2 Feminine Datives Are Animate

There is another aspect where *laísmo* is underdescribed: *laísmo* may only refer to animate indirect objects. As it is well known, dative constructions in Spanish show up not only with transfer verbs, typically restricted by the animacy constraint (Green 1974), but also with other verb classes such as locative verbs. Consider sentences in (8).

(8) a. le/*la puse los tornillos (a la mesa$_{FEM}$)
"I put the screws on the table."

b. le/*la añadí azúcar (a la leche$_{FEM}$)
"I added sugar to the milk."

As can be seen in these examples, dative *la* is not available for non personal IOs. Interestingly, these verbs do accept *laísmo* when the IO is personal, as exemplified in (9).

(9) *le/la puse una inyección
"I gave her an injection."

It has to be noted that the discrimination between animate and inanimate arguments is cross-linguistically quite common, and it is especially well represented in Spanish, where animate objects appear preceded by the preposition *a* (see section 3).

1.3 Feminine Datives Are Arguments

Finally, and in order to complete our description, it has to be noted that *laísmo* is rejected when dative constructions are derived from a transitive verb via benefactive augmentation or any of the other possible adjuncts that may become dative (10).

> (10) a. le/*la preparé un pastel
> "I cooked a cake for her."
>
> b. le/*la empujé el carrito
> "I pushed the cart for her."

The different behavior between arguments and adjuncts in this kind of constructions can also be found in other domains such as passivization (see Quilis et al. 1985, Demonte 1994).

1.4 Summary

Once we consider the whole range of data, the proper characterization of *laísmo* must account for the following properties: (i) it occurs only in ditransitive verbs, (ii) it is restricted to animate/human indirect objects, and (iii) it only shows up in those contexts where accusative can be assigned. Given the nature of this phenomenon, it is the typical situation searching for an explanation in microvariation terms, where different dialects choose between the range of solutions available for an specific problem within a given language. It is basic, in consequence, to properly understand the underlying relations where the problem arises. In this particular case, the relevant context is the relation between the verb and its internal arguments. Among the properties we have overt evidence that take part in this relation, we find animacy, specificity, and case. As far as I know, there is no independent evidence to justify, for instance, that gender plays any role in the relation between the verb and its internal arguments. Therefore, the mere existence of the paradigm described in this section poses an intriguing challenge to our current understanding of Agreement and case relations, because we simply do not expect gender to be a relevant issue.

2. ACCUSATIVE FEMININE DATIVES?

As it is shown in (11), two different clitics may encode the very same grammatical relation when the IO is feminine.

> (11) a. *le / la envié un regalo
> "I sent her a gift."
>
> b. le / *la envié un regalo a la niña
> "I sent the girl a gift."

As previously mentioned in (7), the contrast between (11a) and (11b) is directly tied to the presence of a doubling NP: If dative *la* is actually an accusative pronoun, we expect not to find it in a doubling structure, since doubling is only allowed for datives. Following Roca (1992) and Ormazabal & Romero (2010) I will take this fact to be a consequence of the categorial status of the clitic. According to these authors, and following a proposal originally due to Postal, accusative clitics in Spanish are actually instances of determiner cliticization onto the verb (12). This way it is possible to account for both its semantic interpretation and its morphosyntactic behavior (in contrast, for instance, to first- and second-person pronouns).

(12)

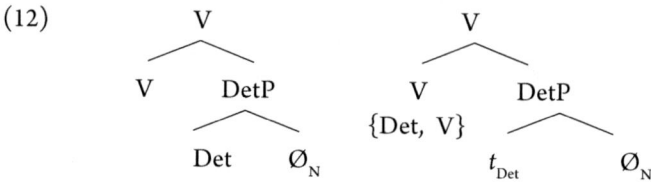

If *la* in *laísta* dialects is an accusative clitic, then it must also be obtained via determiner cliticization. Assuming the base structure in (13a) for ditransitive constructions, the determiner first cliticizes into P (13b), and then the whole cluster P + Det incorporates into V (13c).

(13) a.

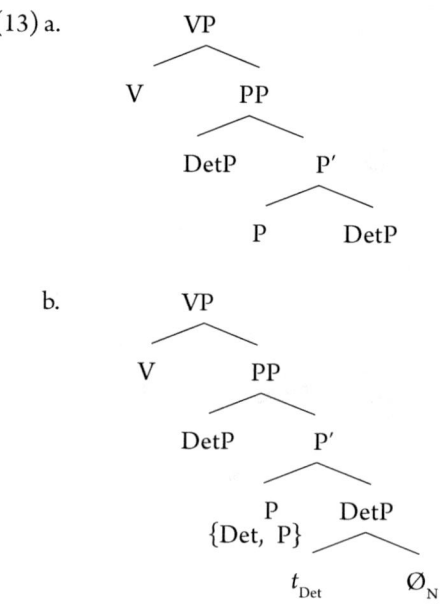

c.

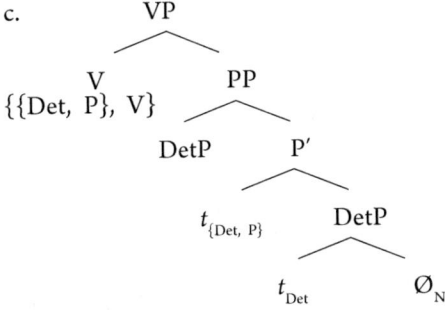

This derivation essentially matches the proposal made by Hale and Keyser (1993) for deriving location verbs such as *shelve*:

(14) put the books on the shelf → shelve the books

In the next sections I will address how this proposal can account for the properties observed:

(i) Why the determiner can only cliticize in accusative contexts
(ii) Why it is restricted to animate nouns
(iii) Why it is restricted to feminine nouns

My proposal is that the two first questions are related, so I am going to deal with them first in section 3, and then I will account for the last one in section 4.

3. ACCUSATIVE

3.1 Accusative vs. Dative: What Difference Does It Make?

As I have previously said, the fact that the IO receives accusative case is by no means an exotic property: it actually happens in languages such as English in double object constructions (DOCs), and, in general, in any language where no morphological distinction is made between accusative and dative cases. According to the proposal in (13), ditransitives have a very interesting structural property, which can be traced back at least to Kayne's analysis of DOCs as small clauses: structurally the verb only takes one complement. In regular transitive clauses the complement is a simple NP (15a), but in ditransitive ones, the complement is complex, a sort of P headed small clause,[2] whose specifier acts as direct object, and its complement as indirect object (15b).

(15) a. $[_{VP}$ V NP]

    b. $[_{VP}$ V $[_{PP}$ NP $[_{P'}$ P NP]]]

According to this analysis, it seems plausible, against what is commonly assumed, to think that since the verb just takes one structural complement, it also only encodes one formal agreement/case relation (Romero 1997). The main argument for this proposal comes from so-called Object Agreement Constraint (OAC), or Person Case Constraint (PCC) (see, for instance, Bonet 1991; Ormazabal & Romero 1998, 2007; Anagnostopoulou 2002). The OAC/PCC describes a situation where there are two internal NPs but only of them can establish a case/agreement relation with the verb.[3]

(16)   *me le llevaron al médico
        1sO 3sD took.they A the doctor
        (Lit.) *They took the doctor me*

Many languages assign just one case, accusative, in this configuration, and the OAC/PCC is expected. But there are other languages that assign two different cases, typically, accusative and dative, and in consequence there seems to be morphological marking enough for both arguments. However, the OAC/PCC arises anyway.

In order to explain this constraint, Ormazabal & Romero (2010) argue that there are reasons to think that dative case is related to a P head incorporated into V. Specifically, consider the sentences in (5) and (6). These examples show that dative case is active in contexts where accusative case cannot be assigned, not just in *laísta* dialects, but in any dialect of Spanish. Actually, in languages lacking dative case, there is no structural case available for this kind of constructions. Consider, for instance, the English version of (5b) in (17a–b).

(17) a. the stone fell on her
     b. *the stone fell her on

---

2 According to (15b), the PP including the theme and the goal is a constituent. As a matter of fact, it acts as a constituent with respect to focus fronting or pseudo-clefting. Furthermore, this constituent may also be embedded within a nominal structure, with similar patterns of derivation (Johnson 1991, Romero 1997).

3 In the last twelve years a growing body of references about this topic has appeared. It seems clear that this universal constraint blocks fairly consistently the possibility of an agreement/case relation with both internal arguments (see Preminger 2011 for an updated reference list, and Haspelmath 2004 for a different view on this subject).

This contrast suggests that this "dative parameter" can be explained in terms of the ability of an incorporated preposition (in a structure like (13c)) to retain its case-assigning properties. If so, languages in which the preposition retains its case assignment properties, do it at the expense of the (accusative) case otherwise assigned by the verb. This can receive a straightforward explanation if, as standardly assumed, structural case is assigned jointly by V and a functional head (V + T or, more generally, V + Agr). Accordingly, there are two potential lexical heads that can trigger structural case assignment, V and P, but there is only one functional head against which the appropriate relation is established. The facts described by the Object Agreement Constraint suggest that P can only incorporate into V if either P or V (but not both) lack case.[4] So the question in Spanish is: when does V lack case?

3.2 No Corpse, No Case

Direct objects in Spanish clearly split into two different kinds: specific animate DOs are necessarily preceded by the preposition *a*, and the rest appear as bare DPs.[5] There is evidence that only *a*-marked arguments receive case. Consider the following sentences:

(18) a. yo he visto las películas
      "I have seen the movies."

   b. se *ha/han visto las películas
      se has/have seen the movies

   c. las peliculas se han visto
      the movies se have seen
      "The movies have been seen."

(19) a. yo he visto a las niñas
      "I have seen the girls."

   b. se ha/*han visto a las niñas
      se has/have seen the girls."

   c. a las niñas se las ha/*han visto
      a the girls se cl3 has/have seen
      "The girls have been seen."

4 When P lacks case, the applied object receives accusative. On the other hand, when V lacks case, the applied object receives dative.

5 The issue is actually much more complex, but the description is enough for the purposes of this article (see Leonetti 2004, and Zdrojewski 2008 for an updated discussion on this topic).

In *se* constructions, the argument that in active sentences satisfies the subject relation has an unspecific/generic interpretation, and it can only be represented by means of the clitic *se* (see Mendikoetxea 1999). When the object is inanimate, it raises to subject position and triggers subject agreement (18b–c), as in passives. However, when the object is animate and specific, and in consequence appears preceded by the preposition *a*, it does not trigger subject agreement (19b), and if it precedes the verb it must appear clitic doubled (19c), as regularly occurs with preposed objects. This contrast receives a straightforward explanation if the verb only assigns case in Spanish when the object is animate and specific. Furthermore, this hypothesis also explains the different behavior between animate and inanimate objects with respect to incorporation. As it is well known in literature about incorporation, only inanimate arguments can regularly incorporate (see Mithun 1984, Evans 1997). This fact suggests that incorporation does not really nullify case and agreement (as argued in Baker 1988), but that, as a matter of fact, it is only possible when there is no formal relation between the verb and the NP.[6]

According to this idea, the animacy constraint for IOs (Green 1974) is essentially the same restriction we find in general for direct objects: there is only case/agreement for animate objects. A restriction that, in the case of Spanish, is made visible by means of the preposition *a*.

3.3 The Derivation of *Laísmo*

I have proposed that *laísmo* is obtained in two steps: First, the determiner in P complement position clitizices into P, and then P incorporates into V. Next I show how this process accounts for the two questions posed at the beginning of this section: (i) Why can the determiner only cliticize in accusative contexts, and (ii) Why is it restricted to animate nouns.

In the previous subsection I have argued that object case is only assigned when the object has certain features. Suppose V encodes some uninterpretable feature related to animacy.[7] The relation underlying this feature can be checked by the object, that in Spanish would appear *a*-marked. But in a structure like (13), in principle, this feature could also be checked by P. As a matter of fact, Rappaport & Levin (2008) propose that certain prepositions

---

6 Note that Baker's hypothesis explains why incorporation nullifies case/agreement in transitive clauses, but not in ditransitive ones, where the IO becomes primary object (Dryer 1986) and receives the accusative case that should have been nullified as a consequence of object incorporation.

7 The precise analysis of this relation falls out of the scope of this article; however, I want to make clear that I do not treat animacy as part of the agreement system. The fact that there is an enormous number of verbs that specifically select animate arguments suggests that animacy is licensed not functionally, but lexically (see note 10).

select animate arguments. That would be the case of the preposition selected by *give* or *say*. If correct, the uninterpretable feature might be checked by the THEME object (Spec, PP) in (13), or by an "animate" P (strictly speaking, by the complement of a P selecting an animate complement).

This way both questions are answered at the same time. On the one hand, the verb encodes formal features that, as seen in the section 3.2, intervene in object case assignment (see note 7). On the other, since these features are the same used for animate objects, *laísmo* is going to be restricted to animate goals. I have proposed that the animacy constraint on dative shift first observed by G. Green is actually an instance of a more general constraint on object case/agreement. This idea can also explain why *laísmo* is restricted to ditransitive verbs (see section 1.3): These verbs are the only ones that select a PP. In the rest of the cases, we can assume that the verb specifically selects an NP, making unavailable this applicative preposition. Furthermore, it also explains why Dative-double object-applicative constructions, if attested in a given language, are always attested for this kind of verbs, transfer verbs. The reason is trivial; the formal apparatus required is independently present in the relation between the verb and the DO. But, it also has a potential drawback: examples in (8–9) show that dative construction in Spanish is also allowed for locative prepositions. Specifically, dative constructions are allowed for locative verbs such as *poner* "put" or *colocar* "tighten" (20).

(20)   le puso los botones a la camisa
       (Lit.) *He put the shirt the buttons

These verbs are ditransitive, and, as shown in (9), exhibit *laísmo*. However, as exemplified in (8a), they are not restricted by the animacy constraint. The reason for this apparent paradox can be explained if we assume that there is another applicative preposition, one specific for locative verbs. This is not really a big assumption: Peterson's monograph on applicative constructions describes many languages that overtly express different applicative overt morphemes for each different semantic value. Furthermore, something like this is required in order to explain why, for instance, English lack DOCs for locative verbs: this "locative" applicative preposition simply does not form part of English vocabulary. Now consider the contrast between (21a) and (21b).

(21) a. *puso la mochila en María
        put.he the backpack in Mary

     b. le puso la mochila a María
        3sD put.he the backpack a María

As far as I know, this is the only instance in Spanish where the dative construction does not have a prepositional variant. This can be explained if the preposition in (21a) selects for locations, and therefore, its complement cannot be animate. On the other hand, suppose that in (21b) the verb encodes the animacy feature. In this situation, the applicative preposition used with transfer verbs would be perfectly compatible with these verbs. Note that in terms of meaning, the applicative locative preposition essentially implements an integral relation (Hornstein, Rosen, & Uriagereka 1995) or a central coincidence relation (Hale & Keyser 1993), and, in consequence, this proposal does not constitute a problem for its semantic interpretation. The difference between the applicative locative preposition and the transfer one is essentially formal: the second requires an animate complement, and the first does not.

In sum, *laísmo* shows up when the verb encodes an animacy feature. This feature is independently needed to explain the behavior of transitive verbs: they assign case when the object is animate, but they do not assign it when the object is inanimate. The relation encoded by this feature can be satisfied either by an animate object, or by an applicative preposition; specifically, by the applicative preposition required by ditransitive transfer verbs.

4. A MATTER OF GENDER

Up to now, we have seen that in *laísta* dialects there are two different ways for satisfying the formal features of the applicative preposition. It can be achieved by means of a regular case/agreement relation. In this case, the dative clitic, *le*, has to be understood as an agreement marker, and as such it does not make a gender difference. Alternatively, it can also be satisfied via determiner cliticization into P. In this case, there are dialects that show gender discrimination. However, there is no independent evidence for restricting incorporation to feminine determiners, and in consequence, we must explore the idea that there is also animate masculine determiner incorporation.

Due to the contexts where *laísmo* shows up, it is hard to find overt evidence for this kind of operation; however, there are two reasons to think that this is in fact what happens. First, *laísta* dialects are necessarily also *leísta* dialects (22).

(22) Standard *leísta* dialects

Masculine DO		Feminine DO	
Animate	Inanimate	Animate	Inanimate
le	lo	la	la

According to Fernández Ordóñez (1994), *laísta* dialects also encode a difference between animate and inanimate DOs. This difference is crucially represented by means of the clitic *le* for animate masculine DOs, the very same clitic used to express dative case. In consequence, independently of how we account for this parametric variation, if masculine determiners also incorporate into P, they are going to show up as the clitic *le*, making it indistinguishable of the dative case/agreement marker, *le*. Ormazabal & Romero (2010) argue that animate masculine DO marker *le* in these dialects is actually an instance of determiner incorporation. From this point of view, and given the contrast between (18) and (19), it can be argued that *laísta* dialects reanalyze the entire clitic system in the following way:

(23) *Laísta* dialects clitic system

	Masculine		Feminine	
	Animate	Inanimate	Animate	Inanimate
DO	le	lo	la	la
IO	le	le	la[8]	le

The crucial point here is that the whole pronominal system exhibits an overt animate/inanimate contrast related to the presence of the *a*-marker. In the case of the direct object, this contrast in encoded in the masculine, and in the case of the IO it is encoded on the feminine. Furthermore, there is syntactic evidence showing that the contrast between animate and inanimate feminine also arise in the case of objects. In Spanish the IO can appear clitic doubled or in a prepositional form (24). However, when the DO is represented by a clitic, dative clitic doubling becomes obligatory (25) (Fernández Ordóñez 1999).

(24) a. el alcalde envió la carta a Sara
"The mayor sent the letter to Sara."

b. el alcalde le envió la carta a Sara
the mayor 3sD sent the letter A Sara
"The mayor sent Sara the letter."

(25) a. *el alcalde la envió a Sara
the mayor 3sfO sent A Sara
"The mayor sent it to Sara."

---

8 As discussed in this article, the feminine IO clitic is *la* when accusative case can be assigned; otherwise it is *le*.

b. el alcalde se la envió a Sara
the mayor 3sD 3sfO sent A Sara
(Lit.) The mayor sent Sara it

Interestingly, the sentence in (25a) becomes grammatical if the third-person accusative clitic references to an animate object, as in (26). As a matter of fact, when the animate clitic is doubled by an NP, (25b) is degraded, if not ungrammatical (26c).[9]

(26) a. el alcalde envió a la niña a Sara
the mayor sent A the girl to Sara
"The mayor sent the girl to Sara."

b. el alcalde la envió a Sara
the mayor 3sfO sent A Sara
"The mayor sent her to Sara."

c. ??el alcalde se la envió a Sara
the mayor 3sD 3sfO sent A Sara

Note, finally, that the same contrast shows up between animate and inanimate masculine objects (27). In this case, when the two clitics coappear, the use of the animate masculine one is barred (27c), and *leísta* dialects resort to the inanimate one, *lo* (27d).

(27) a. el alcalde envió a los niños a Sara
the mayor sent A the boys to Sara
"The mayor sent the girl to Sara."

b. el alcalde les envió a Sara
the mayor 3pmaO sent A Sara
"The mayor sent them (the boys) to Sara."

c. *el alcalde se les envió a Sara
the mayor 3D 3mpaO sent A Sara

d. el alcalde se los envió A Sara
the mayor 3D 3mpO A Sara

This way we can explain why in order to have *laísmo* we first need to have *leísmo*. If so, this correlation may be taken as evidence that there is also masculine determiner incorporation in these cases. Finally, data in (24–27) is common to most varieties of Spanish, suggesting that *laísmo* is probably a matter of morphological representation. If so, the syntactic derivations proposed may

9 It has to be noted that (26c) is perfectly grammatical if there is no clitic doubling.

take place in other dialects. As a matter of fact, it is not clear if it can be avoided, and, as I show next, there is evidence that it is actually the case.

The second argument for masculine determiner incorporation in IOs is based on the behavior of the animacy marker *a*. Consider sentences in (28).

(28) a. llevaron a la niña al general para que informara de nuestra posición
"They took the girl to the general to report about our position."

b. le llevaron (*a) la niña al general para que informara de nuestra posición
"They took the general the girl to report about our position."

c. le enviaron *(a) la niña para que informara de nuestra posición
"They took him the girl to report about our position."

As seen in (28a), if there is no dative clitic, the specific animate DO appears preceded by the marker *a*. However, when the dative clitic appears doubling the IO, the use of this marker is barred. Interestingly, when there is no doubling NP, as in (28c), the marker *a* must appear again attached to the DO. If the structure of (28c) were the same that the one in (28b), except by the fact that the IO is an empty category, this contrast would be unexpected. However, if *le* is a cliticized determiner, it does not require case. In consequence, the verb could still assign the case marker *a* to the DO.[10] In other words, the verb assigns its case to one arguments, and checks its animacy with the other. Since the paradigm in (28) is common to *laísta* and non *laísta* dialects, it suggests that the two derivations are available in general. Note that if third-person object clitics are determiners clitiziced into the verb, then there is no obvious way for restricting the derivation proposed for *laísta* dialects in other varieties of Spanish. In consequence, it seems reasonable to conclude that *laísmo* is essentially a morphological issue related to the representation of a cluster of syntactic features at the cross-road of the internal arguments of the verb.

5. CONCLUSION

In this article I have presented the elements needed to explain the inner workings of those dialects that have a special form for certain feminine

10 Let me speculate with the idea underlying this process. In V, animacy is an interpretable feature (necessarily, for instance, for psych verbs) that triggers the presence of an uninterpretable feature A that probes for an animate goal. This split is due to its semantic nature: it is interpretable both in the verb and in the NP. On the other hand, the interpretable feature in V acts as a goal for the probe in a functional category responsible for case assignment.

indirect objects. Essentially, I have shown that *laísmo* is just a possible microparametric option in those dialects of Spanish where an animate/non animate distinction is made between third-person accusative clitics. Furthermore, I have also shown that *laísmo* may find a natural account in a general theory for dative constructions that has the following two features: dative constructions are obtained derivationally via P incorporation, and third-person object clitics are instances of determiner cliticization. As long as these hypothesis are true, *laísmo* can be understood as an instance of determiner cliticization onto P. From this point of view, the explanation of *laísmo* simply forms part of the explanation of dative constructions.

ACKNOWLEDGMENTS

I am very thankful to the organizers and audiences of the 4th European Dialect Syntax Meeting at the University of the Basque Country. Very special thanks to Javier Ormazabal and Richard S. Kayne for valuable comments, to Almudena Muñoz and Francisco Díaz for data elicitation, and to two anonymous reviewers. This work was financially supported in part by the institutions supporting the research activities of the Basque Group of Theoretical Linguistics (HITT): the Basque Government grant number GIC07/144-IT-210-07 (*Euskal Unibertsitate Sistemako Ikerketa-taldeak*), the Spanish Government's Ministry of Science and Development grant numbers FFI2008-04786 and FFI2011-29218, and the Basque Government's *Ayudas para la consolidación de Grupos de Investigación, cara a establecer redes de investigación y cooperación 2006* (project *Análisis comparativo y tipológico de la cartografía de la oración*, ref.: HM2006-1-8), 2007 program (project *Condiciones de Legitimidad en las Interfaces Lingüísticas*), 2008 (project *Sobre la construcción e interpretación de las estructuras lingüísticas* ref.: HM2008-1-10), and 2009 (*Universal Grammar and Linguistic Variation*, ref.: HM-2009-1-1).

REFERENCES

Anagnostopoulou, Elena. 2002. *The syntax of ditransitives: Evidence from clitics*. Berlin: Mouton de Gruyter.
Baker, Mark C. 1988. *Incorporation*. Chicago: University of Chicago Press.
Bleam, Tonia M. 2000. "Leísta Spanish and the syntax of clitic doubling." PhD diss., University of Delaware.
Bonet, Eulalia (1991). "Morphology after syntax: Pronominal clitics in Romance." PhD diss., Massachusetts Institute of Technology.
Demonte, Violeta. 1994. "La ditransitividad en español: Léxico y sintaxis." In V. Demonte (ed.), *Gramática del español*, 431–470. México: El colegio de México.

Dryer, Mathew. 1986. "Primary objects, secondary objects, and antidative." *Language* 62: 808–845.

Evans, Nicholas. 1997. "Role or cast? Noun incorporation and complex predicates in Mayali." In Alex Alsina et al. (eds.), *Complex predicates*, 397–430. Stanford: Center for the Study of Language and Information (CSLI).

Fernández-Ordóñez, Inés. 1994. "Isoglosas internas del castellano: El sistema referencial del pronombre átono de tercera persona." *Revista de Filología Española* 74: 71–125.

Fernández-Ordóñez, Inés. 1999. "Leísmo, laísmo y loísmo." In Ignacio Bosque and Violeta Demonte (eds.), *Gramática descriptiva de la lengua española*, vol. 1, 1317–1397. Madrid: Espasa Calpe.

Green, Georgia M. 1974. *Semantics and syntactic regularity*. Bloomington: Indiana University Press.

Hale, Ken, and Samuel J. Keyser. 1993. "On argument structure and the lexical expression of syntactic relatons." In Ken Hale and Samuel J. Keyser (eds.), *A view from Building 20: Essays in linguistics in honor of Sylvain Bromberger*, 53–109. Cambridge, MA: MIT Press.

Haspelmath, Martin. 2004. "Explaining the ditransitive person-role constraint: A usage-based approach." *Constructions*, February.

Hornstein, Norbert, Sarah Rosen, and Juan Uriagereka. 1996. "Integral Predication." In *Proceedings of the 14th West Coast Conference on Formal Linguistics*, 169–184.

Johnson, Kyle. 1991. "Object positions." *Natural Language and Linguistic Theory (NLLT)* 9: 577–636.

Kayne, Richard S. 1984. *Conectedness and binary branching*. Dordrecht: Foris.

Lapesa, Rafael. 1968. "Sobre los orígenes y evolución del leísmo, loísmo y laísmo." In *Festschrift W. von Wartburg*, 523–551. Tübingen: Max Niemeyer.

Leonetti, Manuel. 2004. "Specificity and object marking: The case of Spanish *a*." *Catalan Journal of Linguistics* 3: 75–114.

Mendikoetxea, Amaya. 1999. "Construcciones con *se*: Medias, pasivas e impersonales." In Ignacio Bosque and Violeta Demonte (eds.), *Gramática descriptiva de la lengua española*, vol. 2, 1631–1722. Madrid: Espasa.

Mithun, Marianne. 1984. "The evolution of noun incorporation." *Language* 60: 847–894.

Ormazabal, Javier, and Juan Romero. 2007. "The objects agreement constraint." *Natural Language and Linguistic Theory* 25(2): 315–347.

Ormazabal, Javier, and Juan Romero. 2010. "Object clitics and agreement." Unpublished ms., UPV-EHU/U. de Extremadura.

Ormazabal, Javier, and Juan Romero. 1998. "On the syntactic nature of the *me-lui* and the Person-Case Constraint." *Anuario del Seminario Julio de Urquijo* 32(2): 415–434.

Peterson, D. A. 2007. *Applicative constructions*. Oxford: Oxford University Press.

Preminger, Omer. 2011. "Agreement as a fallible operation." PhD diss., MIT.

Quilis, Antonio, Margarita Cantarero, María José Albalá, and Rafael Guerra. 1985. *Los pronombres le, la, lo y sus plurales en la lengua española hablada en Madrid*. Madrid: Consejo Superior de Investigaciones Científicas.

Rappaport, Hovav M., and Beth Levin. 2008. "The English dative alternation: The case for verb sensitivity." *Journal of Linguistics* 44: 129–167.

Roca, Francesc. 1992. "On the licensing of pronominal clitics: The properties of object clitics in Spanish and Catalan." Unpublished ms., Universitat Autònoma de Barcelona.

Romero, Juan. 1997. "Construcciones de doble objeto y gramática universal." PhD diss., Universitad Autónoma de Madrid.

Torrego, Esther. 1998. *The dependencies of objects*. Cambridge, MA: MIT Press.

Uriagereka, Juan. 1995. "Aspects of the syntax of clitic placement in Western Romance." *Linguistic Inquiry* 26(1): 79–124.

Uriagereka, Juan. 1998. "On government." PhD diss., University of Connecticut.

Zdrojewski, Pablo D. 2008. "¿Por quién doblan los clíticos?" PhD diss., Universidad Nacional del Comahue.

INDEX

-a. See Basque determiner -a

à, 41–43. See also à-DPs

√A (absolutive root), 259, 259n4, 272, 273

abiatu (depart), 58

ablative, Basque suffix, 50n1, 64, 71, 75, 76, 77, 82, 83

aboutness topic, 10n6

absolutive root. See √A

abstract Case. See Case

abstract Path, verbs of comparison and, 61

accusative and nominative morphology. See German determiner/adjective agreement paradigm

accusative case realized as nominative case, 132–36. See also DAT-NOM to DAT-ACC change

accusative datives in Spanish, 283–99. See also laísmo

  conclusion, 297–98

  feminine datives, accusative, 284–86

  feminine datives, animate, 286

  feminine datives, arguments, 286–87

  laísmo as accusative, 284–86

  summary, xix

accusative object, DAT-NOM to DAT-ACC change and, 133n30

acquire (áskotnast), 104n10, 105–6, 107, 108, 108n12, 110, 112

acquire (hlotnast), 97, 106, 107, 112

across (zehar), 68, 70

adjectival declension alternation, weak/strong, 189, 193, 209

"Adjective Correspondence" constraint, 193. See also Parallel Inflection

adnominal à-DPs, 24n1

adpositions in Basque. See Basque adpositions

à-DPs

  adnominal, 24n1

  clause-level, 24n1

  core datives and, 24

  indeterminate status of, 41–43

  noncore datives and, 24, 27–29

adverbial complex postpositions, 69

affectedness, noncore datives, 13, 25, 41

against (contre), 68n11

against (kontra), 68, 68n11, 70, 86–87

agreement. See number agreement; person agreement

agreement controllers

  √A (absolutive root), 259, 259n4, 272, 273

  √DA (dative-absolutive root), 259, 259n4, 260, 273, 276n22

  √EA (ergative-absolutive root), 258–59, 259n4, 264t, 272, 275

  √EDA (ergative-dative-absolutive root), 259, 259n4, 259, 261, 262n9, 264t, 273, 274, 275, 276n22, 278

  ergative, 258–59

  root allomorphy and, 258

aitzin (front), 65. See also aurre

allative, Basque suffix, 64, 71, 73–74, 75, 76, 77, 81, 82, 83, 89, 90, 91

allomorphy, 76n16, 78, 189, 192–93, 192n5, 258, 263, 263n10, 270

Amharic, 264

anaphoric Evaluative Dative Reflexive, 6

Ancient Greek dative, xiv, 212, 215t

animate, feminine datives as, 286

animate masculine determiner incorporation, 294–97

annihilate (eyða), 149

antisymmetry, in Basque, 67n10, 80n17

ApplP, 26, 33
approach (*hurbildu*), 58
arbitrary gaps, 269, 277
arguments
    external, Evaluative Dative Reflexives
        and, 6n2, 17
    feminine datives as, 286–87
    laísmo as, 286–87
    nonargumental datives, xiii, 5
    PRO, 96n2, 123, 123n24
Arregi and Nevins (forthcom-
    ing), 270n15. *See also* dative
    displacement
arte (space in between), 66, 66n9
Asia Minor Greek dialectal group, 215n1,
    231
áskotnast (acquire), 104n10, 105–6, 107,
    108, 108n12, 110, 112
aspectual datives. *See* Basque aspectual
    datives
aspectual verbs, complements of, 54, 56,
    86
asymmetries in complement of P, Basque
    adpositions, 76–81
attachment, verbs of, 62, 87
aurre (front), 65, 66, 67, 77
axial parts, 66–68, 71, 85, 90

bakaði (baked), 148
baked (*bakaði*), 148
ballistic motion, verbs of, 146–47, 153,
    155, 159
ball verbs, 153, 154–56, 159
barði (hit), 148
bare postpositions, 70–71
barna (through), 68, 68n12, 68n13, 70
barren (inside), 68n12, 68n13
Barss & Lasnik's (1986) diagnostics, 223,
    223n8, 224, 232, 244
Basque. *See also* Basque dialects; dative
    displacement
    antisymmetry in, 67n10, 80n17
    axial parts, 66–68, 71, 85, 90
    Database Basyque, 52, 93
    ergative-absolutive language, 258–59
    grammatical cases, 52, 52n4
    Long Distance Agreement, number
        features, 92
    Navarro-Labourdin variety, 51–52,
        52n2, 54n5, 55, 56
    northeastern, 51, 52

pro-drop, 68n14
    Souletin variety, 76, 76n16, 77, 82
Basque adpositions
    asymmetries in complement of
        P, 76–81
    case suffixes compared to, 50–51,
        50n1
    lexicalizing adpositional field, 75–83
    null Path, 51
    Place feature, 51, 66–67, 75–85,
        89–92
    primary, xiv, 50n1, 71
    silent Path, 83–92
    spatial datives compared to, 63
    types of, 71
Basque aspectual datives
    in invariant directional postpositions,
        71–72
    silent Paths and dative case, 87–91
Basque dative case
    properties, 52–53
    silent Paths and, 83–92
Basque datives and adpositions, 50–95
    dative arguments, 53
    grammatical cases, 52, 52n4
    introduction, 50–52
    microvariation study, xiv
    sources for data, 51–52
    summary, xiv, xvi–xvii
Basque determiner -*a*, 78, 79, 80, 81,
    82, 85
Basque dialects. *See also* dative
    displacement
    dative displacement DD, 260
    as dative-IO systems, 257–58
    Hondarribia Basque, 268, 276, 276n22
    Oiartzun Basque, 261–63, 262t, 268,
        269, 276, 276n22, 277
    Oñati Basque, 261, 262n9, 268, 269
    Sara Basque, 260–61, 260n7, 261,
        264n11, 264t, 268, 269
    Standard Basque, xix, 256, 258, 259,
        259n4, 260, 261, 262–63, 264,
        276, 277
    Zuazo's classification of, 260n6
Basque invariant directional postpositions,
    68–71
    adverbial/nonadverbial, 69
    aspectual datives in, 71–72
    bare postpositions, 70–71
    described, 55

locational nouns and, 68–70
recapitulation, 71
spatial datives in, 56, 57, 71–72
Basque locational nouns, 64–67
invariant postpositions and, 68–70
nonreferential interpretation for, 66
noun compounding and, 64–65
projective interpretations of, 66
referential use of, 65–66
as regular nouns, 64
Basque Paths, 72–77
abstract, verbs of comparison and, 61
null Path, 51
overview, 51
silent, dative case and, 83–92
unbounded, motion verbs and, 56–59
Basque spatial nonagreeing datives, 54–56
adpositions compared to, 63
axial parts, 66–68, 71, 85, 90
canonical dative DPs compared to, xiv, xvi–xvii, 51
in complements of aspectual verbs, 54, 56, 86
conceptual structure of distribution, 62, 62n7
contribution of, 72–73
crucial ideas for analysis of, 51
directed change of state and, 60
distribution of, 51, 56–62
how does dative arise? (section), 63–73
motion verbs and, 56–59
predicate classes and, 56–62
silent Paths and dative case, 84–87
stative verbs and, 59–60
verbs of comparison and, 60–61
verbs of contact and, 61–62
Basque spatial suffixes
ablative, 50n1, 64, 71, 75, 76, 77, 82, 83
allative, 64, 71, 73–74, 75, 76, 77, 81, 82, 83, 89, 90, 91
forms of, 64, 64n
inessive, 64, 70, 71, 75–76, 77, 78, 79, 80, 81, 82, 83, 84, 85, 86, 87, 89, 91
locational nouns and, 64–67
topological conditions on, 73–75
be (egon), 59, 73
beat the crap out of (buffa), 148, 148n7

be bored by (leiðast), 102, 104, 105, 106, 107, 109, 112, 129, 133n30
begiratu (look at), 70n15
behera (down), 68, 68n12, 71, 72, 88, 90
believe (trúgva), 114
benefactives
c-command relations in benefactives (Standard Modern Greek), 225t
nonselected datives and, 1–3
in Romeyka varieties of Pontus, 233–36, 234f, 236t
berast (receive), 102, 103, 104, 107, 108, 109, 112
Bhatt, Rajesh, 133n30
biconditional, 150–51
bíða (wait), 114
biddslappa (punch, bitch-slap), 148, 148n7
bihurtu (return, turn against), 57
bitch-slap (biddslappa), 148, 148n7
blanda (mix), 157–58
blast (prusa), 156
body-parts as predicates, 37–41
bored. See be bored by (leiðast)
Borer/Chomsky conjecture, ix–x
breyta (change), 149
buffa (beat the crap out of), 148, 148n7
Bulgarian, 221
Burzio's Generalization, 285
butter verbs, 148–49, 148n6, 150, 153

canonical ditransitive verbs, 22, 28
capsize (hvolfa), 127, 128
carrying, verbs of, 147n5
Case (abstract Case)
analysis (DAT-NOM to DAT-ACC change) and, 126–38
defined, 96n1
quirky Case feature, 214
case (morphological case)
analysis (DAT-NOM to DAT-ACC change) and, 126–38
defined, 96n1
case in disguise, xv, xvii, 100, 138, 139. See also DAT-NOM to DAT-ACC change
case suffixes, adpositions compared to, 50–51, 50n1
causativization, dative displacement and, 273–75
CAUSED-MOTION structures, 30

CAUSED-POSSESSION, 30

c-command relations

in benefactives (Romeyka varieties of Pontus), 236t

in benefactives (Standard Modern Greek), 225t

Evaluative Dative Reflexives and, 16, 20

in goal ditransitives (Pontic Greek in Thessaloniki), 230t

in goal ditransitives (Romeyka), 233t

in goal ditransitives (Standard Modern Greek), 225t

noncore datives and, 32, 33, 41

CDC (Coreferential Dative Constructions), 3, 13. See also Evaluative Dative Reflexives (EDRs)

change (breyta), 149

change of state, spatial datives, 60

change-of-state verbs (degree achievements), 148–50, 153

Chomsky. See Borer/Chomsky conjecture; Principles and Parameters (P&P) model

clause-level à-DPs, 24n1

"clipping" contexts (P-D contraction), 192, 204–5. See also OK paradigm

clitic doubling

Cypriot Greek and, 241, 243, 244

dative displacement and, 265

Greek dialects, 251t

laísmo and, 286, 292, 295

Romeyka and, 234

in Standard Modern Greek, 226, 234n13, 241, 244–45, 249

clitics. See also laísmo

in Cypriot Greek, 217–20

determiner cliticization onto P, 288, 294, 298

Evaluative Dative Reflexives as, 6

French noncore datives as, 24, 27

Greek dialectal variation and, 217–20, 220n7

laísta dialects and, 294–95

noncore datives as, 24, 27

in Romeyka varieties of Pontus, 217–20, 220n7

in Standard Modern Greek, 217–20

in Thessaloniki Pontic Greek, 217–20, 229

cold. See kólna (get cold)

colocar (tighten), 293

come back, return (itzuli), 57

comparable agreement dative displacements, 256

comparative studies

language internal variation and, vii

microcomparative approach, vii, x

comparison, verbs of, 60–61

competing grammars, 163, 185

complements of aspectual verbs, spatial datives in, 54, 56, 86

complex demonstratives, 36

complex postpositions in Basque. See Basque invariant directional postpositions

contact, verbs of, 61–62

contextual allomorphs, 189, 192–93, 192n5

contre (against), 68n11

contributions to volume, xv–xix

control infinitives. See PRO

co-occurrence, noncore/core datives, 43–44

cooled (kældi), 148

copy, merge and, viii

core datives in French. See French core datives

Coreferential Dative Constructions (CDC), 3, 13. See also Evaluative Dative Reflexives (EDRs)

covert accusative Case, 135

covert Nom-Acc Case, 100

covert nominative Case, 114, 115, 131, 135, 136

Covert Nominative Hypothesis, 114–15, 131

creating, verbs of, 45, 148–49, 156–59

cross-linguistic variation, x, 44

cult laísta dialect, 284

Cypriot Greek (MedCG and ModCG), 238–45

clitic doubling and, 241, 243, 244

clitics in, 217–20

comparative table of properties, 251t

head-first directionality in, 215–16

morphological exponence/distribution in, 238–39

morphological substitution of Ancient Greek dative, xiv, 212, 215t

passives and, 222

PCC and, 244

syntax of dative arguments (MedCG
  versus ModCG), 239–45
wh-formation and, 220–21

dæla (pump), 156
dáma (like), 115, 177, 179, 179*f*
dansa (dance), 127n29
√DA (dative-absolutive root), 259, 259n4,
  260, 273, 276n22
Database Basyque, 52, 93
DAT-ACC. *See also* DAT-NOM to DAT-
  ACC change
  in the active, 102–7
  in ditransitive passive, 98–99
  in the passive, 110–11
dative-absolutive root. *See* √DA
dative and genitive morphology. *See*
  German dative and genitive morphology (*m, r, s*)
dative arguments
  in Basque, 53
  Cypriot Greek, syntax of, 239–45
  nonselected, xiii
dative case. *See also* Basque dative case;
  dative *versus* accusative
  in passives of ditransitives, 122
  in passives of monotransitives,
    121–22
dative constructions across Greek dialects, 212–55. *See also* Cypriot
  Greek; Romeyka varieties of
  Pontus; Standard Modern Greek;
  Thessaloniki Pontic Greek
  aim of article, 250
  clitic doubling, 251*t*
  clitics and, 217–20, 220n7
  comparative table of properties, 251*t*
  concluding remarks, 250, 252
  correlations in, 245–50
  Cypriot Greek data (MedCG and
    ModCG), 238–45
  empirical findings summary, 250, 251*t*
  generalizations about, 245–50
  head directionality and, 215–17
  inherent case and, 214, 246–50, 252*t*
  m-case and Active *vs.* Nonactive dis-
    tinction across Greek varieties, 252*t*
  microvariation study, xviii
  morphological substitution of Ancient
    Greek dative, xiv, 212, 215*t*
  passives and, 221–22

person restrictions and, 212, 245–47,
  251*t*
piacere-type psych predicates, 213,
  226, 239, 244, 249
properties (comparative table), 251*t*
proposal overview, 213–14
Romeyka data, 231–38
scope/structure of article, 212–13
SMG dative constructions, 222–28
strong PCC, 212, 245, 246–47
summary, xiv–xv, xviii
syntactic isoglosses relating to, 215–22
theoretical implications, 245–50
Thessaloniki Pontic Greek data,
  228–31
weak PCC, 237, 245–46
wh-formation and, 220–21
dative displacement (across Basque dialects), 256–82
  allomorphy of elements, 263n10
  arbitrary gaps and, 269, 277
  Arregi and Nevins (forthcoming) and,
    270n15
  causativization and, 273–75
  comparable agreement, 256
  conclusion, 277
  defined, xix, 256
  ergative displacement compared to,
    265, 265n12, 271, 277–78
  Faroese and, 271–72, 271n16
  Hondarribia Basque, 268, 276, 276n22
  introduction, 256–58
  Itelmen and, 264
  morphological approach to, 265,
    270–71
  Oiartzun Basque, 261–63, 262*t*, 268,
    269, 276, 276n22, 277
  Oñati Basque, 261, 262n9, 268, 269
  Sara Basque, 260–61, 260n7, 261,
    264n11, 264*t*, 268, 269
  Standard Basque, xix, 256, 258, 259,
    259n4, 260, 261, 262–63, 264,
    276, 277
  summary, xv, xix
  syntactic approach, 265–71
  syntactic effects of, 271–77
  systematic factors' influence on,
    268–69
  varieties of, 256
dative displacement DD, 260
dative-flag, 53

dative intervention, 109n13, 262
dative-IO systems, 257, 257–58, 264
dative-marked DPs (dative DPs)
   characterizing, issues in, vii
   defined, xii–xiii
   distinctive properties of, xiii
   reasons for focusing on, xii–xv
dative-nominative. *See* DAT-NOM
datives and adpositions in northeastern
   Basque. *See* Basque datives and
   adpositions
Dative Sickness (DS). *See also* interspeaker and intraspeaker variation
   age and, 179
   dative substitution, 99, 99n5
   defined, ix, 167
   IceDiaSyn and, 170, 170n4
   increase in, 169
   intraspeaker variation and, 185
   langa (want) and *vanta* (need, lack),
     178, 179–81, 180*f*
   mean evaluation of dative subjects
     with typical DS verbs, 168, 168*f*
datives of interest, 2, 52, 263, 276
dative substitution, 99, 99n5. *See also*
   Dative Sickness; nominative
   substitution
dative *versus* accusative and the nature
   of inherent case, 144–60. *See also*
   Icelandic verb classes
   alternation in, 153, 153n9
   biconditional, 150–51
   datives and event structure, 150–51
   introduction, 144–45
   object case in Icelandic, 146–52
   summary, xv, xvii
   themes *versus* goals, 151–52
   variation in, 152–59
   verb classes, 146–50
DAT-NOM (dative-nominative), 96, 96n2,
   98
DAT-NOM questionnaire, 101–12
   age ranges, 101
   bigger surveys, 106n11, 112
   goal of, 101n6
   New Passive, 106, 111n14
   number of participants, 101
   purpose of, 101–2
   REAL survey, 106–7, 112
   results of, 97–98, 102–11
   sentence types compilation, 107

structure, 101
summary, 112
test sentences in, 102
"Variation in Syntax" project,
   109n13, 111
DAT-NOM to DAT-ACC change (case in
   disguise), 96–143. *See also* number
   agreement
   accusative case realized as nominative
     case, 132–36
   accusative object and, 133n30
   analysis, 126–38
   áskotnast (acquire), 104n10, 105–6,
     107, 108, 108n12, 110, 112
   berast (receive), 102, 103, 104, 107,
     108, 109, 112
   case in disguise, xv, xvii, 100, 138,
     139
   comparison, with other Germanic
     languages, 112–26
   conclusion, 138–39
   defined, 102n7
   early stages, 98, 101n6, 102,
     124, 138
   English, 112, 118–22, 125
   Faroese, 112, 113–17, 125
   further investigation, 112, 138
   German language and, 123–25
   goal of article, 100
   henta (suit), 103, 104, 107, 108, 112
   hlotnast (acquire), 97, 106, 107, 112
   Icelandic A speakers, 97, 108, 109,
     109n13, 128, 131, 132, 133, 134
   Icelandic B speakers, 97, 108, 109,
     109n13, 110, 128, 131, 132, 133,
     134
   Icelandic C speakers, 97, 108, 109,
     109n13, 115, 126, 126n28, 131,
     132, 133, 134, 134n31, 137, 138
   introduction, 96–101
   leiðast (be bored by), 102, 104, 105,
     106, 107, 109, 112, 129, 133n30
   líka (like), 97, 100, 103, 104, 104n10,
     105, 106, 106n11, 107, 108,
     108n12, 109, 112, 123n24, 125,
     126, 131, 133, 135n31, 137
   in literature, 97
   nægja (suffice), 102, 102n8, 103, 104,
     104n10, 106n11, 107, 112, 134
   NOM-ACC, 100, 112, 121, 122, 125,
     126, 128, 135n32, 138

nominative case realized as dative
case, 129–32
OV-to-VO change, 124
senda (send), 110
summary, xv, xvii
Swedish, 112, 117–18, 125
sýna (show), 110–11
texts cited, 139–41
variation between different verbs
in, 112
degree achievements (change-of-state
verbs), 148–49, 153
Dekanyi (2009), 85n18
demolish. *See rústa*
demonstratives, 36, 36n6, 193, 284
de nouveau, 33–34
depart (*abiatu*), 58
determiners
Basque determiner -*a*, 78, 79, 80, 81,
82, 85
determiner cliticization onto P, 288,
294, 298
French core/noncore datives and, 37
masculine determiner incorporation in
laísmo, 294–97
diachrony
DAT-NOM to DAT-ACC change,
136–38
Navarro-Labourdin contrasting properties, 54, 54n5
two nominatives at different diachronic stages, 136n32
diglossia, syntactic, 163
directed change of state, spatial datives, 60
discourse update, 11, 19
disguised case, xvii, 100, 138, 139. *See
also* DAT-NOM to DAT-ACC
change
Distributed Morphology (DM), 190–91.
See also German determiner/adjec-
tive agreement paradigm
distribution over subjects, Evaluative
Dative Reflexives and, 5, 11, 16, 19
ditransitives
canonical, 22, 28
c-command relations in goal ditransitives (SMG), 225*t*
laísmo in, 286–87, 293, 294
in Romeyka varieties of Pontus,
231–33, 233*t*
in SMG, 222–25

in Thessaloniki Pontic Greek, 228–29,
230*t*
DM (Distributed Morphology), 190–91.
See also German determiner/adjec-
tive agreement paradigm
DO>>IO, 225*t*, 230*t*, 233, 233*t*, 242
double object constructions
English, 30, 45, 46n8
French, 30
laísmo and, xv, xix, 285, 289, 294
microvariation studies and, xiv
down (*behera*), 68, 68n12, 71, 72, 88, 90
"down-home"-type verbs, 4
dreyma (dream), 129
drift (*reka*), 127, 128
DS. *See* Dative Sickness
dugna (help), 114

EA (external argument), 256
√EA (ergative-absolutive root), 258,
259n4, 264*t*, 272, 275
Early Middle English, 119
Early Modern English, 120
ecco, 9n5
economy of derivations, 162
economy of representations, 92
√EDA (ergative-dative-absolutive root),
259, 259n4, 259, 261, 262n9, 264*t*,
273, 274, 275, 276n22, 278
[+EDR effects], 3n1
EDRs. *See* Evaluative Dative Reflexives
eggja (encourage), 116, 116n17
egon (be), 59, 73
eman (give), 59, 262, 262n9, 262*t*, 273
embedded clauses, 15, 134
emission verbs, 146–47, 146n3, 153, 159
encourage (*eggja*), 116, 116n17
Enga, 127
English. *See also* double object
constructions
DAT-NOM to DAT-ACC change, 112,
118–22, 125
double object constructions, 30, 45,
46n8
Evaluative Dative Reflexives in, 4, 5,
6, 12, 20
Middle English, 119, 120, 121, 264,
271n16
noncore datives and, 44–46
Old English, 118, 121, 125, 139–40
epithets, 7n3

EPP (Extended Projection Principle), xi, 81, 246
ergative-absolutive language, Basque, 258–59
ergative-absolutive root. *See* √EA
ergative agreement controller, 258
ergative-dative-absolutive root. *See* √EDA
ergative displacement, 265, 265n12, 271, 277–78. *See also* dative displacement
erori (fall, inclined to), 58
ethical datives, xiii, 2, 13, 52, 212–13
evaluated eventuality, by clausal subject, xvi, 1, 5, 6, 11, 16–17, 20
Evaluative Dative Reflexives (EDRs), 1–21
  anaphoric, 6
  c-command relations and, 16, 20
  CDC, 13
  as clitics, 6
  core characteristic, 3
  Coreferential Dative, 3, 13
  in embedded clauses, 15
  English, 4, 5, 6, 12, 20
  evaluative focal elements and, 5, 7, 7n4
  evaluative mood, xiii, xvi, 13
  explaining (and reexamining) properties of, 16–20
  external arguments and, 6n2, 17
  ForceP and, 13, 14, 15, 16
  IHDs and, 13–15, 16
  intentionality of subject in, 5, 6, 16, 18, 19, 20
  interested speaker dative and, 13
  interpretive effects of, 6–7, 16
  isolation effect and, 17–18
  low informational relevance and, 1, 5, 7–8, 9–10, 11, 13, 18, 19n8, 20
  Modern Hebrew, 4, 6n2, 11, 12, 20
  monosyllabic "down-home"- verbs and, 4
  Mood$_{evaluative}$, 16
  MoodP$_{evaluative}$, 13, 18, 20
  MoodP$_{evidential}$, 18
  negation and, 5, 7, 7n3, 12, 17
  nonargumental datives, 5
  as nonselected datives, 3–4
  NP counterpart and, 5
  Palestinian Arabic, xvi, 20
  Personal Dative, 3

  positively evaluated eventuality by clausal subject, xvi, 1, 5, 6, 11, 16–17, 20
  properties of, 4–12, 16–20
  purpose of, 8
  Reflexive Datives, 3, 12
  reflexive nature of, 3, 4–5, 6, 20
  resisting distribution over subjects, 5, 11, 16, 19
  restrictions, 1, 7, 10, 12, 14, 19
  in SESC, xvi, 1, 3–7, 9, 11–14, 20
  summary, xiii, xvi
  syntagmatic priming and, 12
  Syrian Arabic, 4, 8, 11, 12, 18, 20
  terms for, 3
  thematic role and, 5
  third-person pronominals and, 5
  topical subject and, 5, 10–11, 10n6, 14, 19, 20
  TP and, 13, 15, 20
  truth conditions and, 4
  verbs and, 5
  as weak pronouns, 5
evaluative focal elements, 5, 7, 7n4
evaluative mood, xiii, xvi, 13
event structure, datives and, 150–51. *See also* dative *versus* accusative
eventuality positively evaluated by clausal subject, xvi, 1, 5, 6, 11, 16–17, 20
Evo, 9, 9n5
exerting force, verbs of, 147n5
experiencer subjects, 99, 104, 106, 108, 109, 112, 113, 120
experiencer verbs, 104, 104n10, 120n21
expletive null operator, xvi, 26–27, 34–35
extend (*framlengja*), 154, 175, 175t
Extended Projection Principle (EPP), xi, 81, 246
external arguments, EDRs and, 6n2, 17. *See also* EA
eyða (spend, annihilate), 149
Eythórsson study, in Faroe Islands, 116–17, 116n18, 135n32

façade of the house, 65, 66
fall, fall under (*erori*), 58
familiarity topic, 10n6
Fanselow, Gisbert, 201n16
FarDiaSyn (syntactic variation study in Faroese), xvii, 161–62, 161n1.

See also IceDiaSyn; interspeaker and intraspeaker variation
indicators of reliability, 166–72
main method, 164–66
precautionary measures, 165–66
reporting on intuition, 166
RÍN results compared with, 166
Faroese. See also dative displacement; interspeaker and intraspeaker variation
dative displacement and, 271–72, 271n16
DAT-NOM to DAT-ACC change, 112, 113–17, 125
Faroe Islands study, 116–17, 116n18, 135n32
quirky datives, 271
faxa (faxa), 175t
feature transmission, syntactic approach to dative displacement, 265
feminine bleeds dative. See German determiner/adjective agreement paradigm; OK paradigm
feminine datives. See also *laísmo*
as accusative, 284–86
as animate, 286
as arguments, 286–87
Figure, 57, 60–64, 74–75, 83, 85–87. See also Basque datives and adpositions
file-card semantics, 19
finish (*ljúka*), 149
[+Fission], 196
fjölga (increase in number), 149
flétta (twist), 156
focal elements, evaluative, 5, 7, 7n4
follow (*jarraiki*), 58
forceful contact, verbs of, 148–49, 148n7, 153, 154–55, 155n10, 156, 159
ForceP, 13, 14, 15, 16
four-way typology, inherent case, 214, 250, 252t
framed (*innrammaði*), 148
framlengja (extend), 154, 175, 175t
French core datives, 22–49
à-DPs and, 24
analysis, 29–31
CAUSED-MOTION structures, 30
co-occurrence with noncore datives, 43–44
determiners and, 37

differences in noncore/core datives, 24–25, 25n2, 46–47
nominalizations and, 25
passivization of internal argument, 25n2
previous analyses, 25–27
similarities in noncore/core datives, 23–24
structure for, 30–31, 30n4
summary, xiii, xvi
French noncore datives, 22–49. See also lambda abstraction (λ-abstraction)
à-DPs and, 24, 27–29
affectedness and, 13, 25, 41
analysis, 29, 31–41
body-parts as predicates, 37–41
as clitics, 24, 27
co-occurrence with core datives, 43–44
determiners and, 37
differences in noncore/core datives, 24–25, 25n2, 46–47
English and, 44–46
hierarchy of participants, 32–34
"high" and "low" properties of, 26
high applicative analysis and, 26
low applicative analysis and, 25–26
new data, 27–29
nominalizations and, 25
nonraising analysis for, 27
optional datives, 22
passivization of internal argument, 25n2
previous analyses, 25–27
raising analysis for, 26
Roberge and Troberg's analysis, xvi, 26–27, 33, 34–35
as second subjects of stative predicate, 31, 44, 46, 47
similarities in noncore/core datives, 23–24
summary, xiii, xvi
fresta (postpone), 149
front (*aitzin*), 65
front (*aurre*), 65, 66, 67, 77
full *à*-DPs. See *à*-DPs
fyrirgjöf (pass), 155

Gallman's phonological proposal, 194–95. See also Parallel Inflection
gaus (spewed), 147

gefallen (like), 123, 124n24
gender motion, *laísmo* as, 283, 284
generative approach, to linguistic variation, 162
generative grammar, vii, 96n1, 162
genitive and dative morphology. *See*
  German dative and genitive morphology (*m, r, s*)
genitive *s*, 192, 205–7. *See also* OK
  paradigm
German
  DAT-NOM to DAT-ACC change and,
    123–25
  oblique subjects and, 123–24
  possessive determiners/pronouns, 192,
    199–204
German dative and genitive morphology
  (*m, r, s*). *See also* OK paradigm
  as contextual allomorphs of OK
    (Oblique Kase), 189, 192–93,
    192n5
  distinctness between nominative/accu-
    sative morphology and dative/geni-
    tive morphology, 191–92, 208, 209
  weak/strong adjectival declension
    alternation and, 189, 193, 209
German determiner/adjective agreement
  paradigm (syncretism pattern), 190t
  baseline analysis, examples for,
    189–90, 208–9
  distinctness between nominative/accu-
    sative morphology and dative/geni-
    tive morphology, 191–92, 208, 209
  Distributed Morphology analysis of,
    190–91
  as epiphenomenal, 189, 190
  fundamental split in, 208
  German four-way case distinction and,
    189–90
  as morphological paradigm, 190
  [+oblique] stipulation, 191
  as part of grammar, 190
  summary, xiv, xviii
  syntax of, xviii, 189–211
  weak/strong adjectival declension
    alternation and, 189, 193, 209
Germanic languages
  DAT-NOM to DAT-ACC change and,
    112–26
  Old Norse, 124, 124n24, 141, 179
get cold (*kólna*), 113n15

give (*eman*), 59, 262, 262n9, 262t, 273
give (*giva*), 117, 135n32
goals, themes *versus*, 151–52. *See also*
  dative *versus* accusative and the
  nature of inherent case
gora (up), 68, 68n12, 71, 72, 88, 89, 90
grammatical cases, in Basque, 52, 52n4
Greek dialects. *See* Cypriot Greek;
  dative constructions across Greek
  dialects; Romeyka varieties of
  Pontus; Standard Modern Greek;
  Thessaloniki Pontic Greek
Grounds, 55, 57–63, 66–67, 70–78,
  80–92. *See also* Basque datives and
  adpositions

head (*skalla*), 145, 154, 155
head directionality, Greek dialectal variation and, 215–17
head-final directionality, 216
head-first directionality, 215–16
Hebrew, EDRs in, 4, 6n2, 11, 12, 20
Hellenistic Greek, 231, 233
hellti (spilled), 147
help (*dugna*), 114
henta (suit), 103, 104, 107, 108, 112
henti (threw), 147
hierarchy of participants, noncore datives
  and, 32–34
"high" and "low" datives, xiii, 26, 277
high applicative analysis, 26, 26n3
Hindi, 127
hit (*barði*), 148
hlakka til (look forward to), 173, 173t
hlotnast (acquire), 97, 106, 107, 112
hnífa (stab with a knife), 148, 148n7
hnoða (knead), 145, 156–57, 158
Hondarribia Basque, 268, 276, 276n22
hræra (mix, stir), 156
Hungarian. *See also* OK paradigm
  possessive determiners/pronouns,
    202–3
  postpositions, 85n18
hurbildu (approach), 58
hvolfa (capsize), 127, 128
Hyow, 264

IceDiaSyn (syntactic variation study in
  Icelandic), xvii, 161–62, 161n1. *See
  also* FarDiaSyn; interspeaker and
  intraspeaker variation

all generations seem reliable (reliability indicator), 166, 167–68, 167f, 167n3, 168f
example from, 164–65, 164n2, 165t
hlakka til, 173, 173t
indicators of reliability, 166–72
main method, 164–66
New Passive and, 170–72, 171n5
precautionary measures, 165–66
prescriptivism and, 166, 168, 170, 170n4
reporting on intuition, 166
RÍN results compared with, 166
subjects' judgment is reliable (reliability indicator), 166, 168–72
systematic *versus* random variation, 166, 167
Icelandic
New Passive, 106, 111n14, 170–72, 171n5
Old Icelandic, 124, 124n24, 124n25, 125
predicates, xvii, 136n32
quirky datives, 237, 271
as V2 language with T-to-C movement, 98n4
Icelandic verb classes, 146–50. *See also* dative *versus* accusative; DAT-NOM to DAT-ACC change; interspeaker and intraspeaker variation; oblique subjects
with accusative objects, 148–49
ballistic motion verbs, 146–47, 153, 155, 159
ball verbs, 153, 154–56, 159
butter verbs, 148–49, 148n6, 150, 153
change-of-state verbs, 148–50, 153
creation verbs, 45, 148–49, 156–59
with dative objects, 147–48
emission verbs, 146–47, 146n3, 153, 159
forceful contact verbs, 148–49, 148n7, 153, 154–55, 155n10, 156, 159
mixing verbs, 156–59
motion verbs with accusative objects, 147–48, 147n5
pour verbs, 146–47, 146n4, 153, 159
preparation verbs, 148–49, 153, 157, 158, 159
social interaction verbs, 147–48
summary (variation between dative and accusative), 153

transformation verbs, 148–49, 153, 157
translational motion verbs, xvii, 147, 150
two-place verbs, 145, 146, 147, 152, 153, 159
ideal linguists, 161n1
ideal speakers, 161n1, 185, 186. *See also* interspeaker and intraspeaker variation
identity criteria, for parameters, x–xii
IHDs. *See* interested hearer datives
I-languages, ixn4, 161. *See also* internal grammars
inclined to/toward (*erori*), 58
increase in number (*fjölga*), 149
indefinite article, Swiss German, 192, 197–99. *See also* OK paradigm
inessive, Basque suffix, 64, 70, 71, 75–76, 77, 78, 79, 80, 81, 82, 83, 84, 85, 86, 87, 89, 91
inflectional parallelism generalization, 192, 193. *See also* Parallel Inflection
informational relevance, EDRs and, 1, 5, 7–8, 9–10, 11, 13, 18, 19n8, 20
inherent case (semantically predictable case), 144. *See also* dative constructions across Greek dialects; dative *versus* accusative and the nature of inherent case
on external/goal arguments, 144
four-way syntactic typology and, 214, 250, 252t
lexical case compared to, 144, 153
with theme objects, xvii, 144, 159
inherent case, dative constructions across Greek dialects and, 214, 246–50, 252t
innrammaði (framed), 148
inside (*barren*), 68n12, 68n13
Insular Scandinavian-Mainland Scandinavian, syntactic variation between, xi–xii
intentionality of subject, EDRs and, 5, 6, 16, 18, 19, 20
interested hearer datives (IHDs), 13–15, 16
interested speaker dative, 13
internal grammars, 161–62, 163n1, 164, 176
internal variation, language, vii, ix

interpretive effects, of EDRs, 6–7, 16
interspeaker and intraspeaker variation (in
    subject and object case markings-
    Icelandic/Faroese). *See also* Dative
    Sickness; FarDiaSyn; IceDiaSyn;
    langa; vanta
    approaches to, 162–64
    ideal speakers, 161n1, 185, 186
    internal grammars, 161–62, 163n1,
        164, 176
    introduction, 161–62
    methodology of syntactic surveys,
        164–72
    prescriptivism, 166, 168, 170, 170n4
    questions addressed in, 161
    RÍN, 161–62, 161n1, 166, 182–84,
        183n9
    rústa (demolish), 175t, 175–77,
        176t, 177f
    sources for data, 161–62
    spontaneous speech recordings, 168,
        169, 169t, 176, 182, 182t, 184
    summary, xvii–xviii
    summary of results and claims,
        184–86
interspeaker variation
    in case marking, 173–76
    object case of DAT-NOM verbs
        (Icelandic), 97
    verb placement (Faroese), 186
intraspeaker variation
    in case marking, 176–83
    competing grammars, 163, 185
    Icelandic C and DAT-ACC variety,
        109
    Kroch's approach, 162, 163
    minimalist approaches, 163
    in phonology, 182–84
    P&P approach, 162–63
    summary of, 184–86
    two grammars, 163, 163n1
    Yang's approach, 162, 163–64
invariant directional postpositions.
        See Basque invariant directional
        postpositions
IO>>DO, 225t, 228, 230t, 233, 233t,
        242, 243
IO systems
    dative-IO systems, 257, 257–58, 264
    with multiple IOs, 257n1
    primary-IO systems, 257–58, 264, 267

symmetric IO systems, 257n1
isolation effect, EDRs and, 17–18
Itelmen, 264
itzuli (return, turn toward), 56–57

jarraiki (follow), 58
jós (scooped), 147

kældi (cooled), 148
kanpo (out), 68, 70
kastaði (threw), 147, 152
kiksa (mishit), 156
knead (*hnoða*), 145, 156–57, 158
kólna (get cold), 113n15
kontra (against), 68, 68n11, 70, 86–87
Korean
    case stacking, 271n16
    two nominatives at different dia-
        chronic stages, 136n32
kreista (squeeze), 156
Kroch's approach, intraspeaker variation,
        162, 163
Kupferman, Lucien, 36n6

lack. *See mangla* (lack); *vanta* (need,
        lack)
laísmo (feminine dative clitics), 283–99
    accusative, 284–86
    accusative/primary-IO syntax and,
        271n16
    animate, 286
    as arguments, 286–87
    characterization of, 287
    clitic doubling and, 286, 292, 295
    conclusion, 297–98
    derivation of, 292–94
    determiner cliticization onto P, 288,
        294, 298
    in ditransitive verbs, 286–87, 293, 294
    double object constructions and, xv,
        xix, 285, 289, 294
    as gender motion, 283, 284
    leísmo and, 296
    masculine determiner incorporation in,
        294–97
    nested microparametric option, xix,
        298
    properties of, 287
    reconsideration of, 284–88
    summary, xv, xix
    unaccusatives and, 285

laísta dialects, 283
  clitic system, 294–95
  cult, 284
  as *leísta* dialects, xix, 294–95, 296
lambda abstraction (λ-abstraction). *See also* French noncore datives
  motivation for, 34–37
  null expletive operator and, xvi, 26–27, 34–35
  stative elements and, 44
langa (want). *See also* interspeaker and intraspeaker variation
  accusative/dative subjects (acceptance rate), 170, 173*t*, 174
  accusative subjects (mean evaluation), 174, 174*f*
  cases in subject position (acceptance rate), 173, 173*t*
  dative object (acceptance, selection), 176, 176*t*
  dative subjects (acceptance, selection, usage), 169–70, 169*t*
  dative subjects (distribution of means), 178*f*, 180*f*
  dative subjects (mean evaluation), 174, 175*f*
  rústa (demolish) and, 175–77, 176*t*
  subject cases (in corpus of spontaneous speech), 182, 182*t*
  vanta (need, lack) and, 177–80, 178*f*, 180*f*
language acquisition, viii, 163–64
language change, viii, 163–64
language internal variation, vii, ix
large-scale parameters, vii–ix
large-scale syntactic variation surveys, xvii, 161
láta (let), 134, 135n31
leiðast (be bored by), 102, 104, 105, 106, 107, 109, 112, 129, 133n30
leísmo, 296
leísta dialects, xix, 294–95, 296
Lekeitio, 268
let (*láta*), 134, 135n31
lexical case, 144, 153. *See also* inherent case
lexicalizing adpositional field, 75–83
like (*dáma*), 115, 177, 179, 179*f*
like (*gefallen*), 123, 124n24
like (*líka*), 97, 100, 103, 104, 104n10, 105, 106, 106n11, 107, 108,

108n12, 109, 112, 123n24, 125, 126, 131, 133, 135n31, 137
liketh, 179n7
"Linguistic change in real time in Icelandic phonology and syntax" project, 106. *See also* REAL survey
linguistic variation. *See also* interspeaker and intraspeaker variation
  cross-linguistic variation, x, 44
  generative approach to, 162
  Principles and Parameters model, vii–ix, viii, viiin3, 162–63
little (*malo*), 8, 9, 10, 18, 19n8
ljúka (finish), 149
locational nouns in Basque. *See* Basque locational nouns
Long Distance Agreement in Basque, number features, 92
long-range parameters, vii–ix
look at (*begiratu*), 70n15
look forward to (*hlakka til*), 173, 173*t*
"low" and "high" datives, xiii, 26, 277
low applicative analysis, noncore datives and, 25–26
low informational relevance, EDRs and, 1, 5, 7–8, 9–10, 11, 13, 18, 19n8, 20

m, r, and *s* morphs. *See* OK paradigm
macroparameters, vii–viii, x
Mainland Scandinavian-Insular Scandinavian, syntactic variation between, xi–xii
malfactive datives, 2–3
malo (little), 8, 9, 10, 18, 19n8
mangla (lack), 177, 179, 179*f*
masculine determiner incorporation, 294–97
Medieval Cypriot Greek (MedCG), 212. *See also* Cypriot Greek
medioparameter, viiin1
meig (urinated), 147
merge, copy and, viii
metaparameters, vii–viii
microcomparative approach, vii, x
microparameters
  nested microparametric option, xix, 298
  parametric variation and, vii–x
microvariation scale, vii, x
microvariation studies, xiv, xviii. *See also* Basque datives and adpositions; dative constructions across Greek dialects

Middle English, 119, 120, 121, 264, 271n16

Milafranga, 273

minimalist approaches, viii, 163

Minimalist Program
Borer/Chomsky conjecture, ix–x
economy of derivations, 162
economy of representations, 92
parameters and, viii, x
Universal Grammar and, vii, viii, ix

mishit (*kiksa*), 156

mix (*blanda*), 157–58

mix (*hræra*), 156

mixing, verbs of, 156–59

Modern Cypriot Greek (ModCG), 212. *See also* Cypriot Greek

Modern Hebrew, EDRs in, 4, 6n2, 11, 12, 20

moka (shovel), 156

monosyllabic "down-home"- verbs, 4

Mood$_{evaluative}$, 16

MoodP$_{evaluative}$, 13, 18, 20

MoodP$_{evidential}$, 18

morphological approach, to dative displacement, 265, 270–71

morphological case. *See* case

morphological exponence/distribution, in Cypriot Greek, 238–39

morphological paradigm, 190. *See also* German determiner/adjective agreement paradigm

motion verbs. *See also* Icelandic verb classes
with accusative objects, 147–48, 147n5
Basque spatial datives and, 56–59
subclass of, xviii, 144

movement of syntactic constituents, syntactic approach to dative displacement, 265

Müller's reaction, 197

multiple grammars, viii–ix, 163–64

Muslim Pontic, 231. *See also* Romeyka varieties of Pontus

nægja (suffice), 102, 102n8, 103, 104, 104n10, 106n11, 107, 112, 134

nail (*negla*), 154, 175t

nanosyntax approach, xiii, 75, 86n19, 192n3

Navarro-Labourdin variety, 51–52, 52n2, 54n5, 55, 56

need (*þurfa*), 179. *See also* nýtast; *tørva*; *vanta*

negation, EDRs and, 5, 7, 7n3, 12, 17

negla (nail), 154, 175t

nested microparametric option, xix, 298

New Impersonal. *See* New Passive

New Passive (New Impersonal), 106, 111n14, 170–72, 171n5

Niš, 3

Niuean, 127

NOM-ACC, 100, 112, 121, 122, 125, 126, 128, 135n32, 138. *See also* DAT-NOM to DAT-ACC change

nominalizations, 25, 80, 81

nominative and accusative morphology. *See* German determiner/adjective agreement paradigm

nominative case realized as dative case, 129–32. *See also* DAT-NOM to DAT-ACC change

nominative substitution (NS)
dative substitution compared to, 99, 99n5
DAT-NOM to DAT-ACC and, 127–28
oblique subjects and, 99–100

nonadverbial complex postpositions, 69

nonagreeing datives. *See* Basque spatial nonagreeing datives

nonagreement. *See* number nonagreement

nonargumental datives, xiii, 5

noncore datives in French. *See* French noncore datives

non-inflected postpositions. *See* Basque invariant directional postpositions

nonraising analysis, 27

nonreferential interpretation, for Basque locational nouns, 66

nonselected datives. *See also* Evaluative Dative Reflexives (EDRs)
benefactive datives, 1–3
datives of interest, 2, 52, 263, 276
defined, 1–2
EDRs as, 3–4
ethical datives, xiii, 2, 13, 52, 212–13
malfactive datives, 2–3
possessive dative, 2
types, 2–3

nonstructural case. *See* oblique case

Nordic Center of Excellence in
Microcomparative Syntax, 161n1
northeastern Basque, 51, 52. *See also*
Basque
noun compounding
adverbial postpositional phrases and,
69
locational nouns, 64–65
NPs (noun phrases)
EDRs and, 5
movement, xiii
NS. *See* nominative substitution
null expletive operator, xvi, 26–27, 34–35
null Path adposition, 51
null subject parameter, vii
number agreement. *See also* DAT-NOM
to DAT-ACC change
with accusative object, 105, 111,
166n18
with dative plural subject, 130–31
with dative subjects, 115, 116, 120,
121, 126n27, 127, 129, 130
with nominative objects, 96–97, 98,
100, 102, 105, 107, 108, 109, 110,
128
with nominative plural objects,
108n12
with oblique subjects, 129
in the passive, 111
"Variation in syntax" project, 109n13
number Long Distance Agreement in
Basque, 92
number nonagreement
with nominative objects, 96–97, 100,
102, 105, 107–10, 125n26
in the passive, 110
nýtast (need), 177, 179, 179f

O1/S1, 257, 260, 263, 264
O2/S2, 257, 259n4, 260, 262, 264, 268
Object Agreement Constraint. *See* Person
Case Constraint
object case markings in Icelandic and
Faroese. *See* interspeaker and
intraspeaker variation
oblique case (nonstructural case), vii. *See
also* inherent case
dative-marked DPs and, xiii
kinds of, 144, 144n1
lexical case, 144, 153

oblique case markers *s, m, r. See* OK
paradigm
Oblique Kase. *See* OK paradigm
[+oblique] stipulation, 191
oblique subjects. *See also* DAT-NOM to
DAT-ACC change
diachrony and, 136–38
English, 112, 118–22
Faroese, 112, 113–17
German and, 123–24
Icelandic, 96, 99
Insular Scandinavian, xii
Mainland Scandinavian, xii
nominative substitution and, 99
NS and, 99–100
number agreement with, 129
Old Icelandic, 124, 124n24, 124n25
OV-to-VO change and, 124–25
person agreement with, 129
sjálfur (self) and, 130
Swedish, 112, 117–18
Of, Romeyka of, 212, 231. *See also*
Romeyka varieties of Pontus
Oiartzun Basque, 261–63, 262t, 268, 269,
276, 276n22, 277
OK paradigm (Oblique Kase, German
dative and genitive case marker
morphs: *s, m, r*). *See also* German
determiner/adjective agreement
paradigm
adjectival agreement analysis and, 189,
193, 209
analysis, important properties in,
206–8
as contextual allomorphs, 189,
192–93, 192n5
defined, 189, 192
genitive *s*, 192, 205–7
indefinite article (Swiss German), 192,
197–99
Parallel Inflection, 192, 193–97
P-D contraction ("clipping" contexts),
192, 204–5
possessive determiners/pronouns, 192,
199–204
summary, xiv, xviii
wh-morpheme and, 193
Old English, 118, 121, 125, 139–40
Old Icelandic, 124, 124n24, 124n25, 125
Old Norse, 124, 124n24, 141, 179

Old Scandinavian, xi, 117
Old Swedish, 117
Oñati Basque, 261, 262n9, 268, 269
operator-variable relation, noncore dative
    and, 27
optional datives, 22. *See also* French
    noncore datives
ORIENT, 57, 59, 60
out (*kanpo*), 68, 70
OV-to-VO change, 124–25. *See also* DAT-
    NOM to DAT-ACC change

Palestinian Arabic, EDRs in, xvi, 20
"Parallel (NP, A-Infl)" constraint, 193
Parallel Inflection, 192, 193–97. *See also*
    OK paradigm
parameters
    Borer/Chomsky conjecture, ix–x
    identity criteria for, x–xii
    large-scale, vii–ix
    long-range, vii–ix
    macroparameters, vii–viii, x
    medioparameter, viiin1
    metaparameters, vii–viii
    microparameters, vii–x, xix, 298
    Minimalist Program and, viii, x
    nested microparametric option, xix, 298
    null subject, vii
    polysynthesis, viii, x
    underspecification of UG, viii
parametric variation, vii–x, xi, xii, xvi
pass (*fyrirgjöf*), 155
passives
    Greek dialectal variation and, 221–22
    in Romeyka varieties of Pontus,
        221–22, 236
    in SMG, 221–22, 225–26
    in Thessaloniki Pontic Greek, 221–22,
        230
passivization of internal argument, 25n2
Paths. *See* Basque Paths
PCC. *See* Person Case Constraint
P-D contraction ("clipping" contexts),
    192, 204–5. *See also* OK paradigm
person agreement, 115, 129, 133. *See also*
    number agreement
Personal Dative, 3. *See also* Evaluative
    Dative Reflexives
Person Case Constraint (PCC, Object
    Agreement Constraint, person
    restrictions), xv, xviii

dative constructions across Greek dia-
    lects, 212, 245–47, 251t, 252
dative displacement and, 259
Icelandic A, B, C, and, 133
laísta dialects and, 290–91
Romeyka and, 220, 229, 237–38
SMG and, 227–28, 228n9
strong PCC, 212, 245, 246–47, 252
terms for, 290
Thessaloniki Pontic Greek and, 229
weak PCC, 237, 245–46
person restrictions. *See* Person Case
    Constraint
PF, underspecification of UG and, viii
Phase Impenetrability Condition, 241
phonological variation study in Iceland.
    See RÍN
phrasal Spell Out, 51, 75
piacere-type psych predicates, 52, 213,
    226, 239, 244, 249
pied-piping, 82, 89n20
Place-external -*a*, 91, 92
Place feature, 51, 66–67, 75–85, 89–92.
    See also Basque adpositions
PolP, 6–7, 15, 16
polysynthesis parameter, viii, x
polysynthetic languages, x
poner (put), 293
Pontic Greek, 212. *See also* Romeyka
    varieties of Pontus; Thessaloniki
    Pontic Greek
positively evaluated eventuality, by clausal
    subject, xvi, 1, 5, 6, 11, 16–17, 20
possessive dative, 2
possessive determiners/pronouns in
    German and Swiss German, 192,
    199–204
possessor raising, 26, 38, 41, 52
postpone (*fresta*), 149
postpositions. *See also* Basque invariant
    directional postpositions
    bare, 70–71
    Hungarian, 85n18
pour verbs, 146–47, 146n4, 153, 159
P&P model. *See* Principles and
    Parameters model
pre-dative affix, 53
predicates
    classes, Basque spatial datives and,
        56–62
    in Icelandic, xvii, 136n32

PredP, 31, 32, 34, 39
preparation, verbs of, 148–49, 153, 157, 158, 159
prescriptivism, 166, 168, 170, 170n4
primary adpositions, xiv, 50n1, 71
primary-IO systems, 257–58, 264, 267
Principles and Parameters (P&P) model
   criticisms of, viii
   described, 162–63
   general discussion, viiin3
   large-scale parameters, vii–ix
PRO, 96n2, 123, 123n24
pro-drop, 68n14, 274
projective interpretations, of Basque locational nouns, 66
þrusa (blast), 156
psych predicates, piacere-type, 52, 213, 226, 239, 244, 249
pump (dæla), 156
punch (biddslappa), 148, 148n7
þurfa (need), 179
put (poner), 293
putting, verbs of, 147n5
Pylkkänen, Liina, xiii, 15, 25, 26, 234, 235

quantifier variable binding
   SMG, 223
   Thessaloniki Pontic Greek, 229
quirky Case feature, 214, 247, 250
quirky datives, 214, 271
quirky subjects. See oblique subjects

r, s, and m morphs. See OK paradigm
raising analysis, 26
REAL survey, 106–7, 112
receive (berast), 102, 103, 104, 107, 108, 109, 112
Reference Term, 60–63, 85
referential, EDRs as, 5, 11, 19
referential use, of Basque locational nouns, 65–66
Reflexive Datives, 3, 12. See also Evaluative Dative Reflexives
reflexive detransitization, 272
reflexive nature, of EDRs, 3, 4–5, 6, 20
regular nouns, locational nouns as, 64
reka (drift), 127, 128
resisting distribution over subjects, EDRs, 5, 11, 16, 19
restrictions, EDR, 1, 7, 10, 12, 14, 19

return (bihurtu), 57
return, come back (itzuli), 57
RÍN (phonological variation study in Iceland), 161–62, 161n1, 166, 182–84, 183n9. See also interspeaker and intraspeaker variation
Roberge and Troberg's analysis, xvi, 26–27, 33, 34–35. See also French noncore datives
Romeyka of Of, 212, 231. See also Romeyka varieties of Pontus
Romeyka varieties of Pontus (Of, Sürmene), 231–38
   Asia Minor Greek dialectal group and, 215n1, 231
   benefactives in, 233–36, 234f, 236t
   c-command relations in benefactives, 236t
   c-command relations in goal ditransitives, 233t
   clitics in, 217–20, 220n7
   comparative table of properties, 251t
   ditransitives in, 231–33, 233t
   head-final directionality in, 216
   morphological substitution of Ancient Greek dative, xiv, 212, 215t
   passives in, 221–22, 236
   person restrictions in, 220, 229, 237–38
   Superiority effects, 221, 232
   Tonya, 219n6
   unaccusatives in, 236–37
   weak crossover in, 232
   wh-formation and, 221
root allomorphy, 258. See also agreement controllers
RSür. See Romeyka varieties of Pontus
rústa (demolish), 175t, 175–77, 176t, 177f

s, m, and r morphs. See OK paradigm
Sara Basque, 260–61, 260n7, 261, 264n11, 264t, 268, 269
S-C. See Serbo-Croatian
ScanDiaSyn (Scandinavian Dialect Syntax), 161n1
Scandinavian
   Old Scandinavian, xi, 117
   syntactic variation between Mainland Scandinavian-Insular Scandinavian, xi–xii

Scandinavian Dialect Syntax. *See*
     ScanDiaSyn
Schlenker's model, 196–97
"*SCHWA-m," 194
scooped (*jós*), 147
second subjects of stative predicate, 31,
     44, 46, 47
selected datives, 1–2. *See also* Evaluative
     Dative Reflexives; nonselected
     datives
self (*sjálfur*), 115, 130
semantically predictable case. *See* inherent
     case
senda (send), 110
sending, verbs of, 147n5
Serbo-Croatian (S-C), 1, 9, 10n6, 13
SESC (southeastern dialects of Serbo-
     Croatian), xvi, 1, 3–7, 9, 11–14,
     20. *See also* Evaluative Dative
     Reflexives
set in motion to a goal (*abiatu*), 58
shovel (*moka*), 156
si, EDRs and, 6
silent Paths, dative case and, 83–92
singular case marker exponents of
     German determiners. *See* German
     determiner/adjective agreement
     paradigm
sjálfur (self), 115, 130
skalla (head), 145, 154, 155
slice (*sneyða*), 156
SMG. *See* Standard Modern Greek
sneyða (slice), 156
social interaction, verbs of, 147–48
sópa (sweep), 150
Souletin, 76, 76n16, 77, 82
southeastern dialects of Serbo-Croatian.
     See SESC
space in between (*arte*), 66, 66n9
Spanish accusative datives. *See* accusative
     datives in Spanish
spatial nonagreeing datives. *See* Basque
     spatial nonagreeing datives
spatial roles, 51, 56, 63
spatial suffixes. *See* Basque spatial suffixes
spend (*eyða*), 149
spewed (*gaus*), 147
spilled (*hellti*), 147
spontaneous speech recordings, 168, 169,
     169t, 176, 182, 182t, 184. *See also*
     interspeaker and intraspeaker variation

squeeze (*kreista*), 156
stab with a knife (*hnífa*), 148, 148n7
Standard Basque, xix, 256, 258, 259,
     259n4, 260, 261, 262–63, 264,
     276, 277
Standard Modern Greek (SMG)
     c-command relations in benefactives,
          225t
     c-command relations in goal ditransi-
          tives, 225t
     clitic doubling in, 226, 234n13, 241,
          244–45, 249
     clitics in, 217–20
     comparative table of properties, 251t
     dative constructions in, 222–28
     ditransitives in, 222–25
     head-first directionality in, 215–16
     passives in, 221–22, 225–26
     Person Case Restraint and, 227–28,
          228n9
     quantifier variable binding, 223
     Superiority effects in, 224
     unaccusatives in, 226–27
     weak crossover in, 224
     wh-formation and, 220
statistical learning model, 163
stative elements, λ-abstraction and, 44
stative verbs, Basque spatial datives and,
     59–60
stir (*hræra*), 156
strong PCC, 212, 245, 246–47, 252
strong/weak adjectival declension alterna-
     tion, 189, 193, 209
structural "side effects" of topical con-
     stituents, in S-C, 10n6
subclass of motion verbs, xviii, 144. *See
     also* Icelandic verb classes
subjacency, viii
subject case markings in Icelandic and
     Faroese. *See* interspeaker and
     intraspeaker variation
suffice (*nægja*), 102, 102n8, 103, 104,
     104n10, 106n11, 107, 112, 134
suffixes in Basque. *See* Basque spatial
     suffixes
suit (*henta*), 103, 104, 107, 108, 112
Superiority effects, 221, 224, 229, 232
Sürmene, Romeyka of, 212, 231. *See also*
     Romeyka varieties of Pontus
surveys. *See also* DAT-NOM question-
     naire; FarDiaSyn; RÍN

New Passive studies, 106, 111n14, 170–72, 171n5
REAL, 106–7, 112
syntactic variation, xvii, 161
"Variation in Syntax" project, 109n13, 111
Swedish
    DAT-NOM to DAT-ACC change, 112, 117–18, 125
    Old Swedish, 117
sweep (sópa), 150
Swiss German. See also OK paradigm
    indefinite article, 192, 197–99
    possessive determiners/pronouns, 192, 199–204
symmetric IO systems, 257n1
sýna (show), 110–11
syncretism pattern. See German determiner/adjective agreement paradigm
syntactic approach, to dative displacement, 265–71
syntactic diglossia, 163
syntactic effects, of dative displacement, 271–77
syntactic isoglosses across Greek dialects, 215–22. See also dative constructions across Greek dialects
syntactic microvariation: dative constructions in Greek. See dative constructions across Greek dialects
syntactic variation
    between Insular Scandinavian and Mainland Scandinavian, xi–xii
    "Variation in Syntax" project, 109n13, 111
syntactic variation surveys, xvii, 161, 164–72. See also FarDiaSyn; IceDiaSyn
    all generations seem reliable (reliability indicator), 166, 167–68, 167f, 167n4, 168f
    indicators of reliability, 166–72
    main method, 164–66
    precautionary measures, 165–66
    reporting on intuition, 166
    subjects' judgment is reliable (reliability indicator), 166, 168–72
    systematic versus random variation, 166, 167
syntagmatic priming, 12
syntax of dative arguments, Cypriot Greek, 239–45

syntax of syncretism pattern. See German determiner/adjective agreement paradigm
Syrian Arabic, EDRs in, 4, 8, 11, 12, 18, 20
systematic factors, 268–69. See also dative displacement

takka (thank), 114
thematic role, EDRs and, 5
themes, goals versus, 151–52. See also dative versus accusative and the nature of inherent case
Thessaloniki Pontic Greek (TPG), 228–31
    benefactives in, 229–30
    c-command relations in goal ditransitives, 230t
    clitics in, 217–20, 229
    comparative table of properties, 251t
    ditransitives in, 228–29, 230t
    head-first directionality in, 216
    morphological substitution of Ancient Greek dative, xiv, 212, 215t
    passives and, 221–22, 230
    Person Case Restraint and, 228–29
    quantifier variable binding in, 229
    Superiority effects, 229
    unaccusatives in, 230–31
    weak crossover in, 229
    wh-formation and, 220–21
theta-marking head, 34
third-person pronominals, EDRs and, 5
threw (henti), 147
threw (kastaði), 147, 152
through (barna), 68, 68n12, 68n13, 70
tighten (colocar), 293
Tonya, 219n6
topical constituents in S-C, structural "side effects" of, 10n6
topical subject, EDRs and, 5, 10–11, 10n6, 14, 19, 20
topological conditions, on Basque spatial suffixes, 73–75
tørva, 177, 179, 179f
TP, EDRs and, 13, 15, 20
TPG. See Thessaloniki Pontic Greek
transformation, verbs of, 148–49, 153, 157
translational motion, verbs of, xvii, 147–48, 150

trúgva (believe), 114
truth conditions, EDRs and, 4
turn against (*bihurtu*), 57
turn toward (*itzuli*), 56–57
tvinna (twist), 156
twist (*flétta*), 156
twist (*tvinna*), 156
two grammars, 163, 163n1
two nominatives at different diachronic stages, 136n32
two-place verbs, 145, 146, 147, 152, 153, 159. *See also* Icelandic verb classes

UG. *See* Universal Grammar
unaccusatives
   laísmo and, 285
   in Romeyka varieties of Pontus, 236–37
   in SMG, 226–27
   in Thessaloniki Pontic Greek, 230–31
unbounded Paths, motion verbs and, 56–59
underspecification. *See also* German determiner/adjective agreement paradigm; Universal Grammar
   of Universal Grammar, viii
   of Vocabulary Items, 190–91
unexpressed argument in a control infinitive. *See* PRO
Universal Grammar (UG), vii, viii, ix
up (*gora*), 68, 68n12, 71, 72, 88, 89, 90
urinated (*meig*), 147

V2 language with T-to-C movement, 98n4
vanta (need, lack). *See also* interspeaker and intraspeaker variation; *langa*
   accusative/dative subjects (acceptance rate), 173t, 174
   accusative subjects (mean evaluation), 174, 174f
   cases in subject position (acceptance rate), 173, 173t, 173t
   dative object (acceptance, selection), 176, 176t

dative subjects (distribution of means), 178f, 180f
langa and, 177–80, 178f, 180f
variation. *See specific variations*
"Variation in Syntax" project, 109n13, 111
verbs. *See also* Icelandic verb classes; motion verbs; *specific verbs*
   attachment, 62, 87
   carrying, 147n5
   comparison, 60–61
   contact, 61–62
   exerting force, 147n5
   putting, 147n5
   sending, 147n5
Vocabulary Items (VI), 190–91. *See also* German determiner/adjective agreement paradigm

wait (*bíða*), 114
want. *See langa*
Warlpiri, 127
weak crossover effects
   Romeyka, 232
   SMG, 224
   Thessaloniki Pontic Greek, 229
weak low informational relevance, EDRs and, 1, 5, 7–8, 9–10, 11, 13, 18, 19n8, 20
weak PCC, 237, 245–46
weak pronouns, EDRs as, 5
weak/strong adjectival declension alternation, 189, 193, 209
wh-formation, Greek dialectal variation and, 220–21
wh-morpheme, 193
Wood, Jim, 106n11

Yang's approach, intraspeaker variation, 162, 163–64
zehar (across), 68, 70

Ziburua, 268
Zuazo's classification, of Basque dialects, 260n6